Constructive Guidance and Discipline

Preschool and Primary Education

FOURTH EDITION

Marjorie V. Fields
University of Alaska Southeast

Debby Fields

Foreword by Constance Kamii

PEARSON
Merrill
Prentice Hall

Upper Saddle River, New Jersey
Columbus, Ohio

Library of Congress Cataloging in Publication Data
Fields, Marjorie Vannoy.
   Constructive guidance and discipline : preschool and primary education / Marjorie V.
Fields, Debby Fields ; foreword by Constance Kamii.—4th ed.
      p. cm.
   Includes bibliographical references and index.
   ISBN 0-13-151256-0
      1. School discipline. 2. Behavior modification. 3. Educational counseling. 4. Education,
Preschool. 5. Education, Primary. I. Fields, Debby. II. Title.

LB3012.F54 2006
372.15—dc22   2004061112

Vice President and Executive Publisher: Jeffery W. Johnston
Publisher: Kevin M. Davis
Acquisitions Editor: Julie Peters
Editorial Assistant: Michelle Girgis
Production Coordination: Becky Barnhart, Carlisle Publishers Services
Senior Production Editor: Linda Hillis Bayma
Design Coordinator: Diane C. Lorenzo
Cover Designer: Keith Van Norman
Cover Photo: Marjorie V. Fields
Production Manager: Laura Messerly
Director of Marketing: Ann Castel Davis
Marketing Manager: Amy Judd
Marketing Coordinator: Brian Mounts

This book was set in Bookman by Carlisle Communications, Ltd. It was printed and bound by
Courier Stoughton, Inc. The cover was printed by Courier Stoughton, Inc.

Photo Credits: Marjorie V. Fields: 2, 8, 19, 28, 32, 38, 40, 46, 49, 51, 61, 63, 66, 72, 75, 79, 85,
89, 91, 102, 105, 108, 112, 116, 122, 127, 135, 148, 155, 162, 166, 169, 173, 177, 181, 184, 188, 191,
196, 208, 211, 220, 224, 229, 233, 236, 242, 252, 260, 263, 271, 276, 281, 288, 292, 295, 299, 304,
307, 312, 318, 323, 327; Debby Fields: 15, 22, 26, 35, 54, 58, 82, 98, 132, 140, 144, 204, 246, 255;
Eileen Hughes: 267.

Pearson Education Ltd.
Pearson Education Singapore Pte. Ltd.
Pearson Education Canada, Ltd.
Pearson Education—Japan

Pearson Education Australia Pty. Limited
Pearson Education North Asia Ltd.
Pearson Educacíon de Mexico, S.A. de C.V.
Pearson Education Malaysia Pte. Ltd.

10 9 8 7 6 5 4 3 2 1
ISBN: 0-13-151256-0

For the cause of
worldwide peace and harmony.
May it begin in the
hearts of children
and spread.
And may teachers be
sowers of the seeds
of peace and harmony.

Foreword

This is a practical book with many examples and contrasts. It is not, however, a mere collection of recipes, but a book full of instructive examples based on sound, theoretical reasons. It also communicates a way of thinking about young children and attitudes of empathy.

The approach the authors recommend is good because it solves problems in positive ways and promotes the development of healthy personalities. In addition, though, the authors have a vision of autonomy as the aim of education that goes far beyond the development of healthy personalities. Since this vision may not have been articulated as forcefully as it could have been, I would like to take this opportunity to discuss autonomy as intended by Jean Piaget as the aim of education.

Autonomy, in Piaget's theory, means something different from its common meaning. Autonomy usually means the *right* to make decisions for oneself, and many people mistakenly think that it means the *right* to do whatever one pleases. In Piaget's theory, autonomy does not mean the right, but instead the *ability* to make decisions for oneself about right and wrong, independently of reward and punishment, by taking relevant factors into account. When one takes relevant factors into account, one is not free to lie, steal, break promises, disturb other people, or be irresponsible.

Parents and teachers have traditionally tried to teach right and wrong by using reward and/or punishment. Reward and punishment give the appearance of working but the result, in the long run, is either blind conformity or susceptibility to manipulation through reward and/or punishment. The Watergate cover-up affair, for example, happened because the men under President Nixon expected to be rewarded for doing what they knew to be morally wrong. As far as the effects of punishment are concerned, we all know how the possibility of punishment leads to the calculation of risks.

A clear example of moral autonomy is Martin Luther King's struggle for civil rights. He took relevant factors into account, concluded that the laws discriminating against African Americans were unjust, and fought to put an end to these laws. Many people tried to stop him with incarceration, dogs, water hoses, and threats of assassination, but he could not be manipulated by reward or punishment.

The important question for parents and teachers is: How can we raise children to become morally autonomous adults who make decisions based on what is right, rather than on what is rewarded or punished? Piaget's answer to this question was that we foster the development of autonomy first by refraining from using reward and punishment. By giving stickers to children for completing worksheets, for example, we unwittingly teach them to become susceptible to manipulation by reward. If we punish children for lying, to cite another example, children can learn only to avoid being punished. Piaget would suggest that, instead of punishing a child for telling a lie, we might look him or her straight in the eye and say with affection and skepticism, "I can't believe what you are saying because . . . I want you to sit down and think about what you might do next time if you want me to believe you." This appeal to the human relationship between the child and the adult and to the direct consequence of the act has the effect of motivating the child to construct from within, over time, the value of honesty. Children who are thus supported in building their own convictions about the importance of honesty cannot tell lies, even for a president who might dangle rewards.

A discussion of specific techniques is beyond the scope of the present context, and the reader is urged to read this book. I also recommend *The Moral Judgment of the Child* (Chapters 2 and 3) by Piaget.

Today's children live with many serious potential problems, such as drug abuse, AIDS, teenage pregnancies, and guns in schools. Although these may all look like separate problems, they are actually all symptoms of the inability to make decisions for oneself by taking relevant factors into account. Children who can take relevant factors into account do not take drugs, for example.

The belief that rules and values must be put into children from the outside through lectures, rewards, and punishment is outdated. Rules and values must be constructed (made) by children from the inside if they are to become the children's own. Only when children have convictions of their own do they have the moral courage to say "No" to drugs, sex, and violence. Children need the same strength of internal conviction Martin Luther King had when he stood up to the punishment heaped upon him.

The time to start fostering the development of autonomy is at an early age. Through building strong human relationships, exchanging points of view with children, and allowing them to learn from their own mistakes, we can help children develop the capacity to take relevant factors into account. Autonomy is a complicated goal, and I congratulate the authors for going beyond the perspective of what seems to work in the short run. What seems to work in the short run often defeats our long-range goal of turning out adults who can decide for themselves between right and wrong.

Constance Kamii
Birmingham, Alabama

About the Authors

Marjorie Fields Dr. Marjorie Fields has just retired after teaching in the field of early childhood education for over 30 years. She first taught kindergarten, then first grade, then began teaching teachers. Thanks to her own children, she also had experience in co-operative preschools and various types of child care.

Marjorie has a doctorate in early childhood education with research in parent involvement. She has been active in early childhood professional organizations at the national and local levels and has served as vice-president of the National Association of Early Childhood Educators. She has also served on the national governing board for the National Association for the Education of Young Children. She has published extensively in the field of emergent literacy, including the textbook *Let's Begin Reading Right* (Merrill/Prentice Hall), as well as in the field of child guidance.

This book is the outgrowth of over 25 years of reading and thinking in conjunction with developing and teaching early childhood discipline courses. Dr. Fields credits her two sons with helping her learn what is most important about child guidance and discipline initially; now she continues to learn from her grandchildren—and with their mother, her new co-author.

Debby Fields Debby Fields is a temporarily retired mental health counselor and a stay-at-home mom of two daughters. Debby has worked as an elementary school counselor and as a teen-parent counselor. Through her work and life, she has learned a great deal about child development. Early intervention and attachment were the focus of her work with teen parents. This work allowed her a window into the lives of young adults with attachment problems and the obstacles they face in raising their own children.

Debby has a master's degree in Marriage, Family, and Child Counseling. She presented her master's thesis on multicultural counseling at a national convention for the American Psychological Association. In addition to her training in attachment issues, she has focused on developing culturally sensitive practices and has a degree in anthropology. Debby currently works in cooperative preschools with both her children.

Contributing Authors

Eileen Hughes   Dr. Eileen Hughes is a faculty member in the early childhood program at the University of Alaska Anchorage. She teaches both undergraduates and graduate students working in child care or public school settings. She has been a teacher and a speech therapist, and has worked in early intervention, traveling to Alaskan villages. For the past 15 years, she has studied principles underlying the Reggio Emilia approach to support teachers in their own study of young children to plan meaningful curriculum. Dr. Hughes is the author of Chapter 13.

Lory Britain   Dr. Lory Britain has 30 years of experience developing curriculum materials and teaching children, parents, student teachers, and professionals in a variety of settings, including the university, community college, and private sector. She has been published internationally and her works include *My Grandma Died*, *The Young Child as Scientist* (with co-author Christine Chaille), and *It's My Body* and *Loving Touches* (under the name of Lory Freeman). Dr. Britain is Director of Evaluation and Training for the Relief Nursery, Inc., of Lane County (Eugene, Oregon), a nationally recognized and replicated therapeutic and family support program for families and children from high-risk environments. Dr. Britain and her daughter, Sierra Freeman, collaborated on Chapter 14.

Sierra Freeman   Sierra Freeman is a special education inclusion teacher in Portland, Oregon, and works with elementary school children. She received her master's degree from Wheelock College after completing the Teaching Students with Special Needs program. Ms. Freeman has extensive experience working with children with special emotional needs and their families, both at early intervention and elementary day treatment levels. Sierra Freeman co-authored Chapter 14 with her mother, Lory Britain.

Preface

Constructive Guidance and Discipline: Preschool and Primary Education attempts to bring together the best of what is known about helping young children become happy, responsible, and productive people. We present guidance and discipline concepts within a framework of child development, developmentally appropriate practices, and Constructivist education. Thus, only discipline approaches that are consistent with all three aspects of this framework are recommended here. We take a stand about what is best for young children, rather than merely presenting an impartial overview of various approaches. We are convinced that adults cannot effectively assist children's moral development through the coercive approaches of punishment or behavior modification.

We emphasize guidance for children ages 3–8, rather than 0–8, which is the entire scope of early childhood. Appropriate guidance and discipline must be tied to developmental level, and infant and toddler development is uniquely different from that of children in the preoperational years of 3–8. The approaches presented in this text require more emotional, social, and cognitive maturation than that attained by most toddlers. The developmental level identified by Piaget as the preoperational stage presents its own set of guidance challenges. These challenges are our focus here.

MAJOR THEORETICAL INFLUENCES

The information and ideas presented in this text come from a number of respected sources. We see four theorists as having major influences on child guidance concepts in this century: Alfred Adler, Carl Rogers, B. F. Skinner, and Jean Piaget. Rudolf Dreikurs's recommendations of logical and natural consequences extended Adler's concepts; Thomas Gordon popularized Rogers's ideas through his Parent Effectiveness Training work; Skinner's work founded the widespread behavior modification techniques; and Piagetian scholars such as Constance Kamii and Rheta DeVries are spreading the word about Piaget's views on the development of morality. Although we reject Skinner's approach for the reasons explained in Chapter 9, we believe that the other three theorists have compatible views. Adler, Rogers, and Piaget all perceive the child as actively seeking understanding. This is in contrast to the Skinnerian view, which sees education as something that happens to a child from outside sources. Adler and Rogers, as well as Piaget, respect the child's personal rate and style of developing social understanding. All three perceive the proper adult role as facilitating rather than controlling the child's gradual development as a constructive member of society. Piaget's theoretical framework is much broader than that of Rogers or Adler, including all moral development as well as intellectual development. Thus, Adlerian and Rogerian concepts can be included as part of a Piagetian perspective, although the reverse is not true.

The research and writing of Jean Piaget and Constructivist scholars regarding intellectual and moral autonomy are central to the message in this book. We have also adapted Thomas Gordon's recommendations for effective communication and interpreted Rudolf Dreikurs's concept of logical and natural consequences into our discussion of a Constructivist approach to discipline. In addition, we have drawn on Erik Erikson's emotional development studies, referred to guidelines from the National Association for the Education of Young Children, and often quoted Rheta DeVries. Many other sources used in this book are listed at the end of the chapters.

We look at guidance and discipline as teaching activities; therefore, the principles of effective early childhood education apply as much to guidance and discipline as to academics. In addition, we discuss the ways in which effective early childhood education practices prevent or alleviate many common discipline problems.

Like any other aspect of teaching, guidance must acknowledge diversity among youngsters. In our recommendations, we have considered individual differences due to innate temperament or individual physical and intellectual capabilities. We also discuss the implications of culture, class, family problems, and gender.

We recognize that teachers must often deal with youngsters in crisis, creating major new challenges in guidance and discipline. Two chapters are devoted to providing background and support to teachers whose classrooms include youngsters with special physical and emotional needs or learning difficulties.

CHANGES IN THE FOURTH EDITION

When first confronted with the task of writing this fourth edition, I thought I had already said all I had to say about the topic. However, I am happy to say that I discovered I had learned a few things in the four years since the last revision. I was also pleased to discover interesting and new relevant research. This edition shares those discoveries and once again attempts to present previous ideas with enhanced clarity.

Content Changes

New research on emotion regulation, emotional development, and the impact of temperament adds significantly to this edition. Understanding these issues is crucial to discovering the causes of child behaviors. We have further explored multiple causes of behavior problems and how those factors interconnect. The importance of adult-child relationships and classroom communities is also explored further in this edition.

Recognizing the influence of family and culture on behavior and appropriate intervention, we have strengthened discussions of family involvement and culture. We have also shared fascinating new information about how brain development and gender impact behavior. In addition, we discuss the behavioral implications of an ever-increasing emphasis on test scores in schools.

This edition continues and strengthens the approach of the previous editions. We have continued to work at making the message of the book clear and understandable. Since behavior modification is so pervasive in our society, the recommendations in this book require most readers to radically alter their thinking. Assisting students in a major paradigm shift requires that principles be carefully documented and clearly explained. We have found that the examples of classroom practice are most effective in helping students understand the concepts; therefore, we have carefully reviewed the classroom vignettes, adding more and better examples. This edition works to better balance the preschool and primary-grade-level examples.

Contributors to This Edition

This edition has benefited from the fresh perspective of Debby Fields, who has a master's degree in counseling and has worked with at-risk young parents. She is also the mother of two young children and has worked in their cooperative preschools. This edition also once again brings you the expertise of Dr. Lory Britain and Sierra Freeman, M.A., for the chapter on children with serious emotional problems. Both Lory and Sierra have been working in the "trenches" with at-risk children and their families and have first-hand insights to share as well as a solid research base. Dr. Eileen Hughes, author of the chapter on children with disabilities, has added to and strengthened that chapter for this edition.

Expanded *Instructor's Manual and Test Bank*

An *Instructor's Manual* is available for this edition, with tips for teaching. Some of the ideas are from other college faculty who use this book to teach about guidance and discipline. In addition, we offer some "hand-out" materials that we and others have found useful. The test bank added to the third edition has been expanded. These are not test items requiring mere rote memory; they simulate actual classroom situations where problem solving is required for effective discipline. Even the multiple choice questions require higher-level thinking. This approach to testing is congruent with a Constructivist approach to education, allowing the college teacher to model the principles recommended.

ORGANIZATION OF THE TEXT

The first three chapters of the book constitute the foundations section. Chapter 1 begins to explain a view of discipline as a way of teaching autonomy and self-discipline while promoting self-esteem. Concepts introduced in Chapter 1 are more fully addressed throughout the book. Chapters 2 and 3 consider stages in children's physical, emotional, intellectual, and social development as they relate to discipline problems and solutions. We consider a clear definition of discipline and its goals, plus knowledge of child development, to be the basic understandings for a discussion of discipline.

Part Two presents various approaches to discipline in descending order, from most positive to negative. This sequence can also be considered as an ascending order, from least intrusive to most intrusive. Chapter 4 discusses how to prevent behavior problems by creating an emotional and physical environment most supportive of children's healthy development. Chapter 5 explains the role of developmentally appropriate programs in preventing discipline problems. Chapters 6 and 7 emphasize both the prevention of problems and intervention when problems do occur. Chapter 6 explains how the examples shown by adults influence child behavior and shows how to help children use those examples during conflict situations. Chapter 7 presents effective ways to communicate with children both to prevent conflict and to address problems that arise and how to negotiate solutions to existing problems. Chapter 8 explains changing unproductive behaviors by using related consequences to help children understand why certain behaviors are unacceptable, Chapter 9 analyzes behavior modification approaches, and explains why rewards and even praise are counterproductive to goals of self-discipline. The dangers of punishment are presented in Chapter 10.

Chapters 11 through 15 constitute Part Three, which builds on the previous two parts. Child development knowledge from Part One is used to determine the cause of behavior problems. Then information about guidance approaches from Part Two is used to select an appropriate response. Part Three analyzes typical causes of discipline problems and relates them to the approaches relevant to each. These chapters emphasize the necessity of dealing with the cause of problems rather than just the symptoms. Chapter 11 discusses the relationship between maturational level and acceptable behavior, and Chapter 12 looks at how unmet needs cause problem behavior. Chapters 13 and 14 explore serious problems with causes outside of the classroom and offer helpful suggestions for the teacher or caregiver. Chapter 15 presents an overview of possible causes of discipline problems and identifies which causes pertain to a particular situation. This chapter also provides a guide for matching causes with the discipline approaches that are most likely to be effective for each.

PROVIDING EXAMPLES

Because we want to balance theoretical explanations with real-life examples, we use typical scenarios to illustrate ways of facilitating self-discipline and moral autonomy through approaches to discipline. Many of these examples are quite long to provide the context surrounding the situation. This is congruent with our message that teachers must not respond just to the behavior, but must consider the many factors that might relate to the cause of the behavior. These "stories" have proven extremely useful to college students trying to visualize the practical applications of text material and struggling with abstract concepts.

Meet the cast of characters: Dennis, Maureen, Sheri, Nancy, and the rest of the staff of the Midway Children's Center, a composite of typical preschool/child-care centers in the suburbs, who provide examples of discipline with 3- and 4-year-olds. Mrs. Jensen, her first-grade students, and the staff of a typical city school demonstrate the same concepts with primary-grade children. Second-grade teacher Mr. Davis and his student teacher, Beth, are at the same school, as is the kindergarten teacher, Mrs. Taylor. Mrs. Jensen and Mrs. Davis represent all the caring and effective public school teachers we have known. Contributing authors for Chapters 13 and 14 introduce other sets of teachers and students as they describe appropriate interventions for children with special physical and emotional needs.

Because contrasting desirable with undesirable practices often helps us define the desirable, we have also provided examples of common practices that we do not recommend. For this purpose, we have created two fictitious characters, preschool teacher Joanne and first-grade teacher Miss Wheeler, and described them in some very real situations. Miss Wheeler is at the same elementary school as Mrs. Jensen. Teacher Joanne is at the same children's center as Dennis, but she is in charge during the afternoon and Dennis is the lead teacher during the morning preschool session. Having Dennis and Joanne sharing the same students and support staff allows examples of how different approaches affect the same children. All teachers are fictional, but the good and bad situations described are real. We use first names for the child-care staff and last names for public school staff, not to imply more respect for the latter, but only as a reflection of common practice.

Examples from readers' own experience will be the most instructive. We believe that spending significant time with youngsters, preferably enough to establish an authentic relationship with them, is necessary for internalizing theories about guidance and discipline. We believe that personal observation and experience are crucial to learning, whether in preschool or adulthood.

We use the term *teacher* throughout the book to refer to caregivers as well as other teachers. Any adults who guide children through their day are teaching them. We firmly believe that adults working with children in child care must be as knowledgeable about child development as any other teachers. Since youngsters are so profoundly influenced by the adults in their lives, it is essential that all teachers have a solid understanding of how to influence youngsters in positive directions.

Marjorie Fields

Acknowledgments

I thank the following reviewers of this edition for their insights: Richard Ambrose, Kent State University; Russ Andaloro, University of Arizona; Stacy Burr, Clemson University; Janet Sawyers, Virginia Tech; and Cheryl Wright, University of Utah.

I wish to thank Constance Kamii for her patience and guidance in my quest to better understand Constructivism and moral autonomy. Thanks also to all the teachers whose classrooms I have visited and who have provided models of kind and constructive discipline. These include my sister, Deborah Hillstead, a wonderful early childhood teacher who keeps me in touch with classroom reality. I have learned the most from children themselves, however. All the youngsters in all the classrooms where I have spent time over the last two decades helped me to understand child development and guidance. Raising my own two sons also taught me a lot, and I must thank them for being the subjects of my longitudinal research. Now I have two granddaughters who are teaching me even more about child development.

It has been a joy to work with my daughter-in-law, Debby, on this edition of the book. Our mutual interest in her children—my grandchildren—gave a personal perspective to our research. I am deeply indebted to the many teachers who allowed me to take photographs in their classrooms and then assisted with parental permission forms. I appreciate the guidance of our editor, Julie Peters, and I am grateful for the hard work of Linda Bayma, the production editor. Debby and I both wish to acknowledge generous research assistance from our friend, Ruth Schreckenghost. Finally, many, many thanks to my dear husband for his patience and help.

Marjorie Fields

I would like to thank Marjorie: my mentor, friend, baby-sitter and mother-in-law. Without Marjorie, my contributions to this book would never have been possible. I am so grateful for her guidance and strong faith in me.

My work was also possible because of the support of my wonderful husband, Mike. He rushed home from many mountains to take care of our family. I am grateful for his generous and patient support.

I would also like to thank my children for all that they have taught me. They continue to be my inspiration.

Debby Fields

Discover the Companion Website Accompanying This Book

THE PRENTICE HALL COMPANION WEBSITE: A VIRTUAL LEARNING ENVIRONMENT

Technology is a constantly growing and changing aspect of our field that is creating a need for content and resources. To address this emerging need, Prentice Hall has developed an online learning environment for students and professors alike—Companion Websites—to support our textbooks.

In creating a Companion Website, our goal is to build on and enhance what the textbook already offers. For this reason, the content for each user-friendly website is organized by topic and provides the professor and student with a variety of meaningful resources. Common features of a Companion Website include:

For the Professor—

Every Companion Website integrates **Syllabus Manager**™, an online syllabus creation and management utility.

- **Syllabus Manager**™ provides you, the instructor, with an easy, step-by-step process to create and revise syllabi, with direct links into Companion Website and other online content without having to learn HTML.

- Students may logon to your syllabus during any study session. All they need to know is the web address for the Companion Website and the password you've assigned to your syllabus.

- After you have created a syllabus using **Syllabus Manager**™, students may enter the syllabus for their course section from any point in the Companion Website.

- Clicking on a date, the student is shown the list of activities for the assignment. The activities for each assignment are linked directly to actual content, saving time for students.

- Adding assignments consists of clicking on the desired due date, then filling in the details of the assignment—name of the assignment, instructions, and whether it is a one-time or repeating assignment.

- In addition, links to other activities can be created easily. If the activity is online, a URL can be entered in the space provided, and it will be linked automatically in the final syllabus.

- Your completed syllabus is hosted on our servers, allowing convenient updates from any computer on the Internet. Changes you make to your syllabus are immediately available to your students at their next logon.

For the Student—

- **Introduction**—General information about the topic and how it will be covered in the website.

- **Web Links**—A variety of websites related to topic areas.

- **Timely Articles**—Links to online articles that enable you to become more aware of important issues in early childhood.

- **Learn by Doing**—Put concepts into action, participate in activities, examine strategies, and more.

- **Visit a School**—Visit a school's website to see concepts, theories, and strategies in action.

- **For Teachers/Practitioners**—Access information you will need to know as an educator, including information on materials, activities, and lessons.

- **Observation Tools**—A collection of checklists and forms to print out and use when observing and assessing children's development.

- **Current Policies and Standards**—Find out the latest early childhood policies from the government and various organizations, and view state, federal, and curriculum standards.

- **Resources and Organizations**—Discover tools to help you plan your classroom or center and organizations to provide current information and standards for each topic.

- **Electronic Bluebook**—Paperless method of completing homework or essays assigned by a professor. Finished work can be sent to the professor via email.

- **Message Board**—Virtual bulletin board to post and respond to questions and comments from a national audience.

To take advantage of these and other resources, please visit the *Constructive Guidance and Discipline: Preschool and Primary Education*, Fourth Edition, Companion Website at

www.prenhall.com/fields

Brief Contents

Contents

CHAPTER 2
Physical and Emotional Development
Affect Child Behavior **22**

CHAPTER 3
Intellectual and Social Development Affect Discipline **46**

PART 2
Discipline Approaches   71

CHAPTER 4
Creating Environments That Prevent Discipline Problems   72

CHAPTER 5
Planning Programs That Prevent Discipline Problems   98

CHAPTER 7
Effective Discipline Through Effective Communication   144

CHAPTER 12
Unmet Needs   242

CHAPTER 13
Children Experiencing Disabilities   260
by Eileen Hughes

Contents

CHAPTER 14
Special Emotional Needs   *288*
by Lory Britain and Sierra Freeman

Note: Every effort has been made to provide accurate and current Internet information in the book. However, the Internet and information posted on it are constantly changing, so it is inevitable that some of the Internet addresses listed in this textbook will change.

Constructive Guidance and Discipline

PART 1
Discipline Foundations

The first three chapters of this book provide the basic information necessary to study the topic of discipline. In Chapter 1, we define discipline as discussed in this text, comparing the concept of Constructivist discipline with authoritarian and permissive discipline. As part of this definition, we examine discipline in terms of the goals or outcomes desired. Chapter 1 also introduces the two basic premises of the book. One of these is working toward long-term discipline goals rather than only immediate concerns. The other is matching the discipline approach to the cause of the problem behavior.

Chapters 2 and 3 focus on child development issues that directly affect discipline in preschools and primary grades. Understanding how children grow, learn, and think helps adults to live more harmoniously with youngsters. This understanding not only creates more tolerance for normal childish behaviors, but it also reduces inappropriate adult expectations. Adults who lack this understanding often unknowingly create discipline problems by putting children in situations where they are sure to have problems. Adults who understand child development are able to use that knowledge to determine what skills are appropriate to teach children at various ages. We believe that effective discipline approaches must be based on knowledge of children's physical, emotional, intellectual, and social development and also on the individual characteristics of each child.

1

Thinking About Guidance and Discipline

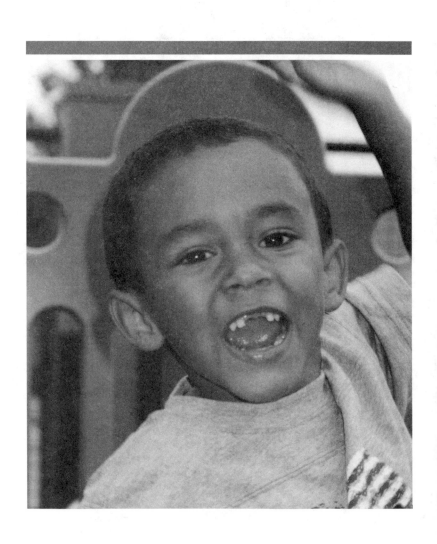

*S*ome books tell you they have the perfect formula to solve all your discipline problems; this one doesn't. This book says there is no one approach to discipline that will work for all problems, let alone for all children. Child guidance and discipline are incredibly complex, confusing, and frustrating. The many books and programs that offer simple solutions to discipline problems ignore the reality of individual differences, emotion-laden situations, and over-burdened caregivers. In this book we do not offer any simple solutions, but instead acknowledge that effective child discipline is multifaceted, requiring a sophisticated set of understandings and skills. We try to provide the basics of the necessary understanding and skill.

This first chapter is supposed to help you understand everything else in this book and give you our definitions for the terminology used throughout subsequent chapters. Ideally, as you read this chapter, you will begin to understand the differences between internal regulations and external controls for behavior. There are big differences in the outcomes and in the processes leading to each.

DEFINING DISCIPLINE

Notice that the title of this book includes both guidance and discipline. The term *guidance* is usually associated with helping youngsters deal with problems (as in guidance counselor) and the term *discipline* is too often associated with punishing children for doing things adults don't like. As you read, you will see that the term *discipline* is used broadly in this book, and that it includes what people generally think of as guidance, but it does not include punishment.

What do you think discipline is? Have you always thought of it as punishing a child for doing something wrong? Many people think that discipline is a smack on a child's bottom. You may have heard a (sick) joke that refers to a paddle as the "board of education." This book defines discipline differently: *helping children learn personal responsibility for their behavior and to judge between right and wrong for themselves*. The emphasis is on teaching as we help youngsters learn responsible behaviors, rather than merely stopping unproductive actions. Did you know that the word "discipline" comes from the word "disciple," which means to lead and teach? Teaching and leading are what adults should be doing when they discipline a child.

Instead of just enforcing rules about what not to do, we want to help children learn to make wise choices about what they should do. Note that learning to make wise choices for themselves is very different from just doing whatever they want. We are not advocating a lack of behavior controls or permissive approaches. Instead, we are advocating approaches that help children understand why certain behaviors are better than others, and that help children choose to act in a desirable manner, whether or not an adult is there to "catch" them at it.

This book is about how to support children in becoming responsible, kind, and productive citizens; it is not about forcing or otherwise coercing children to behave in certain ways. We will explain why we are convinced that external controls, such as reward and punishment, counteract the behavior and attitudes our

This book defines *discipline* as helping children learn personal responsibility for their behavior and to judge between right and wrong for themselves.

society so desperately needs. We don't just tell you not to reward or punish children, we also explain better ways of reaching behavior goals.

A key element in the process is determining the cause of undesirable behaviors and working to eliminate that cause. Our approach to discipline is like diagnostic teaching: individualized to the needs and abilities of each child. This type of guidance and discipline requires extensive knowledge of child development and also of various guidance approaches. This book attempts to assist readers in obtaining the necessary knowledge in both areas; it then presents ways of using them together for child guidance.

Because we view discipline as teaching, not merely controlling, we recommend that school discipline be planned at least as carefully as other aspects of the curriculum. Schools long ago gave up punishing students for not knowing how to read or do a math problem (Butchart & McEwan, 1998). Instead of punishing children for missing skills and understanding, teachers now teach what is missing. This is the same process we advocate for helping children with missing social skills and for teaching them understanding related to behavior.

High Stakes

Can we afford to spend school time teaching social skills and caring attitudes? Evidence shows that we can't afford not to (Charney, 2002). Experienced teachers know that other areas of the curriculum won't get covered if discipline is not taught appropriately. But more importantly, observers of human nature and human development researchers (Coie & Dodge, 1998; Eisenberg & Fabes, 1998; Williams & Shaps, 1999) know that it doesn't really matter what else people learn if they don't learn to become caring, principled, and responsible; their lives will be lived in shambles. In addition, it is becoming increasingly clear that schools must teach caring, communication, negotiation, and other violence-prevention lessons in an effort to make schools and neighborhoods safe (Bebeau, Rest, & Narvaez, 1999).

Teachers report that classroom discipline is their biggest challenge. This challenge appears to be growing greater each year as more and more children arrive at school with unmet needs and insufficient social skills. Things have changed a lot since 1965 when the first author of this book was teaching kindergarten in a low-income neighborhood. Despite having 42 students in the morning and 38 in the afternoon, the classes functioned quite well. Today, teachers struggle with classes of 25 children, many of whom lack impulse control and have little ability to manage their frustration and anger (Brady, 2003).

Teachers of young children need to spend time on discipline not only in self-defense, but because they have the children at the most opportune time. Brain research shows that the early years offer a critical window of opportunity for learning complex functions related to behavior, such as logical thinking and emotion regulation (Shonkoff & Meisels, 2000). During the years from age 3 to age 10, the brain has more synapses connecting brain cells than at any other time. Brain imaging shows conclusively what early childhood teachers have said all along: the early years are the critical years for learning.

THE GOALS OF DISCIPLINE

Discipline approaches must be determined by our goals. As Butchart says, "The ends and means are inseparable" (1998, p. 2). Start by asking yourself, "What is the purpose of discipline?" It may be tempting to look at discipline merely as a means to keep control so you can teach other things, but children and society need so much more.

Long-Term Goals

Whenever you teach something, you need to start by clarifying your long-term educational goals. Teaching discipline or anything else without long-term goals is like trying to plan a trip route without knowing where you are headed. In order to examine long-term goals, you may find it useful to ask yourself what kind of people you value. Notice that the word is *people*, not *children*. Is there a difference? If you are thinking about children, you might be attracted to the goal *obedient*; however, you are not likely to choose that label for an adult characteristic. Keep in mind that early discipline influences character for a lifetime; therefore, it is essential to think about what kind of people function best in society rather than merely considering what kind of children are easiest to manage. What traits will make the best contribution to a democratic society?

Self-Concept and Self-Esteem

Many people list positive self-concept as a goal, but this seems to confuse the difference between self-concept and self-esteem. Self-concept is an understanding of who we are and what we can do; self-esteem is how we feel about that. A realistic self-concept is essential to mental health (Landy, 2002) and can provide the basis for developing good self-esteem.

There is general agreement that we want youngsters to grow up feeling good about themselves. Although almost everyone voices this goal, many still use discipline methods that damage self-esteem. Children are routinely treated with much less respect than adults are. They are lectured, ignored, bullied, and bribed in ways no adult would ever put up with. Children often aren't really listened to, either. Later chapters will discuss how punishment and other coercive tactics— even praise and other rewards—can damage a person's self-esteem.

Self-Discipline

Nearly everyone also agrees that self-discipline is a goal for children. Most approaches to discipline describe themselves as promoting self-discipline (Charney,

2002; Nelson, Lott, & Glenn, 2000). Disagreements center around what leads to this goal. Many believe that rewards for acceptable behavior, and punishments for unacceptable behavior, will lead to self-discipline. Such viewpoints do not recognize that being manipulated by reward and punishment is vastly different from learning about what is right and how to make wise, caring decisions (Kohn, 1999). In contrast, this book is based on the view that children can't learn to regulate their own behavior as long as others are regulating it for them.

Moral Autonomy

A more sophisticated and little known version of self-discipline is called *moral autonomy*. This is a concept presented in Jean Piaget's classic book, *The Moral Judgment of the Child* (1932/1965), and elaborated for modern audiences by Piagetian scholars DeVries (e.g., DeVries, Hildebrandt, & Zan, 2000) and Kamii (e.g., Kamii & Ewing, 1996). According to these sources, *autonomy* means being governed and guided by your own beliefs and understanding. It is much more than merely "internalizing" a set of conduct rules and making yourself follow them. The morally autonomous person is kind to others out of personal feelings of respect for other human beings. The opposite is *heteronomy*, which means being governed or ruled by someone else. The heteronomous person would be kind to others only if that behavior would be rewarded, or if its absence would be caught and punished.

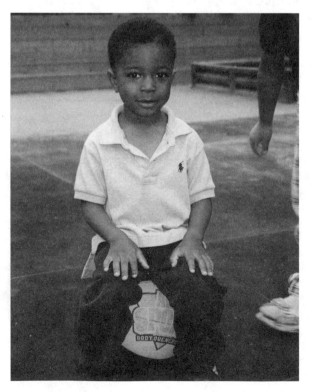

Moral autonomy means having the ability to make decisions about right and wrong, regardless of any rewards or punishments, yet taking into consideration the rights and needs of all involved.

Some people misinterpret this concept and get worried when they hear about autonomy. They think that being governed by yourself means doing whatever you want. However, Kamii points out in the foreword to this book that Piaget's theory of autonomy doesn't mean just the right to make decisions for yourself but the "ability to make decisions for oneself about right and wrong, independent of reward or punishment, by taking relevant factors into account." If you think about the meaning of that statement, you see that a merely self-serving decision would be excluded because it wouldn't take into consideration the "relevant factors" of other people's needs. It is important to note that being governed internally also means that children are not so susceptible to peer pressure; therefore, morally autonomous persons would not join in inappropriate group activities in order to be accepted by their peers.

Therefore, it is a person without moral autonomy who is likely to act irresponsibly when there are no external controls. In fact, that description fits some young college students away from home for the first time. College dormitory life testifies to the fact that some well-meaning parents and teachers deny young people an adequate opportunity to develop inner controls. Inexperienced at self-regulating their work, play, and sleep, some first-year college students find themselves unable to achieve a workable balance.

Autonomy does not mean lack of control; rather, it refers to the source of control. Autonomous people carry those controls within themselves. They are never without them, even when alone. Heteronomous people, by contrast, experience control only when someone else is present. They depend on an external judge to reward or punish their behavior. When you help youngsters develop moral autonomy, you affect how they behave, even when misbehavior isn't likely to be caught. Autonomous people don't need policing to keep them on the right path.

Long-Term versus Quick-Fix Solutions

Are teachers responsible for keeping children safe and orderly and also for helping them develop positive self-esteem, self-discipline, and moral autonomy? That's a tall order! Don't forget that teachers have to teach, too. Can they really be blamed if they have a hard time thinking about long-range discipline goals and are attracted to control for the moment? After all, teachers usually have a student for just one year.

Parents, however, are generally aware that they will be dealing with this child through the teen years and beyond. One mother reports that she was powerfully motivated to help her son Michael learn self-discipline when she thought about his getting a driver's license in 10 years. While Michael was little, she could protect him from harm by watching over him herself, but she doubted that she could ride along to make sure he was driving safely when he was 16. She knew that inner controls would stay with Michael long after she couldn't. Therefore, she focused on discipline approaches that fostered inner control rather than obedience. Nevertheless, even parents are sometimes tempted to ignore the future and concentrate on making their lives easier for now.

Teachers may be under the added pressure to present a "well-disciplined" class, in the old sense of appearing quiet and controlled. This can make a difference at evaluation time with principals who don't understand how young children learn best. As a result, discipline methods that boast quick, short-term results at the expense of children's self-esteem and autonomy remain popular. You will read about some of these methods in Chapter 9.

Fortunately, many teachers care too much about children to give in to temptation. They resist quick-fix approaches and work on positive alternatives. They know that helping children live together peacefully now and preparing them for the future can be compatible goals. Skillful teachers know how to work toward long-term discipline goals while maintaining a peaceful and productive learning environment. They know they don't have to make a choice between protecting children's self-esteem and keeping order. With the guidance of these knowledgeable and dedicated teachers, children can learn from experience to make wise decisions. In the process, they can also develop the positive self-esteem and moral autonomy necessary for becoming "competent, caring, loving and lovable people" (Noddings, 1995, p. 366).

DISCIPLINE MODELS COMPARED

Common approaches to discipline vary—from the very authoritarian, in which the adult makes all the rules and punishes any deviation, to the very permissive, in which the child makes all the decisions. Too many people think they have to choose one or the other of those models. One teacher says she plays the "heavy" until she can't stand herself; then she switches to the opposite until she can't stand the kids. Too few adults (teachers as well as parents) are even aware of any other options. We do not recommend trying to combine permissive and authoritarian styles in an attempt at a middle ground, but there are alternatives that balance the power of adult and child. You don't have to choose between either the adult or the child having all the power. A shared power model best meets the needs of all. The needs and views of both the adult and the child can be accommodated when discipline is viewed as teaching.

Discipline Theory Terms

Many terms have been used to describe the different approaches to discipline. *Authoritarian* and *permissive* are commonly understood terms and concepts. Alternatives to these extremes have been harder to define and to understand. Baumerind (1967) wrote about authoritative discipline and explained how it differed from the authoritarian model through a focus on teaching rather than punishment. However, many people get confused by the similarities between the words *authoritarian* and *authoritative*.

Greenberg (1992b) compares forms of discipline with forms of government. The *autocratic* holding of power by the adult is compared to a dictatorship, and *anarchy* is the label for the overly permissive style that grants too much power to the child. In contrast, Greenberg describes a shared power approach that she labels *democratic*. This term may leave readers with the incorrect idea that behavior is decided by vote and the worry that the teacher will be outvoted.

COMPARING DISCIPLINE TERMINOLOGY

The following list categorizes the various models of teaching and guidance discussed in this chapter and shows their relationship to one another.

Obedience models	Respect models	Passive models
Authoritarian	Authoritative	Permissive
Behaviorist	Constructivist	Maturationist
Boot camp	Community	
Autocratic	Democratic	Anarchist

DeVries and Zan (2004) use yet another way of explaining discipline styles. They contrast three classroom situations and label them: (1) the *boot camp*, (2) the *factory*, and (3) the *community*. The boot camp uses reward and punishment to enforce obedience. The factory model has the same controlling goals as the boot camp, relying heavily on reward and punishment, but with a kinder and gentler touch. The factory model describes the majority of elementary grade or grade school classrooms we have seen. The community, in contrast, uses the Constructivist model to assist children's development of moral autonomy. Fortunately, few teachers are as harsh as those in the boot camp model but, unfortunately, too few have the skills to create a true community of learners.

Because we view discipline as teaching, we believe it makes sense to base guidance and discipline on learning theory. Therefore, we compare the various approaches according to which learning theory they most closely reflect: Behaviorist, Maturationist, or Constructivist. The authoritarian style is consistent with the Behaviorist philosophy of education, with its emphasis on molding behavior via reward and punishment. The permissive style is compatible with the Maturationist philosophy of education, with its belief in time as the best teacher. The best alternative to these extremes of too much and too little adult intervention is the Constructivist approach to education.

Constructivism does not reflect a "middle ground" between Behaviorism and Maturationism; rather, it is a whole different view of learning and of guidance and discipline. It is not a "nicer" way to get obedience; instead, it strives for much more than obedience. Constructivism helps children learn from their experiences and from reflecting on those experiences (DeVries, Zan, & Hildebrandt, 2002; Duckworth & Cleary, 1990; Kamii & Ewing, 1996; Piaget, 1965). Through this process, the learner is assisted in gaining increasingly sophisticated levels of understanding. Thus, children gradually develop the ability to take many relevant factors into consideration when deciding what action is best for all concerned. The word "gradually" is important because it reflects the developmental basis for Constructivist teaching. Constructivists recognize that teaching young children involves accepting immature thinking and requires working in conjunction with maturation to help children move to greater understanding.

Although creating community in a Constructivist classroom is more similar to the Authoritative and Democratic models of discipline than to any obedience or

---

 THREE THEORIES OF DISCIPLINE

Behaviorist: Molds behavior via reward and punishment
Constructivist: Helps children learn from experience
Maturationist: Believes that time is the best teacher

---

passive models, it is not identical. (See "Comparing Discipline Terminology" box.) Because Constructivist learning theory is the basis for Constructivist guidance and discipline, Constructivist discipline has some unique traits. These traits are described throughout the book.

Discipline Goals Compared

In essence, each discipline style is based on the same motive: love and/or concern for the child. However, each has very different goals. Obedience is the target behavior in the authoritarian model, preferably unquestioning and immediate obedience (Kohn, 1999). The permissive model overemphasizes individual freedom (Baumerind, 1967), though it can also be a result of neglect. The constructivist model works toward moral autonomy: self-determined, responsible behavior, reflecting concern for the good of others and for oneself as well (Kamii, 1984). Rewards and punishment are incompatible with these goals. The Constructivist approach acknowledges the complexity of the ever-changing world; therefore, it teaches children to think for themselves about desirable or undesirable actions rather than telling them predetermined answers to current dilemmas. "When we simply tell children how they must behave, reward their good behavior and punish their bad, we fail to build their understanding of moral concepts that can guide their behavior when they encounter new situations to which these values might apply" (Williams & Shaps, 1999, p. 28).

Differences in Discipline Forms

Not surprisingly, each model uses very different forms of discipline (Bronson, 2000). Punishment and reward are used almost exclusively in the authoritarian model (Canter & Canter, 1992; Dobson, 1970). Lack of discipline is the distinguishing feature of the permissive model. In contrast to these two extremes, but definitely not a blend of them, the Constructivist model offers a multifaceted set of discipline options that will be explained in this book.

These Constructivist options focus on teaching and, like all good teaching, begin with good human relationships. Adults who are responsive, warm, and comforting are essential to children's healthy development (Gurian, 2001; Howes & Ritchie, 2002). Good relationships between teachers and children do not mean the teacher tries to be a "pal," just one of the group. The Constructivist teacher is still the adult in charge, responsible for setting necessary limits and keeping children safe. However, this is done in a caring and respectful way. Mutually caring and respectful relationships with adults and peers encourage youngsters to think about the effects of their behavior on other people. Teaching children to think critically is an essential aspect of Constructivist teaching about discipline, and about other topics as well. Constructivist discipline strategies are aimed at helping children construct socially productive behavior rules and values for themselves. As Pritchard (1996) says, "We hope the result is that children become better able to reason, and thus more reasonable human beings."

Differences in Results

What are the results of the different discipline models? We can never be certain about research findings concerning human beings because we cannot ethically control the variables in a person's life. Each person is a unique blend of genetics, family dynamics, societal influences, and individual experiences. However, certain trends occur frequently enough to suggest a relationship. The authoritarian model is associated with anger and depression, as well as low self-esteem and the inability to make self-directed choices (e.g., DeVries, 1999; Howes & Ritchie, 2002; Landy, 2002). Likewise, those people with an overly permissive background usually demonstrate low self-esteem and difficulty getting along with others. The shared power model results in high self-esteem, good social skills, general competence, and self-discipline (Butchart & McEwan, 1998; DeVries, 1999).

Constructivist discipline approaches help most children quickly learn to negotiate solutions to problems, to resolve their own conflicts (e.g., Siccone & Lopez, 2000), and to self-direct their learning activity (DeVries & Zan, 1994).

Family Concern: Shouldn't They Learn to Obey?

Many people think in black or white terms; they think that you either make kids obey or they are "disobedient" and run wild. Some cultures emphasize obedience at home, enforced with punishment. Therefore, you will get worried questions about this guidance approach from your students' families.

You need to help families understand that working for obedience is settling for much less than moral autonomy. Explain what you have learned about long-term versus short-term goals. Point out that obedience without understanding requires external enforcement of some sort, a reward or punishment (DeVries, Zan, & Hildebrandt, 2002). Teachers can introduce parents to the research provided in Chapters 9 and 10, which describe the negative effects of reward and punishment. Be sure to warn families about one of the most common and most devastating reward/punishment approaches: making parental love and approval conditional on obedience. However, remember to listen to what families want for their children and to be respectful of differing views.

Teaching for Moral Autonomy: The Constructivist Approach

Certain basic ideas are central to a Constructivist approach to discipline:

1. A relationship of mutual respect between adult and child is the foundation for development of moral autonomy (Kamii, 1982). *Mutual*

respect means that it is just as important for you to treat the child with respect as it is for the child to treat you with respect.

2. Constructivist teachers always strive to help children understand why a behavior is desirable or undesirable.

3. Providing age-appropriate choices for youngsters and supporting them in solving their own problems is a way of showing respect for children and also a way of teaching thinking and assisting understanding.

4. When undesirable behavior occurs, your discipline efforts must address the cause of the behavior for effective teaching to take place.

Now let's examine these concepts in more detail.

Mutual Respect

Constructive discipline involves respect and affection for the child. The quality of the relationship between child and adult is crucial to the success of any discipline approach. Unless a child knows you care about him or her, and unless that child is concerned about maintaining a relationship with you, there is really no reason for the child to pay attention to what you ask. Having a relationship with a child requires investing time in getting to know children as individuals and attempting to understand them. If you are going to be effective during a behavior crisis, you need to first build a relationship by spending time on pleasant interaction. Spending time with a youngster and listening to that child not only helps an adult understand the child but also demonstrates respect. Too often adults expect youngsters to listen to them but don't reciprocate. Respecting children and their viewpoints helps them to respect our viewpoints (Kamii, 1984). According to DeVries and Zan (1994), "Children do not develop respect for others unless they are respected" (p. 76).

Mutual respect is an essential ingredient of effective discipline. Any discipline response can turn into punishment if accompanied by put-downs, which, of course, are inherently disrespectful. For instance, to call a child "sloppy" for spilling something, or "mean" for knocking down some blocks, would destroy the educational value of your discipline teaching. The child would focus on self-defense rather than on the problem behavior. It is also important to be aware of how your attitude is projected. Anger or disgust in your tone of voice can override even the most carefully chosen words. Listen to yourself as you talk to the children in your care: Are your words something they would want to listen to? Or are you teaching them to tune you out by a steady stream of commands and criticism?

Helping Children Understand

Often it seems obvious to an adult why a certain behavior is inappropriate. But young children have little experience in the world and don't automatically know all that seems obvious to you; therefore, you need to help youngsters learn the reasons behind rules and requests. Sometimes words are helpful teaching tools, but usually young children need experiences to help them understand the explanations. You can teach without punishing by asking Aaron to mop up the

Mutual respect between teacher and child is an essential ingredient of effective discipline.

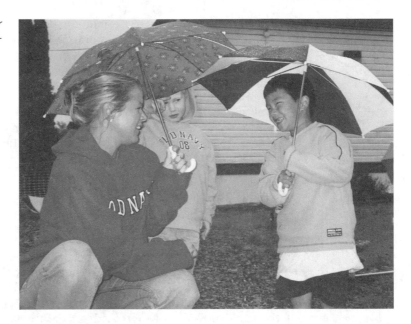

puddle he made when he splashed water on the floor during exuberant water play. Similarly, you can help Kenji learn a better way of showing he wants to play than by knocking over other children's buildings. The teacher's role in developing moral autonomy is to help children figure out why their behavior is causing a problem and provide them with the opportunity to help resolve the problem.

Mrs. Jensen discovered one day that she had not helped Lesa to understand why she was asked to leave group time: Lesa came up to Mrs. Jensen after the group meeting and said, "I'm sorry. I won't do it again." Mrs. Jensen asked her, "Won't do what again?" She was astounded at the child's honest reply, "I don't know." Too often, youngsters learn to mouth meaningless words of apology or appreciation with no idea about what they mean or why they would be appropriate.

Perhaps the most crucial understanding for young children is that other people have needs and wishes different than their own. Dennis's approach to the following doll bed dilemma was aimed at helping Sara and Sophie each begin to think about a viewpoint other than her own. Learning to consider the viewpoints of others in making decisions is part of learning moral autonomy. According to Piaget, we also teach moral autonomy and the necessary understanding of others' views when we help children realize the effects of their behavior rather than merely punishing it. Following is an example of this principle in action.

When preschoolers Sarah and Sophie were tugging on the same doll bed, each screaming, "I had it first!" Dennis, their teacher, resisted coming over and immediately taking the toy away, although it might have been simple to say, "If you can't play nicely, I'll have to put this away." Nor did he start the usual inquisition trying to determine which child had it first so that he could make the fairest decision. Those approaches are common where the teacher's goal is simply to solve the problem for now and where the discipline approach is authoritarian.

Because Dennis's goals are long-term, he wanted to help the children learn to think about their behavior and to develop skills for solving their own conflicts. His discipline approach is constructivist. Therefore, he facilitated decision making on the part of the children instead of making the decisions himself. He helped the girls to clarify the problem by stating what it appeared to be: "You both want a bed for your dolls." He further identified the dilemma: "There's only one of these beds and two sleepy babies." Then Dennis asked them what they thought they could do to solve their problem. In this way, he helped the girls learn to think about fairness for both sides.

Problem solving takes practice, just as other complex skills do. It is also dependent on levels of maturity. Young children have limited reasoning ability, but they become more capable when encouraged to discuss their different views. The teacher works with children at their levels of maturation, demonstrating ways of expressing their feelings and suggesting possible approaches to solutions. The teacher may ask questions, such as, "Where else could a baby doll sleep in this house?" This method still leaves the children in charge of a search for alternatives. Even if they aren't immediately successful, Dennis doesn't take over. However, if the children's frustration and anger appear to be getting beyond their ability to control, he might resort to taking the doll bed and putting it out of reach until they cool down. He then would assure the girls that they could have it as soon as they come up with a solution.

Guiding Choices

Constructive discipline encourages children to make as many of their own decisions and choices as possible. This helps children to learn from their mistakes as well as their successes. In other words, your job is to help children learn how to make wise choices, not to make all the choices for them. In the process of learning to regulate their own behavior, children make both good and bad choices for themselves. It is hard, but necessary, to let youngsters make some poor choices as well as good ones. No matter what their age, people tend to learn best the lessons learned through their own experience—especially from analyzing their mistakes. Think about your own mistakes: Probably someone older and wiser warned you, but you had to find out for yourself, didn't you?

Of course, adults must monitor the choices; not all choices are safe or appropriate. For instance, children don't have the choice of putting their fingers in an electrical socket to experience a shock. But they do have the choice of not eating their snack and getting a little hungry, or the choice of not cooperating in play and subsequently being rejected by peers. Teachers whose goal is helping children learn to think for themselves don't help by thinking and acting for their students. They do not instantly step in and solve conflicts for youngsters. Instead, conflicts and problems are seen as potential learning situations and opportunities for you to offer meaningful teaching (Bronson, 2000). The children work at problem solving. The teacher's job is to facilitate the process as needed.

Treating the Cause Rather than the Symptom

No amount of respect, teaching, or choice will make discipline effective *unless your approach deals with the reasons why the behavior occurred.* If you only stop the behavior without treating the cause, the behavior problem will probably continue to be repeated (Kaiser & Rasminsky, 1999). Discipline is like weeding a garden: If you don't get the roots out with the weeds, the weeds will be back in a few days. Effective approaches to discipline work to get at the root of the problem. Yet, very few discipline/guidance approaches involve considering the cause of a behavior problem before deciding on an intervention. A main focus of this text is matching guidance and discipline approaches to the causes of behavior problems.

It isn't easy to figure out why children do the things they do. You certainly can't determine the cause simply by seeing the behavior. For instance, there could be several reasons why Aaron might have spilled water during water play:

- Perhaps he was just having such a good time that he didn't think about where the water was going.

- It is also possible that he spilled because of immature coordination, which made it hard for him to pour the water where he intended.

- Then again, maybe he knew what he was doing and did it on purpose. He might have spilled to get attention or to alleviate boredom.

A useful way to think about the cause of undesirable behavior is to think about what the child needs in order to act in more appropriate ways. You may find it useful to ask yourself the questions in the box, "Discovering Causes of Behavior Problems," as you work toward helpful interventions for each youngster. Each different cause of behavior problems points to the need for a different solution. Yet, there are many teachers and caregivers who have one solution for any and all infractions of the rules.

Think about how the commonly used time-out bench would affect Aaron in the case of each suggested cause for the spilled water:

- How would the time-out bench affect his feelings about preschool fun if the spill was caused by his eagerness to explore?

- How would time-out affect his feelings about himself if the spill was caused by poor coordination?

- If attention-getting or boredom was the cause, would time-out keep Aaron from spilling water again?

As you read later chapters, you will find suggestions of appropriate responses to each of these and other causes of undesirable behavior.

Observing to Discover the Cause

The best way to determine the cause of a child's behavior is to observe the child carefully and record your observations (Flicker & Hoffman, 2002). You need to know a lot about a child to plan effective discipline. You need to note whether this is usual or unusual behavior, and also under what circumstances it occurs. Are

DISCOVERING CAUSES OF BEHAVIOR PROBLEMS

Ask yourself the following types of questions as a guide toward discovering the causes of a behavior problem: (There may be several "right" answers.)

Is the environment meeting this child's needs?
Enough movement?
Enough privacy?
Enough space?
Sufficient materials?

Is the program meeting this child's needs?
Appropriate challenge?
Personal interest?
Meaningful?

Are behavioral expectations appropriate for this child?
Developmentally?
Culturally?
Temperamentally?

Does the child have unmet physical needs?
Hungry?
Tired?

Does the child have unmet emotional needs?
Friendship?
Trust?
Self-esteem?
Personal power?
Attention?

Is this child missing some social skill?
Perspective taking?
Entering play?

Does this child need help with communication skills?
"I messages"?
Negotiation?

Is the behavior a result of inappropriate role models?
Television?
Admired adults?
Admired peers?

Does this child understand why a behavior is important?
No experience with outcomes?

Has this child learned negative ways of getting needs met?
Received attention for inappropriate behavior?

The best way to determine the cause of a child's behavior is to observe the child carefully and record your observations.

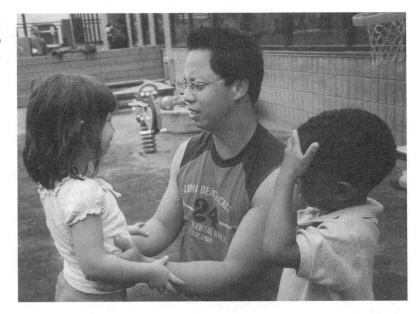

certain activities likely to trigger it? Is there a pattern of when, where, or with whom behavior problems are most likely? What do you know about the child's home routine, health, or family situation that might provide some clues? Communicating with parents and keeping careful records of child behavior are both indispensable parts of determining the cause of problems. You assess the child's social learning needs through this process of finding causes for behavior problems. This assessment is an essential guide for effective teaching.

Never overlook the possibility that you may have caused a discipline problem. Chapters 2 and 3 illustrate how teacher expectations that don't reflect child development, temperament, or culture cause discipline problems. Chapters 4 and 5 discuss how inappropriate school environments and programs often cause behavior problems. Chapters 6 and 7 raise the issue of undesirable adult examples and communication styles as sources of undesirable child behavior. Chapters 9 and 10 explain how coercive and punitive discipline approaches backfire and create worse behavior problems. Chapters 11 and 12 examine various situations, demonstrating the process of finding the cause and matching it to an appropriate response. Chapters 13 and 14 explore causes outside the realm of the classroom. Chapter 15 helps you keep it all together.

Targeting the cause of a behavior problem is a difficult task, compounded by the fact that there are usually multiple and interactive causes. The information presented in Chapters 2 through 6 is especially crucial to determining the causes for undesirable behavior.

As you read this text, you will be guided to match probable causes of behavior with appropriate approaches to discipline. Selecting the right approach requires that you understand many different approaches, as well as understanding children and the many different reasons for their actions. This text presents a set of guidance/discipline strategies; each related to a specific cause. These are explained throughout the text as we explore various behavior problem causes.

CONCLUSION

This chapter has attempted to stimulate your thinking about your values as they relate to guidance and discipline. Our comparison of discipline approaches resulted in the recommendation of Constructivist discipline, rather than an authoritarian or a permissive approach. We began an introduction to ways of implementing Constructivist approaches to discipline, with more complete explanations to come in the following chapters.

This chapter offers an overview of ideas presented in the rest of the book. If you can't visualize how all this works yet, don't worry; that's what the rest of the chapters are for. We hope that you will supplement what you read here with further reading from the recommended reading list at the end of the chapter. We also hope that you will spend significant time with young children, proving guidance and discipline concepts to yourself through your own observation and experience.

If you haven't read the foreword and preface to this book, we suggest you do so. Constance Kamii's discussion of moral autonomy in the foreword should help you better understand the idea. The preface should provide further explanation about the theory-base and intent of the book. The preface also gives an overview of the three-part organization of the text: (1) discipline foundations, (2) discipline approaches, and (3) matching discipline causes to discipline approaches. Be sure to also read the introductions to each section of the text; they will help you understand what you are reading about. We hope you will also read and think about the dedication at the front of the book.

As you continue to read and think, remember that going to school represents the child's entry into our society (Watson, 1999). For the first time, young children may be encountering the necessity of following basic rules and of respecting the rights of others. The skills of problem solving, predicting consequences, and planning ahead are vital for children to escape the culture of violence (Dill, 1998).

If you are now saying to yourself, "But don't kids need limits?" or "I know people who grew up with complete freedom and they felt their parents didn't care," then go back and re-read the chapter. If these are new ideas for you, it will take careful reading and thought to understand that there are helpful alternatives to forcing obedience. The choice isn't just between power-tripping children or letting them run wild.

As you begin to implement the ideas presented here, you should be prepared for less-than-instant success. Understanding complex ideas involves hard work accompanied by trial and error. Changing established ways of interacting with children is also very difficult, requiring time and commitment. At first, you may even find that your discipline efforts seem less effective than before. As they are learning new approaches, some people report feeling "paralyzed" by indecisiveness about what to do. Just as we urge you to be accepting of children's gradual learning processes, we urge you to accept your own gradual progress. When, inevitably, you forget your new plans and don't live up to your expectations, just try again. That's what we do.

∞ *FOR FURTHER THOUGHT*

1. Create your list of desirable goals for discipline. Compare your list with those of others. Select the three characteristics you would most want to encourage through child guidance. Explain your choices and compare them with a friend's.

2. Think about your own parents' approach to child rearing. What characteristics do you think they most valued? How did those values influence your own childhood? Do your choices reflect those of your parents or are they different?

3. How would you rate yourself on a continuum from heteronomy to autonomy? How does this rating reflect the discipline approaches of your parents and teachers? If you are heteronomous, can you help children become autonomous?

4. A problem to solve: Carlos is using the playhouse broom. Betsy wants it and grabs it away. Carlos hits Betsy, and the battle is on.

   a. Describe a response that solves the problem but does not teach autonomy or self-discipline.
   b. Describe a response that solves the problem and does teach autonomy and self-discipline.

∞ *RECOMMENDED READINGS*

DeVries, R., & Zan, B. (1994). *Moral classrooms, moral children.* New York: Teachers College Press.

Kamii, C. (1982). Autonomy as the aim of education: Implications of Piaget's theory. In C. Kamii (Ed.), *Number in preschool and kindergarten* (pp. 73–87). Washington, DC: National Association for the Education of Young Children.

Noddings, N. (January 1995). A morally defensible mission for schools in the 21st century. *Phi Delta Kappan*, 365–368.

Piaget, J. (1965). *The moral judgment of the child.* New York: Free Press. (Originally published in 1932.)

2 Physical and Emotional Development Affect Child Behavior

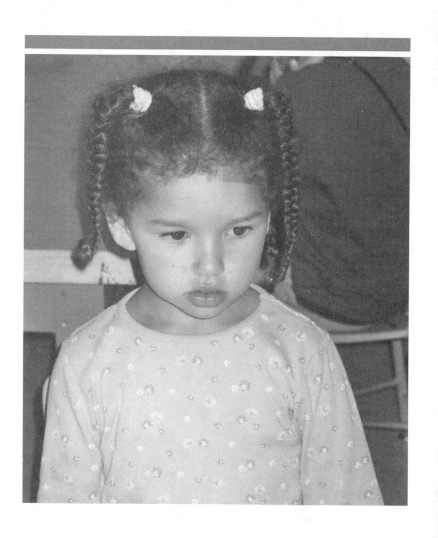

ach stage of child development brings its own set of needs, abilities, and perspectives. Your knowledge of children's physical, emotional, intellectual, and social development will help you guard against adult-caused behavior problems. In this chapter we will examine physical and emotional development; Chapter 3 looks at intellectual and social development.

Child care and teaching are much easier when you are knowledgeable about child development. As we will repeat many times in this book, effective discipline addresses the causes of behavior problems. When you know more about child development, you can determine if immature development may be the cause of a behavior problem. Then, it will be easier to find an effective solution. You can eliminate many discipline problems by matching your expectations of children to their individual maturation levels. In other words, you will not expect children to be successful at tasks beyond their developmental level. Nor will you blame children for behavior that is a result of maturational level.

Effective child guidance and discipline require knowledge of factors that affect emotional development: Temperament strongly contributes to children's unique paths of emotional development. Attachment is also a key factor in emotional development. Children have basic human needs that must be met for healthy growth and development. If these needs are not met, then children will have difficulty developing emotion regulation. Information about emotional development, temperament, attachment, and basic needs will also provide useful guidelines for discipline interventions.

In this chapter, we will examine how the factors above contribute to healthy child development and how they are related to discipline issues. We will revisit these developmental issues again in Part Three (Chapters 11–15) as we look for the cause of and possible solutions to real-world classroom issues. Chapters 2 and 3 are not intended to be a comprehensive coverage of child development. Please refer to the recommended readings at the end of each chapter for more comprehensive coverage sources.

RELATED PHYSICAL DEVELOPMENT ISSUES

It is obvious that young children's physical needs and abilities are different from those of adults. We know that young children are often unable to handle new tasks when their needs for adequate rest and nourishment are not met. Also, children repeatedly demonstrate that they are not able to sit still for very long. However, teachers sometimes forget this last fact and cause trouble for themselves and their students.

Need to Move Around

Devon and several of his classmates in Miss Wheeler's first-grade class routinely upset their teacher's day. They simply won't sit still and listen during group time. They are always getting up and wandering around when they are supposed to be working in their seats. Miss Wheeler constantly reminds them to sit still or to go back to their seats. She just doesn't understand that most young children have difficulty sitting still for very long.

Next door, in Mrs. Jensen's first-grade room, children are free to move around between learning centers. There is very little enforced sitting in that room, and very little need for the teacher to reprimand anyone. In addition to movement indoors, lessons often include outdoor activity. Sometimes, a parent helper and Mrs. Jensen take the class outdoors for a gardening session on the school grounds, allowing physical movement as well as some hands-on lessons about plant life.

Miss Wheeler feels like a police officer instead of a teacher, but she thinks it is the children who are at fault. Matching her expectations of the children with their level of development would make her life much easier, as well as eliminate a lot of needless tension for her students.

Children need to move, not only for their physical development, but also for their intellectual development (Planinsec, 2002). Brain research shows that physical movement stimulates the myelinization process critical to development of neural pathways in the brain. The process of myelinization allows young children to gain control over their muscles and their sensory abilities; it also facilitates their cognitive processes (Berger, 1998). Physical movement also assists the delivery of oxygen and glucose to the brain, optimizing its performance (Leppo, Davis, & Crim, 2000). An assessment of how girls and boys learn differently points out that movement is even more important for boys and their reduction of emotional stress (Gurian, 2001). Some children with little physical movement experience are delayed in both body and space awareness. The spatial confusions can contribute to reading and writing difficulties (Corso, 1993; Hannaford, 1995), as well as to behavior problems. Some young children are continually getting into trouble because they are not aware of where their body is in relation to other people.

Rather than trying to keep children still, adults help children better by promoting physical activity (Pica, 1997). Physically active children are healthier and eventually grow up to be more active, healthy adults. Increased physical activity is needed to counteract the problem of childhood obesity in the United States (Steinbeck, 2001). In addition, physically competent children tend to have higher self-esteem than less-competent peers. Competence in performing motor skills boosts children's confidence. Success and enjoyment associated with physical activity affect how children feel about themselves and how they interact with peers. Having good agility, balance, coordination, power, and speed can promote social interaction and peer acceptance. Children with physical disabilities that affect their gross-motor development often share their classmates' interest in physical activities. Therefore, playgrounds and outdoor equipment should be accessible for children with disabilities (Bredekamp & Copple, 1997).

Small-Muscle Coordination Takes Time

Not only do young children have a need to exercise their large muscles regularly, but they also need practice with small-muscle skills. Young children typically are not very adept at small-muscle work (Bredekamp & Copple, 1997). Both the need for large-muscle activity and the lack of small-muscle ability create problems in classrooms where children are expected to sit at their seats and do paperwork much of the day. Such a schedule focuses on the children's areas of weakness and, therefore, puts a huge pressure on them.

Individual differences and gender play a role in the development of dexterity. Girls tend to be more advanced than boys in fine-motor skills and in gross-motor skills requiring precision, such as hopping and skipping. Boys generally excel in skills that require force and power, such as running and jumping (Berk, 2002). For most children, it is a fact of physical development that fine-motor coordination lags behind gross-motor coordination. Tyler, who is a fast runner and a great climber, may not be able to tie his shoes yet; and Tera, the best rope jumper in kindergarten, may not be able to make a pencil do her bidding. Placing pressure on these children to perform above their current level of development will result in frustration and feelings of failure. Negative behaviors will surely follow. Matching your expectations to the children's abilities will avert some potential discipline struggles.

Although you want to be careful not to push fine-motor tasks too early, fine-motor development can be encouraged appropriately (Bredekamp & Copple, 1997). Ample opportunities for practice, appropriate tools (scissors that actually cut, for instance), and adult support assist children's fine-motor dexterity. Children with certain kinds of identified disabilities may require adaptations or assistive technologies for activities such as writing and drawing. By the time they enter the primary grades, children are usually much more capable of fine-motor work than when they were preschool age, when it often generates neurological fatigue.

Needs for Food and Rest

Young children also have a need for nutritious food and rest in order to work and play cooperatively at school. Many children today are "misnourished," with a large amount of their calories coming from non-nutritive foods (Bhattacharya & Currie, 2001). Eating too many non-nutritive foods contributes to our ever-growing rate of childhood obesity, and also affects children's behavior (Steinbeck, 2001). Too much sugar or a lack of protein or complex carbohydrates can lead to a sugar crash. This crash may affect individual children differently. You may know a child who falls apart completely if he or she has too much sugar or gets too hungry. Some may become impulsive, more likely in boys, while others may become withdrawn or distracted. Girls more often have the latter reaction (Gurian, 2001).

Sometimes Kelsey cannot seem to focus on any of the morning classroom activities, and Dennis, her teacher, figures that she didn't eat much breakfast that day. When this happens, he allows her to have her mid-morning snack a little early. Dennis is taking into consideration Kelsey's individual needs as well as the group's needs. The standard practice of snack time acknowledges the fact that children in general can't eat much at one time and can't go as long between meals as older people can.

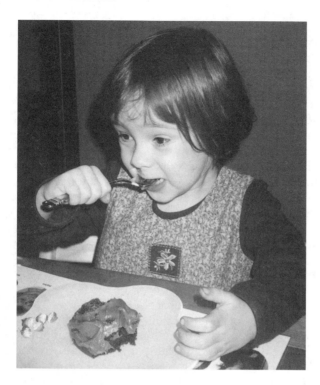

Many children are "misnourished," with a large amount of their calories coming from junk food.

Scheduled rest time at the preschool level acknowledges a need at that age, but formal rest periods tend to disappear once children enter kindergarten or first grade.

Yaisa attends the before- and after-school child-care program at Lincoln Elementary. She gets to school at 7:30 in the morning and doesn't go home until 5:30 in the evening. Sometimes she gets crabby and picks a fight or bursts into tears for no apparent reason. Fortunately, her teacher understands that when Yaisa acts that way, she needs a break, not a punishment for being difficult. Mrs. Jensen sees Yaisa's need and encourages her to find a comfortable pillow and a good book in the secluded classroom book nook. After a short rest, Yaisa is able to participate with the group again.

Mrs. Jensen is trying to teach Yaisa and others with similar needs how to take a break when they need it, rather than push themselves beyond their limits. Her classroom offers several soft, secluded spots, and her schedule offers the flexibility to use them.

EMOTIONAL DEVELOPMENT AND GUIDANCE

Each child experiences the world in different ways. Children's relationships with family members and others, their cultural context, and their brain development are just some of the factors that affect their unique path of emotional development. Temperament, gender, and individual strengths and weaknesses also affect emotional development (Hyson, 2004). In the following pages, we specifically explore some of these factors and how they may play into discipline issues in the classroom. Meeting children's basic emotional needs is essential to creating a peaceful learning environment. Meeting their needs is also essential to children's overall success in school and life beyond.

Temperament

The definition of *temperament* continues to evolve as we gain understanding about children and their individual differences. Most theorists today agree that temperament is an individual's behavioral style or personality traits. These include expressions of emotions, reactions to stimuli, ability or inability to regulate reactions and emotions, activity level, adaptability, and sociability (Landy, 2002). The temperament a child is born with has a primary influence on emotional development. It not only determines much about how the child behaves, but also about how others react to the child (Reinsberg, 1999). This interactive process between youngsters and those around them shapes emotional development and self-concept in positive or negative directions. The challenge for the caring adult is to respond positively to the more difficult child.

Research has identified nine characteristics of temperament, or traits, that are apparent from birth and tend to remain stable over the individual's lifetime (Chess & Thomas, 1996). Some of these traits make children easier to work with than others do. Some children adapt easily to change, have a pleasant mood, and their emotions are easy to read, making them a joy for caregivers and teachers. However, some children who are born with a high energy level, a short attention span, difficulty with change, or a negative outlook, are often in trouble with their teachers. These individual differences influence the child's interactions throughout life, and certainly are a factor in behavior and discipline (Hyson, 2004).

Some temperament differences appear to have underlying biological roots. For instance, one study demonstrated that shy children have different heart rhythms than others (Kagan, Reznick, Clarke, Snidman, & Garcia-Coll, 1984). Another study found that "irritable" children may have different levels of certain hormones than more even-tempered children (Gunnar, Mangelsdorf, Larson, & Hertsgaard, 1989). While temperament traits may be expressed differently depending on an individual's developmental stage, researchers agree that these traits are genetic, inherited differences that will be part of the individual's personality throughout life (Landy, 2002). In other words, if Corrie has a difficult temperament, it is not her fault. She needs your help and understanding because her difficult temperament is making life more difficult for her, too.

Temperament differences such as degree of sensitivity to stimuli, pleasant or unpleasant mood, and intensity of reactions are determining factors in children's ability to regulate their emotions. Temperament often also determines how well a child is received by peers and caregivers. When Corrie cries at the drop of a hat, her friends tease her, calling her a "crybaby." Children like Corrie will need significant support with social skills and emotion regulation to prevent them from developing low self-esteem, or other emotional or behavioral problems. What we

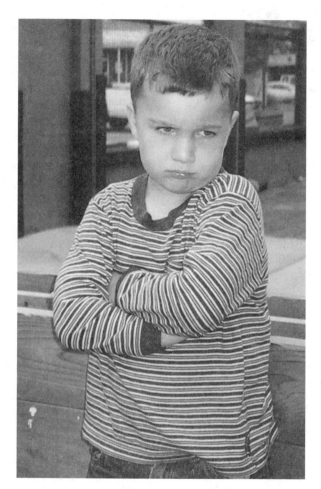

It can be challenging to respond positively to a child with a difficult temperament.

know about temperament traits tells us that children will not change their basic behavioral style; therefore, caregivers must focus their interests on adapting the environment and teaching styles to accommodate the needs of the children involved. This is part of making the school fit the child, as opposed to trying to make the child fit the school.

When behavior problems arise, we assess the cause of the problem to determine our action with the child. Temperament traits are a possible cause for many behavioral issues.

Corrie and Jack are attempting to build a road system together, each with her and his own idea of where the road should go. When Dennis sees that Corrie's frustration level is beginning to rise, he knows from prior experience that she may need some help calming herself down. Dennis calmly approaches Corrie before she rises completely out of control, and invites her to continue building her road in the sand at the sensory table. Dennis knows that the sand play and some time alone will help to calm Corrie. Dennis does not attempt any negotiation between Corrie and Jack when he knows that Corrie's intensity of emotion is too high for this to be effective.

Chapter 12 further discusses temperament issues as a potential cause of behavioral problems.

Developmental Stages

Though individual differences play a significant role, children nonetheless progress through various, predictable developmental stages in their emotional development. Children must build upon what they learn in one stage to progress onto the next, and as they do so they lay the foundation for their mental health throughout their lives. It is important to note, however, that one developmental stage is not completed, like a closed book, when the child moves on to another stage. All stages will be continually revisited and built upon as the child grows and continues developing for the rest of his or her life. Erikson's (1963) theory of personality encompasses the entire lifespan and attempts to explain patterns of behavior throughout every stage of life.

According to Erikson's widely respected theory, each of these stages has a particular focus, or developmental task, that influences the child's responses at this time. We find Erikson's explanation of emotional development especially relevant to discipline issues. Understanding child behavior in terms of the stages that Erikson describes can help us prevent discipline problems; this understanding also can be used to guide intervention when problems do occur (Gordon & Browne, 1996). We will discuss only the stages relevant to early childhood, although Erikson's stage theory continues through adolescence, adulthood, and old age.

These stages are roughly correlated to ages, but individual differences and diversity of experiences create variations from this norm. As mentioned, as children proceed along their developmental path, they are continually building upon and continuing their growth in previous stages of emotional development. Teachers and parents also may notice a child who is in an emotionally stressful situation at home regressing to a previous developmental stage. Some serious problems, such as family crises and how they affect learning, will be discussed in Chapter 14.

Trust versus Mistrust　　Even if you never plan to work with babies, you need to know about the trust versus mistrust stage of development, which Erikson relates to infancy. When babies are making their first discoveries about what kind of world they have entered, they are forming the foundation of emotional health for the rest of their lives. Many are welcomed into homes where they are the center of attention, and their slightest protest is met with efforts to alleviate distress. These babies begin early to trust that they are important and that someone cares for them enough to meet their needs. For these babies, the world is a safe and friendly place. Some babies aren't so lucky, however. Their parents may be overwhelmed with personal problems, and a baby is just one more worry, or their caregivers may be overworked and untrained. These babies may continually cry from hunger or other discomfort without any response. What a different image of themselves and their world these babies get!

ERIKSON'S STAGES OF CHILD DEVELOPMENT

- Trust versus mistrust: Babies learn whether or not the world around them is safe and nurturant.
- Autonomy versus shame: Toddlers learn to define themselves as individuals or feel shame about their independent urges.
- Initiative versus guilt: Children learn to test their individual powers and abilities or feel guilty about making "mistakes."
- Industry versus inferiority: Children extend their ideas of themselves as successful workers or learn to feel inferior and incapable.

Children's early efforts to communicate their needs deserve a response. Responsive adults are setting the stage for children to build trusting, cooperative relationships throughout their lifetime. When a child's needs are unmet, the child feels insecure and does not trust in others to care for him or her. Trust develops along with attachment to a significant adult. Later in this chapter we will talk more about attachment as a basic human need and a foundation for healthy emotional development.

Children continue to actively work on developing trust during preschool and in the early school years, especially if they had a problem with it earlier. They are looking for evidence that they can count on people in their larger world. Some have had negative experiences in their past that lead them to expect continued disappointments from everyone they encounter (Watson, 2003). You may see some of these children constantly checking to see if someone is still their friend. They may also frequently seek the reassurance of the teacher's attention. Others just expect rejection, as in the following example:

September 29th was the first child's birthday in her class. However, Mrs. Jensen didn't see Eli's mother put party invitations into six of the children's cubbies. As the first child discovered hers, a mad rush of others hopefully checked their cubbies. There were a few shouts of delight and many disappointed faces. "Oh dear!" Mrs. Jensen thought. "I should have made it clear that party invitations should not be distributed at school unless all children were included." Mrs. Jensen noticed that Cole didn't even bother looking. He didn't expect to be invited, just as he couldn't believe that other children would let him join in their play.

Cole's life hadn't made him feel secure or wanted. He had been in four foster homes in two years. Mrs. Jensen wondered what his birthdays had been like. Mrs. Jensen reached for her circle time basket and removed the story she'd planned to read, replacing it with A. A. Milne's *The World of Pooh*. She put her bookmark on page 70, "In which Eeyore has a birthday party and gets two presents." She also changed her plans for the topic of the group discussion, deciding to discuss feelings of being left out.

Mrs. Jensen begins group time by sharing a short, humorous but sad, personal story of a time she remembers feeling left out as a child. Two children share similar experiences. When Mrs. Jensen reads the part of the story where Piglet wishes Eeyore "Many happy returns of the day" and Eeyore can hardly believe that his friends remembered his birthday and even gave him presents, Cole giggles especially loudly.

After the story, the group discusses how Eeyore felt and they come up with a list of ways to help him trust his friends next year. Mrs. Jensen then points out how she put paper candles on her calendar to mark all the children's birthdays. She ends with an explanation about most homes not being big enough to invite a whole class, so they will have birthday celebrations in the classroom for everyone. (Class parties are acceptable this year because she doesn't have any children in her class from families who don't celebrate birthdays or holidays.) She mentions the birthdays coming up during the next few months, and Cole beams as she ends with, "and December 6th we'll celebrate Cole's birthday!"

If a child's experiences lead to a lesson in mistrust rather than trust, that child's whole life can be affected. Future friendships, and even marriages, may suffer from this lack of trust. It first appears as insecurity with friends and excessive demands on teachers. Later in life, an inability to trust co-workers and the suspicion of spouses can undermine relationships. As relationships fail to withstand the pressure, a vicious cycle of self-fulfilling prophecy is perpetuated. We have all known children and adults who fit this pattern: They expect others to reject them, so they behave in ways that invite rejection. Your challenge is to help children have experiences that will reverse this cycle before it is too late.

Autonomy versus Shame   Erikson's autonomy stage is the period when youngsters work at defining themselves as separate from the adults they have, until now, completely depended on. (Erikson's use of the term *autonomy* to describe emotional development is different from Piaget's concepts of intellectual and moral autonomy, which were discussed in Chapter 1.) The toddler years are the time for development of autonomy, as Erikson defines it. As infants, children are so dependent that they actually consider themselves a part of their parents or caregivers. But toddlers suddenly begin to see that they are separate people, with ideas and wills of their own. They need to test this new revelation to make sure it is true and to convince themselves of their independence. This period is known as the "terrible twos" and can create serious discipline problems for the unwary adult. It doesn't necessarily disappear at age 3, so beware. The formerly docile child suddenly says an emphatic "No!" to all suggestions and tests the limits that are set.

Andrew is so caught up in his ability to say "No!" that he sometimes says "No!" to things he really wants. "Do you want some ice cream?" his mother asks. "No," says Andrew proudly. Because Andrew is her sixth child, Debbie has been through this behavior before. She knows that right now her 2-year-old is focusing on his power to say "Yes" or "No," not on whether or not he really wants some ice cream. When Andrew inevitably changes his mind and does decide to have ice cream, Debbie doesn't lecture him about the fact that saying "No" means he doesn't get any. Instead, she encourages his new independence by respecting his decisions, either way.

In addition, Debbie gives Andrew as many opportunities as possible to make decisions and choices. These opportunities not only help him feel proud of his

Children cooperate better when they have enough opportunities to assert themselves.

independence, but they also help him cooperate during times when there is no choice. Children who routinely have a chance to exercise their personal power are more able to accept times when adults must make the decisions. Conversely, children who don't get ample opportunities for making choices can be incredibly stubborn. In other words, Debbie knows that letting Andrew make decisions such as whether or not to have ice cream or which shirt to wear will make it easier when he doesn't get to decide what time he goes to bed.

Children in preschool, and even primary grades, still have the need to assert themselves. If you understand this need and learn to give lots of choices, it is often incredibly easy to get children to cooperate. One of Olivia's child-care providers, Nancy, used this understanding to solve a problem that Olivia was having at her child-care center.

It seemed that Olivia was asserting herself by refusing to cooperate when getting ready to go home, antagonizing her tired and hurried father. Nancy didn't give any attention to the undesirable behavior by wheedling and bribing her to get her boots and coat on, nor did she take away Olivia's independence by forcing her to put them on. Instead, Nancy gave Olivia some choices. The choice was not whether to get ready to go home, but rather how to get ready. "Do you want to put on your boots first or your coat first?" asked Nancy. "Would you like me or your daddy to help you with your zipper?" was the next question. "Can you put on your own boots, or would you like help?" was another. In no time at all, Olivia was ready to go and feeling proud of herself.

Erikson's theory says that when children do not develop emotional autonomy, they develop a sense of shame instead. Shame can be caused by their experiences with adults who don't understand what is happening when children assert themselves; these adults think that their job is to stamp out "naughtiness." Unfortunately, they may only be successful at making children believe they are being bad, when really the children are just working at being grown-up. As a result, the children develop feelings of shame about the natural urges of independence.

Initiative versus Guilt   Erikson's next stage of emotional development is called initiative versus guilt. Most preschool and many kindergarten children are in this stage. You will see them further testing their individual powers and abilities. As their physical and intellectual abilities increase rapidly, they try out new and more challenging skills. This stage is like a bridge that children may continually move back and forth across trying out being a "big kid" and then moving back into the security of their dependency on caregivers (Koplow, 2002). Children in this stage want to feel involved and powerful as they try out new tasks. They may be competitive and want to be the best at everything they do. Likewise, they may be intimidated and fear failure when tasks are too difficult for them. It is helpful to offer children appropriate opportunities to feel successful, as in the following examples.

Megan is always right there when it is time to prepare the morning snack. She takes great satisfaction in setting the table or spreading peanut butter on celery sticks. She practices small-motor coordination, and even math skills, as she meticulously places five raisins on each celery stick. Her feelings of accomplishment and confidence are also growing.

Megan and her classmates are invited to assist with many necessary jobs in the morning session of preschool. They care for the guinea pig, cleaning her cage and feeding her. They water the plants, sweep up under the sand table, and organize the dress-up clothes on hooks. They take pride in this work because their teacher, Dennis, communicates his belief in the children's abilities. The teacher accepts the children's ability levels and doesn't make a fuss if a job isn't done perfectly, or if a little something is spilled in the process.

Whenever the morning staff thinks about developing a new learning center, they first discuss the plan with the students. Dennis knows from his classes in early childhood education, as Nancy knows from raising four children, that children will learn much from the planning process and that their involvement will help ensure that the new materials are used appropriately. After a field trip to a bank, the children want to play bank in the pretend play area. Instead of looking all weekend for materials, Dennis and his assistant Nancy invite children to bring things from home that could be used in a bank. The weekly newsletter explains the plan to parents and asks them to contribute. On Monday, the children arrive with old checkbooks, deposit slips, canceled checks, a real cash box, and play money. Aaron's mom works in a bank, so she contributes a pad of loan application forms.

As the interested youngsters work to arrange these materials in a way meaningful to them, they cooperate in problem solving and planning. They are willing to invest effort to resolve disagreements in their bank. Before long, things are set up to their satisfaction, and several youngsters are busily scribbling on the checks, making important banking transactions. These children are feeling good about the work they have done, and it shows in their behavior.

When teachers save all the work for themselves, no one "wins."

In the afternoon session at Midway Children's Center, the teacher makes the snack in advance and pours juice for each child. Joanne, the teacher, discourages the children's offers to help, telling them that they will only spill if they try to pour their own juice. Joanne spends long hours after school and on weekends preparing materials and rearranging the classroom. She prides herself on always having everything ready for her students when they arrive. She wouldn't dream of using class time to set up a new activity; everything is strictly preplanned and scheduled. She doesn't have pets in her class because she doesn't have time to care for them, and the children "are too young to do it properly." Everything is under control: hers. In spite of all her careful planning, Joanne has many more discipline problems than the morning staff does. The students often seem disinterested in what Joanne has planned for them. They frequently "misuse" the materials, pursuing their own ideas instead of copying the model at the art table. When the children don't follow Joanne's plans, she tells them how disappointed she is.

Joshua and his friends feel ashamed when they disappoint their teacher. They don't understand that it is their healthy curiosity and energy that is getting them into trouble. They only know that what they are interested in doing is "bad." They assume that they are bad children. Because Joanne's training is with older children, she isn't familiar with this stage of child development. Thus, she often misinterprets the children's actions.

What a different kind of experience this teacher and her young students would have if Joanne only knew how to harness their constructive energy into activities that would develop their sense of initiative.

Industry versus Inferiority   School-age children are working through an emotional development stage that builds on the preschool stage of initiative versus guilt. Erikson calls this next stage industry versus inferiority. During this phase, children are extending their ideas of themselves as workers and contributing members of society. If they feel successful, their behavior mirrors their good feelings about themselves; negative behaviors go along with negative feelings about themselves. Their tasks now focus on earning recognition by producing things and mastering the tools to do so. In a subsistence society, this stage means learning to hunt, fish, cure skins, gather berries, and preserve food. For today's mainstream society, it means learning to read, write, think quantitatively, and work cooperatively. Feeling successful at this age means seeing yourself as a capable person. Once again, children need to have opportunities for real work that is meaningful to them and that they are allowed to do on their own.

Children need opportunities to do their own real work that is meaningful to them.

Mrs. Jensen's first graders were planting seeds this afternoon as part of their study to learn how things grow. They had read about what plants need to grow and now they were reading the specific directions on the seed packets. They had a variety of fast-growing seeds available: beans, radishes, lettuce, and alfalfa. They also had access to a variety of planting materials and containers.

Some were interested in the idea of watching bean sprouts grow in a jar of water. Others liked the idea of growing an alfalfa crop in a paper cup filled with dirt. The prospect of actually growing a radish to eat was attractive to many. The youngsters had the opportunity to explore as many of the options as they wished. They also had the freedom to do their planting in their own way. The parent helper was worried because some of the seeds weren't being planted at the recommended depth. Mrs. Jensen reassured him that the variety of planting approaches and the varying results were an educational experience. The children certainly weren't worried. They felt very important to know that they were starting the process of making something grow.

When the seeds were planted, the youngsters began making journals for recording the growth of their plants. The children made the books themselves, counting out the agreed-on number of pages, choosing a cover color, and then folding and stapling the pages into booklet form. The parent helper noticed that the children could not keep the pages lined up as they stapled. He offered to help with folding and stapling. Mrs. Jensen explained to the well-meaning father that the children took pride in doing this work themselves. Sure enough, the children all loved their books, crooked and crumpled as they were. Everyone felt like a success.

Too many children are labeled as failures at this stage. You certainly have seen the devastating consequences for the child who fails to begin reading on society's schedule. This is the child whom others shun for being dumb. This is the child who disrupts class out of frustration and anger. This is the child the teachers are eager to send off to the reading specialist. Many students who eventually become school dropouts begin dropping out in first grade (Schorr, 1989). Lifelong inferiority complexes begin early. The children in the following examples were spared:

Emily had a narrow escape. She came home in tears, saying, "I'm dumb now." Her teacher had said she wanted Emily to go to the reading specialist for help on her phonics skills. Fortunately, this step couldn't be taken without a parent conference. Miss Wheeler explained to Emily's mom that Emily didn't seem able to do the daily phonics worksheets; therefore, she obviously needed special help. Emily's mother was puzzled by this report, because her daughter was already reading at home and wrote wonderful stories, too. Her teacher was surprised to hear about Emily's success at home. She couldn't figure out how a child could read and write but not be able to do phonics sheets. Miss Wheeler was new to first grade after teaching in the upper grades and wasn't knowledgeable about beginning reading. She didn't realize that phonics sheets are much more abstract than actual writing is, and that most children learn phonics through meaningful writing experiences. Miss Wheeler listened to the child's mother, however, and did not further damage Emily's belief in herself as a learner.

Blake not only couldn't do worksheets, but also really wasn't interested in writing when he was a first grader. Mrs. Jensen met with his parents and decided that Blake just wasn't ready yet. They knew he was a bright child and would become a reader and writer in time. They made sure that he had plenty of opportunities to experience books and many purposes for writing, but they made no demands for a certain level of performance from him. Most of all, they made sure that he never felt like a failure. If Blake couldn't read in the first grade, it was not the end of the world. However, feeling like a failure could endanger his self-esteem and his future ability to learn. This child was supported as he negotiated the industry versus inferiority stage in his own time.

Feeling successful at new tasks can even help to heal a child's damaged emotional development, as in this story about Robert:

Robert's behavior had become progressively more aggressive as the school year continued, and Mrs. Jensen was very concerned. In fact, things were getting out of control. Last week, when she had to remove Robert from the block area where he was hitting other children with blocks, he had hit and kicked her uncontrollably. She tried to hold him soothingly, but his outburst didn't stop until he was exhausted. He refused to be comforted by her.

Mrs. Jensen planned an activity she thought Robert would enjoy. The class had enjoyed the book *Philomena*, which made them want to have a lemonade stand, so they were going to all help make lemonade. Mrs. Jensen brought the lemons and other ingredients to school and set them out. When Robert arrived, she encouraged him to come and make some lemonade. She modeled how to push down hard on the lemon to make the juice come out, commenting that she could feel the muscles in her arms get harder as she pushed on the lemon. Robert looked interested and then pointed out his big muscles in his arms as he squeezed a lemon. "You can feel my muscle if you want," he said proudly. Since Robert had been the first to start making lemonade, the other children allowed him to tell them how to do it. Robert had a great time, and even cheerfully helped with the cleanup. Mrs. Jensen told him, "I enjoyed working with you today, you really know a lot about making lemonade."

Robert was feeling so good about himself; he was friendly and cooperative at story time and saved the teacher a place to sit next to him at snack time, giving her a hug as she did so.

Notice that Robert is beginning to bond with Mrs. Jensen as well as to feel proud of himself. Of course, one day doesn't undo years of problems, but each step toward meeting a child's emotional development needs is a step in the right direction.

Families and Attachment

A secure attachment is the foundation for healthy progression through all the stages of emotional development. Secure attachment is a loving relationship with special people; interacting with these people is pleasurable and their nearness is comforting in times of stress (Berk, 2002). Very young children need to be supported, accepted, and comforted as they begin to learn about the world. When a parent provides this type of environment for a child, the child forms a secure attachment with his or her parent (Ainsworth, Blehar, Waters, & Wall, 1978). Developing a secure attachment includes giving a child room to explore while also being aware of and sensitive to the child's needs (Landy, 2002). This is the beginning of trust development, as mentioned when we discussed Erikson's stage of trust versus mistrust (Erikson, 1963).

Some of the most difficult children you will encounter as a teacher come from family situations where their attachment experience has been stressful, dysfunctional, or even dangerous (Gurian, 2001). Children with attachment issues may not be able to express their own feelings; they may be aggressive toward or reject others. They may be whiny, impulsive, needy, or disorganized and unpredictable. Typically they are not well-liked due to their behavior (Landy, 2002).

For instance, Tomas may be very successful at pushing other people away when they try to engage him. He may act quite nasty to others and appear unworthy of affection and attention. If Tomas's parents abandoned, rejected, or abused him, his behavior is understandable. If he was not cared for and therefore unable to trust in a parent or other caregiver, then his repulsive behavior is only a protective mechanism. He is attempting to protect himself from what he believes will ultimately be rejection from everyone he encounters.

A secure attachment is the foundation for healthy emotional development.

Teachers and Attachment

Fortunately, during the preschool and early school years it is not too late to intervene in the life of children with attachment problems. In fact, it is critical that attachment issues be addressed at this age. Developing a secure attachment stimulates actual connections in the brain. Sadly, the reverse is also true. When connections in the brain do not receive stimulation, these synapses are disposed of, and are no longer available for use (Shonkoff & Meisels, 2000). The window for forming trust is slipping shut, and not much can be done to open it later in life.

When a child enters into a school or child-care setting without the foundation of a secure attachment, the most important task for the teacher is to focus on building a positive, consistent, and trusting relationship with that child. Research demonstrates that children who are more securely attached to their teachers get along better with other children and have fewer behavior problems (Howes & Ritchie, 2002). Even if Tomas doesn't have a consistently available adult at home, a secure relationship with his teacher can help. His caring teacher can disprove his expectation of rejection. He can learn to trust his teacher.

Rather than reinforcing Tomas's belief that he is unworthy of love and caring, your task is to provide Tomas with a predictable and safe environment, consistently respond to his needs, and show positive feelings toward him. He can learn valuable relationship skills from you that will help him succeed in all areas of his life.

Human Needs

Forming a secure attachment is a basic need for healthy emotional development. Beyond attachment, there are other emotional needs that all humans continue to have throughout life. Adler (1927) proposed that power, attention, and acceptance are basic human needs required for individuals to feel personal significance and a sense of belonging. When these needs are met, people feel good about themselves and tend to interact with others in positive ways. This creates a cycle of positive interaction that further convinces them that they are significant in their world. When these needs are not met, the reverse is true: Human nature leads people who feel insignificant to behave in ways that further alienate them from the acceptance and approval they desire. These needs apply to adults as well as children.

Power   A need for being in charge of your own actions, also known as personal power, is central to feeling significant (Adler, 1917). Children and adults who experience too much external control over their behaviors have unmet power needs. This may make them bossy and controlling of others, or it may overwhelm them to frustration and anger. Sometimes temper tantrums are a result of feeling powerless. You may have seen situations when children began screaming and crying when told they had to do something that seemed insignificant.

If you have spent much time with young children, you will recognize these statements as common: "I don't have to!" "My mom said!" "You're not the boss of me!" These are clear evidence of children's attempts to get personal power. This need for power is often evident when watching children play. Themes of invincibility and control are very attractive to kids. Unfortunately, this play is often violent and may reflect the violence that children have seen in their homes, communities, or the news. The children most likely to play out these violent themes are those who feel the most powerless and vulnerable (Levin, 2004).

Young children are especially vulnerable to unmet power needs because they are able to make so few actual decisions for themselves. This is another reason why it is important to give them choices as often as possible and to say "No" to them as seldom as possible. Children whose power needs are met are definitely easier to get along with.

Attention   A major indicator of significance and social recognition is having other people pay attention to you. Being ignored is painful because it makes you feel unimportant. Having someone listen to what you have to say, or be interested in what you are doing, is incredibly validating. Unfortunately, many adults unwittingly teach children to misbehave in order to get the attention they crave. They pay no attention to children who are getting along well or who are working productively; they only give attention when there is a problem. This means that many children have no idea how to get attention in positive ways; therefore, they strive to get it in negative ways. Interestingly, the drive for attention is so strong that people would rather have others mad at them than ignoring them.

Jarod has been sitting in group time waving his hand wildly, hoping to get a turn answering a question. He knows all the answers, but never gets a chance to show it. He is getting very disgusted at listening to other kids who don't know the right answer. Why won't Miss Wheeler call on him? He could tell her the right answer. Jarod decides not to wait to be called on anymore; he yells out the answer to the next question. Miss Wheeler instantly reprimands him for breaking the rule about raising his hand and sends him to the time-out bench. As he sits there all alone, he sees the plants that the class planted last week. Some are starting to sprout. Jarod breaks the tender shoots off the plants.

Acceptance Being accepted by others, having friends and playmates, is another essential human need. Some people behave in ways that makes others want to be with them, and others do the opposite. Young children generally lack understanding of others' feelings; this often causes them to act in ways that result in rejection. Teachers of young children see variations of the following situation over and over again. Social skill problems such as this will be discussed in Chapter 3:

> Adam wanted to play with Shaun, an older, admired playmate, so he ran up to him and exuberantly banged into him. Shaun didn't see this as a friendly gesture, so he shoved Adam away—hard. Adam fell against the wall and cried brokenheartedly, not just from the bump but also from the rejection.

Motives of Misbehavior

Dreikurs (1964) expanded on Adler's theory of basic human needs to specifically discuss children's behavior. Dreikurs proposed that children will often misbehave in an unconscious attempt to have their basic needs met. Specifically, behavior problems may be the result of a need for power, attention, revenge, or an attempt to avoid failure. "Avoidance of failure" means a child has totally quit trying. This is the result of experiencing too many failures in the quest to fulfill personal needs, becoming convinced there is no hope of success.

As children's brains and nervous system mature, they can better control their emotions.

Emotion Regulation

Emotion regulation refers to our ability to control our internal reactions and outward expressions of our emotions (Landy, 2002). Specifically, our emotion regulation involves the ability to verbalize feelings, cope with emotional highs and lows, or stop from reacting to our impulses. It also may mean that we can delay gratification of desires or motivate ourselves into action. Some research expands on emotion regulation and discusses emotional intelligence or emotional competence. Emotional competence goes beyond emotion regulation; it involves having an awareness of our own and other's emotions, reading social cues, and showing empathy (Gottman, 1997; Hyson, 2004).

Whether it is easy or difficult for a child to learn to regulate emotions depends on many factors. Adults who become impatient with very young children's lack of such control need to know that it is partly dependent on physical maturation of the brain and central nervous system (Hyson, 2004). The elements of emotional development we have discussed in this chapter, primarily temperament and attachment, also play a major role in the development of emotion regulation. In fact, children's temperament may largely determine their ability to regulate their emotions. If negative mood and an intense reaction style are elements of Nicole's temperament, then learning to regulate her emotions will be a more difficult task than for a more even-tempered child. In addition to temperament, developing a secure attachment with a caregiver may be one of the most important contributors to emotion regulation. As we discussed earlier, a secure attachment involves a responsive adult who acknowledges a child's emotions and provides comfort when needed. In this way, a child experiences empathy from the caregiver and begins to learn how to express empathy for others, a critical element in developing emotion regulation (Landy, 2002).

Behavior Problems Many behavioral problems involve emotion regulation issues (Landy, 2002). As mentioned, there is a lot for young children to learn: how to deal with frustration, cope with fear and anxiety, and express pleasure are just parts of developing emotion regulation. When Zach throws himself on the floor, kicking and screaming, he demonstrates that he cannot control his emotions. When Meadow puts her thumb in her mouth instead of crying after her mother drops her off, she demonstrates progress in emotion regulation. When Dylan is able to wait his turn on the slide, he shows the progress he has made. Min Ho's nonexpressive style is evidence that he has learned his family's cultural standards for emotion regulation.

Educators and psychologists agree that success in developing emotion regulation is crucial for success in school and life beyond (Hyson, 2004). When we are under stress it is more difficult to remember and understand what we learn. Therefore, children who can manage their emotions are more able to concentrate on learning new skills. With emotional competence, children are able to be better problem solvers and be a better friend to their peers. Children who can soothe themselves emotionally have fewer behavior problems and are less likely to commit acts of violence (Gottman, 1997). When schools focus on helping children develop their emotional competence, academic achievement increases, quality of relationships with peers and teachers improves, and behavior problems decrease (Slavin & Madden, 2001).

Helping Children Develop Emotional Competence

With adult assistance, children become more able to behave in socially acceptable ways as they mature. We have already mentioned that attachment is crucial to developing emotional competence. Therefore, forming a positive and supportive relationship with children in your classes is the first and possibly most important step in assisting in their emotional development. If kids trust you, then they will be able to express their emotions to you much more easily. For children who have not experienced a secure attachment, learning to express their emotions in an acceptable and healthy way may not come easily. If you work on developing your relationship with them as the first step, their emotional competence will gradually begin to grow as well. Relationship building is discussed further in Chapter 4.

There are many other proactive ways to help children learn more about emotions and develop skills for controlling them. As a class, talk about emotions, incorporate this discussion into storytelling, and allow children to express their emotions in play time with puppets or figures. Talk about children's emotions during conflicts with each other, asking about or pointing out the facial expression of the other child, and help them to name the feelings they are expressing. Likewise, acknowledge your own emotions and model techniques for calming yourself, like taking deep breaths or a quiet time. How to accept children's emotions and model appropriate expressions is discussed further in Chapter 6.

As children develop emotion regulation, they learn not to cry at minor disappointments and how to comfort themselves when upset. They also gain the ability to control impulsive behavior. Impulse control is needed for a social skill such as taking turns, which requires that a child be able to postpone the immediate gratification of desires. Good teaching assists children in gaining impulse control, as Mr. Davis shows here:

> The second-grade classroom is abuzz with activity as children work on their electricity projects. Chris is trying to build a working flashlight, but it only works some of the time, and Chris is getting more frustrated by the minute. Chris finally reaches the end of his patience and begins to pound the table with

 HELPING CHILDREN DEVELOP EMOTION REGULATION

- Build positive, respectful relationships with each individual child
- Integrate discussions about emotions into curriculum
- Acknowledge children's feelings (don't minimize or ignore emotions)
- Help children put their feelings into words they understand
- Model appropriate expressions of your own feelings

his materials and rip his flashlight apart. His face gets red and he looks as if he might cry.

Mr. Davis sees what is happening and goes over to Chris, kneeling down next to him. He talks in a low, calm voice, "Looks like you're feeling pretty frustrated with this project, Chris." Chris stares at the table, blinking back his tears unable to respond. Mr. Davis asks, "Would you like to take a break from working on the flashlight and go relax in a calming place?" Chris gladly accepts and goes to the classroom's designated quiet place. Here he is able to get the privacy he needs as he works on cooling down and getting his feelings under control.

At lunch time, Mr. Davis and Chris work together rebuilding the flashlight. They are relaxed and laughing together when Mr. Davis says to Chris, "Boy, it's a lot easier working on this now when we aren't upset, isn't it?" Chris smiles and agrees. They continue to work, laughing at their mistakes along the way. With the support of Mr. Davis, Chris is learning about how to deal with frustration.

Acknowledging and accepting children's emotions can go a long way. Have you ever been very angry with your boss? Remember a time when a friend talked about that anger with you, allowed you to feel it, and even commented that they would feel the same way if they were in your shoes. Many times your anger is more manageable after you have expressed it to someone who understands. Instead of minimizing, criticizing, or denying children's emotions, allow them a time and place to feel all of their emotions. Continually communicate the message that no emotions are prohibited, only certain behaviors are off limits. You can enforce limits of behavior, but acknowledge the child's emotion as valid. Listen to children's verbal and nonverbal expression of emotions, and help them put their true emotions into accurate words.

Sarah and Sophie are playing house. Sarah is being "the Mommy" and pushing her baby in the buggy, when Sophie decides she is ready for her turn. She grabs the buggy away, knocking Sarah over in the process. As Dennis approaches, Sarah is crying as she tells him, "I hate Sophie. She is mean." Dennis sits beside her, putting an arm around her and says, "I can see you are really angry with Sophie for taking your baby buggy. I feel angry too when someone takes away something I really want. I'll go with you while you tell Sophie that you will finish your turn with the buggy and then she may have her turn after you."

Dennis also acknowledges Sophie's feelings, "I can tell you are sad that you don't have that baby buggy right now. Sometimes it is hard to wait, and it's okay to be sad. It isn't okay to grab toys from our friends. Next time I know you'll ask or wait your turn."

CONCLUSION

Children's physical and emotional needs affect their behavior. Understanding child development is necessary for dealing with discipline issues. Many factors contribute to emotional development in children; temperament and attachment play a major role in the development of emotional competence. Most children have parents and teachers who help them develop trust in others and belief in their own abilities. Knowledgeable adults meet these children's basic needs and support them in developing emotional competence. Some children are not so lucky. Guidance by knowledgeable and supportive caregivers is necessary for children's healthy emotional development.

∽ FOR FURTHER THOUGHT

1. Observe an early childhood setting, watching for examples of young children's inability to sit still for very long. What problems do you see when adults forget this aspect of child development?

2. As you observe young children, try to identify different temperaments as described in this chapter. What is the difference between a person's current mood and that person's temperament?

3. Think about people you know well. Do any of them exhibit signs of an insecure attachment as described in this chapter? How does that problem affect their social interactions?

4. Observe toddlers, watching for expressions of developing emotional autonomy as described in this chapter. How do adults respond? Do you recommend any different responses based on your understanding of this aspect of emotional development?

5. Observe preschoolers, watching for expressions of their desire for real work. Does their environment meet this need? What changes could be made to assist their development of initiative?

6. Observe young children in public schools, looking for the differences between those who are succeeding with school tasks and those who are not. In what ways do the youngsters express their feelings about their abilities?

7. A problem to solve: Jeremy isn't working on his writing assignment. He is fooling around and bothering others instead.

   a. What are some possible causes of this behavior?
   b. How would you address the various causes?
   c. How might the problem have been avoided?

∞ RECOMMENDED READINGS

Erikson, E. (1963). *Childhood and society* (2nd ed.). New York: Norton.

Gottman, J. 1997. *Raising an emotionally intelligent child.* New York: Fireside.

Gurian, M. (2001). *Boys and girls learn differently.* San Francisco: Jossey-Bass.

Hyson, M. (2004). *The emotional development of young children: Building an emotion-centered curriculum.* New York: Teachers College Press.

Landy, S. (2002). *Pathways to competence: Encouraging healthy social and emotional development in young children.* Baltimore: Paul H. Brookes.

Pica, R. (1997). Beyond physical development: Why young children need to move. *Young Children, 52*(6), 4–11.

Schorr, L. (1989). *Within our reach: Breaking the cycle of disadvantage.* New York: Anchor Books/Doubleday.

3

Intellectual and Social Development Affect Discipline

Young children are not miniature adults. That idea is central to early childhood education and basic to the constructivist view of learning. It reminds us that children have unique needs that must be considered in their care and education. The statement also cautions us against adult egocentricity in assuming that children's thinking is the same as ours.

In this chapter we examine some ways in which children's ways of thinking influence their behavior and affect your discipline decisions. Information about young children's intellectual and social development will not only help you immeasurably in the areas of guidance and discipline, but it will also help you be a more effective teacher in general. This information builds on the discussion of emotional development from Chapter 2; intellectual and social development are intertwined with emotional development.

INTELLECTUAL DEVELOPMENT AND BEHAVIOR

Lev Vygotsky and Jean Piaget, both born in 1896, are two major contributors to the understanding of intellectual development. They are both considered *constructivists* because they emphasized that knowledge is actively constructed by the learner rather than passively received from others. However, neither suggested that input from others is not necessary; both writers acknowledged the essential role of social interaction for the development of understanding. Vygotsky wrote convincingly of social experience shaping how people think and interpret their world (Berk, 1994). Piaget's work frequently discusses the role of social interaction with adults and with peers, as learners exchange viewpoints to construct understanding. Piaget (1932/1965) explained that social interactions between children are necessary for the development of intelligence, morality, and personality.

Both Piaget and Vygotsky also described processes of organizing information as central to learning. Vygotsky's work (1934/1962, 1978) describes young children moving from randomly categorizing information in "heaps" to an increasingly more sophisticated classification system based on analysis of the relationship between pieces of information. Piaget's work focused extensively on the significance of individually created logico-mathematical frameworks for classifying relationships between ideas and information (Gruber & Voneche, 1977).

What is commonly known about the work of either Piaget or Vygotsky is only the tip of the iceberg, and their most significant contributions are widely ignored due to their complexity. Both Piaget and Vygotsky are best known for the one aspect of their work that is easiest to understand: Vygotsky is best known for the idea of the *zone of proximal development* (Dixon-Krauss, 1996), which will be discussed later in this chapter. Piaget is known for his *stage theory,* indicating a sequence of maturation in understanding and thinking. Vygotsky agreed with Piaget that young children's thinking differs from that of older children, and that abstract thought is a later development (Berk, 1994). Due to Piaget's life and career lasting much longer than Vygotsky's, Piaget and his associate researchers at the Geneva Institute were able to amass huge quantities of research data about the learning process. Because children were the subjects of the studies, they provided excellent views of children's thinking.

Young Children's Thinking Is Different

The work of Piaget and his colleagues clearly shows that a child's view of the world and reality is different from an adult's. Children's limited reasoning ability, coupled with their limited experience, often bring them to conclusions inconsistent with adult logic. This situation often gets children into trouble. Teachers and parents get angry at youngsters for what adults perceive as disobeying rules, telling lies, being selfish or inconsiderate, and behaving in totally irrational ways. To make matters worse, the children don't realize that they have done anything wrong. For a parent or teacher who doesn't understand what Piaget (1964) has explained about intellectual development, this behavior can be totally infuriating. However, it is often just normal behavior for a young child.

Breaking Rules

Part of Piaget's (1965) famous and extensive studies of children's thinking involved their understanding of rules in games. He focused on rules in the game of marbles, finding out that children's views of rules differ with age. The younger children weren't able to follow the rules but believed that they were quite sacred and imposed by adults. Piaget pointed out that these youngsters nevertheless seemed unconcerned about following the rules. Older children felt free to change the rules by mutual consent, but then felt bound by them. Piaget related this concept to the difference between guidelines for life that are imposed by others and those that children reason for themselves. The latter situation signals moral autonomy.

The way children deal with the rules of a game can help adults understand how children deal with societal rules and expectations (Piaget, 1965). As you watch youngsters playing games, you can see for yourself that their ideas about rules vary with their ages.

Dennis is amused at how his 3-year-old students think about rules for their games. When they play hide-and-seek, they tend to yell out, "Here I am! Come find me!" If some adult sets up a race, the children don't wait for "ready, set, go." After the race, if someone asks who won, they all say with conviction, "I won! I won!" It is clear that young children respond according to their perceptions of what is important, not according to adult rules.

Most preschool youngsters don't understand, or can't cope with, the competitive aspect of games. The first time Dennis set up a game of musical chairs with 4-year-olds, he quickly learned a better way of structuring the game. He was faced with torrents of tears when youngsters were "out" after not finding a chair. Dennis immediately changed the rules so that there was a chair for everyone; the challenge was simply to find a seat quickly when the music stopped. The important thing was that no one was forced out of the game.

Primary-grade children become concerned about rules and about winning. The desire to win often colors the interpretation of rules, and each child wants to

Most young children don't under-stand or can't cope with competitive games; avoiding such games avoids some behavior problems.

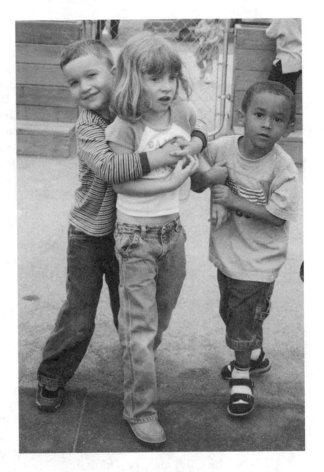

change the rules in his or her favor. Mrs. Jensen values the arguments and discussions that are an inevitable part of board games among her first-graders. She recognizes that learning to resolve their own disputes about rules helps children learn to reason. She appreciates that young children can learn about cooperation from these opportunities to consider each other's position (e.g., DeVries & Zan, 2006; Siccone & Lopez, 2000). By learning to consider the viewpoint of others, children learn about behaving in ways that are compatible with the needs of others. This lesson takes time and careful adult assistance, but it is an important part of the long-term goals of discipline.

It is important for adults to realize that children who break rules, whether in play or elsewhere, may not understand that they have done so. Much of what adults take for granted is unknown to children. Piaget's (1965) studies of moral development indicate that young children are not capable of understanding why certain behaviors are acceptable or unacceptable; therefore, many behavior problems are caused by a lack of understanding, and the child truly has no idea of wrongdoing.

Being Selfish

Parents and teachers tend to get very cross at young children who don't share; however, intellectual maturation plays a big role in learning to share. It is normal for young children to see things only from their own viewpoint. This aspect of their intellectual development affects their interactions with others. They are not necessarily being inconsiderate when they overlook a playmate's feelings; a very young child is often not even aware that someone else has feelings (DeVries & Zan, 2006). It's not surprising, then, that young children have many conflicts and that their teachers spend a great deal of time dealing with those conflicts. Teachers who understand child development don't get upset at these normal misunderstandings. Instead, they use the situation as a teachable moment, as Dennis does in this next example:

> Luis is playing by himself in the sandbox, carefully filling a dump truck with sand and emptying it, creating a hill. Celeste is playing next to him with a toy bulldozer. She suddenly drives her bulldozer over Luis's hill to flatten it out for a road. Luis immediately starts to cry and to hit Celeste.
>
> Dennis arrives on the scene and comforts both children. He has observed enough from across the room to say to Luis, "I don't think Celeste knows why you are upset; can you use your words and tell her?" But Luis is too upset to talk yet, and so Dennis gives him more time by rephrasing the question. By then, Luis is able to say that he didn't want Celeste to touch his hill.
>
> Dennis realizes that neither child had considered the intentions of the other. Luis thought Celeste was being mean, and Celeste was shocked that he was mad at her. Having encouraged Luis to express his view, he then asks Celeste to explain what she was doing. It turns out that she was trying to be helpful in building a road, not understanding what Luis was doing. With help from Dennis, Luis is able to say, "I don't want a road, I'm making a hill." With this information, Celeste is happy to work on her road in another part of the sandbox and all is peaceful, for the moment.

Conflict is an opportunity for an alert teacher to help youngsters tune in to the feelings and viewpoints of their playmates. Knowledgeable teachers do not blame the children or make anyone feel guilty for being thoughtless of others; they understand that this behavior is normal for young children.

Mrs. Jensen also works at helping her young students grow beyond their egocentricity by encouraging them to tell one another how they feel. Often she needs to help children find the words to express themselves; they learn from her example as she walks them through the process of communicating their feelings in a constructive way. (Effective communication of these useful "I messages" are discussed further in Chapter 7.) This is part of effective guidance, which teaches lifelong interpersonal skills. As children's intellectual ability to understand the views of others develops, their social development is enhanced as well. Learning to think about how others feel, called perspective taking, is discussed further in the Social Skills section of this chapter.

The goal is voluntary unselfishness, but many adults force children to share instead. Few adults would be as generous with their prized possessions as parents and teachers often insist youngsters must be. Would you turn your new car over to someone you barely know because "she doesn't have one"? Why should Rosa let Samantha ride her new bike? Rosa's right of ownership and right to decide whether or not to share must first be respected in order to prepare her to voluntarily share. Children often think that sharing means giving something away permanently (Landy, 2002); their generosity may be increased by reassurance of getting the object back again.

Only when sharing is a real choice and not coerced can a child make the choice to be generous. Even with classroom materials not owned by any individual, the rights of possession must be respected. Youngsters should also be encouraged to stand up to aggressors who attempt to take things by force (Slaby, Roedell, Arezzo, & Hendrix, 1995). Of course, we need to teach them how to do this assertively rather than aggressively.

Lying and Stealing

Our society takes lying and stealing seriously; they are moral as well as legal issues. Adults without child development knowledge usually believe their role is to punish children for lying and stealing, not realizing those behaviors are linked to maturation (Landy, 2002). As a child, seeing things from your own viewpoint may mean

A child can learn to be generous only when sharing is a real choice and not forced.

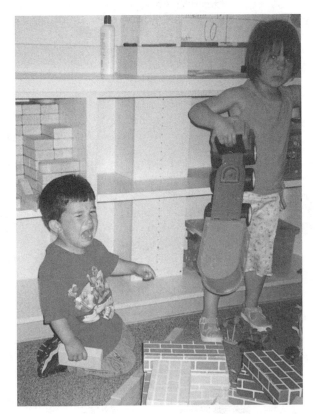

that something is true because you want it to be true and that something is yours because you want it. These beliefs cause children to tell "lies" that they genuinely consider truths and guiltlessly take things that don't belong to them. An adult who understands how children think can help a youngster learn from these situations.

When Sophie tells her teacher that she is going with Olivia to Disneyland next week, Dennis understands and is able to respond with empathy: "You really wish you could go to Disneyland." This response helps Sophie separate her wishes from reality without making her feel bad about herself. The following example presented an actual problem of disappearing preschool material:

> Madeline was in her favorite dress-up outfit from the playhouse. She announced to Sheri that the outfit she was wearing was her own and that she was going to wear it home and even to bed. Sheri said, "Dressing up is one of your favorite things to do at school, isn't it?" Madeline agreed and then repeated that the outfit was hers.
>
> Sheri tried again, "I recognize those clothes as preschool dress-up clothes. It sounds like you wish they were your very own. You want to be able to take them home with you." Madeline held her ground, and Sheri tried explaining, "If everyone took their favorite clothes home, we wouldn't have any dress-up clothes to play with at school." Finally, Madeline seemed to be listening.
>
> Yet Madeline still insisted that the clothes were hers, but she was very attentive as Sheri continued to discuss the problem. "I remember a few times when you went home with the dress-up clothes you were wearing. When I found out, I felt bad. I was worried that there would not be enough dress-up clothes at preschool anymore."
>
> After listening carefully, Madeline put her arms around Sheri's neck and whispered in her ear, "Sheri, I know they are preschooler clothes." Then she smiled and danced away.

Madeline's struggle with fact and fantasy is not unusual. Piaget (1965) found that young children really do not understand the nature of a lie. Even 6-year-olds in his study could not differentiate between an honest mistake and a purposeful mistruth. Additionally, they tended to judge how bad it was to tell a mistruth in relation to how likely it was to be found out and therefore punished. Thus, with this line of reasoning, a believable lie is acceptable, yet a lie that stretches the truth too far is bad. Piaget's research about children's thinking should help teachers and parents understand why explaining their adult logic to youngsters doesn't work. Instead, children need to experience the problems that come from deceiving others. As they get older, they can be helped to realize the impact of untruths on relationships. They can also be helped to understand that taking something from others makes them sad. For these lessons to be effective, children must have caring relationships with others (DeVries, 1999).

Schoolwork Problems

Intellectual development stages determine what kinds of materials and activities best help children learn. If you don't match the experiences and materials to the children, you are sure to have behavior problems as well as academic problems.

Piaget's (1960) work explains the importance of young children having real experiences with real materials to construct their knowledge about the world. The term *concrete* is often used to describe the type of materials children need for productive explorations. They include the water in the water table, the hammer and nails in the woodworking center, and the blocks in the block center.

Some teachers present letters, numbers, and other symbols to children who cannot yet make sense of them. This developmentally inappropriate instruction can create discipline problems. When children are not capable of doing what they are asked to do, they are likely to behave in ways adults dislike. Certainly they are not likely to complete the work on schedule. Often youngsters who are frustrated and discouraged by school tasks that are beyond them are then punished for not doing the work. It is common to see these children sitting dejectedly at their desks during recess, staring helplessly at a worksheet. Is it any wonder that they are tempted to be less than cooperative or even to lash out in anger?

Some people get confused and think that plastic magnet letters or wooden letters that fit into puzzles are concrete. These letters can be touched and moved around, but they are still only *representational symbols*. Some representational materials are more easily recognized than letters or numbers are. For instance, a doll is more recognizable as a symbol for a baby than are the letters in the word *baby*. Pictures of real things are not concrete either, but they may be useful symbolic representations.

Sometimes teachers are striving for developmentally appropriate education but don't realize that their teaching materials are not concrete. Not everything that a child can touch and manipulate is concrete. Clocks and quarters are examples of apparently concrete materials that are actually representational rather than concrete. Young children can't construct knowledge of time or money through manipulation or observation of clocks or coins. No wonder lessons in telling time and making change are such difficult activities for young children. They involve both *symbolic representation* and arbitrary *social knowledge*. (Social knowledge is explained in Chapter 5 as one of three kinds of knowledge.) As such, they cannot be learned through an exploration of materials.

Teachers who understand how young children learn have fewer problems with child behavior because they provide age-appropriate learning activities and materials for children. They provide many real-life experiences and choices. (See Chapter 5 for further discussion of this topic.) A classroom that provides choices for children allows them to decide for themselves what type of materials and activities make sense. Mrs. Jensen's first grade has a wide assortment of concrete and representational materials accessible on open shelves for children to make selections. Miss Wheeler next door keeps everything but the worksheets in closed cupboards and rarely brings out anything else. She doesn't realize that the worksheets are entirely representational and meaningless to many of the children in her classroom.

Dylan was in Mrs. Jensen's room, and his identical twin brother, Devon, was in Miss Wheeler's class. Devon tried to pretend he was Dylan so he could get into the room with all the interesting things, but he was sent back. Dylan was having a happy and productive year while Devon was in trouble constantly. One day Devon took matters into his own hands and got out an armload of special things from the teacher's cupboard, placing them enticingly on the tables as he had seen them in Mrs. Jensen's

Teachers who understand how young children learn have fewer problems with child behavior because they provide age-appropriate learning activities.

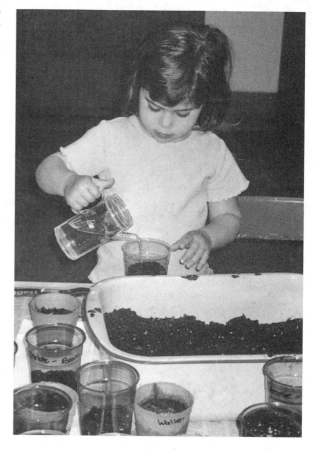

room. Now his room was a nice place to be, just like his brother's. But Miss Wheeler didn't appreciate his efforts. She was upset that he would dare to get into the cupboard without permission. How sad that she missed the important message Devon was sending about his learning needs.

SOCIAL SKILLS AND GUIDANCE

Missing social skills is the single most common cause of discipline problems. Children's squabbles over materials and their unskilled efforts to make friends cause frequent disruptions to both preschool and primary classrooms. Social skills are discussed last because we see them as an outgrowth of the previously discussed aspects of development. Physical abilities, emotional development, and levels of intellectual understanding all combine to determine current levels of social skill and understanding.

Teachers of young children have a big responsibility because the early years are crucial for social development. Youngsters who do not develop social competence in the early childhood years typically continue to experience difficulty with peer acceptance throughout the school years (Howes & Ritchie, 2002; Johnson, Ironsmith, Snow, & Poteat, 2000). Not surprisingly, these children are at risk as adults for social and emotional problems (Denham et al., 2001; Yanghee, 2003). Helping youngsters learn how to make a friend and be a friend is crucial to their life-long happiness. It's also a big help to teacher happiness when children learn how to get along.

Constructing Knowledge for Social Skills

Children construct knowledge as a result of reflecting on their experiences. As they experiment with blocks, for instance, they observe the results of trying to stack, balance, and bridge structures. Thinking about the results helps children revise erroneous ideas. This process helps them construct understanding about such concepts as gravity, balance, and measurement. Children construct their theories of how the social world works in the same sort of trial-and-error situations.

As youngsters experiment with different ways of interacting with others, they observe the results of various approaches. Reflecting on the results of their social overtures can help children figure out how to play with others successfully and how to make friends. We have remarked previously on the value of peer conflicts as teaching situations. You may be surprised to hear that children's fights are useful teaching tools. Conflicts tend to challenge children's assumptions and encourage an exchange of viewpoints. They help youngsters realize that not everyone sees things their way. Thus, conflicts provide the necessary experience for learning and they provide the teachable moments. Helping children deal with their disputes gives the teacher an opportunity to guide children's thinking about the experience. The adult role varies, depending on the child's individual levels of emotional, intellectual, and social development.

Teaching children to think critically about their behavior and to use reasoning abilities to learn to solve interpersonal problems is consistent with current recommended approaches to teaching other subjects. National guidelines in every area of the curriculum urge teaching for critical thinking and problem solving instead of old approaches of memorized learning. Some adults think it is enough to simply tell children how they are expected to behave and then punish them if they do not. That approach would be the same as a teacher merely demanding mastery of mathematics without instruction, assessment, and reteaching (Butchart & McEwan, 1998).

Adults who are focused only on immediate outcomes will use punishment to get desired behaviors, believing that the teaching approach is too slow. Keeping long-term goals in mind is especially important and difficult when dealing with behaviors linked to maturation. True, you won't get 4-year-olds (or even 5-year-olds) to truly understand the feelings of the child they just hit; but that doesn't mean you stop working toward your goals. If you resort to coercive tactics, you will make it more difficult for the child to eventually become considerate of others.

Have you noticed that we are not talking about social skills as learning to say *please, thank you,* and *I'm sorry?* These are polite ways of speaking, but they are only superficial behaviors and do not necessarily reflect true feelings (Flicker &

Hoffman, 2002). Some adults and children confuse these memorized phrases with the understanding needed for true social competence. You have certainly seen children who are caught doing something wrong and who automatically say, "I'm sorry," yet show no signs of remorse. These children have merely learned the magic words for getting out of punishment. Too many adults focus on teaching socially acceptable words instead of helping children understand others and develop caring feelings.

> Mrs. Jensen realized the uselessness of teaching words instead of understanding several years ago when she rescued Isabel from Jason's physical aggression. Jason was angry with Isabel and was gripping her wrists very hard, hurting her. After Mrs. Jensen pried his hands off Isabel and helped Isabel to tell Jason how she felt, she asked Jason what he could do to make Isabel feel better.
>
> Jason said "Thank you," and Mrs. Jensen asked Isabel if that made her feel better. Isabel replied in a disdainful voice, "No. Jason, you have to say 'sorry.'" So Jason said, "Sorry." However, Mrs. Jensen could tell that one platitude was as meaningless as the next.

How Children Develop Social Competence

As in other teaching topics, we need to start with the "basics" when we teach social skills. Like any other learning, the ability to successfully master social skills requires that children's physical and emotional needs are met. A child who lacks security and confidence has difficulty working on anything else. Children are most likely to be secure, confident, and socially competent if their parents are warm and attentive and also help them understand limits (e.g., Hart, Olsen, Robinson, & Mandleco, 1997; Landy, 2002). If these needs cannot be met adequately at home, schools must try to fill the gaps (Koplow, 2002).

 BASICS OF PROSOCIAL BEHAVIOR

1. Successfully "entering play," which leads to
2. Having friends, which leads to
3. Caring how your actions affect others, which leads to
4. Willingness to work at "perspective-taking," which leads to
5. Prosocial behavior

Consider The Alternative:

1. Being unsuccessful at entering play, which leads to
2. Not having friends, which leads to
3. Not caring how your actions affect others, which leads to
4. Unwillingness to work at perspective-taking, which leads to
5. Antisocial behavior

We need to think about a child's motivation for prosocial behaviors, such as sharing or otherwise compromising. You have surely seen youngsters who don't care one bit whether they hurt other children or make them mad. These are usually the children who feel rejected by others, and who reject others in return. If a child doesn't care about others, you aren't going to have much luck with lessons about getting along. Being able to consider another person's feelings is a different issue than wanting to (Pritchard, 1996). It really isn't until children have something to lose, such as a playmate, that they have reason to consider how their actions affect others. You have probably noticed that, as children develop the idea of friendship, they often use the "friendship threat" ("I won't be your friend!") in an effort to get their way (Wheeler, 2004).

Therefore, a "basic" for learning social skills is having friends, which for children means having playmates. In order to have playmates, children must be able to successfully enter into play with others, which may be the most "basic" part of developing social skills. The process of playing with others not only provides motivation for learning social skills, it also provides excellent practice (Lillard & Curenton, 1999). Play provides many opportunities for conflict and negotiation, which help children learn to consider the needs and feelings of others. Considering the needs and feelings of others is called *perspective-taking*, and is also basic to developing social skills.

Though each piece contributes to the other, we see a necessary initial sequence to the components of learning social competence: first comes the ability to enter play successfully, which creates feelings of being accepted by others, which leads to friendships and to caring about others. These relationships make youngsters more willing to consider the perspective of others instead of just their own. When these pieces are in place, a child is generally open to teacher assistance with social skills and behaves in a fairly socially acceptable manner. Let's look now at how to help get these pieces into place.

Learning How to Enter Play

How many times have you seen a child crying because of not being allowed into a play situation? Research indicates that approximately 60 percent of attempts to enter on-going play are rejected (Landy, 2002). Asking "Can I play?" is often ineffective and can even invite rejection because it offers the power to say "no." Instead, children can be helped to learn more productive strategies for being accepted as a playmate.

Children first must be helped to avoid advances that disrupt the ongoing play. Too often a child will barge into a play situation like a bull in a china shop and be totally surprised and crushed when the other children get mad. It may be useful in these cases to teach a beginning strategy that does not interrupt: simply playing alongside a potential playmate, doing a similar activity (Ramsey, 1991). Five-year-old Seanne expressed this idea clearly. She told her teacher, "I learned how to play with a boy today." When her teacher asked her what she did, Seanne explained, "I just watched what he was doing with Legos and then I played like him."

Another useful approach is to first observe what the desired playmate is doing; in other words, to work at seeing things from the other child's viewpoint. This

Asking "Can I play?" often gets "No" for an answer. Teachers can help children learn more productive approaches to being accepted as a playmate.

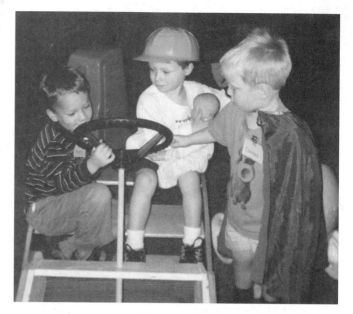

observation provides information that the child can use by offering a way to contribute or fit into the existing play. When the child's goal is to join a group at play, it is worth the effort to figure out what the others are doing first. The child who joins a group with a contribution to ongoing play is most likely to be accepted (Howes & Ritchie, 2002; Landy, 2002). Six-year-old Diego explained this very well to his 5-year-old brother, Antonio.

> Antonio was complaining to his mother that Diego wouldn't let him play with his group at recess that day. Diego quickly defended himself, saying, "You could have played with us if you had just started playing what we were playing. But instead you tried to make us stop our game and listen to what you wanted to do. Next time, Antonio, just start doing what we are already doing, OK?"

It is important to help youngsters experience success in these efforts and so develop confidence that they will be accepted. A child who approaches playmates with confidence is more likely to gain entry to play. Conversely, the unsure child is more likely to experience rejection. Rejection starts a cycle of unproductive behaviors that lead to increased rejection (Denham, Mason, Caverly, Schmidt, & Hackney, 2001). Teachers can make a difference with careful teaching and coaching, as in the following example:

> Peter and Sasha are deeply engrossed in their play. They have created elaborate boat replicas with Legos and have made pretend spears and spear throwers out of Unifix cubes. More Unifix cubes have been used to represent the seals they are now playing at hunting with their spears. Their cries of "ya ya ya" accurately capture the tone used by their fathers when they pursue seals on the Yukon River by their village.
> Joe comes over and wants to play with Peter and Sasha. He picks up one of the "seals" and starts adding Unifix cubes to it, saying, "Look how long a road

I can make with this." Sasha grabs back the pretend seal that he was about to spear and tells Joe to stop. Joe starts to cry, saying, "I wanna play too!" Peter and Sasha ignore him as they continue with their seal hunt.

Mrs. Akaran, the children's first-grade teacher, sees there is a problem and comes to help. She has been admiring the quality and complexity of Peter's and Sasha's pretend play, and doesn't want to disturb them. She realizes that the problem is caused by Joe's inept attempts to join the two more socially adept boys. Therefore, she focuses her attention on helping Joe begin to learn some important missing skills. The teacher goes to Joe, puts her arm around him comfortingly, and whispers conspiratorially to him as she pulls him aside. "Come over here and let's figure out what you can do." Joe stops crying and listens as Mrs. Akaran urges him to watch what Sasha and Peter are doing.

"What are they using those Unifix cubes for?" asks his teacher as she assists Joe's observation of his desired playmates. She gets Joe to think about what others want instead of just considering his own desires. Then Mrs. Akaran asks Joe what he could do to help with the seal hunt; she is proposing a strategy for entering play that is often successful. With a little help, Joe decides that he could make a seal and a spear for himself out of the Unifix cubes not currently in use. He makes his own pretend play props, and then his teacher encourages Joe to go over where Sasha and Peter are playing and try them out. She watches to see what happens, noting with satisfaction that the other boys allow Joe to join in on the hunt.

Notice that the teacher didn't use her adult power to get Joe accepted as a playmate. She knew that it wouldn't work anyway; it would probably break up the play because Peter and Sasha would go elsewhere. Well-meaning teachers often insist that no child be left out (Paley, 1999), but such intervention overlooks a teachable moment and may actually make things worse for that child. There is usually a reason for a child not being allowed to play, and it is the teacher's job to assess the situation and figure out that reason. Usually there is a missing skill or understanding on one side or the other; the teacher needs to identify what needs to be learned and then teach it. Insisting that a child be allowed to play just covers up the problem, teaches no skills or understanding, and may make other children more resentful of the child forced upon them. You may also want to consider how you feel when you are having a meaningful conversation with a best friend and an uninvited acquaintance joins you. Is it perhaps reasonable at times for children to ask not to be disturbed by others?

 HOW TO HELP CHILDREN DEVELOP SOCIAL COMPETENCE

1. Coach youngsters in successful play-entry strategies.
2. Encourage close friendships and caring relationships.
3. Use children's disputes to help them exchange viewpoints and learn perspective-taking.
4. Teach negotiation skills for conflict resolution.

Encouraging Friendships

Teachers and parents also help children become socially competent by encouraging friendships (Jalongo & Isenberg, 2004). Friendships are important for a variety of reasons. Children are more likely to be successful when initiating contact with friends, thus increasing their confidence (Howes & Ritchie, 2002). Children's play is more sophisticated and mature when they are playing with friends, which improves their competence. Children care more about the feelings of friends than about those of other people (Corso, 2003), thereby encouraging them to practice perspective-taking. By early elementary school, many children have established a best friend. These relationships are important because they offer the best opportunities for developing the interpersonal understandings needed for socialized behavior.

Learning Perspective-Taking

Once children experience the joy of friendships, they are motivated to work at keeping them. As stated previously, this gives a reason for trying to understand another child's viewpoint in a conflict.

The ability to see things from another's viewpoint, *perspective-taking*, is essential to social competence. Without this ability, youngsters remain self-centered and unable to relate to the interests, needs, and rights of others. Until children can take into consideration the viewpoint of another person, they cannot make progress in reasoning about fairness. When they can only see their own views, their idea of justice consists of that which they desire for themselves. Obviously, this perception will not endear them to playmates.

There is considerable difference of opinion about how early children are able to understand another person's thoughts and feelings. Examples of empathy from toddlers are often used to dispute Piaget's research findings that perspective taking does not emerge until around age 6 (e.g., Lillard & Curenton, 1999). Although frequently discussed together, empathy is not the same thing as perspective taking. We agree that certain forms of empathy appear early, such as sympathizing with another child who is sad. However, true perspective taking, the ability to take another person's view into consideration even when it conflicts with your own, is another matter. A 3-year-old who gives a cookie to a hungry child when there are plenty of cookies is not likely to do so when there is only one cookie, especially if that 3-year-old wants the cookie for himself or herself. Though very young children have been observed sharing and helping others (Eisenberg, 1992), it is not clear that these are demonstrations of true perspective-taking. Positive social behaviors may be motivated from other sources.

Despite differences in the research literature, there is agreement that awareness develops gradually from an egocentric perspective to the ability to respond to and even predict how others will feel (Hyson, 2004). Anyone working with young children is aware of their egocentricity (Flicker & Hoffman, 2002). According to Selman (DeVries, Hildebrandt, & Zan, 2000; Selman, 1980), with experience and guidance, people move through five levels of perspective taking as follows: Level 0, not recognizing that others have feelings or ideas different from your own, is common during preschool. During the primary grades, most children operate at level 1. At

Learning to consider another person's needs and feelings is a huge task—especially if those needs and feelings are in opposition to your own.

this point, young children realize that others have their own feelings, but can't consider someone else's feelings while thinking about their own. Our observation shows that this is particularly true when their own feelings are in opposition to the other person's. As they move into upper elementary school, level 2 thinking is more common. This brings the ability to consider another person's views as well as their own. Levels 3 and 4 bring increasing decentering and the ability to coordinate mutual perspectives. However, these generally do not emerge until adolescence and adulthood. Theory of mind research points out the role of maturation as children develop understanding of their own and others' thinking (Flavell & Hartman, 2004).

This information about children's thinking should help you to be more accepting of how they behave. You will respond differently when you realize that young children probably aren't being mean when they disregard another child's feelings; they're just being young. This information about levels of intellectual development also offers essential guidance for helping children move to higher levels. The message is not to just accept the child's lack of perspective-taking, but to aim your teaching one level higher than what the child is doing (DeVries, Hildebrandt, & Zan, 2000).

Working with young children, you will often see situations like the following:

Jessie is working on a drawing, using the only yellow marker at the table. Jack reaches over and grabs the marker out of Jessie's hand. He seems somewhat startled when Jessie yells at him and tries to grab the marker back. Soon the two are in a tug-of-war, with both sides claiming they need the marker.

Dennis stops the struggle and calms the children with his gentle presence. He works at getting each child to explain his or her feelings, trying to get them to use the "I messages" he consistently models. (See Chapter 7 for more detail on "I messages.") Then Dennis shows Jack where he can get another yellow marker.

When Jack grabbed Jessie's marker, he demonstrated that his perspective taking was at level 0. He took the marker simply because he wanted it, with no thought about Jamie. Therefore, Dennis aimed at helping Jack realize that Jessie has wishes and feelings, too. It probably wouldn't be worthwhile trying to teach higher-level cooperative negotiation to Jack because it would be too far above his level of understanding.

Children can make better than normal progress through these levels of understanding with the support of understanding teachers (DeVries & Zan, 2006). And, as Vygotsky (1962/1934) reminds us, children can perform at higher levels with assistance than they can alone. Vygotsky's writings about the *zone of proximal development* and *scaffolding* refer to how adults help children to do things, and thus teach them to perform independently. Puppets, role playing, and storybooks may also provide assistance to children as they learn to think about the feelings of others. In *Jamaica's Blue Marker* (Havill, 1995), Jamaica comes to understand why Russell was acting mean; this type of story may help your young students think about how others feel. Use of children's literature for guidance is discussed further in Chapters 11 and 12.

The ability to understand and empathize with others is crucial to adult society as well as children's interactions. "Children are less likely to behave aggressively toward someone if they can put themselves in the other person's place and imagine that person's thoughts and feelings" (Slaby, Roedell, Arezzo, & Hendrix, 1995, p. 145). This statement seems equally true for adults.

Learning Conflict Resolution

Children who have some perspective-taking ability can be helped to learn conflict resolution skills. The ability to avoid and resolve conflicts constitutes another essential aspect of social competence. It involves the ability to communicate personal needs and to listen to others expressing theirs. It also involves willingness to compromise as well as the capacity to manage aggression (Siccone & Lopez, 2000). All these aspects of negotiation require the child to take into consideration the viewpoint of others. These sophisticated abilities require significant practice.

> "You dummy!" yells Megan as Sam pours rice into the funnel at the rice table. Her teacher calmly walks over and asks Megan, "You don't like something Sam is doing?" The the teacher guides Megan's words from merely expressing anger to clear communication of what is upsetting her. Sam needs help hearing this message and deciding what to do about it. The teacher is there to make this a valuable learning experience for both children.

As mentioned in Chapter 1, children do not get this practice if adults solve problems for them. Instead, adults must guide youngsters in age-appropriate ways and help them to resolve their own differences. For very young children with limited language ability, the teacher may do the talking for both parties in reflecting the two viewpoints. As children mature, they can gradually take a more active role in the expression of their different views. The goal is for the teacher or parent to intervene as little as possible. Effective communication for conflict resolution is discussed further in Chapter 7. In the following example, Stephen seems to have learned a lot:

> Kyle had grabbed a truck from Stephen and wouldn't give it back. Then he took a larger truck and hit Stephen with it. The first impulse of the teacher, Maureen, was to go to Stephen and see if he was all right. But the chain of events that happened next kept her out of it.
>
> Stephen stood up, looked at Kyle with an angry face, and said, "What's my face telling you? I'm mad and if you hit me again or won't play nice I'm going someplace else to play!" Then Stephen sat down and began to play again. Kyle looked surprised, gave back the truck, and they were off playing together again. Maureen caught Stephen's eye, smiled, and winked a congratulatory message. She felt wonderful to see the results of the teaching she had been doing.

The Teacher as Coach

A variety of teaching methods are useful in helping children develop social competence. The teacher who respectfully considers children's viewpoints is teaching by example. When children are involved in a dispute, the teacher's appropriate role might be more of a coach, providing encouragement, critiquing the performance, and recommending strategies for improvement. Sometimes the most helpful adult role is to stand back and let children experience the social consequence of their actions. Kyle might need to learn from experience that other kids don't want to play with him when he grabs things from them. Chapters 6, 7, and 8 in Part Two of the text explain these teacher roles more fully.

When children have disputes, the teacher can be a coach for problem solving: recommending useful approaches, providing encouragement, and critiquing performance.

Although it is important not to intervene more than necessary, it is also important to be there as needed, both for safety and support. Therefore, when Dennis sends Colette over to the playhouse with a suggestion for joining in play there, he also tells her to come back and talk to him if it doesn't work. Dennis helps Colette to watch what Kelsey and Megan are playing and to think of how she can help. He helps her plan her entry into the play activity, and stays nearby to lend her confidence while she carries out the plan. Dennis could simply tell Kelsey and Megan they have to let Colette play, but that wouldn't teach Colette useful social skills. It certainly wouldn't make her more popular with her peers, either.

The playground at recess definitely offers the richest opportunity to help children learn social skills. Yet, in most schools, teachers are given recess time as part of their preparation time, leaving playground supervision to aides. The problems with this situation are many: the ratio of children to adults is likely to be at least 100 to 1, making it impossible to do any teaching. Even mere crowd control is a challenge with those numbers. Even if the numbers were appropriate, the aides can't know the children well enough to provide guidance aimed at the needs of individuals. In addition, very few aides have adequate background and training to provide the kind of guidance that will be beneficial. No wonder kids just get sent to the principal when a fight breaks out. The opportunity for on-the-spot problem solving is lost. For this reason, more and more teachers are choosing to go out to recess with their students. They report that they are able to observe natural peer dynamics and diagnose the causes of many social problems as a result.

Issues to Discuss with Families

Your success in enhancing the social skills of your students will be greater if you can bring the child's family into the process. Research shows that the type of discipline techniques used by both teachers and parents relates to children's social skills (e.g., Butchart & McEwan, 1998; Landy 2002). Parents may not be aware that children who are disciplined through punishment tend to show aggression and hostility toward peers. On the other hand, children who are helped to understand the harmful effects of their behavior on others exhibit more positive social behaviors. Children who are aggressive to others are generally rejected, but those who show consideration for others are sought-after playmates. Therefore, teaching children why certain behaviors are acceptable or not, instead of just punishing undesirable behavior, can lead to better social skills and better relationships with peers.

Parents may be anxious because their child doesn't share toys and grabs from others. Information about maturation can help families accept and support the developmental process. Though young children are not maturationally capable of functioning at high levels of interpersonal understanding (Selman & Schultz, 1990), they grow toward higher levels with adult assistance. As Vygotsky says, "The only good kind of instruction is that which marches ahead of development and leads it" (1962/1934, p. 104). This can be compared to how we help babies learn to talk: Just because they can't talk yet doesn't mean we don't talk to them. Just because their early efforts aren't very good doesn't mean we don't respond and encourage further effort. In these ways, families effectively teach oral language. Similarly, adults at home and school can effectively teach higher levels of thinking by modeling and scaffolding; aiming just a little above the level the child is capable of independently.

ACCOMMODATING INDIVIDUAL DIFFERENCES

There are some basic developmental accomplishments that apparently transcend cultural differences. These include learning how to make friends, learning language, learning to organize and integrate perceptions, and how to think, imagine, and create. But how these accomplishments occur varies according to the cultural context in which they occur (Lillard & Curenton, 1999). Therefore, it is important to remember that appropriate social behavior varies from group to group. Family expectations for children vary according to the child's culture, family background, economic status, and gender. The teacher who holds all children to one standard of behavior is actually being unfair to some.

Cultural Differences

Culture is not skin color or ethnic origin; it is the context within which we view the world. We don't assume that all people of European ancestry are the same, nor can we say that all Latinos or African Americans are the same. Culture is the product of multiple sources: not just race, language, ethnicity, and religion, but also experiences, educational level, socioeconomic status, gender, age, lifestyle, political orientation, geography, and temperament (Kaiser & Rasminsky, 2003). Each of us has a culture, but generally we are not aware of it until we experience a conflict with someone else's. This lack of awareness creates interpersonal misunderstandings, between teachers and children as well as between teachers and families. When a teacher finds a child's behavior unacceptable, one question in discovering the cause must be whether it is the result of a cultural mismatch. Teachers who hold all youngsters to one standard inadvertently cause some to fail socially and academically.

The culture of school reflects the dominant culture of the setting. Those children whose homes and family expectations are most similar to those of the school have the least adjustment to make. Increasingly, schools host children from multiple cultures, making the teacher's role immensely complex and the children's adjustments equally complex. Cultural differences affect all expectations and interactions. Communication can be hampered due to differing ideas about such things as when and how speech is used, what body language means, whether a direct question is rude, and whether it is polite to look directly at the speaker. Culture differences affect relationships, too. Different groups hold varying ideas about the proper relationship between children and adults, acceptable styles of peer interaction, and about whether it is better for children to be cooperative or competitive. Differing expectations of children at home and school cause confusion and mistrust. For instance, western European culture expects children to be independent, but interdependence is valued in most of the world's cultures. There are enormous implications for different behaviors based on this one set of expectations

Culture is not skin color or ethnic origin; it is the context within which we view the world. Teacher expectations of children must reflect the world view of each child's family.

(Kaiser & Rasminsky, 2003). Following are examples of some of the kinds of cross-cultural misunderstandings that can cause problems.

> Rabia's teacher is upset because Rabia is not able to put on her own coat or shoes for going outside. Her teacher discovers that Rabia's parents dress her at home and also carry her to and from the car at school.
>
> Ahmed gets into trouble because he won't stay on his mat at rest time. His teacher discovers that he has never slept alone but always with his parents.
>
> Miriam doesn't talk at school and she doesn't say when she needs to use the bathroom. Her teacher discovers that Miriam relies on nonverbal cues that the teacher misses.

Another example of differing cultural styles was recorded by Rizzo and Corsaro (1991). They noted that white, middle-class preschoolers tend to exhibit very different interaction styles from African American and Latino children they observed in Head Start. The Head Start youngsters were observed teasing each other and using competitive and oppositional talk without being upset by it. On the contrary, this interaction style seemed to cement friendships within the group. In contrast, the white, middle-class preschoolers were very concerned about hurt feelings and were easily upset by negative comments. Rizzo and Corsaro concluded from their research that interaction perceived as friendly among one group would be perceived as aggressive and intimidating by the other. Many white, middle-class teachers would misunderstand and squelch the social interactions of a child who used teasing as a friendly overture.

For some people, fitting in with their own culture and succeeding in the dominant culture are not compatible. In addition, learning a new set of expectations can be very stressful for young children who are still learning their home expectations. Sensitive teachers will help by eliciting information from families and by being accepting and respectful of children's home values. They will also help children bridge the culture gap by being explicit about their expectations, instead of assuming that everyone knows what is expected and being upset when some don't conform. Teachers who respect all cultures will also educate themselves about their students' cultures and modify expectations to assist all children in feeling comfortable (Barrera & Corso, 2003).

Socioeconomic Differences

Cultural differences based on family income, jobs, and educational background also result in different behavioral goals and patterns. These variations may cause children from different backgrounds to be less comfortable with each other, causing social interaction problems (Ramsey, 1991). Adults, too, are often less comfortable with those from different backgrounds (Kaiser & Rasminsky, 2003). This discomfort can inhibit the flow of communication between home and school and disadvantage the child.

Disturbingly, research has shown that some pre-service teachers have an unfounded bias about children from poorer families. Pettit and Sugawara (2002) found this bias among the group of teacher education students they studied. The future teachers rated children from lower socioeconomic backgrounds as less competent socially and cognitively than peers from families of higher socioeconomic status. These ratings occurred despite the fact that the children actually had similar competencies.

Teachers who remember that "different" is neither better nor worse will help more children succeed in school. The youngsters whose background values are different from their teachers' are most at risk for school failure and dropping out (Schorr, 1989). As Ramsey (1991) says, "We must be sure that we do not exacerbate economic disadvantage by undermining the social skills and styles that children have developed, even though they may be less compatible with the current structure of the classroom" (p. 61).

Gender and Brain Development

The fact that a child is a boy or a girl also affects behavior. Although we acknowledge that sex-role stereotyping contributes to behavior differences between boys and girls, brain research explains why our efforts at gender neutrality have failed (Gurian, 2001). Buying dolls for boys and trucks for girls has had limited success.

The differences begin early prenatally, as soon as gender is determined. The parts of the brain develop differently, different chemicals and hormones dominate, and developmental rates are different. Female brains develop more quickly than male brains; this is especially evident in the rate at which girls develop verbal skills. This gives girls an edge in resolving disputes through negotiation, while boys tend to rely on nonverbal communication. Male brains secrete less of the chemical serotonin, making boys more impulsive and more fidgety than girls. The chemical oxytocin is more constantly stimulated in females, making girls more empathic. Male brains deal with emotion more in the brain stem (where fight-or-flight responses are stored), while female brains move emotion to the upper brain where complex thought occurs (Gurian, 2001). Of course, boys have more of the testosterone hormone, making them more aggressive; the female growth hormone, progesterone, is considered the bonding hormone. Given this information, it is no wonder that teachers often complain when they have more boys than girls in their classes.

Teacher complaints about too many boys are related to viewing typical "boy behavior" as problem behavior (King & Gartrell, 2003). Boys tend to be developmentally younger than the girls in their class and they do need more physical activity than girls. Girls fit better into a quiet and controlled school environment. As a result, normally active little boys may be mislabeled as having attention deficit hyperactive disorder (ADHD). Instead of drugs, these children need more physical activity in their daily agenda. Block play, woodworking activities, outdoor learning, and large-motor opportunities will help little boys be more cooperative. Teachers who understand and accommodate for normal gender differences are better able to appreciate the social competencies of boys (Pettit & Sugawara, 2002).

Although boys and girls don't often choose to play together, they may benefit from interacting with one another. Children with at least one playmate of the opposite sex demonstrate higher levels of social competence (Howes, 1988). Interacting with male friends may help girls become more independent and assertive (Powlishta, 1995), and interacting with girls may help boys become more caring, cooperative, and less aggressive. Therefore, you may want to do something to minimize gender segregation. Group projects that interest both boys and girls can encourage cooperative interaction between them. In contrast, organizing games as "girls against boys" emphasizes gender distinctions.

CONCLUSION

This chapter and Chapter 2 examine some aspects of child development only as they directly pertain to discipline issues. Knowledge about children's thinking can help you distinguish between immature thinking and purposeful misbehavior. Information about the development of social competency will help you intervene in more productive ways. Realization of how behavior is affected by differences such as culture, socioeconomic status, and gender will give you more realistic expectations of children. When teachers understand child development and match their expectations to what individual children can comfortably do, teachers are happier with their work and they have more cooperative students. Matching your expectations to child development can make the difference between dreading to go to school and looking forward to each new day. Following the guidelines in this chapter is not an easy task; be patient with yourself as you strive toward the goals presented.

Social development tends to be the primary content for teaching discipline. Children who have trouble getting along with peers and cooperating in a group create common discipline problems. Therefore, the topic of social development leads us into our next section, which discusses approaches to discipline. See the sources in the Recommended Readings at the end of the chapter for more comprehensive coverage of the topics introduced in this chapter.

∞ FOR FURTHER THOUGHT

1. Observe young children playing games. What evidence do you see of their unique perception of rules?

2. As you interact with young children, watch for examples of their inability to think about another person's viewpoint. Try to help youngsters learn to express their views and to hear those of another child. Analyze this experience and discuss with your peers how you might improve your approach.

3. Listen to young children. Do you hear them confusing personal fantasy with fact? What is the best adult response?

4. Do you know a youngster who has difficulty being accepted into play with other children? Practice the coaching techniques described in this chapter. What are the results? What did you learn?

5. Have you or someone you know experienced difficulty in school because of a mismatch with the culture of the school? How did you or your friend respond? What were the long-term effects?

6. A problem to solve: Conrad accidentally spilled the paint at the easel, but he denies that he did it.

   a. What is the probable cause of this "lie"?
   b. What is the best adult response to the situation?

∞ RECOMMENDED READINGS

Asher, S. R., & Coie, J. D. (Eds.). (1990). *Peer rejection in childhood.* New York: Cambridge University Press.

Barrera. I., & Corso, R. M. with D. Macpherson. (2003). *Skilled dialogue: Strategies for responding to cultural diversity in early childhood.* Baltimore: Paul H. Brookes.

Corso, W. A. (2003). *We're friends, right? Inside kids' culture.* Washington, DC: Joseph Henry Press.

Edwards, C. P. (1986). *Promoting social and moral development in young children: Creative approaches for the classroom.* New York: Teachers College Press.

Johnson, C., Ironsmith, M., Snow, C. W., & Poteat, G. M. (2000). Peer acceptance and social adjustment in preschool and kindergarten. *Early Childhood Education Journal, 27*(4), 207–212.

Kaiser, B., & Rasminsky, J. S. (2003). Opening the culture door. *Young Children, 58*(4), 53–56.

Kemple, K. M. (1991). Research in review: Preschool children's peer acceptance and social interaction. *Young Children, 46*(5), 47–54.

Lillard, A., & Curenton, S. (1999). Research in review: Do young children understand what others feel, want and know? *Young Children, 54*(5), 53–57.

Piaget, J. (1965). *The moral judgement of the child.* New York: Free Press. (Originally published in 1932.)

Ramsey, P. G. (1991). *Making friends in school: Promoting peer relationships in early childhood.* New York: Teachers College Press.

PART 2
Discipline Approaches

Chapters 4 through 10 present an overview of approaches to discipline. We present these approaches in sequence, from most to least positive; this presentation also moves in sequence from least intrusive to most intrusive.

Chapters 4 and 5 examine ways to prevent discipline problems from occurring—the most pleasant discipline option. Chapter 4 looks at the interpersonal environment as well as the physical setting of the classroom. Chapter 5 explores prevention of behavior problems through the school program: its content and implementation. Chapter 6 shows how adult examples can teach children desirable behaviors, including how to accept and regulate their emotions. Chapter 7 explains how to teach communication and negotiation skills so that youngsters can manage potential behavior problems for themselves. Chapter 8 presents ways to enforce limits while helping children learn why certain behaviors are more desirable than others. Chapter 9 discusses the problems of behavior modification, an approach we do not recommend but that is widely used. In Chapter 10, we explain why punishment is damaging to the discipline goals of most people in society.

We do not believe that any one discipline approach holds all the answers for all children at all times. Determining the cause of the behavior is essential to selecting the appropriate discipline approach. We have confidence that teachers and caregivers with a wide knowledge of possible discipline approaches and a good understanding of child development are best prepared to respond appropriately in a given situation. However, we do not believe that all approaches are good ones. This section warns against counterproductive approaches as well as recommends productive ones.

4 Creating Environments That Prevent Discipline Problems

*S*ome people think of discipline as just dealing with misbehavior. It is much more productive to think about how to avoid behavior problems in the first place. You may have visited a classroom where things went so smoothly that you envied the teacher for having such a well-behaved group of students. Chances are that the children were normal, but the teacher was very skilled at creating an environment that made it easier for kids to cooperate. This skill is a much more sophisticated approach to discipline than simply reacting to problems. In this chapter we will look at ways you can prevent the cause of many behavior problems by creating a classroom emotional environment and physical environment that help children get their needs met.

THE EMOTIONAL ENVIRONMENT

The adults set the tone in school and determine whether it is a caring community or a "dog-eat-dog" society. "Achieving a sense of community entails that children understand that they are part of a larger group and that being thoughtful and cooperative with others benefits both themselves and the entire group" (Howes & Ritchie, 2002). As part of a caring community, children acquire the judgment, sensitivity, self-control, and skills to be able to treat others well (Watson, 1999). Although classroom communities support academic learning, teaching children caring and kindness may be the most important mission of our schools (Noddings, 1995). This chapter begins the description of how to create a caring community through establishing relationships, respecting children's uniqueness, and meeting children's needs. Future chapters will discuss other aspects of the caring community.

Relationships

Relationships provide the foundation for building community and for effective teaching in general (Fox, Dunlap, Hemmeter, Joseph, & Strain, 2003). Classrooms include multiple types of relationships: between teachers and children, between children, and between the teacher and the child's family. All of these relationships play an important role in building community and creating an environment that supports children's social, emotional, and intellectual development.

Teacher-Child Relationships   Teacher-child relationships are a critical part of teaching, whether teaching science or social skills (Koplow, 2002). Teachers need to build positive relationships with children in order to influence their behavior and thought. The same teaching approaches that develop good relationships with children also create harmonious classrooms conducive to learning. In addition, supportive relationships with the teacher are important for children's self-esteem, confidence, and feelings of security. Children need to know you care about them, will keep them safe, and can help them succeed. When they know these things, children have many fewer behavior problems (Fox et al., 2003).

How do you establish good relationships with children? First you get to know them. There are many ways to do this: You can follow a child's lead in play, listen to children talk about their interests and experiences, give hugs and high fives, hold a child's hand, have a conversation over snack or lunch, and greet each one individually. Be sure to tell children how much they were missed when they miss a day of school. You could also call a child after a bad day and say "I'm sorry we had a bad day today—I know tomorrow is going to be better!" (Fox et al., 2003).

Building relationships with children has much in common with making friends of your own age. Relationships are based on sharing, caring, attention, and trust. Sharing some of your own personal life with children also helps build relationships: show pictures of your children or pets, talk about your weekend activities, and share your related experiences during conversations about children's experiences. In other words, be a "real" person, not detached and remote. Children can tell whether adults want to be with them, therefore it is necessary that teachers of young children actually like them and accept their immature behaviors (Koplow, 2002). Children can also tell if you are not really paying attention to them; being physically present is not the same as being mentally present. Too often teachers get busy and only pretend to be paying attention. We know that pretense and other deceit damage relationships; but adults are often guilty of not being truthful with children. Usually this is an effort to protect children by making light of their fears and concerns. However, denying children's observations and feelings is counterproductive. Sometimes children have bad experiences with other adults; they need to have someone they can trust to listen and care. Other times, the problems are among peers. In the following example, acknowledging Max's feelings is the teacher's first step in working with him to try to solve his problem.

> Max comes crying to Sheri, telling her that the other kids don't like him. Sheri's first thought is to reassure him by telling him "Of course they do!" But she has seen Max being rejected and knows he has a reason for his feelings.
> So she says, "It makes you feel bad when Zach won't let you sit by him, doesn't it?"

Children's Relationships with Peers   If children aren't getting along, learning is disrupted and so is the sense of community. Children who have difficulty with peers, either through aggression or withdrawal, are lonely and become victims of other children's aggression. When they are preoccupied with social problems, children lack motivation for learning (Howes & Ritchie, 2002). Helping children learn social skills, as discussed in Chapter 3, is crucial to creating a harmonious learning environment. As a teacher who has good relationships with children, you are in the perfect position to assist children with their peer relationships.

Two additional ingredients are needed for effectively promoting peer relationships: knowledge of child development and freedom to focus energy on the task. Child development knowledge is essential to appropriate expectations and to accurately diagnosing the learning need. Chapters 2 and 3 of this text summarize some of the relevant child development information. School administrators and directors must allow teachers the freedom to put energy into assisting peer relationships. Unfortunately, too many teachers are pressured to focus only on academic performance (Koplow, 2002). A focus on academic performance at the expense of building relationships is counterproductive, since academic achievement is linked to healthy relationships.

How do you help children build positive relationships with their classmates? First you have to make sure that children have time to interact with one another. Teacher-directed classes often keep children so busy responding to teacher-assigned tasks that there is little time for peer contact. Open-ended activities and play time are not only important for children's learning, they also offer opportunity for in-depth interaction between children. Observing such interaction gives the teacher information about individual children's abilities and about group dynamics. This information is then used to plan the types of social skill building described in Chapter 3.

Family-School Relationships   Supportive relationships with children's families are also essential to an effective early education program. Young children are tightly linked to their families, and their families are the main source of information about the child's life so far. Teachers who know students' families are much better able to build relationships with the children and to help them learn.

How do you build relationships with families? Home visits are a start. Home visits have been routine for Head Start teachers for years. Other preschool teachers, and even elementary teachers, have begun to adopt this valuable approach for getting to know their students. A home visit is a good chance to learn from parents. You can find out what the parents want from their child's educational experiences, and you can learn special information about the child. For instance,

Supportive relationships with children's families are essential to an effective early education program.

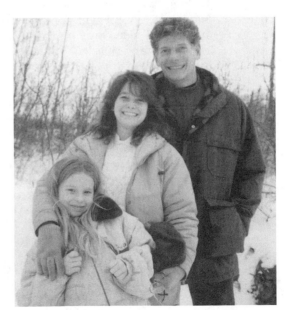

knowing the child's pet name at home and something about his or her favorite family activities will help you relate more personally to the child. You might also want to ask parents to bring family photos to school for their child to share. Families could help make "All About Me" books with their children. You could find out if a child has a favorite book and then read it to the class.

This kind of planning is difficult when the family and teacher do not share a language. A translator can help bridge the gap; a community volunteer, a professional translator, or a friend of the family could provide needed assistance. A translator should be available to families for formal teacher conferences and also for times of informal communication.

Inviting family members to school and to school events or outings is another way to connect with them. Evening events allow working parents to be involved. Potluck dinners are a great way to help families have time for evening events and also are a great way to build community among families. No matter where you meet, the key to establishing relationships is being respectful of what the other person knows, wants, and believes.

Mutual Respect

A caring classroom community requires a teacher who is kind and respectful to children, but who is nevertheless clear about her authority. As DeVries and Zan (1994) say, "Children do not develop respect for others unless they are respected" (p. 76). Children are also more likely to go along with what you want if you are willing to go along with what they want sometimes. In other words, you encourage children to respect your wishes by showing respect for theirs (Miller, 2004).

Most adults are pretty clear about why they want kids to respect adults, but perhaps you haven't thought about adults showing respect for children. Your model of respect will spread and encourage respect between youngsters. Your model will also come back to you as respect from children. Learning to respect the needs and rights of others is basic to treating others well. Treating others well is central to what our society views as acceptable behavior. The construction of moral values is widely believed to be based on learning respect for others (De-Vries, Hildebrandt, & Zan, 2000).

Respectful Communication   What does it mean to respect children? An obvious indicator of respect is how we talk to children. Too often adults speak to children in ways they would never consider speaking to an adult. Respecting children also involves accepting them for who they are instead of trying to make them into what you want. Chapter 2 describes how some children's innate temperament requires more careful handling. Chapter 3 explains some ways in which young children's thinking differs from adults'. Many adults have trouble accepting children's reasoning; they try to get youngsters to parrot adult reasoning instead. Respectful interaction involves listening to children to understand their viewpoints and asking them honest questions about their thinking.

How does an honest question differ from a "dishonest" one? An honest question is one you don't already know the answer to. "What color is your dress/shirt?"

is a dishonest and patronizing question from any adult who is not color blind. "Why do you think that happened?" is an honest question unless you have a pre-conceived "right" answer in mind. If we ask others what they think, we need to accept their answer. What they think may not be what you think, but certainly it correctly describes their thinking.

Respecting Children's Needs   Chapter 2 describes how young children's physical development needs affect their behavior. Adults demonstrate respect for children by allowing for these needs. Matching the physical environment to children's needs will be discussed further in the second part of this chapter. Chapter 2 also explains children's emotional development and needs in terms of their behavior. For instance, young children may need transitional objects such as a teddy bear from home to help them feel safe at school (Hyson, 2004). Respect for youngsters means accepting that they are still small children and also accepting their strong needs to be "big": important, successful, and contributing members of the group. Endless shouts of "Watch me!" demonstrate how important it is to be big when you are small.

The human need to be significant is one reason why respect for children involves letting them have choices and be decision makers. In Chapter 1, we discuss choice as crucial to the development of moral and intellectual autonomy, as described by Piaget. In Chapter 2, we discuss the role of choice in the emotional autonomy stage, as described by Erikson, and in the need for power, as described by Adler. Choices are essential for feeling good about life and about your position in it (DeVries, Hildebrandt, & Zan, 2000).

Teachers who make all the decisions in their classrooms have more rebellious students. Teachers who involve children in deciding how best to accomplish goals have a much easier time. Occasionally, even the most enlightened teachers find themselves in a power struggle. Power struggles occur when you give an ultimatum and a child decides not to go along with it.

Dennis learned a lesson on the day he said, "No one eats lunch until your mess is cleaned up." Amy flatly refused to pick up the dress-up clothes she had been trying on. Now what? Dennis didn't really intend to deprive anyone of lunch; his remark had just been thoughtless. But the other children had picked up on it and were telling Amy she wasn't going to get any lunch. Amy was wailing hysterically over the thought of missing lunch, but she was not picking up any dress-up clothes.

Would the children ever believe him again if he let Amy have lunch without picking up? He couldn't in good conscience actually deny her food. What could he do?

He decided that he could teach a really valuable lesson to his young students. He could demonstrate how to admit an error graciously and to remedy it. This social skill is pertinent to the lives of preschoolers as they work at getting along. Dennis congratulated himself on modeling something much better than the "might makes right" concept, which his threat of missing lunch had perpetuated. So he went over to Amy and gently touched her shoulder to get her attention. He sat down on the floor beside her and explained that he had spoken without thinking. He assured Amy that she would not miss lunch.

Feeling calmer, Amy was able to listen as Dennis clarified his intent: to get the playthings out of the way so there would be space for eating lunch. With the ultimatum removed, Amy was able to problem-solve and reason. She proposed to move her dress-up clothes out of the way for now and finish putting them away after lunch when she wasn't so terribly hungry. Dennis was pleased to accept the compromise, realizing that it was not only logical but also a mutually face-saving solution.

Later, as he thought about the incident, Dennis examined the issue of saving face as it relates to power struggles. He acknowledged that his own pride was involved and he thought about children's pride. He decided that if he got himself into a similar situation again, he would not hesitate to back off. He analyzed his reasons for going against the common assumption that adults must not lose in a battle of wills with a child. Dennis's conclusion was that losing such a battle meant damaged pride and, therefore, damaged self-esteem. Were his own pride and self-esteem more important than the child's? Because enhancing children's self-esteem was one of his major educational goals, Dennis was clear about the answer. He didn't want to make himself feel important at the expense of a little child. His was a respectful solution and one that took courage on his part.

Respecting Differences

Feeling good about yourself requires that you be accepted for who you are. A caring community accepts all members of the group. In Chapter 3 we discuss the danger of teachers not understanding and accepting behavior patterns from a culture other than their own. Classrooms that accept and honor cultural differences meet the needs of minority students while teaching other children concepts of cultural pluralism (Copple, 2003; Hunt, 1999). In respecting the cultural background of the child, it is also important to see the child as an individual and not just as a member of a certain group. Seeing children as individuals helps guard against stereotyping them according to their culture. The teacher's attitudes can affect the attitudes of children and may counteract prejudiced ideas (Derman-Sparks, 1999).

Most teachers find that they have a lot to learn to avoid common, well-intentioned, but generally counterproductive efforts toward multiculturalism. Copple (2003) shares explanations of the mistaken and limited assumptions about diversity demonstrated by most teachers. Teachers find that learning how to achieve true cultural plurality, as opposed to "pseudomulticulturalism," requires significant study.

Mrs. Jensen is working within her school to help her colleagues move away from pseudomulticulturalism. Her school as a whole is very proud of its annual Multicultural Fair. For this event, each grade level represents a different country or culture. Each group makes costumes to wear and learns songs and dances to perform. They form a huge parade, winding through the school and into the multipurpose room for the songs and dances. Though this is quite spectacular, Mrs. Jensen is convinced that the way it is done teaches nothing helpful and probably creates stereotypical thinking.

Remember to see each child as an individual, not just as a member of a certain ethnic or cultural group.

What do the kindergartners think or understand as they are instructed in making "mukluks" from paper bags as part of their Eskimo costumes? Do they realize that mukluks are made from animal skins, not paper bags? Do they understand why people living in cold climates, without access to shoe stores, would make and wear mukluks? Do they realize that their classmate Mollie, who wears velcro-fastened sneakers, is half Eskimo? When they join the school parade right behind the Chinese dragon created by the third graders, what connections do they make between dragons and mukluks?

Remember, young children are not capable of understanding abstract issues involving different time periods and faraway places. They create their theories based on what they see and experience. More on this topic in Chapter 5.

Cultural stereotyping is not limited to minority groups. One of the common misconceptions is that all white children are from a common culture, a perception that overlooks different backgrounds among them. As explained in Chapter 3, no matter what skin color or ethnicity a child has, family patterns, religious beliefs, and class differences create unique cultural backgrounds for each (Kaiser & Rasminisky, 2003). In addition, Caucasian children may be recent immigrants from a variety of countries: Russia, Romania, and Croatia are represented in Mrs. Jensen's school in addition to children with Asian, Native American, and Latino backgrounds.

Each child comes to school with a unique set of prior experiences that include a set of family values. Many of these values relate to guidance issues. Remember that different families have different ideas about acceptable and unacceptable behavior; they also have different ideas about how to teach children to be better behaved. Understanding these differences is another reason for teachers to get acquainted with parents. Getting acquainted is also essential for dialogue about how to deal with differing expectations between home and school.

Some children speak languages other than English at home and come to school with limited English proficiency. Not only does a language difference complicate communication between teacher and child, it puts the child at great risk for social isolation. Lack of a mutual language certainly gets in the way of play and other interaction with peers, often leading to frustration and/or withdrawal for the child unfamiliar with the dominant language. Tabors points out that these children are caught in a "double bind of second language learning: To learn a new language, you have to be socially accepted by those who speak the language; but to be socially accepted you have to be able to speak the new language" (Tabors, 1998 p. 22). Group play that requires little verbalization is essential for counteracting the social isolation that inhibits language learning. Mrs. Jensen notices that block play offers an ideal opportunity for second language learning. Other helpful teacher strategies include having a predictable schedule and using repetitious songs and rhymes; these strategies help the preschool and primary grade children learning English as a second language just as they help younger children learning English as their first language.

Language and cultural differences are not the only things that make individual children unique. Different temperaments and individual histories cause children to respond differently to new experiences and school routines. Teachers who respect such differences respond to each child in ways appropriate for that child's needs.

Including Children with Special Needs   Children with special needs who are included in regular classrooms add another dimension of diversity. The teacher's example will help counteract children's fears of this and other kinds of differences. When you focus on the child and not the disability, you will more easily integrate the child with special needs into your group (Bredekamp & Copple, 1997). You can help your other students become comfortable with a wheelchair, prosthesis, or whatever special assistance a child requires. Then your students, too, can focus on the child as a person. Children with special needs often are rejected by peers because they are different (Ramsey, 1991). Sensitive teachers can help with this problem by modeling acceptance and honoring the strengths of all children. (See Chapter 13 for more detailed explanations.) The mother of a child with Down syndrome spoke with tears of joy about the friends her son had found after he was included in a first-grade classroom with a helpful teacher. The little boy just couldn't stop talking about his friends.

All people have needs for friendship, success in worthwhile endeavors, and recognition for their efforts. A classroom community does not exclude any members due to a disability. It is the teacher's responsibility to make sure such exclusion does not occur (Elswood, 1999). Children spend a large part of their day in the school setting and must be able to find friends, success, and recognition at school. It is essential that a teacher understand these needs and know how to provide for them. Books such as *Creative Resources for the Anti-bias Classroom* (Hall, 1999) may offer ideas for activities to counteract stereotypical thinking; however, we caution you to be selective and avoid substituting paper-and-crafts activities for real experiences.

Children's Emotional Needs

Fostering the emotional well-being of young children requires that teachers, administrators, aides, and guidance counselors learn about emotional development and commit to supporting children's emotional health (Koplow, 2002). A classroom that nurtures children's good feelings will encourage "good" behavior (Siccone & Lopez, 2000). Conversely, damage to pride or self-esteem generally is expressed in some undesirable behavior. In fact, bad feelings of any kind are likely to show up as "bad" actions. Helping children in your classroom feel good about themselves and their school experience is an important part of effective classroom management, community building, and harmonious group dynamics.

Friendship   Classrooms and child-care centers where friendship and socializing are encouraged tend to be happy and harmonious places (Honig, 2004). Important social studies lessons occur constantly as the teacher assists youngsters in their efforts to work cooperatively. Disagreements are viewed as teaching opportunities instead of reasons to keep kids apart. These classrooms are places where the teacher isn't continually telling children to be quiet. The teacher's energy is directed into more useful ways of helping children use their time productively.

With building community as a goal, the children's energy isn't wasted by trying not to talk to one another. Teachers who understand the need for friendship and the value of peer interaction don't go around being mad at kids for doing what comes naturally. And kids don't end up feeling bad about wanting to communicate with their peers. Happier teachers and children create a friendly, relaxed atmosphere more conducive to learning of all kinds.

In fact, schools truly committed to building caring communities schedule time for children to enjoy one another in a relaxed atmosphere (Watson, 1999). Mrs. Jensen's school encourages teachers to take their students on a two-day overnight outing to a nearby camp that offers cottages for sleeping and a lodge for group gatherings. She schedules this event for early in the school year to maximize its benefit. Many parents go along, helping to supervise the children, but also creating bonds among parents and between parents and the teacher. We also know teachers who schedule Saturday family hikes for their classes, contributing their own time to the important goal of building community.

Such events help children make individual friends as well as create group camaraderie. As we have stated before, having friends is essential to children's healthy social and emotional development. Children who have difficulty making a friend need the teacher's assistance. Friendship skills include sharing, turn taking, contributing to play, giving and receiving help, paying compliments, and

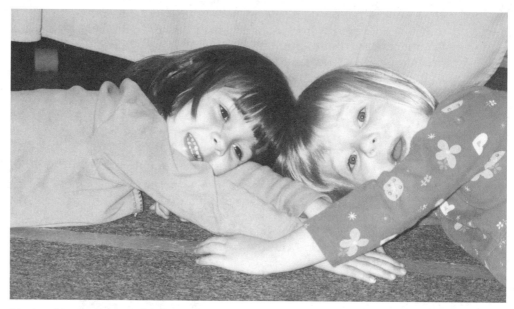

Having friends is essential to children's healthy social and emotional development. Children who have difficulty making friends need the teacher's help.

coping with teasing or bullying (Honig, 2004). Sometimes missing skills are the problem, and other times it is a lack of contact due to shyness. You can encourage the interaction of shy children by setting up small groups for cooperative learning activities (Phillipsen, Bridges, McLemore, & Saponaro, 1999).

In spite of the importance of having a friend, you probably have seen situations when best friends have been separated in school so that they will not disturb one another's work. This well-intentioned intervention ignores the importance of friendship for the child's intellectual and emotional development. Youngsters learn a great deal as they strive to get along with a friend: They learn to think about another person's views, they learn much about compromise and problem solving, and they learn about caring and being cared for. They also practice emotion regulation. These things don't happen with just any peers; they require someone who is special to the child. As we have said before, a child must care enough about another child to be willing to examine egocentric views and work out disagreements.

Mrs. Jensen works to ensure that children in her first-grade classroom find friends. She doesn't have a seating chart at first. Instead, she encourages youngsters to try different places for a couple of weeks. After they have had a chance to get acquainted, the children are asked to choose a place to sit for a while; Mrs. Jensen puts their names at those places for the time being. There is always an opportunity to make new choices as new relationships blossom. Mrs. Jensen says, "The most important thing you can do for some kids in a school year is to make sure they have friends."

Some teachers are not tuned in to friendship as a legitimate need and overlook its educational value. Miss Wheeler is not only unaware of the importance of friendship, but she also doesn't know that children need to interact with their peers as a part of learning. She spends much of her energy each day in futile efforts to keep children from socializing. Her attempts to enforce an unnatural quiet in her classroom are counterproductive to academic and emotional development.

Mrs. Jensen, however, enjoys the busy hum of children sharing ideas and discussing experiences. In this environment, the several children who came to her class speaking a language other than English are fast becoming fluent in English. The interactive learning style of this classroom is perfect for their language-learning needs. Sometimes individual children need to be reminded to talk more softly, but they are not told to be silent in Mrs. Jensen's classroom. She notices that adults talk while they work and wonders why so many try to impose silence on children.

Recognition   When they come to school, children enter a big new world and have the task of finding some way not to be lost in the crowd (Koplow, 2002). If most teacher interaction with students is as part of a group, many children will feel lost or invisible. When the teacher interacts with children as individuals, they know that they have the teacher's attention. Communicating on an individual basis also makes it easier for the teacher to interact appropriately with children of various cultures. Mrs. Jensen makes sure to notice and comment to each child about his or her activity during free-choice time and lets children know she is tuned-in to them at other times. Her comments and questions help each child feel important and valued. Her students don't need to engage in inappropriate attention-getting behaviors to get her to notice them. Because each child has her undivided attention at some time, they more easily share her attention during group times or when she is working with another child.

Conferences between teacher and child provide for both individual attention and focus on individual progress. Mrs. Jensen usually manages to meet with each of her students once a week for 5 or 10 minutes. She is convinced that the weekly one-on-one time is much more valuable than meeting with all children daily in a group. Interacting with children individually in this way also assists in building the relationships with them that are crucial to the teaching-learning process.

Mrs. Jensen found time to meet with Nick after making the rounds of the room during quiet reading time. Everyone seemed engrossed in a book, so she hoped that she and Nick wouldn't be interrupted too much. During their conference, Nick told Mrs. Jensen about the books he had read recently and showed her how long his list of books completed had become. Then he read a particularly funny part from a book about King Bidgood in the bathtub. He also showed his teacher the letter he was writing to his pen pal in the third grade. They discussed whether or not Nick's letter clearly explained the way the classroom snake shed its skin. A copy of the final polished version of the letter would go into Nick's writing portfolio. Mrs. Jensen suggested some books about snakes that Nick might be interested in. Nick went back to his work with confidence and a renewed sense of purpose. During the conference, Mrs. Jensen made brief notes about Nick's progress and what skills he was ready for next.

Conferences like the one between Mrs. Jensen and Nick are increasingly being used as an alternative to tests for assessment and diagnostic purposes (e.g., Fields, Groth & Spangler, 2004). Traditional, competitive ways of assessing children's progress make only the best students feel proud and accomplished. All except the top few feel just the opposite. Too many minority youngsters are evaluated without regard for cultural influences (Bloch, Tabachnick, & Espinosa-Dulanto, 1994). Evaluation systems that compare children to one another have a much different effect than systems that compare children's current work with their own work a few months earlier.

When a child competes with a past personal record instead of with classmates, each child can feel a sense of accomplishment. Each can feel motivated to keep trying. For instance, children who look at a folder containing their writing and drawing for the year can see for themselves how much progress they have made. New approaches to evaluation help youngsters to set personal goals for themselves and take pride in their progress toward those goals (McAfee, Leong, & Bodrova, 2004). The ways in which you assess children's educational progress can help each child feel individually important and can help each feel successful.

Success   Children experience feelings of success or failure during many different kinds of activities in school, during playground games, as well as through teacher assignments. Staley and Portman (2000) urge us to look at the kinds of games we encourage, pointing out that games such as Duck, Duck, Goose and Red Rover, Red Rover may be games of waiting, rejection, failure, and humiliation for many children. Noncompetitive games and those that don't require being "picked" are a better choice.

Competitive situations are a set-up for failure, since not everyone can win. Therefore, the others become losers. In addition, competition is incompatible with the goal of building a caring community. If you pit children against one another, you undermine the development of kindness and cooperation. In order to foster the caring community and help everyone feel successful, you will want to arrange for cooperative games, contests, and projects. Situations where children work as a team for a common goal are productive. If you can't do without competition, have children try to "beat the clock" instead of one another (Clayton, 1997).

When all children are expected to complete the same assignment in the same way, comparisons are inevitable, with results similar to those of competition. Open-ended activities allow for individual differences and discourage comparison by allowing children to use their creativity in how they complete a task. Open-ended activities are those with no one right outcome, and therefore no possibility of failure. Success is ensured because children can choose to work at their own appropriate level of challenge. Some children will easily succeed at almost any task the teacher comes up with, but they may not be sufficiently challenged to feel good about succeeding. Other youngsters are more vulnerable to failure. In both cases, open-ended activities can help all children experience feelings of success.

Open-ended activities do not have set limits and they allow for extension beyond the expected levels, creating an additional challenge where needed. In this case, youngsters can make a project as challenging as they wish. Open-ended activities are also an important aspect of inclusion. Often children with special

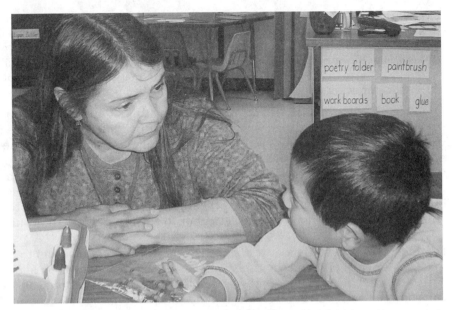

Assessing and supporting children's learning through individual conferences can help each child feel important and successful.

needs require open-ended activities in order to participate with the other children. Feelings of success do not result from easy schoolwork; they result from the appropriate match between the challenge and the child's ability.

The writing center in Dennis's preschool class provides for many levels of abilities and adapts to a variety of interests. It has a selection of paper in many sizes and colors, both with and without lines. There are also pencils and markers, staplers, and hole punches. Children are free to use these materials as needed for their work and play. Naomi's "pretend" writing, Joshua's scribbles, and Shakir's drawing are all acceptable. Each of the children uses writing for different purposes. Naomi uses writing for social purposes, putting a combination of pictures and symbols on a scrap of paper and giving it to a friend to establish contact. Joshua is interested in how different types of crayons and markers make different kinds of marks. Shakir shows an impressive literary background in the picture stories he creates and makes into books. Children frequently choose to spend time at the writing center and they are making progress in their understanding of how print works.

Contrast Dennis's open-ended options with Joanne's closed-ended activity described next. Joanne thinks the only important thing about writing is learning the correct way to make letters; she decided it was time the children learned the right way to write.

Joanne got out the lined paper and some charts showing proper letter formation. She told the children they could make any letters they wanted, as long as they made them look like those on the charts. Sarah wanted to make "her" S and tried hard to make it look like the chart. Somehow it kept coming out more like a backwards C; sometimes it was a C with a tail. However, it looked fine to Sarah until Joanne told her it was wrong. Sarah resisted Joanne's efforts to show her the right way; she choose to leave the writing center. Similarly, Naomi's pretend writing didn't meet Joanne's standards; and neither Joshua's scribbles nor Shakir's drawing were allowed. None of the children wanted to write any more.

Certainly, there is also a need for activities with just one correct response; but these need to be implemented with care for individual differences. You need to provide a balance of open and closed activities in your classroom to meet the needs of all youngsters. Sometimes Kelsey seeks the challenge of closed tasks in preschool, such as putting a puzzle together or learning how to weave paper mats at the arts and crafts table. As she challenges herself with the specific task and succeeds, she builds her feelings of competence. At other times she seeks the freedom to test what she can build with various manipulatives or to explore freely with art materials.

Choice   How can you, as a teacher, possibly provide just the right activity and material for each child all the time? You can't. What you can do is allow children a freedom of choice among a wide variety of interesting educational activities. You can count on each child almost always choosing the appropriate level of challenge and the right type of activity for the moment. Here is another value of child choice: Not only does it enhance the development of autonomy, but it also is invaluable for matching the curriculum to the child. Obviously, providing choice for your students is an important teaching strategy.

Allowing children to match their level of personal challenge to a variety of open-ended activities is a good classroom management strategy (e.g., Bredekamp & Copple, 1997; Feeney, Christensen, & Moravcik, 2006). Self-selection of an academic challenge also provides an alternative to ability grouping, which is a less effective effort to match the task to the child's ability. Research has demonstrated the negative effect of ability grouping on self-esteem and classroom dynamics (Cunningham, Hall, & Defee, 1998). It doesn't take much time in a classroom to notice that children in the "low" group are most likely to act out or quit trying academically.

If you follow youngsters onto the playground, you also see that children in the low group are frequently rejected as playmates by children from the other groups. This rejection creates a segregation effect among youngsters of different academic achievement levels. It is especially disconcerting in light of the fact that a disproportionate number of minority children tend to be placed in the low group (Bloch

---

∞ INSTEAD OF CONTROLLING, YOU COULD BE TEACHING

- Encourage choices
- Allow talking
- Provide for movement
- Accept more than one right way

et al., 1994). Teachers need to take special care that being a child from a certain ethnic group doesn't disadvantage the child academically. Teachers also need to take care that children are not socially disadvantaged because of academic labels.

The purpose of ability grouping is for supposed efficiency when the teacher is giving information. Ability grouping, with its many negative side effects, is part of a teacher-centered classroom where the teacher makes most of the decisions about what happens. In contrast, child choice is basic to what is known as a child-centered classroom. The teacher moves among the youngsters as they work at their choice of activities with their choice of friends; the teacher's role is to ask questions and make comments to encourage thinking. There is no place for ability grouping here. Instead, children choose learning activities based on their interests, and children of various ability levels work together to contribute in their own ways. This approach builds community.

The teacher is responsible for the external order and rhythm of the classroom, but giving children the freedom to make choices within that structure helps children find learning experiences that are individually appropriate (Koplow, 2002). We don't recommend allowing children to make all the choices, but children cannot grow emotionally in an overly rigid setting. Both chaos and rigidity damage children's ability to grow emotionally (Koplow, 2002).

Positive Teacher Expectations

The teacher's attitude can create an environment that encourages either positive or negative behavior (DeVries & Zan, 1994). Naturally, no teacher would deliberately encourage negative behavior, yet it is possible to send messages unconsciously that are better not sent. Nonverbal communication is especially likely to reveal your inner feelings. Body language, tone of voice, and intensity often speak louder than words.

If you are convinced that children want to work and play constructively, your whole manner of relating to them communicates that expectation. However, you may be convinced that children want to get away with whatever they can and have no interest in learning. This expectation, too, will be communicated by your tone of voice as you speak to children and by the amount of freedom you give them. You can pretty well count on children to behave according to your expectations.

> Mrs. Jensen's first-grade class has just come in from recess, and the youngsters are moving purposefully around the room as they prepare for their next activity. They have the freedom to choose among the classroom centers and to decide individually whether to eat a snack now or later. The classroom is alive with the sounds of decision making as children refocus their energies. Some go first to wash up before a snack and find a comfortable spot to relax and eat. Beau and Dylan are hungry but want to finish the block structure they were working on before recess. Food isn't allowed in the block area, so they postpone their snack. Yaisa and Shayla take their snack into the playhouse, where eating is allowed, and happily incorporate snack time into their dramatic play. Now that the youngsters have learned the routines and the classroom rules, Mrs. Jensen sometimes feels she really isn't needed. She is able to use this time for observing and recording children's progress.

Mrs. Jensen has trusted her children to self-direct their free-choice time, and they have lived up to her expectations. This makes school more pleasant for her and for her students. Contrast Mrs. Jensen's room with Miss Wheeler's.

Next door, Miss Wheeler has no time for observing. She is busy directing and controlling everyone's behavior. In her first-grade class, all the children must eat their snack as soon as they come in from recess, whether they are hungry or not. This schedule makes a long wait in line for handwashing, with lots of pushing and shoving during the wait. It isn't easy, but Miss Wheeler makes the children all sit still until everyone is finished eating before they are excused for the next activity. Then she assigns them by table to specific centers, where they must stay until she flashes the lights signaling rotation to the next center. Jose is a constant problem, always trying to sneak out of his assigned center to the blocks. Emily cries a lot, saying she doesn't want to play with those "mean kids" from her table. Miss Wheeler is in constant demand to settle disputes and make children stay where they are supposed to be. She sees this situation as clear evidence that these young children aren't capable of self-direction. Actually, she is getting in the way of their self-direction.

Unfortunately, many teachers run their classrooms like Miss Wheeler does, and they create discipline problems for themselves. Their lack of trust in children to make good choices makes them over-controlling, which means individual children don't get their needs met.

Clear Guidelines

It is essential that children understand exactly what behaviors are acceptable in school and which ones are not. Your positive outlook is not enough if children are confused about what they are to do. Young children often do not have the experience to know what is and what is not acceptable. Social norms are not self-evident.

Mrs. Jensen started the school year by reading a book called *Little Monster Goes to School.* Little Monster does a lot of bad things, like sticking his arm out of the bus, tripping other kids, and getting into their lunches. Mrs. Jensen's first graders were properly horrified at this behavior. The story provided a good start for a discussion about how to act at school. Then the class was invited to brainstorm behavior limits. Mrs. Jensen helped them to combine their ideas into a few main ideas and to phrase them in positive instead of negative terms. "Don't run" became "Be careful." "Don't hit, don't shove, and don't spit" became "Be kind and talk things over." Mrs. Jensen wrote these as the children watched. They were displayed on a bulletin board that the children decorated with monster pictures they created at the paint easel. Most of the children learned to read the guidelines and referred to them when a classmate didn't follow one.

Children will more likely follow guidelines they themselves have helped to determine. They may also actively remind other children to do the same. However, young children's ability to describe appropriate and inappropriate behavior greatly exceeds their ability to act accordingly (Koplow, 2002). Therefore, the teacher's role goes beyond the initial determination of rules; regular class meetings must be held for the purpose of problem solving when children do not live up to the guidelines.

Children are more likely to fol-low guidelines they them-selves have helped decide; they may also remind other children to follow the guide-lines too.

Class Meetings   Class meetings help the group function as a community and include discussing ways in which people have been kind and helpful as well as discussing problems. Sharing feelings, working together to solve conflicts, and supporting one another as children strive toward common goals create a unified group (Styles, 2001). Class meetings allow children, and the teacher, to bring problems and concerns to the group for discussion. The goal of these discussions is to find a solution for the next time the issue arises, not to place blame or give out punishment (Rightmyer, 2003). Such meetings allow thoughts and feelings to be expressed without fear of embarrassment or punishment. This feeling of safety has a positive effect on the school day and improves children's ability to concentrate on learning (Vance & Weaver, 2002). We discuss conflict resolution during class meetings more fully in Chapter 7.

Children come to understand the ideas behind class guidelines as a result of on-going discussions that apply the guidelines to problems shared in class meetings. Have you noticed that we aren't talking about making rules, but instead use the terms *guidelines* and *limits*? Reynolds (2000) points out the differences between limits and rules: Limits and guidelines are flexible, taking circumstances into consideration; rules are rigid and tend to apply regardless of circumstances. Limits or guidelines encourage thinking and decision making; rules allow neither. Therefore, limits and guidelines foster moral autonomy, and rules foster heteronomy. Consider the difference between "Be careful" and "Don't run." The rule "Don't run" or even "Always walk" encourages children to test it and see what happens. Obviously there are times when kids can run, and even times when they should. The limit of being careful encourages children to reflect on what it means to be careful; "Being careful" becomes a topic of discussion to encourage children to self-evaluate their behavior according to that standard.

> Nick was driving a toy car on the block road he and Kyle had built. The car zoomed faster and faster as Nick began a fantasy about a jet car. Kyle was absorbed in building a bridge over his part of the road and wasn't paying attention to the jet car. He had finally gotten the right combination of blocks and the right balance to make his bridge stay up when Nick's jet car crashed into it. Dennis heard the heated exchange of words between the boys and managed to get to them before the disagreement escalated to blows. "He knocked down my bridge!" complained Kyle. "I didn't mean to!" exclaimed Nick. What a perfect opportunity for important teaching. Dennis could use this situation to help Nick, and also Kyle, to think about the effects of their actions. His question, "Were you being careful of Kyle's bridge when you drove your car so fast?" is designed to encourage thought. So is the question, "How could you make your car go fast and still be careful of what other children are doing?" Notice, Dennis isn't giving answers—he is helping the kids think.

Young children have much to learn, but you might assume that they should at least know better than to sit up on their knees during class meetings and story time. Surely they realize that sitting that way blocks the view of the person behind them, and that means they are not following the guideline "Be kind." But remember that young children think about their own needs and have trouble considering someone else's position. There are ways to help them understand another person's view during group time.

> Mrs. Jensen doesn't constantly remind children to sit down in the front rows; instead of nagging, she structures a learning experience to help them begin to understand consideration for others. She assigns each table of children to a specific row during the first group meeting of each day. During other group sessions, they are allowed to choose their own places, but for this one group time they take turns experiencing how it feels to be in the back rows with other children in their way. Mrs. Jensen encourages the children who can't see to remind the others politely when they are thoughtlessly blocking the view. This experience provides an important lesson in seeing things from another person's perspective and in communicating a problem. The children soon take responsibility for reminding one another to be considerate, and eventually remember most of the time not to kneel in front of someone.

THE PHYSICAL ENVIRONMENT

Did you realize that the decoration, furnishing, and arrangement of a classroom affect a child's behavior? Have you investigated what effect the room colors and lighting may have on children? (Cool tones are more calming and fluorescent lighting can cause a problem.) Have you considered whether the room's decor may be over-stimulating for some children? Have you thought about whether or not your classroom invites children to do what you want them to do? Have you noticed whether each child can find seating that is the right size? Have you considered the effect on behavior when a child is either physically or emotionally uncomfortable in a school setting? If a child is exhibiting a behavior problem, be sure to examine the physical environment for possible causes of the problem. Following are some examples of common problem areas.

Analyzing for Consistency

Is the classroom arrangement consistent with teacher expectations for children? A teacher-centered classroom typically has desks or tables arranged so that children can see and hear the teacher. In this type of class, the source of information and center of attention is the teacher. Therefore, it is consistent to have the room arranged to help students focus on the teacher. In contrast, a child-centered class is arranged in activity areas, often called centers. This arrangement allows the children's focus to be on the activities and materials provided. Seating arrangements that allow for student interaction are consistent with programs that value peer exchange of ideas.

First-grade teacher Miss Wheeler doesn't realize that her arrangement of desks in small groups facing each other does not match her expectations for children. She knows that it is popular to have desks arranged in groups rather than in rows, but she hasn't thought about why. These groupings are designed to encourage peer interaction and cooperative learning. The problem is that Miss Wheeler doesn't want children to talk in school. Her room arrangement

Is the classroom arrangement consistent with teacher expectations? Consider how children will perceive the space and materials.

counteracts the behavior she desires. Mrs. Jensen has the same desk arrangement, but it works for her because it is completely consistent with her expectations for behavior.

We also send "mixed messages" when we provide wide open spaces and expect children to sit still. When children see a corridor, the message they get is "run!" In addition, little boys will see open spaces as wrestling rings, and use them accordingly. Arranging classroom furniture so there are no long corridors will cut down on unwanted running. However, you do need open space for group gatherings. Perhaps wheeled storage shelves can allow for open space only when needed.

To avoid confusion and conflict, it is important to create an environment that sends clear, nonconflicting messages. Joanne learns this message from Nancy in the following example:

> As she called the children to story time with the xylophone, Joanne dreaded the inevitable power struggle that was sure to follow. Story time just wasn't working for her. The only floor space big enough for story time was surrounded by shelves of toys, and the children just couldn't keep their hands off them. It was impossible to keep their attention. Because the shelves were on wheels, she tried pushing them as far back as she could. But the children just inched their circle back to get to them. She repeatedly reminded them that it was time for a story, not for toys. Still, it was like trying to keep bees from flowers!
>
> Frustrated, Joanne asked Nancy how she dealt with the problem during her story time. "Oh, I gave up long ago expecting them to ignore the shelves," Nancy explained. "When story time is coming, I ask for volunteers to help turn those shelves around to face the wall. They love the powerful feeling of moving furniture. Other children see the change in the room happening and know it's time for a story. And it goes without saying that it's not time to play with shelf toys—they can't even see them!"

Joanne's story-time arrangement gave a mixed message to the children. The toys surrounding them had been purchased and arranged particularly to attract people their age. These materials invited play. Conflicting with this invitation was the person with the book, also requesting their attention. Chances were high that some children weren't interested in that book just then but were fascinated with one of the toys, which were so enticingly near. Placing children in this situation and then asking them to obey the teacher with undivided attention creates needless conflict.

Nancy's solution provides a clear message about the focus of the activity and what is expected during this time. If some children are not interested in the book she is currently reading, she tells them they may go to another area in the room, where shelf choices are still available, and play with the toys quietly at a table. She has clearly defined her story-time space with the turned shelves. The messages from the environment and the teacher are not contradictory. It is easy for the children to recognize what they are to do. It also helps if the doorway is not visible to children from the group gathering spot; this avoids distraction when people come and go. If children in your class are "misbehaving," check to see if the setting is leading them astray with mixed messages.

Many public school lunch rooms offer examples of environmental mixed messages: Hundreds of children are crowded together at long tables, excited about planning their upcoming playground activities, and yet the supervising adults demand quiet. For whose benefit is the quiet? What is the rationale for demanding it? Why are children punished for talking while eating lunch? How quiet is it in the teachers' lunch room? Whenever she can spare the time during her lunch break, Mrs. Jensen invites small groups of her class to have lunch with her in the classroom. This way, at least periodically, they have a more pleasant and civilized lunch experience. She makes a point to frequently include those children who are especially overwhelmed and made anxious by the big, noisy lunchroom where adults yell at the children.

Studying Traffic Patterns

Children thrive best in a classroom with clearly defined learning centers that allow children to explore various types of activities (Koplow, 2002). The locations of learning centers can either make things run smoothly or can be a source of trouble (Curtis & Carter, 2003). If the block-building center is not protected from people walking by, you can bet on frequent yelling, and even hitting, over ruined block creations. If the woodworking area is right next to the reading center, you can predict that quiet reading will be disrupted by noisy carpentry. Teachers work hard at planning their room arrangement. Even then, they are constantly monitoring how well it works and making adjustments as indicated.

> It had been a rough day at Midway Children's Center. Aaron's screeching as he defended his space in the block center had given Sheri a headache—again. Sheri talked with her colleagues while the children were napping and tried to figure out a solution. They decided that the room needed to be rearranged, but realized they should involve the children in the plan.
>
> The next day, Dennis asked the children if they had noticed there were lots of problems with people getting in each other's way in the block center. They had. So the preschoolers and their teachers brainstormed about ways they could rearrange their classroom to make things better. The children thought of ways to use space that their teachers hadn't.
>
> After school that day, the Children's Center staff was busy! They implemented the changes agreed on by the group and ended up with a much larger block area. As a result, the book nook was moved to a more secluded spot. The kids loved it all. In the enlarged block center, Aaron was able to work alongside Zach and Kenji without any conflict. A side effect was more children choosing to read in the book nook. Solving a discipline problem by making a change in the environment worked very well in this case.

Allowing for Movement

Discipline problems can also be a result of keeping kids sitting too long. If youngsters are kept still and quiet most of the day, many will experience real discomfort. Have you ever found yourself simply unable to sit for another moment during

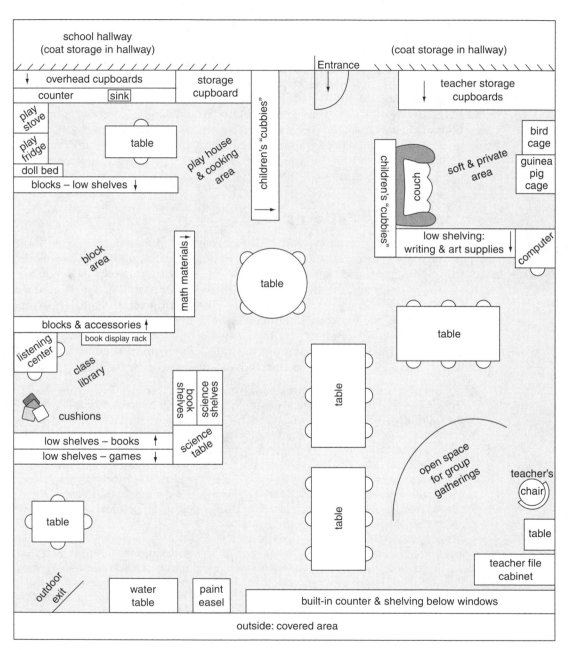

FIGURE 4–1 A sample primary grade classroom arrangement. The floor plan of this small classroom allows for student interaction and for privacy. It also provides protection for block constructions, a quiet spot for reading, and a group gathering spot without distractions. This plan could be adapted for younger children.

94

a long meeting or a long airplane flight? If so, you probably know what kind of physical discomfort young children feel when they are asked to sit longer than they are able. The natural reaction to this discomfort is to get up and move around. In classrooms where moving is allowed and provided for, there is no problem. However, there are classrooms where children are supposed to stay in their seats until the scheduled recess provides relief. Sometimes a child can use a trip to the bathroom as an excuse to walk around, but this often leads to lots of playing around in the bathroom.

> Mrs. Jensen not only allows children to move around quite freely between activities in her classroom, but she also makes an attempt to provide high-mobility activity choices when youngsters need them. Dylan, the lucky twin, is in her room. When he has a special need for activity, he can build with the big, heavy blocks and exercise his arms and upper body. He can challenge himself with the balance beam or pound nails in the carpentry area. His twin brother, Devon, does not have these opportunities in Miss Wheeler's room.
>
> Devon squirmed in agony after sitting at his place endlessly doing worksheets. He was not allowed to get up for a book until he was finished, and he was always the last one done. Finally, unable to take it any longer, Devon stretched his leg and tripped another child passing by. Instantly, he was in big trouble and was sent to the principal's office. At least he got to walk on the way there.

Providing for Privacy

Have you ever experienced strong antisocial feelings after extended periods of interacting with other people? Spending a full day in school, especially a long child-care day, can be extremely wearing psychologically. You will notice youngsters getting crabby as the day wears on. They are more than just tired; they are also tired of people. Some children make hiding places for themselves if given the chance. Madeline built herself a little house in the block area, got inside, and covered the top with a doll blanket. She insisted that others keep out. Sometimes you will see a child simply taking refuge under a desk or a table. One little boy even got into a wastebasket to get away from it all.

Teachers are becoming more aware of children's need for a retreat from hubbub (Bredekamp, 1997). Research on emotional development tells us that children should be allowed to move freely between group activities and individual activity (Koplow, 2002). Many classrooms feature special places for being alone or visiting with a friend by yourself. Mrs. Jensen created a small space between two file cabinets and furnished it with cushions, books, and a reading lamp. Dennis found a spot under a stairway in the preschool that was perfect for one or two small children. It, too, has been cozily fitted with pillows and decorated with pictures. When the demand for the private spots becomes too great, children can either sign up on a waiting list or create their own spots. There is no reason why children can't do the same work in private that they can do in the middle of the room. In fact, sometimes children need a bit of privacy before they feel up to serious work. Some also need to have less stimulation from sights and sounds, as well as from people.

CONCLUSION

Teachers who understand and provide for privacy and mobility save themselves a lot of trouble and also save children from being "naughty." Teachers who plan the environment so that it doesn't create problems have smoother days. Adults who expect the best from children and communicate their expectations clearly find that children behave more positively. Adults who respect individual children, their families, and their cultures create caring classroom communities. Adults who provide choices and otherwise share power with children find them more eager and helpful. Teachers who help youngsters find friendship, success, and recognition help them to learn more effectively. Teachers who make an effort to build relationships with individual children and their families create the necessary foundation for learning social and academic skills. When you meet children's needs in the physical and emotional classroom environment, many common discipline problems never arise.

∽ FOR FURTHER THOUGHT

1. What are the behavior guidelines in an early childhood education program where you have spent time? How were these guidelines determined? Why do you think the youngsters either do or do not follow the guidelines?

2. In what ways have you seen teachers demonstrate respect for young children? In what ways have you seen teachers show lack of respect for youngsters? Which examples most closely match your own interaction with children?

3. How are friendships encouraged or discouraged in an early childhood program with which you are familiar? Would you recommend any changes to help children develop meaningful friendships?

4. Analyze an early childhood program for open-ended and closed activities. Is there a balance or does one type dominate? How do children's responses to the two types differ?

5. Observe teacher-child interaction, watching for the amount of individual attention provided. How do youngsters respond differently to individual interaction with the teacher than they do to interacting as part of a group?

6. Analyze the physical setting of a classroom. In what ways does the room arrangement prevent or create discipline problems? How are mobility needs met? How are privacy needs met?

⌒⌒ RECOMMENDED READING

Bredekamp, S., & Copple, C. (Eds.). (1997). *Developmentally appropriate practice in early childhood programs serving children from birth through age 8.* Washington, DC: National Association for the Education of Young Children.

Derman-Sparks, L., & ABC Task Force. (1989). *Anti-bias curriculum: Tools for empowering young children.* Washington, DC: National Association for the Education of Young Children.

Elswood, R. (1999). Really including diversity in early childhood classrooms. *Young Children, 54*(4), 62–66.

Koplow, L. (2002). *Schools that heal: Real-life solutions.* New York: Teachers College Press.

Okagaki, L., & Diamond, K. E. (2000). Responding to cultural and linguistic differences in the beliefs and practices of families with young children. *Young Children, 55*(3), 74–80.

5 *Planning Programs That Prevent Discipline Problems*

$\mathcal{W}$hen children are interested and involved in learning, they don't have time for troublesome behavior. Which do you think would keep young learners involved better? Tracing and copying a different letter each day or exploring print in books and signs that have an interesting message? Counting the number of dots on a worksheet or figuring out how to divide the raisins equally for snack time? The educational activities and objectives selected for a school or classroom are called its *curriculum*. It has been said that the best discipline is a well-planned curriculum (Greenberg, 1987). Prevention of problems is the idea behind that statement.

Young children are better able to cooperate in school when educational approaches match their developmental stages. Therefore, teacher expectations must be geared to the maturation level of the students, and curriculum must be appropriate to the children involved. When practices and materials created for older students are used for younger ones, many problems arise. Developmentally inappropriate teaching by adults results in inappropriate behavior from children.

Research shows that children in programs that are not developmentally appropriate exhibit more stress (Hart, Olsen, Robinson, & Mandleco, 1998; Ruckman, Burts, & Pierce, 1999). Obviously, stress has negative effects on learning and on behavior. Therefore, it is no surprise that developmentally appropriate classrooms are also more emotionally positive environments (Hyson & Molinaro, 2001). As a result, children in programs that are developmentally appropriate demonstrate higher levels of social skills than those in other kinds of programs (Jambunathan, Burts, & Pierce, 1999; Jones & Gullo, 1999). This chapter describes developmentally appropriate curriculum and program management; such practices will help to eliminate the causes of many behavior problems.

MAKING LEARNING MEANINGFUL

How do children act when they are bored or disinterested? Most likely, you remember from your own childhood how you acted under those circumstances. Most youngsters will create some action when the teacher doesn't offer any. Often, however, these creative efforts do not conform to acceptable group behavior, and teachers call them discipline problems.

The National Association for the Education of Young Children (Bredekamp & Rosegrant, 1995) provides curriculum guidelines for preschool and primary grade youngsters (see Appendix B). These guidelines emphasize the characteristics of developmentally appropriate approaches to teaching young children. The following discussion explains how these guidelines can eliminate many potential discipline problems you might otherwise face as a teacher or caregiver.

Relevance and Interest

The National Association for the Education of Young Children (NAEYC) curriculum guidelines emphasize making curriculum relevant to children (Bredekamp & Rosegrant, 1995). Relevant curriculum allows children to investigate things that affect their lives, things they care about. Cutting out snowflakes in Miami just because it is January would not be relevant. A unit on farming would not be relevant to youngsters in Nome. How the weather affects children's activities is relevant in both locations, as is how people get their food in each place. But kids themselves might be more concerned about the problem of the mudhole beneath the tire swing. That, too, offers an opportunity for meaningful study. Relevant learning helps keep youngsters engaged and on task—a classroom management challenge.

Sometimes the most relevant curriculum deals with unresolved developmental issues such as making friends, separating from parents, dealing with disappointments, or facing fears (Hyson, 2004; Koplow, 2002). If we ignore these emotion-laden issues and try to focus only on teaching academics, children will be unable to learn and may suffer socially and emotionally as well as academically.

Tapping into children's interests is another recommendation in the NAEYC curriculum guidelines. Don't we all get more involved in things we are interested in? Mrs. Jensen is alert to questions and comments from youngsters that indicate their current interests (Hyson, 2004). She knows that children have some well-developed interests by first grade; she encourages children to pursue these ideas and incorporates many child-generated topics into class activities. She is prepared for many of the ideas with collections of books and activity ideas for topics that frequently catch on in her classes. Mrs. Jensen knows from experience that kids are generally interested in dinosaurs, space, animals, and insects.

Ideas from individual youngsters often become a major curriculum focus in Mrs. Jensen's first grade (Jones & Nimmo, 1994). She knows that it doesn't really matter whether they are studying spaceships or turtles; children can practice the basic skills, broaden their knowledge base, expand their interests, and increase their feelings of competence with almost any topic. She uses children's various interests to provide a purpose for learning. For instance, reading to find out why turtles pull their heads inside their shells is a good way for children to practice reading and to learn to value reading skills. When children care about the work they are doing, they are less likely to be disruptive.

Mrs. Jensen also knows how to help children become interested in subjects she is directed to cover. For instance, the topic of nutrition may sound pretty boring. It probably was when you had to memorize the food groups, but it isn't when you take a trip to the supermarket to buy items from each food group and

---

NAEYC Curriculum Guideline #4: Curriculum addresses a broad range of content that is relevant, engaging, and meaningful to children.

NAEYC Curriculum Guideline #6: Curriculum content reflects and is generated by the needs and interests of individual children within the group. . . . Making curriculum meaningful to children helps keep them engaged and on task.

---

use them for class cooking projects. Interest is sustained in the subject when a play store is set up next to the playhouse. Much thought and energy goes into writing grocery lists that reflect nutritious meal planning. These children are going far beyond mere memorized social knowledge; they are constructing logico-mathematical understanding about food and nutrition. When you channel children's energy constructively, they don't have so much excess to burn off inappropriately.

Dennis uses the same curriculum guidelines for preschoolers as Mrs. Jensen does for first graders. The principles are the same, although the expectations for children differ according to their developmental stage. He, too, ensures that the curriculum makes sense to kids. Instead of rote learning about letters, his students have frequent opportunities to see their names and the names of their friends used for labeling artwork and for keeping their place on a waiting list. Many children can recognize their own names and those of their closest friends. Some discuss how confusing it is when names start with the same letter, like the names Aaron and Anna or Kelsey and Kenji. The thinking that goes on during these discussions results in true construction of knowledge and genuine involvement in learning about letters.

Integrated Curriculum

Both Dennis and Mrs. Jensen use *themes* and *projects* to organize their curriculum and help kids make sense of new information. Bredekamp and Rosegrant (1995) refer to themes, projects, and units as *conceptual organizers*. A theme, such as a study of birds, offers a variety of activities related to the topic of birds. However, the theme approach may not be as compelling a reason to learn about birds as a project, such as caring for the classroom finches who just laid eggs. Projects tend to have more immediate applicability to children's lives (Katz & Chard, 2000). Themes and project work are approaches to integrating the curriculum rather than offering disconnected pieces of information and isolated drills in basic skills. An *integrated curriculum* gives a context for learning and therefore makes learning more meaningful, as is recommended in the NAEYC curriculum guidelines. Any way of making learning meaningful increases student involvement and therefore decreases disruptive behaviors.

An integrated curriculum allows children to practice reading, writing, and math skills as they explore topics of interest. The topic itself usually involves social studies or science information. Art, music, and drama are incorporated as children express ideas about their learning. As we explained previously, children

NAEYC Curriculum Guideline #10: Curriculum allows for focus on a particular topic or content, while allowing for integration across traditional subject-matter divisions, by planning around themes and/or learning experiences that provide opportunities for rich conceptual development (Bredekamp & Rosegrant, 1995).

can learn in most subject areas using almost any topic. Dennis knows that actually using arithmetic to explore a subject is more useful than merely practicing arithmetic skills, so he helps children find the mathematics potential in the topics they are interested in.

> When the resident preschool expert on dinosaurs reported that a certain type of dinosaur had 200 teeth, Dennis challenged the child and others who were interested to discover just how many 200 is. They got out Unifix cubes and worked together as a group to identify 200; then they arranged them like top and bottom teeth to visualize the dinosaur's mouth. Ahmed commented, "I'll bet dinosaurs can eat faster than we can!"
>
> That remark led Dennis to suggest the idea of getting a partner and counting each other's teeth. Megan decided that they should count out the number of teeth in their mouths and make a display of them using the smallest Cuisenaire rods. Counting dinosaur teeth and their own teeth turned into quite a project, attracting different children over a period of several days. It led to further reading and further science information as a result.
>
> Olivia was motivated to make pictures representing herself with her teeth and the dinosaur with its teeth. Several other children followed her example. Thus, artistic representation was added to mathematics, science, and reading as the curriculum was integrated around a dinosaur-teeth theme.

The play store in Mrs. Jensen's classroom is another example of a theme for an integrated curriculum. Children thought about foods for good nutrition while playing store. They practiced writing when they made their grocery lists, and they practiced reading both the lists and the labels on the food packages. They extended their mathematical thinking about counting and money as they made

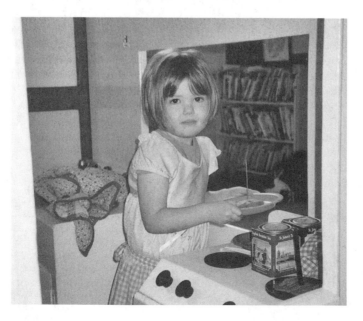

An integrated curriculum allows children to practice reading, writing, and math skills as they explore topics of interest.

price tags and tried to figure out proper payment for each item. The class book in which each child contributed a drawing and a dictated message about the trip to the supermarket also helped children learn to read and write. The children learned more about their community during their field trip to the supermarket. Thus, the trip was part of the subject of social studies. There was also lots of social studies involved in resolving the inevitable disputes during these activities. Important negotiation skills were practiced while making group decisions also. Encountering others' points of view is an important learning experience (Hyson, 2004).

Second graders in Mr. Davis's classroom discovered a project during recess; they ended up using math and literacy in a study of science focused on environmental conservation.

Fall rainstorms were eroding the steep hillside at the end of the playground. During recess, the playground aide told everyone to stay off it so it wouldn't get worse. But the hill was almost everyone's favorite place to play, and she had trouble enforcing the rule. She blew her whistle again and again, sending children inside who wouldn't obey her.

Mr. Davis heard his students complaining about the loss and their doubts that it was really necessary to close the area. The conversation became a topic for a class meeting and Mr. Davis asked the class if they would like to go back outside and study the problem some more. Always eager for any reason to go outside, the children threw their coats back on and grabbed the notepads Mr. Davis handed out.

Active debate ensued as they checked out the hillside, riddled by rivulets of water, with sloughing topsoil and gravel slides. Gradually, the observations became more critical. Mr. Davis encouraged them to write down what they saw and what they wondered about. He helped them focus on what might happen there and what they might be able to do to help the situation. Healthy disagreements arose, and Mr. Davis kept on saying, "Interesting idea. Write that down!"

Regrouping in the classroom, the second graders shared what they'd seen and what they thought might help. Ideas included using rip-rap rock, staking burlap over the hill, putting in drainage, and even letting it slough away to a more stable slope. Some children cited their observations of city projects to stabilize slopes and a couple said one of their parents knew all about how to fix things like that.

They decided they wanted to take on a "save the hill" project, but first they needed more information. Mr. Davis warned them that this project would take some serious planning, work, record keeping, and evaluating. The children were excited and wanted to get right to work. They planned walking field trips to observe some other sites, the children with expert parents said they would invite them as guest speakers, and Mr. Davis worked with the librarian to obtain relevant research materials.

Counting dinosaur teeth, playing store, and saving the trail are authentically integrated activities because the activities help children learn more about the topic they are studying (Fields, Groth, & Spangler, 2004). Not everything labeled

Developmentally inappropriate teaching by adults results in inappropriate behavior from children.

"integrated curriculum" fits this criteria. Too often "A pile of ideas is generated with a superficial connection to each other, and they're used to fill in slots in the weekly schedule" (Jones & Nimmo, 1994, p. 129). Poor Miss Wheeler does just that and wonders why her students don't act interested.

> Miss Wheeler has a different theme each week. This week it is rocks. She brought many different rocks to school for the children. (She thought it would take too much time for them to go outside and collect their own.) For writing time, each child is to write a letter to his or her rock. For art time, children are allowed to paint their rocks. For snack, they get a little piece of rock candy along with something more nutritious.

These activities may involve rocks, but they don't help children learn anything about rocks. This is a *correlated* rather than an *integrated* curriculum (Fields et al., 2004).

Real Experiences and Real Materials

Both Dennis and Mrs. Jensen know that children will benefit more, and the school day will be smoother, if teaching is compatible with how children learn naturally. Integrating the curriculum is one way to match your teaching with children's learning. Children certainly don't separate the world into the categories *science, math,* and *social studies.* They just want to make sense of their world, with all its interrelationships, as they experience it. Therefore, school also needs to reflect the real world and children's own experiences in order for youngsters to perceive school as important. Teachers need to build on the experiences and knowledge that children bring to school with them (for further information, see NAEYC Guideline #8).

> Nathan brought a bird's nest for sharing time, and other children began talking about birds' nests they had seen. Mrs Jensen encouraged the discussion by asking what they knew about birds and birds' nests. Most of the children in this suburban area had some sort of experience to share. Tony told a story about when his mom had cut his hair outside on the patio; he had seen birds come and take the hair for their nests. Other children told about being careful of nests with eggs in them. The teacher decided to follow up on the children's experiences and build on the knowledge they already had.
>
> Mrs. Jensen got out her own collection or birds' nests from past years for the children to examine. She had protected the nests by keeping them in clear plastic bags, which kept the nests from falling apart. A discussion about the kinds of things birds use to make nests was preparation for a field trip around the schoolyard to collect materials for making birds' nests. Each child had the

opportunity to make a bird's nest model with the materials collected. Mrs. Jensen provided the "mud" to hold the material together; she had previously discovered that glue mixed with dirt and water allows for a successful nest-building experience.

As we explained in Chapter 3, children's way of learning starts with real experiences and real objects from which to make sense. Mrs. Jensen's students would not have made much sense out of a lesson on birds' nests without both their personal experience and the concrete materials the teacher provided. Some teachers don't understand this; they waste precious energy lecturing children about topics totally outside their realm of experience, never giving them any real experiences related to the topic. Of course, this approach leads to discipline problems because children don't pay much attention to a discussion they cannot understand.

Some teachers cover the same topics year after year without responding to the enthusiasms and questions of the children in *this* class *this* year. Then they follow up the meaningless lessons with developmentally inappropriate worksheets. Many youngsters will dutifully go along with the teacher and complete these purposeless tasks, but many others will cause classroom problems by trying to find something interesting to do.

Mrs. Jensen not only started with a topic of personal importance to her students when they studied birds, but she also provided opportunities for children to investigate at the concrete level. Examining real nests, collecting real material

Lecturing to children about topics outside their experience, without real experience related to the subject, leads to inattention and discipline problems.

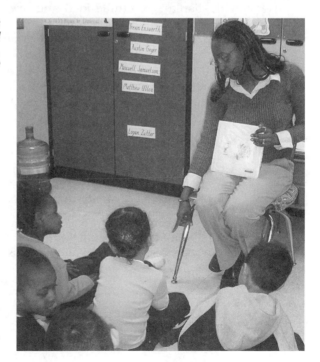

to make nests, and going through the process of creating their own models are the kinds of concrete experiences that match the way young children learn. They have the opportunity to construct their own understanding of birds' nests from the experience of creating replicas. The children engaged in these educational experiences are involved in the business of learning and therefore aren't likely to disrupt anyone else's work. They are also building the base for thinking further about birds and will be better able to make sense of reading material on that subject.

Too often, teachers forget young children's need to focus on the real world of the here and now. Well-meaning teachers frequently lead youngsters into the totally unintelligible world of long ago or far away. Thanksgiving time is particularly likely to motivate teachers to explain the history of the original feast. Young children have notoriously inaccurate ideas about time and space. They may not understand the difference between something happening 300 years ago and something happening last week. Ask a young child who has heard the story of the first Thanksgiving to tell you about it, and you will hear truly amazing misconceptions. Instead of wasting children's time with a presentation of incomprehensible historical facts, you would be wise to help them think about what they are thankful for in their own lives.

Efforts to offer multicultural education can also lead to developmentally inappropriate presentations (Barrera & Corso, 2003). Youngsters carry away distorted pictures of Native Americans as scary people in war paint who live in tepees (Billman, 1992). Some youngsters come to believe that African American people are currently slaves. Even efforts to build an appreciation for different cultures with displays of ethnic food and dress can backfire by emphasizing the differences rather than the commonalities among people. Instead, teachers can enhance acceptance of cultural diversity in the children's own environment. The pictures on the bulletin board, the books in the library corner and at story time, and the dolls in the playhouse can all reflect cultural and racial plurality. The messages that permeate their daily lives will have a positive effect on children's lifelong attitudes (e.g., Derman-Sparks, 1999; Hunt, 1999).

Active Learning

A related curriculum guideline has to do with encouraging children's active involvement in learning. Mrs. Thomas had a recent reminder of how important this is for her students' ability to pay attention to learning.

> The salmon were running in a nearby stream when school started and many children had been fishing with their parents. Interest in fish was high, and Mrs. Thomas decided to capitalize on it. She planned a trip to the local fish hatchery

---

NAEYC Guideline #13: Curriculum engages children actively, not passively, in the learning process. Children have opportunities to make meaningful choices.

---

so that her students could see the salmon fighting their way up the fish ladder. They also got to see the eggs being taken, fertilized, and put in tanks to grow. The field trip was just right for young children: lots of action and the talking limited to answering some questions.

The follow-up portion of the plan went differently. The hatchery donated a few salmon for the children's closer study. One of the children's parents is a fish biologist who has offered to donate her time to help with this study. Back in the classroom, children crowd around a small table to watch the biologist cut open the fish and see what is inside. But first, the fish expert wants to tell the youngsters some things: how fish move through the water, the name and purpose of each fin, how fish breathe, how the gills function, and how fish are marked for study.

Mrs. Thomas personally finds the lecture fascinating, though the Latin names for the various parts go over her head. She realizes, however, that a lecture appropriate for her is not appropriate for her students. Some children have started to talk among themselves, others are jockeying for position to see the fish better. One has wandered over to a table where other fish are displayed; he is engrossed in stroking their scales. A few youngsters are still interested in the biologist, but they want to tell her what they know about fish. The biologist sees that the children are restless and decides to get on with the dissecting. Unfortunately, most children have lost interest. Mrs. Thomas realizes she should have planned more specifically with the guest to ensure that the presentation would allow the children's active involvement rather than require only passive listening.

The Role of Play

Play is a perfect way to meet the NAEYC curriculum guideline for engaging children actively and providing meaningful choices. Play also fits NAEYC Guideline #16, emphasizing social interaction and learning from peers. The social interaction provides valuable practice with expression of emotions and emotion regulation (Hyson, 2004). In addition, play is an excellent way to encourage children's thinking, reasoning, decision making, and problem-solving abilities (NAEYC Guideline #15).

The play store project in Mrs. Jensen's classroom is not only an example of integrated curriculum (Jalongo & Isenberg, 2004) but also has many other benefits. There are lots of important decisions to be made and problems to solve during play, whether it is pretend play, such as the play store, or games such as checkers or cards: Who gets to run the cash register? How do we resolve it when everyone wants to do it now? Which rules for Crazy Eights should we use today? Can Nathan change the rules if he is losing? What an efficient use of time: Children are learning math and essential life skills at the same time.

Vygotsky (1978/1933) points out that play necessarily involves learning about rules and abiding by them. In this sense, play provides practice with controlling immediate impulses in the process of following the rules of the game or of a make-believe context. Rules in a game are pretty common, but you probably are wondering about rules in make-believe play. Think about children playing store: They follow the "rules" of shopping and paying for their purchases. If they are playing fire fighter, they follow the "rules" for putting out a fire. According to Vygotsky

(1978/1933), "Whenever there is an imaginary situation, there are rules" (p. 95). Rules are necessary for guiding behavior in an imaginary situation because children have to agree on the "script" and the cast of characters (Bodrova & Leong, 1998). As children construct the rules necessary to keep their pretend play situation going, they develop logical reasoning skills and also both creative thinking and critical thinking abilities (e.g., Curran, 1999; Kostelnik, Soderman, & Whiren, 2004; McCune & Zanes, 2001). Teachers can enhance children's cognitive and social development by encouraging pretend play.

It is interesting to note that as children get older their play increasingly emphasizes rules. Vygotsky described this development as moving from play that is obviously imaginary and subtly rule-bound (playing house) to play that focuses on rules but has subtle imaginary contexts (chess). Berk (1994) concludes that the rules involved in play help children understand expectations for desirable behavior and encourage children to act accordingly. This is another one of many reasons to include play in your curriculum.

Using Time Wisely

Perhaps the most critical curriculum guideline has to do with making sure that what children are asked to learn is worth knowing. Respect for children should guide us away from the trivial and cute school activities that are all too common. Instead of wasting children's time having them all make identical red flowers for the bulletin board, let's think about what is truly important in their lives. Feeney puts things into perspective by reminding us that one of the most important things any of us can learn might be "how to find a friend when you're sad" (Feeney, Christensen, & Moravcik, 2006). Feeney makes this statement in the

Negotiating rules for play helps children understand expectations and desirable behavior in the real world.

context of a broad view of what is worth knowing; it includes understanding the physical and social environment and yourself in order to better respect and care for the world and its people. She helps us evaluate the importance of colors and shapes in comparison to goals of becoming more human and helping our world survive. Respecting children involves respecting their time and using it wisely. Mrs. Jensen was surprised at how well the birds' nest activity met this goal.

> When the children finished making their birds' nests, Mrs. Jensen called them together for a group discussion. "What did you learn when you made the birds' nests?" she asked. Expecting answers about the way the mud felt and what ingredients worked best, the teacher was astounded to hear a whole different level of response: "Birds' nests are really hard to make!" "I'll never knock one down out of a tree," and "I won't ever shoot a bird" were the type of ideas generated. Making birds' nest models encouraged these youngsters to think about the birds' viewpoint, and it helped them develop an appreciation for birds and their struggle for survival. Certainly, these children will be better able to respect and care for the world they live in.

You also need to ask yourself whether what you are teaching is worth the effort at this time in children's lives. Many teachers have discovered the hard way that learning to tell time in kindergarten is not worth the effort. Others have decided that trying to teach everyone how to make change in first grade is wasted energy. Chapter 3 explained that telling time and making change are confusing to young children because they use arbitrarily designated representational symbols. Trying to teach these symbols too soon is about as productive as trying to teach a 5-month-old baby to walk. Some topics are a waste of time because they are too easy and can be learned without specifically spending school time on them. For instance, directed instruction on colors is not necessary for most children. Colors are a part of life and are generally picked up at a very young age as children decide which color crayon to use, which shirt to wear, or the color of their favorite ice cream. Talking with children about color as they engage in other activities is all the instruction most of them need.

However, some ideas are well worth the time and effort. We hope for greater emphasis on helping children learn to respect and protect the environment and to live peaceably together with respect for individual differences. These areas of study might be called science and social studies; they might also be called basics.

Three Kinds of Knowledge

Other curriculum guidelines can be derived from an understanding of the learning process. Any learner is more engaged and on-task when teaching approaches match the ways in which people learn. Different kinds of knowledge are best learned in different ways. Teachers who understand the differences between *physical knowledge, social knowledge,* and *logico-mathematical knowledge* are able to plan learning activities accordingly (Kamii, 2000).

Experimenting with objects and seeing what happens is the basis of physical knowledge. For example, what will sink and what will float is primarily learned by actually putting various objects in water and observing the result. Information from other people is the basis of social knowledge, also called *conventional arbitrary knowledge*. Information such as the days of the week, the names of the basic food groups, or the polite thing to say when someone sneezes are things we primarily learn from others. (Notice that these all vary from culture to culture; thus, they can be considered cultural conventions and are obviously arbitrary.)

Individual reflective thinking is the basis of logico-mathematical knowledge. This knowledge cannot be found in the objects explored, nor can it be "given" by a teacher. It is a system of relationships that must be constructed by each learner in a way that makes sense to him or her. Logico-mathematical thinking provides the framework for classifying, and therefore making sense of, any information. Physical knowledge and social knowledge are used in the construction of logico-mathematical knowledge, and logico-mathematical knowledge is necessary to construction of physical and social knowledge (DeVries, 2001). According to DeVries "Intelligence can be described as a framework of potential logico-mathematical relationships" (p. 167).

Therefore, in order to truly engage children's minds and help them be successful learners, teachers must ensure opportunities for experimentation and reflection. Too many classrooms trivialize education by limiting teaching to transmitting social knowledge. Recent emphasis on test scores has led to force-feeding children information for tests. Teachers who know this is poor education see the negative effects on children's learning and on behavior, but feel powerless against state and national policies. Planning meaningful learning experiences for young children must take into consideration the three kinds of knowledge, as well as the developmental level of the students.

Several NAEYC curriculum guidelines relate to teaching for construction of knowledge: emphasizing thinking, reasoning, decision making, and problem-solving (Guideline #15), providing experiences for children to succeed from their point of view (Guideline #19), building on what children already know and can do (Guideline #8), and encouraging conceptual frameworks for children's increasingly complex mental constructions (Guideline #9).

A crucial guideline for helping children learn to think is Guideline #14: valuing children's constructive errors, not prematurely limiting exploration and experimentation for the sake of ensuring "right" answers. This means you shouldn't tell Blake that his idea about why things sink or float is wrong; instead, you respectfully listen to his thinking. Then you ask some questions to get him to think further and possibly experiment further. You are willing to wait days or even years for the "right" answer; your goal is Blake's competence as a thinker. The answers that take years are for the type of questions that Blake will still be exploring in college physics classes; if you gave him your adult answer now, it wouldn't make sense anyway.

NAEYC Guideline #14: Curriculum values children's constructive errors and does not prematurely limit exploration and experimentation for the sake of ensuring "right" answers.

Teaching children to think is a component of many anti-violence curriculum programs (e.g., Gibbs, 2001). Creative thinking, intellectual problem solving, and reasoning all develop children's ability to manage social interaction challenges. Authoritarian approaches to academics, with an emphasis on memorizing answers given by authority figures, undermine children's ability to reason about moral issues as well as about academics (Dill, 1998). As you teach children to think critically, you create *intellectual autonomy*, the necessary partner to moral autonomy.

ORGANIZATIONAL STRATEGIES

Experienced teachers know when behavior problems are most likely to occur. They anticipate problem situations and plan ways to keep the day running smoothly. They use combinations of routines and novelty to avoid turmoil during transitions, waiting periods, and group times. They also use group time to discuss ways of preventing problems during other activities.

Routines

Stable routines help children know what to expect and therefore can assist them in being cooperative members of the group. However, it is necessary that the routines offer the proper balance of activities and expectations (Koplow, 2002). Children need both familiarity and novelty; they need freedom and they need limits; they need rest and they need movement.

Routines also provide emotional security through predictability (Hyson, 2004), which is especially important for children who are "at risk" because they come from homes where chaos is the norm (Dill, 1998). Because the children know the routine, it doesn't take any time at all for Mrs. Jensen's first graders to assemble for group time. They have a system for moving smoothly from their seats to the group area, and each child knows just what to do. Routines save the teacher from constantly having to tell the children what to do next; they know what comes next and what they are to do.

Having a routine does not mean being ruled by the clock. It doesn't mean that you stop whatever else is going on at exactly 11:15 each day and have story time. But it is important that children have an idea of the sequence of events and what their role should be. Children in Dennis's preschool class know that they will get to work and play at their choice of activity when they first arrive at school and that there will be a time to gather together about mid-morning. They know where they can fix and eat their snack when they are ready for it. They know where to put their coats and belongings when they arrive, and they know where to find the materials they might need for a project.

Dennis plans his routines around children's needs; he alternates periods of active exploration with more quiet times and plans for outdoor play daily. The exact timing of transitions is based on his observations of the children in his preschool program; using these observations, he can determine when it is time for a change, such as gathering for a group time or going outside. He doesn't rush children from one activity to another, instead he tries to be sensitive to children's needs for extended periods of uninterrupted concentration (Hyson, 2004). He is aware that quality play and exploration take time to set up before the truly productive activity begins. Dennis also knows that children have long attention spans when they are doing something important to them. The myth of short attention spans is the result of giving children trivial activities that are not engrossing and not their choice. Unfortunately, many teachers do not know this fact, and they unwittingly reduce the children's ability to concentrate by making them constantly change activities.

When it appears that most of the youngsters may be winding down on their choice time activities and reaching closure, Dennis moves around the room telling each child that it will be group time in 5 minutes. This advance warning allows children to finish what they are doing and mentally prepare to move on. Occasionally a child will be too engrossed to quit and will ask to be excused from group or to join in a few minutes. Dennis's respect for children and their work comes through as he honors these requests.

Making Transitions

Many discipline problems occur during transition times, when children are moving from one activity or one place to another. Some children's temperaments can't handle the noise and movement associated with transitions in a child-centered classroom (Hyson, 2004). These youngsters need help figuring out how to cope. Most transition time behavior problems happen because teachers unrealistically

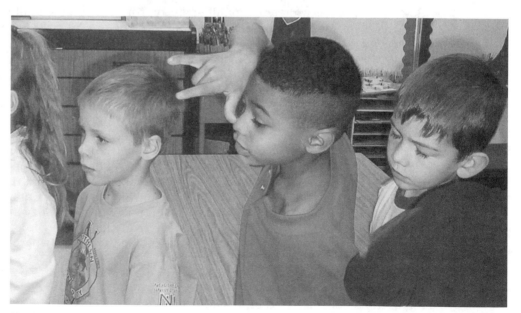

Having children wait and walk in lines invites behavior problems, as children figure out ways to alleviate boredom.

expect children to wait patiently for too long while other children get ready to join them. Adults who respect children do not waste their time with prolonged periods of waiting. If they do, you can almost guarantee that children will be clever enough to find some way to alleviate their boredom. Unfortunately, this activity usually takes the form of poking or pushing the person in front of them. Few teachers appreciate these creative outlets.

Mrs. Jensen dislikes having to line up her students and make them walk all together in a row. She knows that waiting in line is terribly boring for them and invites behavior problems. When her students go out for recess, she lets them leave individually or in small groups as they get ready. At the beginning of the school year, she spent time with her class discussing and practicing good manners when walking through the elementary school hallways. Her children generally remember to walk instead of run and to keep their voices down. When they forget, their classmates remind them. Not having lines is less trouble for Mrs. Jensen and her students and causes many fewer discipline problems.

The librarian, Mrs. Hill, insists on lines, so Mrs. Jensen's class gets practice in lining up when they go to the library. Instead of making the students who get ready quickly wait around and be bored while she gives her attention to the procrastinators, Mrs. Jensen creates some action of her own in the line. She leads the group in their favorite songs and finger plays to head off inappropriate kinds of activity. This approach also hurries the stragglers faster than nagging does; they are eager to join in the fun.

Mrs. Jensen uses a similar approach when she is gathering children together for group time. If it takes a while for everyone to arrive, she engages in a discussion with those who are there. She often uses time to help children evaluate their activities, with questions such as, "What did you do special today at choosing time?" At other times, the children want to do their favorite finger play about the five little monkeys.

Getting to and from the mid-morning gathering are the only significant transitions children must make in the morning preschool component of the Midway Children's Center day. An extra, time-consuming transition is avoided by having outdoor play just before children go home at noon. That way, they are already in their coats when it is time to leave. Dennis's use of advance warning helps most children get prepared for a change of activity. When they are not interrupted in the middle of a project, they are much more agreeable. Keeping transitions to a minimum also keeps disruptions to a minimum. For most of the morning, youngsters are free to change learning activities as they are individually ready to do so.

When group time is over, Dennis avoids a stampede to the snack table by making a game out of sending a few children at a time. Sometimes he says, "Everyone wearing stripes today may go to the snack table." Next it might be those with plaid or print designs on their clothing. On other days, Dennis focuses on hair or eye color. Sometimes he holds up name cards to excuse the children one at a time; the youngsters practice reading their own and their friends' names to determine whose turn it is. These games keep children involved and learning during their short wait. Those who arrive at the snack table first must also have something to do besides waiting. They either need to be allowed to begin eating immediately, or else another adult must be there to engage them in a song or activity.

Those children who remain at the center for the full-day program are faced with a number of transitions: lunch time, nap time, getting up from nap, going outside again, and parent arrival time. Each of these changes requires that children change gears and move from one mode of activity to another. Most also involve movement of groups from one place to another. Both aspects of transition are frequently upsetting to youngsters. Young children need the support of teachers they know and are comfortable with as they move through these activities. Teachers may not consider lunch, toileting, and rest time to be central to their mission but these are very important to the children (Koplow, 2002).

Tuning in to children as individuals will help remind you not to herd them into the next activity. One key to making smooth transitions lies in not unduly rushing children. As soon as you start to hurry kids, they immediately start to rebel. Respecting individual differences in youngsters is another important guideline for smooth transitions. Joshua is always hungry at lunchtime and eagerly gets going on his meal. Anna makes slower transitions and has trouble tearing herself away from the dramatic play she is usually involved in. These two children require different treatment. Forcing Anna into Joshua's schedule won't work for her.

Similarly, Naomi, Jack, and Ahmed are ready for sleep at nap time, while Megan, Tory, and Olivia rarely nap. The staff at the children's center solved their nap-time problems by separating sleepers from nonsleepers; the teachers allowed nonsleepers to play quietly after lying down with a book for 15 minutes. It makes no more sense to attempt to force all children to sleep than to force them all to stay awake. There are real differences in the needs of children. A program with the flexibility to accommodate these differences greatly reduces its discipline problems.

Mrs. Jensen used increased flexibility to allow for differences and solve a problem at the end of daily choice time.

Children in Mrs. Jensen's classroom were not being cooperative about cleaning up after choice time and getting ready to go out to recess. She wasn't interested in Miss Wheeler's approach of giving out candy as a reward to get children to clean up. Instead, she carefully watched to see what was happening instead of clean-up.

What she noticed was that many children were just not ready to stop what they were doing because they hadn't had enough time. Many were bouncing around for about 10 minutes before they settled in to what they wanted to do with their choice time and then didn't really have enough time to complete anything before they were told to clean up. She decided to try something radical for a public school: a choice of staying in or going outside to play. Since the primary playground was just outside her back door, she could allow children to go out during recess if and when they were ready.

This plan worked very well, with clean-up coming after recess instead of before, and going much more smoothly. On nice days, some of the indoor activity flowed outdoors and children didn't have to choose between their choice-time project and being outdoors.

Group Time

Group time serves many different purposes and has many different names. We bring children together in groups for stories, songs, lessons, planning, and problem solving. Whether it is called *story time, circle time, class meeting,* or something else, gathering together as a group is essential for building a sense of community in a classroom. This feeling of belonging and caring for one another is necessary for developing a social conscience. When youngsters meet together regularly, sharing rituals such as favorite songs and stories, they come to see themselves as a group. As a group, they can discuss mutual problems and create solutions that transcend the wishes of the individual (DeVries & Zan, 1994). This process promotes moral reasoning and de-centering from an egocentric viewpoint. Children in classrooms with a sense of community tend to be more cooperative, supportive of one another, and empathetic (e.g., Hyson, 2004; Koplow, 2002).

To get the most out of group time, teachers need to truly encourage student input and get children thinking. Some group times don't really engage children's minds, but instead drag them through a series of repetitive rote exercises. How engaged are children in merely reciting the responses to questions such as, "What day of the week is this?" "What is today's date?" and "How many days have we been in school?" We see lots of bored youngsters and frustrated teachers during this kind of group time. We also see children getting into trouble because they can't sit still and give the desired responses. Group time is much more productive when it is spent helping children work on intellectual or moral issues they care about.

As important as group time can be, bringing young children together often creates trouble. Teachers complain about feeling like police officers as they continually remind children to sit down or pay attention at group time. Young children talk when they aren't supposed to; they wriggle and squirm and poke one another, and they even just walk away. Teachers with child-development knowledge realize that these behaviors are related to children's maturational stage. They understand that young children are not good at sitting still or being quiet, that they have trouble dealing with large groups, and that they aren't good at pretending to be interested when they are bored (Bredekamp, 1997). Many of these teachers seriously question the appropriateness of a group time at the preschool level; some question it in kindergarten as well. Yet, these same teachers usually wish to have at least a brief period of togetherness.

Successful group times cannot be passive listening experiences for youngsters. They must truly involve all children in the group activities and discussions (Vance & Weaver, 2002). Some teachers find that a circle seating arrangement works best with this goal. A circle allows children to see one another during discussions and read body language as well as hear words. The group circle is consistent with a child-centered approach and with the purposes of group interaction; the teacher at the front of a group suggests a different purpose.

Some programs compromise on group time by having several small groups instead of one large group. Instead of two adults with 20 youngsters in a circle, each adult takes 10 children for circle time. This method is a little closer to the guidelines for group size recommended by James Hymes (1990). Hymes recommends the following guide for group size: The right number of children for a child to interact with is no more than the number of birthdays that child has had.

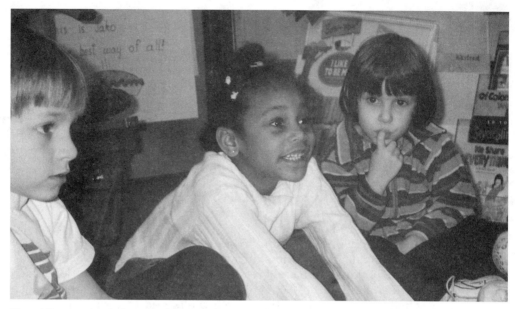

To get the most out of group time, teachers need to truly encourage student input and get children thinking. Children will not pay attention to repetitive rote routines.

Another approach allows choice about participation in some group activities. Dennis is able to allow choice with his preschool group because there are other adults available to supervise children who do not choose to join. Dennis tries to make his circle time so attractive that youngsters will want to join in and stay involved. If he doesn't get much enthusiasm, he treats that response as useful feedback regarding the appropriateness or relevance of what he is offering at group time. For instance, if several children leave during the story he is reading, he might think twice about sharing that story again.

Dennis allows for a partly involved presence at group time as another way of meeting individual needs. Some youngsters can't seem to sit and listen without having something to occupy their hands. Therefore, children in his program are allowed to look at books or work on puzzles at the back of the group area. Only activities that are quiet and do not disturb the group discussion are allowed. Allowing quiet activities lets children who might not otherwise be able to cope with the enforced passivity benefit from the discussions and stories. Through this flexibility, Dennis provides a transition into group time for children who need it.

In other programs, teachers feel strongly about full participation but try hard to make group time more compatible with the needs of young children. They keep the time short and respond to signals from youngsters that they have reached their limit. Frequent opportunities to move and actively participate extend the amount of time children can cope with group times. Songs and rhymes that involve full-body movement provide useful breaks. Nevertheless, 15 minutes may be long enough for most preschoolers to be involved in group time. This time period will gradually increase as children get older, but teachers need to take their cues from the children.

Many will argue that youngsters need to learn the social skills involved in a traditional group gathering because the next teacher will expect it. Others reject that argument on the grounds that children will more easily gain those skills when they are a little older. They believe there is no point in putting everyone through the misery of pushing the skills before youngsters are ready. This argument is similar to the prevailing view of toilet training: Wait until the child is ready, and it will happen quickly and painlessly.

Waiting a Turn

We have already talked about problems caused by waiting in line and waiting for groups to start. They are invitations to discipline problems as well as a serious waste of children's time. However, there is another kind of waiting that causes just as many problems: when children must wait their turn.

Waiting for a turn is incredibly hard on young children for several reasons. One reason is that they don't have a sense of time. Because time is an abstraction, telling a child to wait 5 minutes for a turn with the tricycle is meaningless. Another problem is that young children don't understand why they must wait. They can't see things from another person's viewpoint, so they don't relate to another child's claim. Colin wants the tricycle. That desire is the only reality for him. The fact that Alex also wants it is irrelevant to Colin. With help from adults, youngsters gradually learn about the needs and feelings of others. With experience and maturation, they also learn to approximate time spans. While youngsters are in the process of learning, understanding teachers can help them cope.

> Kenji ran into the large-muscle room. He was eager to get onto the climbing tower, his favorite place to play. Suddenly a teacher came to tell him that he must get off and wait his turn. There were already four other children on the climbing tower. Four is the limit; that's the rule.
> Kenji looked confused and sad but climbed down. He gazed longingly at the children climbing and shouting. He kept asking Sheri, the adult in charge,

 PROGRAMS THAT PREVENT DISCIPLINE PROBLEMS

Avoid:	**Provide:**
rushing	interesting activities
waiting	predictable routines
crowding	appropriate intellectual challenges
regimentation	enough adults to help children

when it would be his turn. Gradually, tears welled up in his eyes. Sheri realized that Kenji was in distress. She tried to explain to him that the other children were in the room first. Seeing that her explanations were getting nowhere, Sheri thought about other alternatives. Center rules allow youngsters to use equipment until they decide they are finished, so she couldn't even promise Kenji a certain time for his turn. She tried to distract him with suggestions about the block-building or woodworking centers. But Kenji was determined to be there to stake his claim as soon as someone got off the climbing tower.

Then Sheri remembered the sign-up sheet that helped children wait their turn to hold the new pet rabbit last week. She asked Kenji if he would like to start a sign-up sheet to use the climbing tower. He agreed to this plan and helped Sheri locate paper, tape, and a marker. Kenji wrote his name 4-year-old style on the page and taped it to the wall near the climber. He seemed to feel better now that his claim to a turn was officially in writing. He said he would wait in the block center nearby. Sheri assured him she would call as soon as someone got off the climber. Without someone hovering nearby waiting for a turn, the pressure to stay on the climber eased. Soon there was a vacancy, and Sheri notified Kenji. He had been helped to cope with a hard situation. His feelings were respected even though he didn't immediately get his way. The experience helped him build understanding and trust in the waiting process.

Many teachers use sign-up sheets to ease turn taking and waiting. This approach fosters literacy development as well as social development. Of course, it works better if there aren't so many children in the group that it takes days for everyone to get a turn. When children are limited to a set amount of time for a turn, the sign-up sheet can be combined with an egg timer. Watching the timer ticking away or seeing the salt pour from one side to the other can help youngsters to experience the passage of time, making it a little less abstract. Of course, these timed waits must be short in order to be humane.

Much of the children's waiting involves waiting for help from an adult. Children have to wait less if there are more adults available to them. Public school classrooms generally not only have larger groups than recommended, but also have too few adults for the number of children. The maximum groups size in kindergarten and the primary grades should be no more than 15 to 18 children with one teacher. If the group size is up to 25, there should be two adults. For preschool age groups, it is necessary to have two adults responsible for no more than 20 youngsters (Bredekamp, 1997). We see much higher levels of social development and involvement in preschools where there is an adult for every five children and the group size is limited to 20.

Family Involvement

Parent volunteers can make a major contribution to a smoothly running classroom. They can improve the ratio of adults to children, cutting down on the length of time children wait for adult assistance and being there to intervene when problems arise. When you involve families in helping children learn, however, you accomplish more than a shorter waiting time for youngsters. A child whose parent or grandparent spends time helping at school gets a clear message that the family thinks school is important; therefore, the child also believes school is important. Additionally, when parents spend time helping, they tend to gain a better appreciation for the school program. Their increased understanding of the teacher's goals and methods makes parents more supportive of the teacher's efforts. Parental attitudes of support for school programs are also communicated to children, and those attitudes about school influence child attitudes and behavior. Families are a vital part of a supportive child care or school community (Koplow, 2002).

There are a variety of approaches to family involvement. Kindergarten and primary-grade teachers generally ask for parent volunteers at the beginning of the school year. Many find that posting a list of specific jobs and asking parents to sign up is a good strategy. Parents whose work doesn't allow them to spend time at school may volunteer for something that can be done at home in the evening. Some preschools follow the same pattern, but cooperative preschools exhibit the ultimate in parent involvement. Cooperative preschools are run by parents who determine school goals and procedures, administer the budget, collect tuition, and hire the teacher. Parents take turns as teacher assistants to create appropriate adult-child ratios for their programs. Child-care programs generally exist because parents are not available during the day. However, with encouragement, parents may find it rewarding to visit during their lunch time and even to take occasional time off to be part of their youngster's child-care day.

CONCLUSION

Prevention of discipline problems is based on caring relationships with children and families. Prevention of behavior problems also has much to do with respecting children. Respecting children involves making it easier for them to meet school expectations; including their parents in their education; accepting their emotional needs as valid; planning programs carefully to fit their level of development; helping them learn to think about others; and using their time and energy wisely. When you do these things, you will find that most children are more cooperative, hardworking, and committed to learning.

∞ FOR FURTHER THOUGHT

1. Conduct or observe a group meeting designed to build community. How effectively are children encouraged to think for themselves rather than repeat adult words? What activities are useful for building group bonds? What strategies are helpful for keeping children engaged and involved?

2. Think about curriculum topics you are familiar with. Identify those that are inappropriate for children too young to know the difference between a day and a week, let alone between one year and 100 years. Identify those that are inappropriate for youngsters who have no idea of the differences between a town and a country.

3. Give examples of developmentally appropriate topics (or inappropriate) for each of the following developmental age groups: preschool (3–5 years), Kindergarten and 1st grade (5–7 years) 2nd and 3rd grade (7–9 years). Explain why you think your topic would be appropriate or not.

4. Observe early childhood teachers' use of transition activities. Practice using some games for guiding children's movement in small groups from one place to another. Learn some finger plays and rhymes and practice using them to assist children during waiting time.

5. Try some techniques described in this chapter to help youngsters wait for a turn. Analyze the successes and the failures to learn from them.

6. A problem to solve: The kindergartners were lining up to go to the library. Tony got into line and immediately began pushing Tim, who was in front of him. Next, Tony grabbed Tim's arm and then began playing with his hair.
   a. What is the probable cause of this problem?
   b. How can you best deal with it now?
   c. How can you prevent similar situations in the future?

∽ RECOMMENDED READINGS

Bredekamp, S., & Rosegrant, T. (Eds). (1995). *Transforming early childhood curriculum and assessment* (Vol. 2). Washington, DC: National Association for the Education of Young Children.

Chaille, C., & Britain, L. (2003). *The young child as scientist: A Constructivist approach to early childhood science education*. New York: Longman.

Davidson, J. (1980). Wasted time: The ignored dilemma. *Young Children, 35*(1), 13–21.

Developmental Studies Center. (1998). *Ways we want our class to be: Class meetings that build commitment to kindness and learning*. Oakland, CA: Author.

Hyson, M. (2004). *The emotional development of young children: Building an emotion-centered curriculum*. New York: Teachers College Press.

Jones, E., & Reynolds, G. (1992). *The play's the thing: Teachers' roles in children's play*. New York: Teachers College Press.

Kamii, C. (2000). *Young children reinvent arithmetic: Implications of Piaget's theory*. New York: Teachers College Press.

Katz, L. G., & Chard, S. C. (2000). *Engaging children's minds: The project approach*. Norwood, NJ: Ablex.

Koplow, L. (2002). *Creating Schools that heal: Real-life solutions*. New York: Teachers College Press.

Vance, E., & Weaver, P. (2002). *Class meetings: Young children solving problems together*. Washington, DC: National Association for the Education of Young Children.

6 *Teaching Desirable Behavior Through Example*

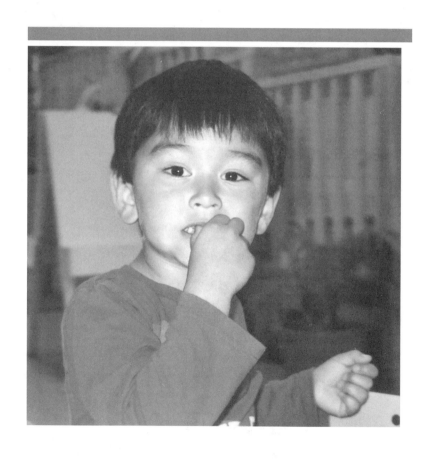

*D*iscipline is a teaching activity, and teaching by example is a powerfully effective method. Children use the examples of admired adults as they construct their own ideas of appropriate behavior. Therefore, teacher and parent examples are productive methods of guidance and discipline. The more that teachers take the time to model appropriate expressions of emotions and action, the less time they will spend on discipline issues as the year progresses (Brady et al., 2003). This chapter will give examples of how models of desirable behavior help children learn to behave in socially acceptable ways.

Sometimes the cause of inappropriate behavior is that children have learned from inappropriate role models. If you doubt that children pick up the example of adults, watch them during pretend play. Parents and teachers are often embarrassed as they see children mimic parts of adult behavior they'd rather not have repeated. Children also imitate the behavior they see on television and movies, with some extremely antisocial results. Positive adult models are crucial to counteracting such pervasive and violent influences.

Adults providing examples and children imitating them are both referred to as *modeling.* Let's look at how your positive modeling can help children learn desirable and useful ways of behaving.

INTERACTION STYLE

Over and over again, research findings demonstrate that children learn how to treat one another from the way they are treated by their teachers and parents (Landy, 2002). A teacher who consistently speaks kindly and respectfully to students tends to have a classroom where children speak more kindly and respectfully to one another. However, a teacher who uses sarcasm and put-downs to keep kids under control will certainly generate more of that type of interaction among students.

Some classrooms and centers have a warm and friendly feeling as you walk into them, and others exude tension. The teacher usually sets the tone for the classroom, with children taking on the interaction style of the adult (DeVries & Zan, 1994). Likewise, parents who are sensitive, responsive, and involved with their children have youngsters who behave in ways that make them more popular with their peers (Landy, 2002; Mize & Pettit, 1997). Children notice when adults respectfully consider children's ideas and feelings. From this example, they gain both attitudes and skills for getting along with other children and peacefully negotiating solutions to disagreements. Teachers and parents who exhibit very controlling behavior are setting an example of demanding their own way without regard for others. If that attitude is the adult example, then youngsters will learn to behave in the same way.

Children's literature is sometimes helpful for providing examples of behavior for discussion and analysis. For instance, *The Grouchy Ladybug* (Carle, 1977) or *Mufaro's Beautiful Daughter* (Steptoe, 1987) might spark discussion about how to treat others.

EXPRESSING FEELINGS

How do you deal with your emotions? Do you hold them in and try to hide the fact that you are upset? Or do you find yourself "flying off the handle," and yelling when things go wrong? The holding-in approach might sound like a more desirable model for kids, but we believe it is actually worse for them—and you—in the long run. You may know from your own experience, or from others who are close to you, that suppressed emotions will eventually surface in some form or other and can cause debilitating emotional and physical problems. As discussed later in this chapter, a person's culture often determines how emotions are expressed. Cultural norms affect how both teachers and students express their emotions, and their expectations of one another. Some people with loving, responsive families are taught to completely suppress their negative emotions. Teachers who had this experience in their childhoods may need to overcome some of their discomfort with expressions of anger or sadness by talking with friends or counselors. Looking at our own life experiences is an important step in our ability to model healthy expressions of our emotions.

While we don't advocate that teachers "stuff" their emotions, throwing a tantrum to express your feelings isn't productive either. Adults who have learned to accept and work with their emotions achieve a socially acceptable medium between the extremes of too little emotional outlet and too much. Many find that it is important to let off steam as it arises instead of allowing it to accumulate into a blowup. Teachers with this kind of self-knowledge can provide a beneficial model for youngsters.

Letting It Show

You teach a lot when you share your feelings with children and allow them to see how you express your frustration, excitement, sorrow, or joy. Children learn the most when adults talk about how they feel, also letting it show in their face, body language, and tone of voice. By listening and observing, children begin to understand what feelings are, what situations are likely to create which feelings, and how to express feelings (Hyson, 2004). The daily life of the school offers ample opportunity for modeling the expression of emotions. But, as Hyson (2004) says, "Early childhood educators should not be content to leave this process entirely to chance. Competent, thoughtful professionals consciously decide what emotions and emotion-related behavior to model" (p. 130).

> Mrs. Jensen was pushed past her limit one day by the several children in her classroom with behavioral disorders. Her friends always told her that the "reward" for being a great teacher is that you get more of the needier children. But that thought was of no comfort when she was being kicked and hit on a daily basis. Then there was the additional problem of trying to keep the other children safe from those who were out of control.
>
> Mrs. Jensen's voice was loud, yet controlled as she told the students, "Kids, I need your help. I am getting too frustrated right now to help anyone. I am going to take 2 minutes to sit and breathe in a calming place. I will talk with those of you who need me when I have calmed myself down." While the kids stared

with curiosity, Mrs. Jensen walked to the window and took some deep breaths with her eyes closed. She reminded herself what her goals were for this class, and that the weekend was almost here. Slowly she opened her eyes and returned her attention to the classroom. She spoke more quietly than before as she told the class, "I feel more calm now and I will try to stay that way while I talk to those of you who need my help. As the children took their turns talking with Mrs. Jensen, her calming mood seemed to be contagious and the frenzy began to mellow.

After all her years of teaching, Mrs. Jensen has learned when she has had enough. This time she could tell she had reached the limits of her patience. She knew it would be good for her, and a good model for the children, to take a break. She really did feel better after stepping away from the chaos and taking some deep breaths.

A personal time-out is often the best answer when you are overwhelmed. Obviously this is more easily accomplished when there are several adults in charge of a group of children. Unfortunately, the option of leaving the scene is seldom available for public school teachers. Even if you are the only adult with a group of children, you can still stop and take a deep breath when things begin to feel overwhelming. You do not need to respond instantly to the problem. However you do it, your model of how to calm yourself will teach your students best if you explain to them what you are doing. Children benefit in two ways when teachers briefly remove themselves, either physically or emotionally, when they become overstressed: The cooling-off period helps the teacher to deal more rationally with child behavior, and the example set by the teacher shows children a useful way of handling their own stress.

This is just one of the many possible lessons that can be taught by adult example. It is helpful to think about the individual needs and developmental stages of children in a class when determining what emotions and behaviors to model. Your priorities and personality will also determine how and what emotions you choose to deliberately express to your class. You can make a point to express some of your emotions during your daily routine tasks or make a special time for dealing with some more complex emotions or issues. Dennis tells the kids around him when he is feeling frustrated with the stapler that won't work. He also uses puppets during circle time to discuss feeling both sad and excited about the vacation time ahead. As mentioned in Chapter 2, there are packaged curriculum programs addressing many of the important lessons about feelings, but observing an adult who is actually coping with an emotional situation is much more likely to help children learn.

Apologizing

Sometimes even wonderful teachers get overwrought and lose control before they have a chance to take a break. This offers a teaching opportunity also, as in the following example:

Dennis usually didn't mind the children's inevitable messes, but the director's reminder to "spruce up" for open house that night had him on edge. It seemed like everywhere he looked was a disaster area. He snapped at Anna when she ripped the border edging on his bulletin board while she was trying to reach the shelf next to it. He complained to Jessie that he was spilling sand from the sand table. Then Dennis saw the easel career forward, with violet, green, and red paint spewed all over the adjacent block area. He let out a "Hey!" so loud it silenced most of the class. Madeline, who had tripped on the easel, cowered and looked fearful of punishment.

Dennis took a few deep breaths, recovered his composure, and smiled to reassure the frightened girl. Then he told the class, "Wow, I'm really getting nervous about all the people coming to see our classroom at the open house tonight. When I saw that paint spill, I got upset. I'm sorry I yelled. I've been pretty irritable about messes all day because I want our room to look nice when your families come to visit tonight. I'll bet you want it to look nice, too. What can we do to fix this problem?" The children were eager to help and immediately got busy cleaning up the paint.

Dennis apologized for frightening the children and explained his feelings to them. Then they worked together on a solution. Because there is so much inappropriate expression of feelings in the world, and in some children's homes, it is essential that schools model better ways. For instance, how we express our anger makes the difference between a violent situation and a nonviolent one, and between a destructive use of anger and a productive one (Lantieri & Patti, 1996).

Children's Literature

What children's books do you know that deal with the expression of feelings? Some children learn from the old favorite *Alexander and the Terrible, Horrible, No Good, Very Bad Day* (Viorst, 1972). Have you read *Spinky Sulks* (Steig, 1988) with children? Both provide examples of how not to have children express their feelings, but offer children the opportunity to be wiser than the book character and offer suggestions for improvement.

ACCEPTING FEELINGS

As teachers acknowledge and appropriately express a wide range of their emotions, they demonstrate to children that no emotions are wrong. Teachers also have the opportunity to model acceptable ways of expressing all emotions. This is particularly important for negative emotions, such as anger, sadness, or even shame. Some children have rarely seen appropriate expressions of these difficult emotions. These emotions may be commonly expressed in violent ways in their household or may be denied altogether in their experience.

Sometimes adults try to deny children's negative feelings because they so desperately want them to be happy, or they don't want to deal with the potential tantrums that could result from children not getting their way. Therefore, some adults try to make bad feelings go away by distracting children with treats or activities. A common response to children's unhappiness is often, "Don't cry, do you want a cookie?" Some adults punish or belittle children when they feel strong emotions. For example, "You do not hate your sister, you will go to your room if I

Acknowledging and accepting feelings helps children learn to deal with them in a healthy way.

hear that again." Although well-intentioned, these responses don't help children learn to deal with their feelings effectively. Instead, they may learn that their feelings are wrong and end up feeling guilty (Plattner, 2003). This guilt, added to repressed feelings, is likely to result in negative behavior.

Instead of trying to make children's bad feelings disappear, you are already helping children learn to accept and express their feelings when you accept and express your own feelings. Beyond modeling, identifying and acknowledging children's emotions are a critical part of teaching them how to deal with their emotions in a healthy way.

Use Your Words

When Christie says, "I hate you!" she is expressing anger. The anger may or may not be justified from your perspective, but she does have that feeling and it needs to come out. Young children usually lack the language skills to express their feelings adequately. Your role as the teacher can be to help the child clarify feelings by modeling more appropriate words. In this case, your response might be "It sounds like you are angry with me."

If you can find out what made Christie angry, you can help her find the words to say specifically what she is upset about. Perhaps she wanted to be the line leader, and you chose someone else. You can accept her feelings while helping her express them more suitably. This approach involves demonstrating expressive language for her, perhaps by saying, "I can tell you are very *disappointed* that you weren't chosen." Then you can let Christie know that it is more productive to tell you that she wanted to be the line leader than to say she hates you. Teaching effective communication will be discussed further in Chapter 7.

By allowing children to experience a range of emotions and helping children to name their feelings, you are teaching them valuable, lifelong skills. Important learning can result from facing negative feelings. For instance, a child who has never faced the loneliness of being left out is less able to feel compassion for someone who is being excluded from a group. Children who experience empathy for their feelings will be able to treat others with empathy as well (Landy, 2002).

Acknowledging and Listening

Sometimes just acknowledging bad feelings and lending a listening ear can help a child get over them. Listening while children talk about their feelings, without telling them what to do, shows your acceptance of the child and their feelings. This is often all that children need. Children then free their energy to begin their own process of problem solving.

We can see the power of acceptance and acknowledgment in the following example. Jealousy of a new sibling is a common problem that most adults don't want to accept; however, Maureen provides Colette with a safe place to feel her jealousy and begin to move beyond it.

Colette was glued to the goodbye window at preschool. She was trying to get her mother's attention for a wave, but her mother's back was to the window as she adjusted the baby's carseat. Maureen noticed the look on Colette's face and asked if she'd like to step outside to catch her mom. Colette spit back, "She's too busy with that baby!" and turned away, her face scrunched in anger and sorrow.

Maureen appreciated Colette's irritation since she had been the only child in her family, too, until her brother came along and burst her bubble. She remembered what adults usually said to her when she was feeling sad about having to share her parents' attention, "You love your baby brother, don't you? He loves you. You are so lucky to be a big sister!" Maureen knew that Colette wasn't feeling lucky. She said gently, "It's not always fun being the big sister is it?" Then she gave Colette some time to respond. Colette looked sad but didn't have anything to say.

Maureen sat down and asked if Colette would like to sit on her lap. Colette quickly accepted and settled into Maureen's lap. Maureen held her for a while and then told her, "I am a big sister too, and I remember feeling pretty angry at my mom when she was always holding my baby brother. I felt sad sometimes too." Colette looked surprised and asked, "Do you like your brother?" Maureen thought for a moment and then said, "I didn't like him much when I was little because he was always taking my mom away from me." Colette seemed relieved, she agreed and began to smile. Maureen was tempted to tell Colette that she would like her sister one day, but she refrained. She knew that Colette was hearing enough of that. Colette then volunteered that her mom was going to pick her up and take her to the park, alone! Maureen cheered for Colette and the two walked to the art table where Colette decided to make a picture for her mom.

Colette needed someone who could understand her and made her feel safe expressing her feelings. This may have been harder if Maureen didn't share a similar experience. Regardless, Maureen could still take the time to identify Colette's feelings and give her some time to feel them without trying to talk her out of her feelings.

Gender and Emotions

Similarities can be particularly helpful in modeling, as we discuss later in this chapter. Male role models are especially important for little boys. Actual brain function and social pressure tend to make it harder for males to deal with emotions. The old idea that big boys don't cry hasn't disappeared from society. Many men not only feel uncomfortable expressing sadness or fear, but they also have trouble expressing positive feelings of affection and caring. For some men, anger is the only emotion they can easily express. Therefore, it may be difficult for teachers to tell when some boys feel sadness, loneliness, or jealousy. Brain research demonstrates that processing emotions is more difficult for males than it is for females. Boys are more likely to become aggressive or withdrawn when confronted with an emotionally difficult situation. Experts propose that boys are slower to process their emotions and may first need a physical outlet to help access their emotions. Due to some boys' inherent difficulties dealing with emotions, helping them identify their feelings and put them into words is particularly important (Gurian, 2001).

Conversely, some females have difficulty expressing anger or have learned to consider anger unfeminine. Male and female role models are important to give all children opportunities to relate to, and be understood by, important attachment figures. When male teachers are not available, bringing in male volunteers from the community or older boys from upper grades can provide male mentors. This is especially important for boys without father figures at home (Gurian, 2001).

Dennis does his part to wipe out the macho stereotypes and gives boys and girls plenty of time and opportunities to express all of their feelings. He freely expresses affection for his young students with hugs, smiles, and verbal feedback, such as "I like being with you." He demonstrates his joy in small things: a sunny day, a delicious snack, or a child's artistic creation. He also shows feelings of sadness when the guinea pig dies. Although Dennis doesn't cover up his feelings of frustration when something goes wrong, he is careful to show negative feelings in ways he wants children to imitate. He knows the children are likely to follow his example, whether it is positive or negative.

Cultural Differences

As always, your cultural background, and that of the children you work with, is an important consideration as you deal with emotions in your classroom. Some children get very different messages at home about how to express emotions than what they get at school. Some children come from a culture that allows aggressive expressions of anger. Others come from a culture that does not allow for any expression of emotion (Hyson, 2004). Cultures also differ in the ways children are taught to show respect for others, about whom they should trust, and polite ways of speaking (Barrera & Corso, 2003). Whether to speak loudly or softly and

BE A ROLE MODEL

- Be kind to others
- Be honest with your feelings
- Be willing to try new things
- Practice what you preach

whether to look at the person spoken to are examples of cultural variations on politeness. The many possible differences between home and school expectations emphasize the importance of getting to know parents and coming to a mutual agreement with them on behalf of their children. Asking families about their cultural norms helps to clear up any confusion or misunderstandings that occur due to differing expectations.

Perhaps your own cultural background makes you disagree with this text about the best ways of dealing with feelings. This book explains one viewpoint; your professional judgment will have to guide you in how to use this information in ways that work best for you and for your students.

CARING FOR OTHERS

You may have noticed that some youngsters have sharp tongues and say cruel things to other children, and others show concern for anyone having a hard time. Much of that behavior is learned through example. "Children use adults as mirrors: they learn from watching others" (Hyson & Molinaro, 2001, p. 115). Because adults are powerful role models for young children, your example has a great impact. When adults model caring behaviors coupled with reminders about people's feelings, children learn to think about the impact of their words. In a classroom where students are being unkind to one another, the teacher needs to examine what type of role models children are experiencing.

Modeling Acceptance

"More and more early childhood teachers have come to recognize that teaching tolerance outright in the curriculum is as fundamental and as far-reaching as teaching children how to read" (Teaching Tolerance, 1997). The tolerance referred to here is actually about appreciating that there are differences and learning to respect the opinions and ways of people who are different from you. This is a lesson clearly not learned in most of the world: wars between people of different religions, skin colors, and cultures throughout the world testify to the lack of tolerance.

How can you, as a teacher, work to counteract ethnic and racial stereotyping that creates divisiveness in the classroom and in the world? In the past, teachers have considered it enough to treat all children the same and ignore differences, with the intent to give the message that everyone is equally acceptable. However, those approaches have not been effective in the face of outside influences. It is now clear that schools must take a proactive stance in combating intolerance. For instance, instead of hushing it up if a child repeats a racial slur, use it as a "teachable moment" for a class discussion. Instead of pretending there are no differences in skin color, offer activities that celebrate those differences. Whole boxes of crayons devoted to various skin colors can contribute to such celebrations. *Starting Small* (Teaching Tolerance, 1997) is one source of activities designed to increase children's appreciation of diversity.

Sometimes you will have students who have personal difficulties that make them the target of cruelty from other children. Maybe a youngster with a bedwetting problem comes to school smelling of urine, and another wears ragged and ill-fitting clothes. Sometimes the child is like Patrick, who has such damaged self-esteem that he actually seems to invite abuse from other youngsters. These children have many needs, but one of them is the teacher's example to encourage their classmates' kindness toward them. These children are often hard to like and unappealing to be around; however, they are the ones who most need your acceptance and caring.

Starting with their families and friends, children can begin to understand and accept differences and similarities. Later they will be able to expand this awareness to the greater world. Learning to care about others and to get along together in our diverse world are central issues in the curriculum area called *social studies*. Some teachers' guides seem to suggest that social studies only covers the food and music of other lands, so youngsters spend time learning trivial facts rather than developing attitudes and understandings that might promote the welfare of humanity (Barrera & Corso, 2003). If educators recognize that compassion and learning how to establish caring relationships are among the most important things anyone can learn, they will spend time in the classroom assisting the development of such social skills.

Modeling Kindness

Children first need to learn these ideas at the concrete level—in their own environment and through their own experience. People and problems far away are too abstract for young children's thinking. Concepts such as compassion become understandable to children when they witness the principles in their own homes, classrooms, and communities (Landy, 2002).

Children learn these lessons best through situations that constantly arise during the course of the day, as 25 people attempt to live and work harmoniously together in a classroom. Because Mrs. Jensen considers that learning to live harmoniously is an important issue, she doesn't hesitate to spend schooltime helping children learn to settle a group problem. She calls it her social studies curriculum and considers it time well spent. By making time for interpersonal relations skills, she shows that she considers such skills important.

She and other educators are concerned about the prevalence of bullying in school. This is a worldwide problem that affects children's ability to feel safe in

Children understand compassion when they experience it in their own lives.

school and to learn (Banks, 1997). The bullies and their victims both feel the negative effects: The bully, left unchecked, learns a pattern of abuse that may carry over into violent relationships in their future (Baumeister, 2001), and the victim suffers from low self-esteem, anxiety, and insecurity. Too often teachers do nothing about bullying, either because they are unaware of it or because they want to discourage tattling (Froschl & Sprung, 1999). Teachers do not ignore bullying if they realize how serious the effects are.

Mrs. Jensen lets it be known that she will not tolerate such behavior. The guidelines in her class emphasize being kind to one another, and any deviation from that is a matter of grave concern for the whole class. Any child who does not feel safe in class, on the playground, in the lunchroom, or even on the school bus is encouraged to let the teacher know. If a child has a pattern of bullying, Mrs. Jensen works with the parents and tries to get help for the child. Often, the intervention needs to focus on the family, since the cause of such problems is often based on family interactions. See Chapter 10 to learn how punishment can create bullies; see Chapter 14 for further discussion of family intervention for children with serious emotional needs.

Mrs. Jensen also takes a proactive approach to bullying: She combats bullying and other unkindness when she creates a classroom climate that fosters cooperation instead of competition, when she helps children learn ways of calming themselves, and when she involves children in discussions about the kind of class they want to have. Whenever you work at meeting children's needs and at creating a caring classroom, you are combating bullying.

Children's books may help you discuss bullying and teasing with your students: We suggest you try *Chrysanthemum* (Henkes, 1991), *Oliver Button Is a Sissy* (de Paola, 1979), *The Meanest Thing to Say*, (Cosby, 1997), and *The Crow Boy* (Yashima, 1976).

Vivian Paley's stories of classrooms (1999) show us that young children are capable of caring and concern for others. Paley encourages understanding of others through the stories she shares with children: stories of helpfulness and compassion to give children the ideas and the models needed.

TAKING RISKS

Teachers can also be role models for risk taking. Why would a teacher want to encourage risk taking? Rest assured, we don't mean dangerous physical risks, but rather intellectual risks. Intellectual risks involve following up on an idea or hypothesis to see if it works. Intellectual risks may be related to science, math, art, music, or other areas. When people talk about intellectual risk in the field of science, they refer to it as generating and testing hypotheses. When they talk about the arts, they refer to intellectual risk as creativity.

Why Bother?

Risk taking is an essential part of the learning process and therefore a highly desirable behavior. Unless people are willing to think about concepts and test out their ideas, they are only able to memorize what other people say is true. Such rote learning is a very limited and limiting aspect of education. People who only learn this way will never add to the knowledge of the world. Throughout history, the great scientists, mathematicians, composers, artists, and others who have made major contributions to civilization have been those who risked questioning the status quo.

Some people might argue that children who don't think for themselves are easier to manage. They might even suggest that encouraging risk taking will increase discipline problems. After all, a child who debates the fairness of adult-imposed rules and consequences can be a real pain. But you can also consider such debates a challenge with valuable teaching potential. How you feel about this idea relates back to Chapter 1 and decisions about your goals for children. Because we, the authors of this book, are committed to the goals of intellectual and moral autonomy, we definitely want to encourage children to think for themselves.

We believe you will find that teaching for autonomy, rather than conformity, makes guidance and discipline easier, not harder. As you help children learn to make their own responsible decisions, you are released from having to make and enforce all the rules. Additionally, children who are challenged intellectually to think for themselves tend to get excited about learning. As they explore their hypotheses, they become self-directed and self-motivated learners, which also makes the job of classroom management easier. The teacher is released from the job of police officer and freed for the role of educational guide and facilitator of learning.

How to Do It?

How does the teacher demonstrate risk taking? The first step is to work on fear of failure or mistakes. This fear is a serious block to trying new ideas of any type. Mrs. Jensen starts by calling attention to all the mistakes she makes herself. She freely shares her failures, such as a fall on her new mountain bike. She doesn't belittle herself for natural human failings, but rather demonstrates acceptance of them. If she misplaces a book or some needed supplies, she might say, "I got so interested in Meadow's block creation that I didn't pay attention to where I put the book for story time today. Can you help me look for it?" Then she might use the situation to encourage children to disclose times when they, too, forgot where they put something. Her acceptance of their forgetfulness, as well as her own, provides an example for them to learn similar acceptance. It is also important for teachers to model taking risks as part of their own learning experience.

> Russian visitors were coming to Lincoln Elementary School. One of the school aides spoke some Russian, so Mrs. Jensen invited him to her classroom to teach some basic greetings. Never having heard the language before, Mrs. Jensen was right with the children at a beginner's level. First, the aide told them how to say, "My name is . . . . " "Menya zavoot," he said. Mrs. Jensen tried, "Menizoot." He repeated, "Menya zavoot." She struggled, smiling, "Menyesavoot?" The children giggled with her as she tried again. She admitted, "This is a little hard for me," and she invited the children to try with her: "Can you help?" Their keen young ears quickly picked up the nuances of sound, and within a few minutes everyone was saying, "Menya zavoot Abby. Menya zavoot Jacob." Eventually, even Mrs. Jensen mastered it!

Relation to Academics

Mrs. Jensen believes that risk taking is especially related to children's progress in writing. Emergent literacy research indicates that children learn about letters and their sounds best when they work on their own hypotheses about writing and spelling (Kamii, Long, & Manning, 2001). Therefore, Mrs. Jensen encourages children to try out their ideas through "kid writing" or invented spelling. This approach involves risk taking. Some children charge into kid writing with gusto, but others hesitate, afraid of making a letter wrong or spelling a word wrong. Some are risk takers and some are not.

The fearless ones produce pages and pages of scribbles; they also include some words they have memorized, such as their own name and *Mom, Dad,* and *I love you.* They proudly tell everyone about what they have written. Soon these youngsters are making good progress on their sound-symbol hypotheses, trying out different ideas about which letter makes which sound (Fields, Groth, & Spangler, 2004). Those children who are afraid of failure may be hampered in their learning.

> Isabel just joined Mrs. Jensen's class and obviously has not done any writing except copying. She is so terrified of making a mistake that she does nothing for most of journal time. As Mrs. Jensen tries to encourage her that "kid writing" is just fine, Isabel blurts out, "What if I mess up?" Mrs. Jensen tries to reassure her, but knows it will take awhile before Isabel gets the courage to try to express herself in writing.

Ideas about perfection in one area, such as writing, can carry over to other topics and get in the way of other learning, too. Some children feel incapable of

Children who are challenged to think for themselves become more self-directed and self-motivated learners.

artistic creativity, always wanting someone to show them the "right" way to approach an open-ended project. Others will read the same book over and over, not just because they enjoy the book, but because they know all the words and it is safe. These children desperately need the teacher to model acceptance of imperfection and the courage to venture into the unknown. They need help becoming more comfortable with learning through their mistakes. They need such help in order to become effective learners and self-directed students.

TAKING RESPONSIBILITY

Adults tend to lecture a lot about being responsible. Picking up after yourself, taking care of materials, finishing what you start, and doing work on time are common themes. A much better way to teach children these important ideas is by modeling them yourself.

Helping with Clean-up

Clean-up time is a good place to start. You read about Dennis's power struggle over this issue, and you may know that cleaning up frequently causes conflict. It is often a problem at home as well as at school. Many young children are simply overwhelmed by the mess; they don't know where to start and think it is impossible to clean up. Adults who tell kids to clean up are assuming that the children know how to do it. That is not a logical assumption. Young children need to be taught how to pick up a mess; the best way for them to learn is for you to show them what you mean by cleaning up. In other words, you work with them. Seeing you help with clean-up also gives children a clear message that the teacher thinks cleaning up is worth doing. You are an effective model. Contrast the following scene with one where the teachers merely tell youngsters to hurry up with the clean-up.

> The block area was strewn with a jumble of blocks and littered with the small toy cars and trucks that had been driving on the block roads. Nancy, one of Dennis' assistant teachers, saw Kelsey and Zach standing in the midst of this mess looking hopeless. Nancy went over to the children and offered to help. She started picking up blocks, handing the long, rectangular ones to Kelsey to put on the shelf and giving the small, square ones to Zach to put away. Nancy made sure the youngsters were able to match the blocks with the outlines painted on the shelves showing what kind of block goes where. She called their attention to the different sizes and shapes as they worked together.
>
> Soon Nancy positioned herself by the shelf and asked the youngsters to hand her all the triangle-shaped blocks. Next, the children got to choose which shape to work on, and before long the job was complete. Kelsey and Zach felt good about their hard work, and they gained skill in organizing the clean-up of the block area. Eventually, they will be able to do it themselves with only a few verbal clues. Having Nancy work with them helped them to value the work they were doing.
>
> Meanwhile, Dennis was working with children washing out paint brushes. As they worked, he talked about the importance of using cold water so as not to loosen the glue holding the brush in the handle. He also encouraged his fellow brush cleaners to experiment with ways that most quickly get the paint out.
>
> While Dennis and Nancy helped with blocks and paint clean-up, Sheri, another assistant, circulated among other clean-up tasks. She stopped to help get the doll babies comfortable in their bed instead of on the floor in the playhouse. Then she complimented Celeste and Anna on how orderly the kitchen cupboard looked before moving on to help Megan and Joshua at the manipulatives table.

Keeping Your Promises

Following through with a plan or a promise is another important area of responsibility. Like clean-up, it, too, contributes to a smoothly running classroom. Mrs. Jensen teaches this behavior effectively through modeling. She starts each day with a discussion of the day's schedule, writing it on the board while the children watch and learn about writing as well as planning. They get practice in reading as they refer back to the schedule during the day. Mrs. Jensen treats the daily plan like a contract, or promise, of what the day will bring.

If weather causes the cancellation of a nature walk that the children are looking forward to, she discusses the change and plans with them to do it another day soon. She makes sure to follow through with this plan, never deciding that the children will soon forget. She models consistent follow-through, and she talks to the children about her commitment to keeping her word. She wants to be sure they realize what she is modeling for them. Some children have no experience with consistency and follow-through in their homes. These children may need help recognizing it when they see it.

Children in Mrs. Jensen's class can count on this same follow-through on an individual level as well. If their teacher is too busy when they want to talk to her, they know she will soon get back to them.

> Mrs. Jensen was deep in discussion with Ling Ling about the story she was reading when Tony came up and tapped his teacher on the shoulder. A tap on the shoulder is an approved signal for a child to communicate the need for teacher attention when she is in conference with another student. Mrs. Jensen smiled at Tony and made a signal with her fingers indicating she would be with him in a short while. To make sure that she didn't forget, Mrs. Jensen wrote Tony's name on a note to herself. Tony went back to his seat, secure in the knowledge that his teacher would soon be with him. As soon as she was finished with Ling Ling, Mrs. Jensen went over to see what Tony wanted. Tony and his classmates have begun writing reminder notes to themselves in imitation of their teacher.

Sometimes Mrs. Jensen's list of requests for attention gets too long, and she knows she can't reach so many children in a timely manner. Rather than keeping them waiting, she makes appointments with them for later on. They can still count on her, even if not immediately. Of course, if children have an urgent need, they communicate it. Mrs. Jensen then helps them find whatever assistance is required. As part of encouraging their autonomy, Mrs. Jensen has shown her students how to use a variety of resources effectively rather than always relying on the teacher. Therefore, these children are quite capable of helping each other when their teacher is working with an individual child.

Independent Use of Materials

Things go smoothly without the teacher's constant attention due, in part, to the time Mrs. Jensen has spent in helping children learn how to use materials in a responsible way. Her students have learned these lessons well because their teacher doesn't just lecture about their proper use. You guessed it: She shows them how instead.

 SHOW, DON'T JUST TELL

Instead of telling kids to do something, show them how to do the following:

- Clean up
- Keep promises
- Be safe

Mrs. Jensen spends time working with children in each learning center as a way of helping them learn the independent use of materials. Independent use is much different than prescribed single use. It is not a way to limit how children use things, but rather to provide guidelines for their creative expression. Mrs. Jensen finds that her students soon take over the modeling job and begin to show one another important points. Dylan learned that a tile is needed under the plastic clay to protect table tops. He then took the responsibility of reminding Nathan when Nathan forgot. Mrs. Jensen also follows the class guidelines when she uses any material. She knows that to do otherwise would undermine her efforts.

Following the Rules

Beth's first day of student teaching taught her a lot about the importance of adult role models. At least some children pay a lot of attention to whether adults follow the rules.

> When the teacher called everyone together for the morning meeting and everyone began to gather, Beth took a seat on the couch in the gathering area. Riley loudly informed her that, "It isn't your day for the couch." Beth asked him how he knew whose day it was, and he pointed to a list. Beth went and examined it and said, "You're right, it's not my day for the couch." Beth joined the children on the floor.
>
> After the meeting, children were dismissed to the designated learning centers. Beth was busy helping a group of children when she noticed that Riley had climbed up onto the table. She looked at him questioningly. He looked back. Beth said, "Are you supposed to be sitting on the table?" He just looked at her, and in that instant she realized that she was sitting on the corner of the table. She immediately acknowledged, "But I'm sitting on the table, aren't I?" Riley nodded yes. Beth replied, "Well, I'll have to get off then, won't I?" Riley waited until Beth stood up, then he jumped back down onto the floor. Later, when Beth forgot and sat down on the table again, Riley started to scramble back up again. Beth quickly got up and Riley got down.

KEEPING SAFE

"Do as I say and not as I do" won't work in teaching safety behavior, either. All the teachers at Midway Children's Center remind each other to carry scissors with points down to keep their example consistent with their words to children. They are also careful not to walk too close to a child on a swing, and they model safe street crossing when taking walks with children. When using a car or van for a field trip, teachers, as well as children, wear their buckles.

Mrs. Jensen makes sure she always pushes in her desk chair when she's not using it. Pushing in chairs is an important safety rule in her school. This rule is primarily to keep passageways clear for fire drills, but it also saves a lot of tripping over chairs on a daily basis. Mrs. Jensen helps her students internalize this safety rule by her example.

Maureen became convinced of the impact of adult models while watching preschoolers in dramatic play one day.

Several youngsters were engrossed in a make-believe trip on the boat in the play yard. Megan ran to get some life jackets that had been donated as props. She offered them to Jack and Tory, who scorned them, saying, "We're the dads! We don't wear those." These children had obviously noticed during family boat outings that the children had to wear life jackets but that their fathers did not wear them.

EFFECTIVE ROLE MODELS

Role models are most effective when they are people whom children look up to: important, powerful, nurturant people (Hyson, 2004). Young children look up to their teachers and their parents. In fact, they tend to consider all adults powerful and infallible creatures. This belief puts a large responsibility on you as an adult who works with young children. Seize the opportunity! As children get older, they look less to adults for their models and turn more to peers they admire.

Someone Similar

The ability to identify with role models is important to all ages. As discussed previously, children are more likely to copy people who are similar to them in some way. Teachers can emphasize similarities with their students by commenting on similarities of interest and feelings. For instance, Anna's favorite color is purple. Nancy makes a special point to tell Anna that she likes purple the best, too. Sheri and Zach both have pet beagles that they talk about.

Older children often look to others of the same age for models, and models of the same gender are important because of their similarities, too. Children whose first language differs from their teacher's or whose skin is a different color are less able to benefit from the model of their teacher (Brazelton & Greenspan, 2000). This tendency is one reason why it is important to recruit more teachers and aides from minority groups.

Someone to Be Like

You are more likely to be an effective role model if children want to be like you (Hyson, 2004). This means that youngsters need to see you as being fun and pleasant. It probably also means having a positive relationship with youngsters. They want to be like you because they like you.

Children often want to be like sports stars, television characters, and superheroes. The companies who use these stars to market their products count on this and use it to their advantage. Advertising can be very powerful and, unfortunately, is increasingly aimed at children (Linn, 2004). At Kidscreen's fifth annual conference on Advertising and Promoting to Kids, some of its stated missions were to teach attendees how to "own kids" and create "lifelong consumers" (*The Lancet*, 2002,

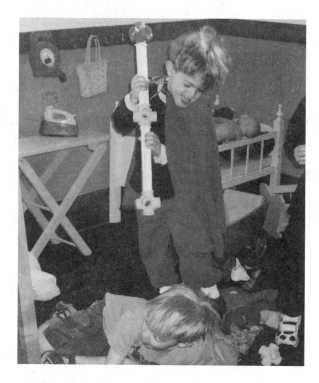

Superhero play can be redirected from violence to more positive themes of being helpful and feeling powerful.

p. 959). The philosophy now in advertising to kids is to "to teach kids to influence their parents' purchases" (McLellan, 2002, p. 1001). Children are inundated with these persuasive role models in games, clothes, foods, and especially toys.

There are other problems with media's strong influence on children. Children pick up whole behavior patterns by emulating the models they see in the media. In some television programs, sarcastic put-downs are presented as humorous and entertaining, teaching impressionable young people that this is a desirable way to interact. The greatest concern with the influence of superheroes and some cartoon characters is the likelihood that children will copy the violent behavior they have observed.

MODELS OF VIOLENCE

The American Medical Association, the American Academy of Pediatrics, the American Psychological Association, and the American Academy of Child and Adolescent Psychiatry made a joint statement about media violence. These health professionals concluded that violence in television, music, video games, and movies can make children more aggressive, fearful, disrespectful, and insensitive to the effects of violence (TRUCE, 2003–2004, in Appendix A). The National Association for the Education of Young Children (NAEYC) has also published a position statement cautioning about the media and violence. Media is clearly a significant influence when we consider the amount of time some children spend watching television or playing video games. Violence affects children of all ages. Children are never too young to have their trust development or desire to explore their world threatened by exposure to violence (Osofsky, 1997).

Organizations such as TRUCE (Teachers Resisting Unhealthy Children's Entertainment) actively work to eliminate violence in children's television and toys. Other coalitions, including CCFC (Campaign for a Commercial Free Childhood), specifically work against marketing aimed at children. A quick search on the Internet will bring up many more groups with similar missions.

When children see violence they will often bring it into their play. This is their way of processing what they have witnessed and trying to make sense of it all. Creating class rules about violence and safety in the classroom is essential. However, when violent play arises, teachers have a great opportunity to help children learn from what they have seen. When children imitate their favorite superheroes, we can use these opportunities to discuss what is fantasy versus reality, the impact of violence, and support positive images of being helpful and feeling powerful (Levin, 2004). Instead of imitating superhero plots seen on the screen, you can encourage children to develop their own plots for superhero play. This may be a great opportunity to discuss true heroism and how our actions affect others. Some children develop real fears from violence they have actually experienced or observed. In some cases, your openness to discuss violence may allow you to help a child who is tormented by fear or who is in real danger.

Working with Families to Combat Media Violence

Families and schools must work together to shield children from harmful advertising and violent media. You can encourage parents and guardians to talk to their children about the content of advertising and media; family involvement can help counteract negative media images. Children need to know that, contrary to what they may be seeing on TV, most people really do not carry weapons—they avoid violence and talk about their disagreements instead of forcing their opinions on others. It is the responsibility of adults to help children think about and analyze the positive and negative models they are sure to encounter both in real life and on television. Youngsters will learn negative behavior patterns from models as easily as they learn positive ones. Teachers and families must work together to ensure that the negative doesn't overwhelm the positive.

Resources are available to help children and families use discretion in choosing positive media images and to facilitate discussion about the effects of media. Workshops and newsletters for parents are great ways to communicate these messages. In Appendix A at the end of this book, you will find some useful handouts to send home; they include some startling statistics about the impact of media on children. These handouts also offer suggestions for facilitating family discussions about potentially negative media images. We can also encourage the use of open-ended toys that allow children to use their imaginations instead of toys that represent specific characters connected with violent media (Levin, 2004). We can all work together to decrease the amount of violence exposure in children's lives.

Fortunately, all media is not harmful. Some books that may be helpful for fostering critical thinking about the media are: *The Bionic Bunny Show* (Brown, 1999); *Mouse TV* (Novak, 1994); and *Box-Head Boy* (Winn & Walsh, 1996). These books may aid a discussion about the harm and good that can come from media and inspire children to consider alternatives to watching television (Hesse & Lane, 2003).

CURRICULUM PROGRAMS THAT PROVIDE EXAMPLES

The principles described in this chapter are accepted pieces of violence prevention (Lantieri & Patti, 1996) and are included in published violence prevention programs. Lesson plans to promote productive expression of feelings, caring for others, and being responsible for yourself can be found in programs such as the *Resolving Conflict Creatively Program* (Lantieri, 2003), *Tribes* (Gibbs, 2001), *Second Step: A Violence-Prevention Curriculum* (Committee for Children, 2003), and *Educating the Heart* (Siccone & Lopez, 2000).

Creating a caring classroom reduces violence by addressing the major causes of violent behavior: unmet emotional needs, values of exclusion rather than inclusion, and lack of skills for peaceful conflict resolution. If a program does not work toward these goals, then we question its worth. A worthwhile program also includes intensive training for teachers as well as for the school administration and staff. The most effective programs have lessons for children integrated throughout the day—lessons that are relevant to their real lives. For best success, schools must commit to a program for a significant span of time (Wheeler, 2004).

Even if your school doesn't adopt a formal program schoolwide, you may find that some of the materials from these programs offer helpful ideas for class discussions and activities to promote kindness, caring, and cooperation. Mrs. Jensen uses many of the esteem-boosting and appreciation expression activities from the *Tribes* curriculum as part of building her classroom community (Gibbs, 2001). We encourage you to critically review published programs and decide the worth of the lessons for yourself. We find that some focus on paper-and-pencil or cut-and-paste activities rather than on actual interpersonal experiences. We prefer activities that involve children with one another, using the skill or disposition to be learned. These include exercises such as practice in giving compliments, expressing and interpreting feelings through pantomime, and partner interviews.

CONCLUSION

Your positive examples will result in more positive child behaviors. If you have a caring relationship with your students, your models of respect and fairness toward children will be emulated in how children treat one another. How you deal with your own feelings and those of others will affect how children handle their feelings. Your demonstrations of caring and kindness will make lasting impressions on young people. Your willingness to take risks in learning new skills and trying out new ideas will help youngsters more bravely try out their emerging skills and ideas. When you set an example of being responsible and of following good safety habits, children are more apt to pay attention than when you lecture about those issues. As an adult you have a powerful influence on young children. You are teaching by everything you do.

∞ FOR FURTHER THOUGHT

1. Observe young children and the adults with whom they spend their days. Note the ways in which the children imitate the examples set by adults.

2. Analyze your own expression of feelings in your personal life. Are you able to express fear or loneliness to trusted friends or family? Do you have a tendency to cover up other negative feelings with expressions of anger? How do you express your anger? Do you need to work on your own ability to express your feelings effectively in order to set an example for children?

3. Notice how adults respond when children get hurt or are upset. Do they deny children's negative feelings or accept them? Do they try to distract children from physical or emotional pain? What is your own common response? Do you need to work at learning new ways to respond to a child's pain?

4. Observe ways in which teachers encourage or discourage children in thinking for themselves. Do you see any relationship between a teacher's own intellectual autonomy and that teacher's encouragement of children's intellectual autonomy? How would you rate yourself for intellectual autonomy?

5. Observe the difference in classrooms where teachers merely tell children to clean up and those where teachers work with youngsters, showing them useful clean-up approaches.

∞ RECOMMENDED READINGS

Froschl, M., & Sprung, B. (1999). On purpose: Addressing teasing and bullying in early childhood. *Young Children, 54*(3), 70–72.

Hesse, P., & Lane, F. (2003). Media literacy starts young: An integrated curriculum approach. *Young Children, 58*(6), 20–26.

Hyson, M. C. (2004). *The emotional development of young children: Building an emotion-centered curriculum.* New York: Teachers College Press.

Levin, D. E. (2004). Beyond banning war and superhero play: Meeting children's needs in violent times. In D. Koralek (Ed.), *Spotlight on young children and play.* Washington, DC: National Association for the Education of Young Children.

Plattner, I. E. (2003). Granting children their emotions. *Child Care Information Exchange, 152,* 34–36.

Teaching Tolerance. (1997). *Starting small: Teaching tolerance in preschool and the early grades.* Montgomery, AL: The Southern Poverty Law Center.

7 *Effective Discipline Through Effective Communication*

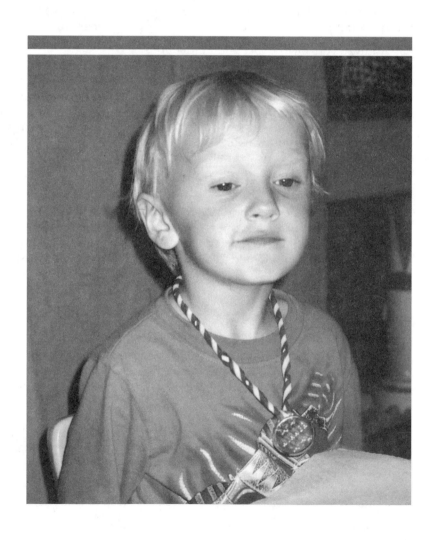

"*G*et to work, young man."
"Stop acting like a baby."
"You're such a good little girl."
"No recess unless that paper is finished."
"You are being rude."
"Everything will be fine; just wait and see."
"Your picture is beautiful."
"You're okay. There's no reason to cry."
"You need to improve your attitude."

Do any of these statements sound familiar? Perhaps you heard them from your parents and teachers as you grew up. Perhaps you have said them to children yourself. You may be surprised to hear that these statements have a negative effect on behavior (Gordon, 1989). Chapter 6 discusses some of these types of responses in terms of negating children's feelings. This chapter will look at how such comments build barriers to communication in addition to teaching children that their feelings aren't okay. In his discipline classic *Parent Effectiveness Training,* Thomas Gordon (1970) calls them "roadblocks to communication."

Many parents and teachers grew up with these counterproductive ways of communicating, which have become second nature to them. These adults automatically resort to the ways of talking to children that they have heard in the past. Knowledge about effective communication can drastically alter relationships between people of all ages. Some people use the information to improve marriages, friendships, or working relationships (Gordon, 1989). Parents and teachers can apply the information to effective communication and better relationships with children. Effective communication is an essential part of effective discipline, as are good relationships.

This chapter helps you build better relationships as you communicate more positively with children. Being a role model of effective communication, plus your explicit teaching, help children learn to use these forms of communication so that they can get along better with others. Your classroom will be a more peaceful place when you and your students talk, listen, and negotiate differences according to the guidelines shared in this chapter.

WHY CHILDREN DON'T LISTEN

Adults frequently complain that children don't listen to them, and they often have no idea why. Few adults ever consider that it might be their own fault. Think about the following situations:

1. You have just warned Nicholas to be careful of that puddle, and now he's splashing right into the middle of it.

2. You have given the directions for the art activity three times, and still individual children are coming up to you and asking how to do it.

3. You hear yourself saying, "How many times have I told you not to do that?!"

145

These incidents may be symptoms of ineffective ways of talking to children. Of course, we can't guarantee that Kenji will stay out of the puddle no matter what you say, but you can improve your success rate. How you talk to kids makes a big difference in whether they listen to you. How you talk to children and other people also makes a big difference in whether they care what you have to say.

Criticizing and Lecturing

It isn't too surprising that people don't listen to what is unpleasant to hear. It seems like a natural self-protective device to tune out what is unpleasant. Yet, many teachers and parents express dismay when children don't listen to their persistent nagging. The adults consider frequent reminders and corrections as forms of teaching. Certainly, teaching is the intent, but the teaching approach obviously is not effective if the teaching is ignored.

No matter what their age, people rarely like to hear someone tell them how badly they have behaved. Similarly, no one wants to be called derogatory names such as *selfish* or *tattletale*. Most people also get irritated at being told how they should be acting. Well-intentioned comments analyzing possible causes of your behavior are perhaps the most infuriating of all. Remember, kids are people, too, and if you want them to listen to you, avoid talking to them in ways that turn off listening. Think about how you would feel in the following situation:

> You were late for work and feeling awful about it. It was a terrible morning: Everything that could go wrong did go wrong. Your alarm didn't go off, the clothes you had washed and put into the dryer last night to wear today didn't get dry, and the bus pulled away just as you got to the bus stop.
>
> You finally arrived at work, frustrated, hungry, and disheveled. Your supervisor pointed out that you were late once last month, too, and said that you have been inconsiderate. She went on to tell you how disappointed she was in your thoughtlessness and suggested that you might have a problem dealing with authority and rules. She finished by lecturing you on the importance of being on time.

Would this supervisor's approach make you open to her instruction? Would you pay close attention to what she says and want to learn more from her? How would it affect your feelings about her in general? How would your attitude about work that day be affected? Most people would get very angry, tune out the supervisor, and have an even worse day as a result. Yet, many teachers regularly talk to students in this way and expect improved behavior to result. Gordon (1970) calls this behavior "sending put-down messages." It is fortunate that kids often tune such messages out because they are so harmful to self-esteem.

Giving Orders

It is fairly easy to recognize the unpleasantness of hearing about your errors. However, you may not have thought about why kids (and adults) also dislike constantly being told what to do and how to do it. These instructions communicate disrespect for the other person's ideas and abilities. When you tell people everything they need to do in a situation, you also tell them that you don't think they are capable of figuring it out for themselves. Gordon (1970) calls this communication approach "solution messages." When you communicate this kind of disrespect, you don't get much cooperation in return. You are more likely to generate resistance to your directions instead. Of greater concern are the long-term effects on the child. Such disrespect not only damages self-esteem, but it also short-circuits growth toward autonomy. When you solve problems for them, children learn not to trust their own solutions. You are creating an unhealthy dependency.

> Ariel couldn't get the glue to come out. She turned the dispenser's end, chewed on it, and squeezed as hard as she could. Finally, she just took off the lid and tried to pour glue onto her collage. When it didn't immediately come out, she shook the container. Glop! As Ariel considered the best way to approach the puddle of glue, Miss Wheeler stepped in and ordered, "Get a sponge!" Ariel frowned. She would have scooped up most of the glue with a scrap of mat board first. Then she would have gotten a sponge to finish the job. Why didn't Miss Wheeler ever let her decide how to do things, Ariel wondered.

Haim Ginott also wrote a child-guidance classic, *Between Parent and Child* (1965). Thomas Gordon and Ginott both discuss how differently adults talk to children than to other adults. They point out that few teachers or parents would talk to a friend or acquaintance in the bossy, rude ways that many speak to children. It tends to sound ridiculous if you think of talking to an adult in the disrespectful terms often used toward youngsters. If Ariel had been an adult, would the teacher have spoken to her that way? More likely, Miss Wheeler would have said, "You may use my table sponge if you'd like."

Inauthentic Communication

Speaking to children with respect, as you would expect to do with adults, can be a helpful guide. But many people don't know the best ways to express themselves to people of any age. You may be one of those people who don't say anything when someone offends or upsets you because you don't want to be rude or unpleasant. Or, you may be bold about speaking up to defend yourself. Too often, it is hard to defend yourself without expressions of anger, which generate anger in response.

If you say nothing when someone hurts or frustrates you, your resentment builds. Your nonverbal communication will be negative, indicating your true feelings. The relationship will be damaged by the unexpressed feelings and the unresolved conflicts. This is not an honest way of relating. Children with parents and teachers who provide this model of behavior do not have productive examples to follow.

If you find yourself speaking in anger frequently, you may also be covering up your true feelings. Anger is often a secondary emotion. It results from a primary emotion such as fear, hurt, or embarrassment. Expressions of anger focus on what the other person did, without acknowledging your own feelings. Some teachers and parents feel that revealing their own fear or hurt is not compatible with their authority role. They may think that the expression of true feelings demonstrates weakness and that their job is to demonstrate power. Like holding in unpleasant feelings, expressing them as anger also damages relationships. It is dishonest and, therefore, a poor role model as well.

The idea that an adult cannot demonstrate fear, sadness, or other feelings associated with vulnerability is linked to the power-based authoritarian discipline style, with its repercussions of negative behaviors and negative self-esteem. The invincible adult role is counterproductive to long-term discipline goals in other ways as well. We have already discussed in Chapter 6 how children's ability to express their emotions in a healthy way is affected by their adult role models. Additionally, the invulnerable adult model gets in the way of authentic relationships with children because the adults cannot reveal their true selves. Authentic relationships between adults and children, like those between peers, encourage cooperation and empathy. These traits are clearly linked to more desirable behavior.

TALKING TO CHILDREN RESPECTFULLY

It is important to communicate your personal needs and limits. Doing so effectively means you state your feelings without labeling the child as bad and without ordering the child to change. In this way you balance the expression of self-respect with that of respect for others. Gordon (1970) was the first to call this simple statement of your own feelings an "I message."

"I messages" are appropriate when the problem is yours: what is happening is upsetting to you personally. Children need to learn to give "I messages" when someone does something that bothers them. Sometimes adults seem to get confused and assume that all problems are the adults' problem; that view gets in the way of teaching children to express their own feelings with "I messages."

In contrast with "you messages," "I messages" do not blame or condemn another person, and they do not contain put-downs. "I messages" also don't tell

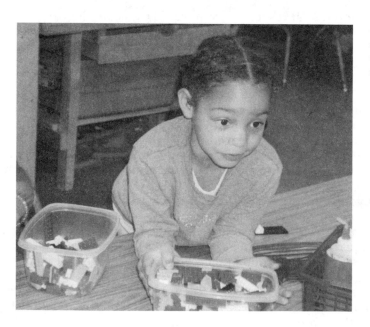

Using "I messages" teaches children how to respectfully communicate their own needs to others.

someone else what to do, thus avoiding a "solution message." They focus on your needs instead of on the other person's actions. Therefore, people are more willing to listen to this type of communication; it generates little argument or defensiveness.

A complete "I message" has three components according to Gordon's book, *P.E.T. in Action* (Gordon & Sands, 1976):

1. It is specific about what the unacceptable behavior is.
2. It states your feeling.
3. It explains why it makes you feel that way.

We add another component:

4. It stops after saying those three things.

Too many people start out with a good "I message" and then ruin it by telling the child what he or she should be doing differently. Some social skills curriculum programs also make this mistake in teaching "I messages:" they actually say to tell the other person how to change his or her behavior. That sends a solution message—another roadblock to communication. If you don't stop after stating the problem and its cause, your listener hears the instructions for improvement and tends to react negatively.

It is more effective and respectful to communicate the nature of your problem and then to back off, allowing the child to make things right. The following examples show three different examples of useful "I messages."

1. While Mrs. Jensen was reading a story to the group, Abby was talking to her friend quite loudly. Mrs. Jensen looked at Abby and said, "I can't read with so much noise in the room. It gives me a sore throat to try to talk loudly enough for people to hear me." Abby had a reason for keeping her voice down and willingly complied.

2. Dennis was bending over to help Anna with her boots when Sam came up behind, threw his arms tightly around Dennis's neck, and hung on his teacher's back. Dennis nearly fell over backward, but understood that Sam was expressing affection and meant no harm. As calmly as possible, Dennis told the affectionate child, "I'm afraid I'm going to fall over with you on my back, Sam, and I can't help Anna with her boots this way." Sam hopped off, and Dennis gave him some attention as soon as Anna had her boots on.

3. Karina was spilling paint on the carpet as she exuberantly worked on the class mural. Mrs. Jensen walked over to where Karina was working and told her, "I am worried that this paint won't come out of our rug, especially after it dries." Karina got a sponge for clean-up and then put down papers to catch the drips.

Relationships

"I messages" assume that the person you are speaking to actually cares about how you feel. If you don't have a caring relationship with Alexis, you can't expect her to be concerned when you tell her you are having a problem. Once again, we are reminded of the central role played by relationships. Piaget (1965/1932) identified mutually respectful relationships as the basis of moral development. In order to be effective with guidance and discipline, you must cultivate relationships with the children in your care.

The children in the previous examples were free to think about their teachers' concerns instead of defending themselves against accusations of wrongdoing. The children were also free to think about how they could make things right again. Did you notice that Mrs. Jensen didn't tell Karina what she needed to do about the problem, but instead respected the child to come up with a solution? This approach helped Karina feel good about herself and increased the likelihood of future desirable behavior. If Mrs. Jensen had tacked on a solution message, it would have taken away from the effectiveness of the communication. Instead, Mrs. Jensen indicated belief in the child's ability and desire to figure out a solution.

Misconceptions

Sometimes people get confused about what an "I message" is. They think that it is any statement that starts with "I feel. . . . " Remember, an "I message" is the expression of your own perspective; it is an "I message" because it doesn't aim the blame at someone else. Be careful, or you might actually send a "you message," fooling yourself into believing that it is an "I message" (Gordon, 1970). For example, Mrs. Jensen might have told Mica, "I feel irritated when you are being such a messy painter." Her "I feel irritated" would then have only been a preface for an insult.

The real key to "I messages" has little to do with using the word *I*. Instead of saying, "I feel hurt when you kick me," it would be much more natural to say, "Ouch, that hurts!" The message is the same: It isn't calling the youngster bad for kicking; it is just expressing your feelings about being kicked. The statement, "I am proud of you" may, at first, sound more like an "I message" than saying, "thank you." Analysis of the two statements, however, reveals just the opposite. "Thank you" actually tells your feelings and means "I feel appreciative of what you have done." The statement "I'm proud of you" really is a judgment of the other person.

Effectiveness

According to Curwin and Mendler (1990), "I messages" are effective for the following four reasons:

1. They say how you feel about what a child is or isn't doing.
2. They give a reason why the behavior is a problem.
3. They never criticize or blame the child.
4. They allow the child to solve the problem.

It takes practice to get good at "I messages," but eventually you can retrain yourself so that it comes more naturally to express your own perspective instead of

DEVELOPING POSITIVE "I MESSAGES"

Can you think of positive "I message" alternatives instead of the "you messages" used in the following examples?

1. You are taking a group of children on a walking field trip that involves crossing a few streets. Sam runs ahead of the group instead of staying with you as instructed. Frantic, you yell to Sam, "You have to stay with us! Come back here right now!"

2. A co-teacher is clearing a counter for a project and doesn't notice that five children behind her have their hands raised. You are overwhelmed by trying to meet their demands for attention alone and say to the co-teacher, "You should be more attentive to the children!"

3. A parent brings in a child late, as is her habit, which disrupts your morning gathering time. Besides, this boy really needs help with the daily separation from his mother. You wish she would bring him either earlier or later so that you could be available for him. You say to the mother, "You really need to be on time."

judging someone else's behavior. You will find that the results are worth the effort. People of all ages will respond much more positively to what you say.

Teaching Children to Use "I Messages"

Your model will go a long way toward encouraging your students to express themselves with "I messages," but coaching them in how to use them will help, too. Remember, the person who has the problem is the one who gives the "I message." So, when Sarah is upset because someone took something she was using, it is an appropriate time to help her use an "I message." Often, the other child involved will have a different perspective on the problem and can be helped to give his or her own "I message" in response. "I messages" are an important first step in conflict resolution. You may recall that Chapter 3 recommended "I messages" for helping children gain perspective-taking ability, too.

BEING A GOOD LISTENER

Maybe one of the reasons why children don't listen to adults is that adults often don't really listen to children. Too often teachers and parents respond to children's problems by brushing them off. The reasons for this attitude, as discussed in Chapter 6, may be varied. Sometimes adults believe that children's concerns are trivial, or they worry too much about children getting upset. Sometimes an adult is unable to deal with real feelings. It is also possible to be so busy that you don't realize you are not truly listening. You may even think you are paying attention to a child and still respond in ways that prove otherwise.

Not Listening

Many common, well-intentioned ways of responding to what a child says amount to quick brush-offs. Trying to distract a youngster from feeling sad is one way of not really listening. Diversions may be something like the old "let's have a cookie" routine or other words that say, "Let's think about something nice instead." Quick reassurances that everything will be fine also communicate that you are not interested in hearing the child's concerns. Therefore, these are roadblocks to communication. Even trying to solve the child's stated problem with advice is a way of not really listening. Think about how you feel when someone does those things to you.

> Maureen has a friend, Jane, who is quick to give out advice. Maureen really hates it when she is upset about something, then confides to Jane, and gets an instant solution. The advice is always shallow and nonproductive anyway, because Jane hasn't had time to think through the problem. Naturally, Maureen has thought of all those obvious and easy solutions and already come to the conclusion that they won't work; otherwise, she wouldn't still have the problem.
>
> Because Jane doesn't know all the complexities of the situation, her thoughts are mostly irrelevant. What Maureen really wants is someone who hears and understands how upset she is. Instead, Jane's response shows that she isn't hearing the seriousness of the problem; her offer of an easy answer clearly says to Maureen, "Your problem isn't any big deal. If I were in your place, I could solve it in a minute. You aren't handling things very well."

No wonder Gordon lists giving advice as one of the roadblocks to communication.

Talking Instead of Listening

Sometimes adults are so busy telling kids what they think that they don't hear what a child is saying. When children bring up a problem, many teachers and parents think it is their job to tell youngsters what to do. Some talk to kids about what they "should" do from a moral standpoint, while others tend to dish out facts, trying to influence young people with logic. Still others just give orders and expect compliance. None of these approaches results in listening to the child or respecting the child's ability to figure out answers to problems. You can surely remember how you felt when you got these kinds of lectures yourself. They didn't make you feel like listening!

Passing judgment on a person confiding in you is another sure way to stop further communication. You have heard responses like "It's your own fault" or "You're not making any sense." You may have even heard worse. One of the worst things anyone can say to a young child striving hard to be grown-up is "You're being a baby." Such name-calling is just one way of shaming children and making them feel worthless. Some teachers unfortunately use ridicule and other forms of humiliation to keep youngsters from challenging authority.

On the opposite end of the spectrum, have you ever noticed that praise is another way of passing judgment? In this case, you have judged that things are good, but the implication is clear that you will continue to judge and next time may come up with negative findings. We further discuss problems with praise, and offer alternatives in Chapter 9. Messages of praise are also counterproductive to the communication process. Gordon (1970) includes praise, along with reassuring, diverting, and probing, in his list of roadblocks to communication. These methods are attempts to help the child feel better; but like the rest of Gordon's 12 roadblocks to communication, they are nonlistening responses.

Adults can teach good listening by being good listeners. Adults can also learn a lot by listening to kids and finding out what they are thinking. In addition, you can build productive relationships with children by showing that you care enough about them to genuinely listen. When you have a good relationship with children, they try harder to cooperate with you. Good listening can reap many rewards.

Passive Listening

One way to show you are listening is to stop talking yourself. Some people just can't seem to be quiet long enough to hear what anyone else is saying. Quiet attention to a child's words with only minimal comments, such as "Is that so?" or "How interesting," can be very effective. Even a sympathetic "hmmmm" is better than a roadblock (Faber & Mazlish, 1996; Porter, 2000). Sometimes more is required, such as asking "What do you think about that?" or "Would you like to talk about it?" These responses indicate acceptance and respect for the child's opinion. They are basically passive listening approaches.

Reflective Listening

Gordon (1989) suggests that "active listening" is even more productive than passive listening. He used the term *active listening* to describe an approach common among counselors and therapists. This process is essentially an extension of the processes highlighted in Chapter 2 and Chapter 6, used to help children express their feelings. "Reflective listening" is essentially another term for the same method, a term we consider more descriptive of the process. *Reflective listening* includes restating and validating the concerns and/or feelings of another person. Reflective listening can be used to ensure the accuracy of communication by reflecting back to the speaker what the listener has heard. Though the term *active listening* is widely used, we prefer the term *reflective listening*.

When you practice reflective listening, you will discover how often misunderstandings occur. When you say what it is you think the other person meant, you allow the speaker to confirm or correct your interpretation. The different experiences and perspectives of the people involved can give totally different meanings to the same set of words. Reflective listening involves the speaker and the listener in a mutual effort to ensure accurate communication. When you give this kind of effort to understanding a child, you show the child you care. You are also more likely to find out what's really going on.

Madeline was often upset when her mother dropped her off at preschool. However, today her reaction was more extreme than usual. As was sometimes the case, Dennis had to gently restrain Madeline from following her mother out the door. Today, Madeline did not stop crying 30 seconds after her mother's departure as she usually did.

Dennis knew that Madeline and her family had been out of town for the last two weeks, and this was probably the reason for her increased difficulty with separation. He settled himself into a seat where he could be eye level with Madeline and said to her softly, "It looks like you really didn't want to come to school today."

Madeline sniffled, "I want to go home."

Dennis reflected, "You went on a trip with your mom and the rest of your family didn't you?" Madeline nodded as Dennis continued, "Sometimes it is hard to come back to school after you've been gone for a while. Everything seems new again."

Madeline just nodded her head, leaning on Dennis' shoulder, and continued sniffling.

Dennis wondered if Madeline was feeling tired too, after her big trip. He told her, "When I go on a long trip, sometimes I feel extra tired when I get back."

Madeline sat up, and said, "I was tired when I got a fever at Aunt Debby's house."

Dennis asked, "Were you sick on your trip?" As, Madeline nodded, all the pieces seemed to fall into place. Madeline's difficulty with separation was exacerbated by her time away from school, and she was recovering from the exhaustion of traveling and being sick. It was easier for Dennis to have empathy for Madeline when he knew why she was feeling so needy. Dennis summed it all up, "It is really hard to play at school when you miss your mom and you're tired."

Madeline offered, "I don't want to play right now." Dennis understood her need and sat with Madeline as she continued to lean on him and look around for a few more minutes. Madeline eventually stopped crying. When her friend Sarah stopped to ask if she wanted to "be Clifford," Madeline accepted and went off barking across the room.

There are many important benefits to reflective listening. In this example, acknowledging and reflecting Madeline's concerns without forcing solutions or attempting to distract her reduced her need to be oppositional and created a connection between Dennis and Madeline (Koplow, 2002). By encouraging children to talk about a problem or concern, you also encourage them to think about it and give them time to deal with their needs. Children are then free to figure out their own solutions. Chances are good that their solutions are similar to yours, but they are more likely to implement them because they are their own. Chances are also good that their solutions are more in tune with the child's perspective.

Cautions about Reflective Listening

When you practice reflective listening, be sure to watch for some common pitfalls. Most people find it very hard to avoid trying to give advice. Sometimes the tendency to take over the problem is shown by inappropriate probing questions, such as "Why do you think that happened?" or "When do you feel this way?"

Reflective listening is appropriate when the problem belongs to the child; remember to use "I messages" for your own problems. When the problem belongs to the child, the best solution is the child's own. If you decide how the problem should be solved, then you communicate a lack of respect for the child's problem-solving ability. You get in the way of children's learning when you try to figure out and solve their problems for them. The experience of personally resolving a problem teaches children how to do it and empowers them in the future. Besides, kids generally don't use adult solutions. If they do use an adult's solution, it only creates dependency.

Feeling Awkward or Phony   You may initially feel awkward when trying to find the right words for reflective listening. This type of listening involves telling the speaker what you heard him or her say, but it should be your own interpretation rather than mere parroting of the same words. When you provide your interpretation, you are asking for confirmation that you did understand the speaker's intent. The process of clarifying the message encourages the speaker to continue and to delve more deeply into the subject. By clarifying the idea for the listener, the speaker tends to clarify his or her own thinking.

The reflective-listening process may sound contrived to you at first, and you may feel like a phony paraphrasing back to someone what he or she just said to you. If you are honestly trying to understand what the other person is saying, however, your sincerity will come through. Keep focused on the other person's feelings and on accurate communication; then you will not only feel more comfortable with reflective listening, but you will also be a more effective listener. Your model will

Reflective listening involves using your own words to tell the speaker what you heard him or her say.

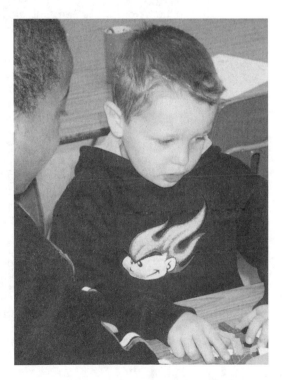

help children learn to be better listeners for one another, but few preschool or even primary grade children are capable of this sophisticated type of communication.

Children's Communication   Very young preschoolers not only can't do reflective listening, but they can't easily use words to tell us what is bothering them. Their vocabulary generally doesn't have precise words for feelings. In addition, they often lack a clear idea of what is bothering them. Reflective listening with very young children requires you to tune in to the children carefully and pay close attention to their nonverbal communication, as we saw in the Dennis and Madeline example. With children you know, you can usually get clues from their behavior about what is bothering them. You can follow up these clues by checking out your impressions with the child.

The process of reflecting these nonverbal messages is the same as reflecting back what you hear being said with words. Just as with oral communication, you may not receive the message accurately. Instead of immediately solving the problem you assume is at hand, you verbalize your hypotheses until you identify the actual concerns of the children involved.

> Jack grabbed the handlebar of Sam's tricycle, yanking him sideways. Sam tried to shove him away and screamed for the teacher. When Nancy arrived, Jack was saying, "Off! Off!" The teacher assumed he wanted to use a tricycle. There were other free trikes she could help him get, and she almost offered. But she thought she'd better check to see if that was really his problem. "You want to ride a trike?" she asked. Jack had planted himself firmly in front of the trike. "No, I want Sam off!" he replied, still clinging to Sam's handlebar.
>
> Nancy thought again, looking around for other clues. Then she saw the chalk dust smeared all over Jack's hands and clothes. Nancy looked ahead on the sidewalk and saw a big colored section. "It looks like you are worried Sam will drive over your picture," she guessed. Jack nodded, "yeah." Nancy then modeled some words Jack could use to ask Sam to please go around his drawing. They communicated to the best of their ability, and the conflict was resolved. Both boys returned to their play.

Cultural differences can present another barrier to reflective listening. For instance, some families discourage children from speaking their minds to adults (Lantieri & Patti, 1996). Some families also teach children not to look at people who are talking. So, if you are trying to use reflective listening with a child and you become frustrated that the child isn't looking at you, be sure to consider whether this is a cross-cultural misunderstanding.

HELPING CHILDREN RESOLVE CONFLICTS

Both reflective listening and "I messages" come in handy when conflicts arise. When your needs and the needs of a child conflict, sophisticated communication skills can help you to negotiate a solution. You can protect your own personal limits and still respect the needs of children. When youngsters experience conflict among themselves, you can coach them in using effective communication to resolve their differences. Your classroom can become a laboratory for learning the fine art of conflict resolution. This skill may be one of the most important subjects you can teach.

Many people think that conflict is bad and should be avoided; however, avoiding conflict usually means repressing feelings. Rarely can people live and work together in total harmony with no one's needs impinging on those of another. Conflict in the classroom and on the playground can be viewed as a learning opportunity. It is a chance for children to learn about the needs and wants of others, and it is also a chance for them to learn lifelong skills for mutual problem solving. In the process of practicing conflict resolution, children have the opportunity to learn more about perspective-taking, empathy, self-control, and collaboration (Landy, 2002; Wheeler, 2004).

Consistency in Schools

Schools have traditionally used a power model rather than a negotiation model (Gordon, 1989). Because children have so often seen adults use threats and intimidation as ways of resolving differences, it may take some effort to teach children a peaceful, respectful alternative. However, you will find it is worth the effort both to enhance the social skills of your students and to increase peace in your classroom.

Many of the social skills curriculum programs adopted by school districts include conflict resolution instruction based on the same principles of negotiation and consensus that Thomas Gordon described (e.g., Siccone & Lopez, 2000). The success of these programs may require that schools let go of authoritarian approaches to discipline. It is difficult to teach students a cooperative approach to resolving their problems if you model a different style when adult-to-child interactions are involved. If adults use a "power-on" model, instead of learning negotiation and cooperation, children learn that "might makes right." Children must feel trust, knowing that they are emotionally and physically safe, in order for conflict resolution to be successful (Levin, 2003).

Everyone Wins

Negotiating mutually acceptable solutions allows both sides to have power and respect. No one says, "You do it my way or else." No group says, "We have more votes. You lose." No one ends up angry and resentful. Therefore, general attitudes and relationships are more pleasant. Because everyone is involved in selecting the solutions, each person is more likely to follow through on them.

In addition, the solutions tend to be higher quality, reflecting the needs and ideas of all involved. The process helps children to consider the views of other people. Consideration of others and the thinking process involved in problem solving both contribute to the long-term goals of intellectual and moral autonomy. It takes a lot more work to get consensus than just to vote, but that's what makes negotiation such a great learning opportunity.

Mutual problem solving not only assists children toward long-term goals, but it also makes life more pleasant in the here and now. It relieves youngsters from the anger and the fear of punishment that accompany teacher-power approaches. It relieves the teacher from constantly having to nag, enforce, and police instead of teach. Mutual problem solving makes school a much more enjoyable and productive place for teachers and children.

Conflict Resolution Programs

The violence-prevention programs listed in the end of Chapter 6 include conflict resolution in their comprehensive approach. Some other programs for teaching conflict resolution are *Peacemaking Skills for Little Kids* (Schmidt & Freidman, 1992); *Teaching Conflict Resolution through Children's Literature* (Kreidler, 1999); and *Conscious Discipline* (Bailey, 2002). Gordon (1970, 1989) presents the basic model for peaceful negotiation and problem solving; many other authors present variations of these steps. Diane Levin's book, *Teaching Young Children in Violent Times: Building a Peaceable Classroom* (2003) is another helpful source on conflict resolution.

These programs are most successful when they are implemented schoolwide, so that not only the teachers, but also the playground and lunchroom aides, the principal, the librarian, and all adults in the school, treat children respectfully and know how to encourage peaceful conflict resolution. When parents are brought onto the team, the benefits are much greater. Even if your school doesn't adopt such a program, you will find that the materials offer helpful ideas for class discussions and activities to promote kindness, caring, and cooperation. Some programs, such as *Peacemaking Skills for Little Kids* (Schmidt & Friedman, 1992), suggest children's literature to help teach ideals of the caring community; others, like *Teaching Conflict Resolution through Children's Literature* (Kreidler, 1999), use children's stories as the main focus. Whether your school uses a formal program or not, you can informally help your students learn conflict resolution. When conflicts arise, you can support children in using the problem-solving approach to conflict resolution. Seizing the teachable moment is often more effective than any formal program (Curtis & Carter, 2000).

The chart "Sample Steps for Negotiating Solutions to Problems" shows the steps for several well-designed programs. We will use Gordon's model to discuss the basic steps.

Identifying the Problem

How does the problem-solving process work? You may begin the process in a class meeting or on the spot during a conflict. When children are very upset or angry, the process will be unsuccessful unless they have some time to calm themselves before beginning (Landy, 2002). In some programs, calming techniques like breathing are taught with the process. In others, children leave the scene of the conflict and go to a peace table (Schmidt & Freidman, 1992). Whatever the setting, the steps are the same. The first step in conflict resolution is identifying the problem. This step is where "I messages" come in to help each side express how its needs or expectations are not being met. Reflective listening is useful for hearing the other side, and often it's necessary for discovering the actual cause of the problem. If you see your role as the storyteller, you can remain objective and let the kids do their own work. Being a storyteller means describing both sides of a situation to all the children involved. You may also point out any feelings that the children are expressing. In the following example,

**SAMPLE STEPS FOR NEGOTIATING
SOLUTIONS TO PROBLEMS**

How are these alike and different?

Thomas Gordon's Steps:	*William Kreidler's Steps:*
1. Identify the problem.	A. Ask: What's the problem?
2. Generate solutions.	B. Brainstorm solutions.
3. Evaluate solutions.	C. Choose the best.
4. Make a decision.	D. Do it!
5. Implement the plan.	
6. Evaluate the plan.	

Peaceworks Steps (Schmidt & Friedman):

1. Keep both hands on the peace table while you are talking and listening. (Hands are for helping, not hurting.)
2. Tell the truth.
3. Listen without interrupting.
4. No name-calling or blaming.
5. List ideas to solve the problem.
6. Choose the best solution.

the teacher helps the children use conflict resolution and effective communication to solve their conflict.

> During the after-school child-care program, Ann, the program director, noticed some tension on the basketball court. "Hey guys," Ann said as she approached, "looks like you've got a problem."
> "They won't let us have the ball!" complained the younger children.
> "They won't, huh?" she reflected. The kids responded by telling her more about the situation. "They never throw the ball to us," said some of the younger children. "They always lose the ball when they dribble down the court," retorted some of the older children. Ann summed up their comments without blaming either side and defined the problem as a shared one (Levin, 2003), "You both have a problem here don't you. Everyone wants a chance with the ball, and the way you were playing doesn't give you both time with the ball. It's no fun for you younger kids to be left out and it's frustrating for you older kids to keep losing the ball to the other team." The kids were obviously glad that Ann understood and confirmed her thoughts about what they were feeling.

Brainstorming Solutions

Once the problem is identified, everyone involved needs to help think of possible solutions. Many conflict resolution programs include setting limits about blaming or criticizing any specific children during this step (Rightmyer, 2003). No idea is too wild, and no ideas are rejected at this point. In fact, no ideas should even be evaluated yet. Be sure to continue getting ideas until everyone has run out of possibilities. Sometimes, writing down all the ideas where everyone can see them is helpful, even if the children are too young to read yet. You can refer to the list as you review, and they will recognize their ideas.

> Ann asked all of the children, "Can you think of what you could do so that everyone can play and have some time with the ball?" The group proposed many ideas, and Ann wrote them on a big piece of paper so all could see.
> "Big kids play and then little kids have a turn," suggested Will, a competitive and competent player.
> "Little kids play an easier game," offered Abby, trying to be helpful.
> "Don't take the ball when we dribble," Eli said assertively.
> That seemed to spark an idea for Blake: "I know!" he said excitedly. "Let's make a rule that the little kids can either dribble the ball or they can hold it and run down the court."
> "OK," chimed in Riley. "And when they dribble, no big kids can try to get it; but if they carry it, we can try to get it away."
> The brainstorming seemed over at this point and it was time for the next step in problem solving.

Evaluating Solutions and Making a Choice

The next step is to evaluate the suggestions. Which ones are just impossible or totally unacceptable to someone? Cross those out immediately. Now what is left? Do any of them stand out as great ideas? Continue the discussion until everyone agrees to try one or a combination of solutions. Make sure the children understand that choosing a solution means a commitment to carrying it out. Voting is not a part of the process. This is a consensus model: Everyone agrees to try a solution, and no one is forced into it by a "someone loses" or "minorities lose" method, such as a vote.

> Choosing among the suggestions for the basketball conflict didn't take long. Will held out a bit for his idea of the big kids playing without the little kids, but the little kids nixed that one. There was lots of support for the idea of new rules that created some equality between older players and younger ones. Consensus soon emerged around that plan, and the new basketball rules were clarified.

Implementing the Plan

There's more to the process than simply determining a solution. A plan isn't worth much unless you figure out how to implement it. Who will do what? When and how often? Where and how? To what standards? Who checks? When children make these kinds of decisions and plan to implement them, they tend to follow through with little teacher direction.

> Blake and Riley felt ownership of the new plan. They took leadership roles in setting up teams of fairly equal ability and getting the game going again. All the children reminded one another of the new rules as they played.

Evaluating the Plan

What if the solution doesn't work? There are many reasons why it might not. Perhaps it was too difficult to implement or perhaps there were conditions you and the children neglected to consider. Evaluating the solution after you have tried it for a while is an essential final step. If you find that things aren't working, that situation isn't a signal for you to take over. It just means that the group needs to try again to generate workable solutions.

> Ann watched with pleasure as the game went on for a full 45 minutes without a single problem. What a relief! Complaints and arguments had been the main event on the basketball court for days. In addition, she noticed that these new rules encouraged the younger children to practice dribbling the ball. The older children were now working in partnership with the younger ones on their team, giving them the ball and urging them to dribble it, since that protected it from being stolen. Everyone seemed to be having a good time.

Ann checked with the group the next day after school, asking them how their new "big kid—little kid" rules worked out. There seemed to be unanimous agreement that they worked great.

Saving Time

Does conflict resolution sound like it takes a lot of time? This is a common concern. Sometimes problem solving can be accomplished in just a few minutes; at other times, it does take quite a lot of time. However, if you have a recurring problem, that takes a lot of time, too. Teachers and parents who use this problem-solving approach report that it saves a lot of time in the long run. Instead of ineffectively dealing with the same problem over and over, time is set aside to deal effectively with the problem until it is resolved. The time spent on this problem-solving session was certainly time well spent for Ann; the problem had been disrupting play and dividing the group for quite some time.

Independent Problem Solvers

You can save yourself time and trouble by teaching youngsters to negotiate solutions to their own problems. The model you provide in group problem solving is an important part of this teaching, but you will need to talk children through the process individually while they are learning. Teaching conflict resolution during class meetings is a great way to work toward fostering independent problem solvers. You can begin teaching the process slowly starting with the first two steps. Later you can work with the kids on evaluating the solutions and choosing the best one. Eventually the kids will be able to do these steps in one sitting. Gradually you can add in the implementation and evaluation of plans.

You can teach these steps as you work on real class issues. Some teachers have a sign-up sheet available for children to record their name or an issue that will be solved through conflict resolution during class meeting (Adams & Wittmer, 2001). The use of puppets and children's literature is also a great way to bring up

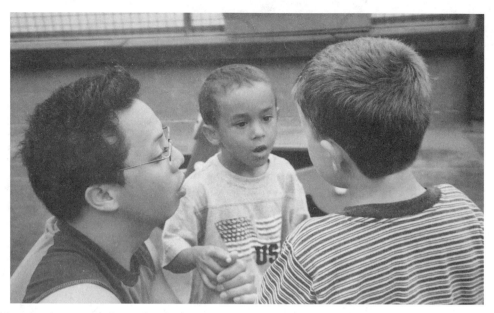

Taking the time to teach conflict resolution skills helps children learn how to solve their own problems independently.

conflicts to discuss with groups of young children. There are many sources for finding meaningful children's books and tips on how to use them, such as *Teaching Conflict Resolution Through Children's Literature* (Kreidler, 1999) and *Class Meetings: Young Children Solving Problems Together* (Vance & Weaver, 2002). When using children's stories, you can ask questions that help children apply the lessons to their own lives.

If you continually practice the same steps for conflict resolution with individual children and in your class meetings, it will come naturally to the children. It takes practice for teachers, too, to ask meaningful questions that allow children to solve their own problems during this process (Koplow, 2002). Kreidler's (1999) simplified *ABCD* version of negotiation is probably easiest for children to remember: A. Ask: What's the problem? B. Brainstorm solutions. C. Choose the best. D. Do it! Let's see how Jacob and Blake work out their problem at the sand table.

Jacob and Blake were trying to play together at the sand table again, but as always, they had very different game plans. Jacob was trying to make carefully groomed patterns in the sand. Blake was chugging around with a bulldozer, trying to get all of the sand up against the edges, exposing the bottom.

Jacob complained as the bulldozer kept undermining his space, making the patterns sluff away. Mrs. Jensen observed the conflict and got things rolling by helping them define the problem. "It looks like you two are getting in each other's way here," she commented. Then she suggested that the boys try to brainstorm a way to play together at the sand table.

Jacob frowned, wishing the teacher would just tell Blake to stop ruining his work. Then Mrs. Jensen reminded him, "You guys have been solving problems so well during our class meeting. I bet you could come up with a way to fix this one!" Jacob brightened up.

Mrs. Jensen then asked, "Do you remember how to brainstorm solutions?" Blake had liked that part; anything you thought of was okay, so you could be silly or serious. Blake was silly: "Measure every grain of sand and divide it exactly!" Jacob got into it and offered, "We could take turns at the sand table." "I know! We could build the Great Wall of China, and neither one could cross it!" Blake said excitedly, remembering a picture he had seen of the wall. Jacob thought again and came up with one last idea: "Blake could play with the funnels instead of the bulldozer."

Mrs. Jensen reminded the boys that choosing the best solution meant they had to both agree on a solution to try. Measuring sounded like a challenge and both boys thought it would be too hard. Taking turns was rejected because neither wanted to be second, and Blake wasn't interested in playing with the funnels. But the "Great Wall" idea intrigued both of the boys. They asked if they could use some blocks in the sand table to make a barrier wall.

Mrs. Jensen thought to herself that the idea might not work but told them to go ahead anyway. They were eager to try out their solution. It didn't perfectly hold back sand, but it was completely effective at resolving the conflict between the boys. Whenever it collapsed, they ignored their patterns and bulldozing to rebuild their barrier cooperatively, the new major focus!

If you teach children how to negotiate their own solutions, soon they will be teaching each other and won't constantly be coming to you with their arguments or to tattle-tale (Rightmyer, 2003). Even preschool-age children are capable of problem solving. In the past, adults generally just separated children who were in conflict, or else the teacher decided who was in the right and would "win." Teaching children to arrive at a mutually satisfying solution to their disagreements is a more productive use of your time (Watson, 1999). In the process of learning to problem-solve, your young students will learn about peaceful negotiation of differences. Perhaps they will even put this skill to work as adults, possibly helping the people of the world to resolve their differences peacefully.

FAMILY AND COMMUNITY

Imagine what a different world it would be if children grew up feeling so cared for that they could never imagine doing harm to themselves or anyone else! What if families, schools, and communities worked together to protect children and teach them, by example, about cooperation and caring for others? Would the United States still spend more on the prison system than on education? Is it conceivable that schools could be a model for families and communities? When children know they are valued, worthy of time and attention, heard, and treated with kindness and respect, they will pass this treatment along to others they encounter throughout their lives.

Comprehensive violence-prevention programs, such as the Resolving Conflict Creatively Program (RCCP), teach effective communication and peaceful conflict resolution to teachers, children, parents, and school administration and staff. Using this program in a school for only one year showed some encouraging results: "92% of children felt better about themselves; and more than 90% of parents reported an increase in their own communication and problem-solving skills" (Lantieri, 2003, p. 84).

We believe that any approach that enables schools to model and teach respectful and peaceful communication to children and parents will have a positive impact that echoes throughout our communities. If children internalize these skills when they are young and continue experiencing and using them throughout their growing years, the implications for their adult years are staggering. Maybe they would become world leaders able to peacefully resolve international disputes, without war? Maybe child abuse and domestic violence would only be a bad memory of our past? These are lofty goals, we realize. However, starting with one classroom in one school, building positive relationships with children and their families is well within your realm of possibility. Through your example, class meetings, and other integrated classroom activities, children can learn how to treat others with kindness. Through workshops, newsletters, community events, and your own interactions with *families*, they can also learn more effective and peaceful communication skills. If more teachers and schools used this approach, the impact would be well worth the effort.

CONCLUSION

When we communicate with children respectfully, we can prevent many discipline problems and solve many others. When we state our own needs respectfully, children are more apt to behave considerately in the first place and are generally more willing to change their behavior if it has become inappropriate. By reflectively listening to children, we can help them resolve their own problems, either before their behavior is adversely affected or in time to remedy the situation. When we teach problem-solving skills, children learn to avoid disputes as well as to resolve them. Communicating with kindness and respect, and teaching children to do the same, has far-reaching implications. Our dedication in the beginning of this book reflects the aim of our interactions with children. This book was written "For the cause of worldwide peace and harmony. May it begin in the hearts of children and spread. And may teachers be the sowers of the seeds of peace and harmony."

∞ FOR FURTHER THOUGHT

1. Listen to adults talking to children. Think about those same words used with another adult. Do they sound ridiculous or reasonable? Analyze your own ways of talking to children. Do you show less respect to children than to your adult acquaintances?

2. Practice using "I messages" when someone upsets you. What are the

results? Were you careful not to send a disguised "you message"? Were you able to stop yourself from also telling the other person what to do or not to do? Keep on trying. It takes time to break old habits.

3. Practice reflective listening with friends who confide in you about a problem. Be careful not to give advice or reassurance, but only to clarify your understanding of the other person's feelings. How does this attitude affect the communication? Is it difficult to do?

4. A problem to solve: Angie comes to you complaining because another child is using the swing and she wants to swing.
   a. Describe a common ineffective response.

   b. Describe a reflective-listening response.

5. A problem to solve: Matt and Jason are experimenting with magnets at preschool. Jason goes off to play elsewhere, and Matt starts crying.
   a. What might a teacher say who is skilled in reflective listening?
   b. What might a teacher say who doesn't understand about roadblocks to communication?

6. Try out the steps to negotiating conflicts as described in this chapter. Analyze the results to learn how to be more effective in the future.

∽ RECOMMENDED READINGS

Adams, S. K., & Wittmer, D. S. (2001). I had it first: Teaching young children to solve problems peacefully. *Childhood Education, 78*(1), 10–17.

Faber, A., & Mazlish, E. (1996). *How to talk so kids can learn at home and in school.* New York: Fireside/Simon & Schuster.

Ginott, H. (1965). *Between parent and child: New solutions to old problems.* New York: Macmillan.

Gordon, T. (1970). *Parent effectiveness training.* New York: Wyden.

Gordon, T. (1974). *T.E.T.: Teacher effectiveness training.* New York: Wyden.

Gordon, T. (1989). *Teaching children self-discipline: At home and at school.* New York: Random House.

Kreidler, W. J. (1999). *Teaching conflict resolution through children's literature.* New York: Scholastic.

Levin. D. E. (2003). *Teaching young children in violent times: Building a peaceable classroom* (2nd ed.). Washington, DC: National Association for the Education of Young Children.

Schmidt, F., & Friedman, A. (1992). *Peacemaking skills for little kids.* Fresno, CA: Peace Works Inc.

Siccone, F., & Lopez, L. (2000). *Educating the heart: Lessons to build respect and responsibility.* Boston: Allyn & Bacon.

Vance, E., & Weaver, P. (2002). *Class meetings: Young children solving problems together.* Washington, DC: National Association for the Education of Young Children.

8 Helping Children Understand and Accept Limits

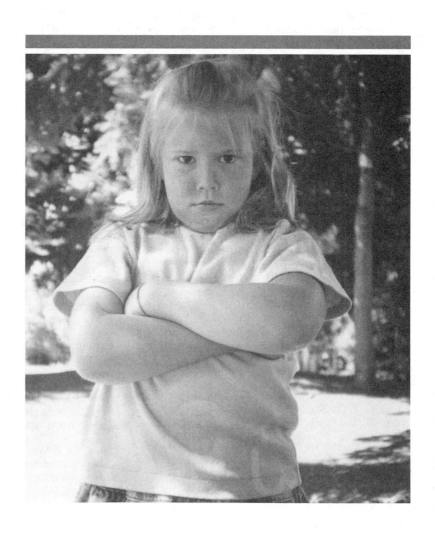

$\mathcal{W}$hat do you do if prevention, modeling, listening, and problem solving don't work? What if you need to change a behavior immediately? What do you do when it's too late to prevent a problem because it is already happening? Do you then turn to punishment?

Natural and related consequences, not punishment, provide the answer. We are definitely making a distinction between consequences and punishment here. It is consequences, not punishment, that provide effective, immediate results compatible with long-term, positive outcomes. Punishment merely affects the immediate response and generally produces negative side effects. With related consequences, you can teach toward long-term discipline goals while still enforcing limits. And don't forget: discipline that ignores the cause of the problem is pretty worthless. The best use of consequences as a discipline tool is when the undesirable behavior is caused by a child's lack of understanding. Children's understanding is the goal of using consequences as a teaching tool.

Related consequences emphasize and clarify limits; they communicate through actions that certain behaviors will not be tolerated. At the same time, related consequences help children learn why that behavior is undesirable, giving them personal reasons to change. Instead of merely forcing children to do what adults know is best, related consequences help youngsters reflect on the consequences of their actions. Related consequences use children's own experiences as the basis for teaching desirable behavior. In the process, this form of discipline helps develop the personal responsibility necessary for self-discipline and moral autonomy. At the same time, this kind of discipline respects the child's right and ability to choose more appropriate action.

The concept of related consequences has been described in different terms by various authors. Publications by Piaget (1965/1932) and Dreikurs (1964) laid the foundation for the idea; subsequently, others have continued to explore why and how this discipline approach works (e.g., Charney, 2002; Flicker & Hoffman, 2002; Kamii, 1982, 1984; Reynolds, 2000).

In *The Moral Judgment of the Child* (1965/1932), Piaget points out the arbitrary nature of punishment and its lack of relation to the misbehavior as reasons for not using this approach. Piaget describes several types of alternative discipline strategies in contrast with punishment. He recommends five results of misbehavior that help children move toward moral autonomy. These results may or may not be imposed by an adult; they may simply occur as the natural outcome of the child's actions or may happen within the child's peer group in response to antisocial behavior.

1. Natural consequences: The child experiences the direct results of his or her own behavior. Piaget uses the example of a child who has a cold room as a result of breaking his or her own bedroom window.

2. Exclusion: The child who is harming others may not play with the other children until the behavior changes.

3. Deprivation: The child may not have access to materials that have been abused or misused until the behavior changes.

4. Restitution: The child pays for, or replaces, that which has been damaged or lost; the child assists a person injured through that child's fault.

5. Reciprocity: What the child has done to another is done back to the child. Piaget is very clear that this response does not mean an adult doing evil for evil, such as biting a child who has bitten another. He says that action is not only a poor model but also "absurd" (Piaget, 1965/1932, p. 208). Instead, he refers to a response such as not doing a favor for a child who has not helped with assigned chores. Thus, if the child doesn't help you, you don't help the child.

Dreikurs's concept of natural and logical consequences is basically the same as Piaget's alternatives to punishment. In his book *Children: The Challenge* (1964), Dreikurs explained consequences and elaborated on the concept in his subsequent writing (Dreikurs, Greenwald, & Pepper, 1998). *Natural consequences* are those that automatically result from the child's behavior with no intervention from an adult. According to Dreikurs, *logical consequences* are those imposed by an adult but linked to the child's actions.

In this book, we blend the viewpoints of Piaget and Dreikurs. We prefer the simplicity of a distinction between consequences that happen without adult intervention and those that require such intervention. Therefore, like Dreikurs, we make a distinction between natural consequences and imposed consequences. To emphasize the necessity of consequences being related to the behavior, we chose the term *related consequences* for imposed consequences that help a child learn. We find Piaget's several categories of consequences helpful in remembering to consider a variety of options in discipline situations. Keep in mind that some outcomes in these categories may also occur naturally or within the child's social group.

It is important to remember that related consequences are designed to help children think: think about why certain behaviors are unacceptable and others are desirable. This is a teaching approach in which punishment has no place; Chapter 10 explains why punishment actually stops such thinking. Consequences are designed to help children view themselves as capable and willing problem solvers. Punishment tends to have the opposite effect, making children consider themselves bad and teaching them to be sneaky to avoid being caught (Kamii, 1984). Punishment will be discussed further in Chapters 9 and 10.

NATURAL CONSEQUENCES

Both Piaget and Dreikurs recommend allowing children to experience the results of their actions when possible. Natural consequences are mostly a matter of getting out of the way and allowing children to learn from their experiences. Too often adults deprive children of the chance to experience the consequences of their actions because they care about the children and don't want them to have unpleasant or disappointing experiences. Unfortunately, the result is that the children don't become responsible for their own actions (Kamii, 1982). The following example is a type that most teachers see frequently:

Travis forgot his gym shoes again. It was gym day, and the P.E. teacher would not let the children participate unless they had on the proper shoes. But Travis wasn't worried; he was confident that his mom would bring his shoes for him. Sure enough, Travis's mother arrived soon, harried and disgruntled at having to fit this errand into her day's schedule. She was cross with Travis and fumed, "Why are you so irresponsible? I even reminded you this morning. You never listen."

What has Travis learned here? Instead of learning that he needs to remember his gym shoes if he wants to participate in P.E., he has learned to depend on his mother. He has become convinced that he is, indeed, irresponsible and that his mother needs to take responsibility for him. Instead of having the experience of not getting to play in the gym, Travis experiences his mother's anger. Anger teaches nothing; it only brings resentment and retaliation. It focuses the child's attention on the "mean" adult instead of on his or her own behavior. It deprives him of the opportunity to think about and learn from the outcome of his own actions.

Avoiding Overprotection

Mrs. Jensen does try hard not to protect children from learning through their mistakes. She reminds herself not to take over their responsibilities when they forget. She doesn't nag, coax, and remind children to do the things they are supposed to remember on their own. Mrs. Jensen thinks that youngsters learning to take responsibility for themselves is more important than making sure everyone remembers to take home the book order list or even the class newsletter. She teaches effectively by helping them to figure out the cause-and-effect relationship between their actions and the results. They soon find out that they don't get to buy a book if they don't take the book order form home, get permission and money to place an order, and then return the form with the money to school. She knows that children learn through their experiences and that learning takes time.

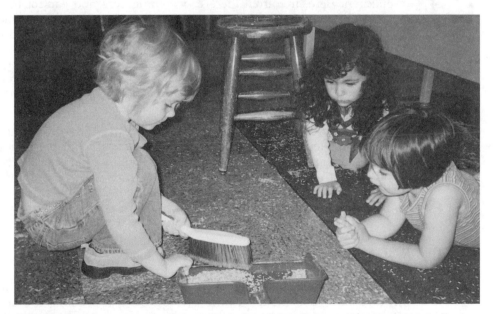

Related consequences are designed to help children figure out the cause-and-effect relationship between their actions and the results.

The real world offers much more opportunity for natural consequences than school does. By its nature, school is an artificial environment that doesn't allow much opportunity for natural responses. At home, Mrs. Jensen can allow her own children to learn much more freely from their mistakes than she can at school with her students. If her own children don't put away their things at home, they naturally get lost. At school, the custodian picks things up and gets cross when they are lying around. When her own children go running outside without a coat on a cool day, she lets them find out for themselves that they need to come back for a coat. At school, she worries that parents will think she is shirking her responsibility if she lets her students go out to recess without coats. Besides, school rules don't allow youngsters to run back inside for coats in the middle of recess. Mrs. Jensen has trouble allowing for natural consequences at school.

The Inevitable Does Happen

Although teachers and parents are often uncomfortable with allowing natural consequences, children still manage to experience them often. They will build an unstable block tower and experience its collapse. From this natural consequence they can begin to learn about balance, physical limits, and maybe the way hard blocks feel when they land in their lap. That is, they will learn if some overprotective adult doesn't stop them by controlling their constructions. Social behavior and friendships are also molded a great deal by natural consequences (Rizzo, 1989). A child who repeatedly hurts others physically or hurts their feelings may reap the consequence of peer rejection, as in the following example:

> On the playground at Lincoln Elementary School, the ratio is 2 aides to 250 children. Here, free from the ever-watching eyes and ears of the classroom teacher, the children learn how to get along on their own. Allison had been particularly bossy to her table mates in class one morning. She told Rosa to get out of the book corner and ordered Ling Ling to clean up her mess. When Allison came out for recess, they all avoided her, leaving her out of their games. She complained, "Why can't I play?" Rosa answered directly, "Cause you always have to be the boss!" Allison was experiencing a delayed natural consequence for her earlier behavior.

The teacher can help Allison by helping her to think through this experience, not by saving her from it. Although showing sympathy for her hurt feelings is appropriate, fixing the problem Allison created will not help her learn. Some adults would insist that no child should be left out; this would ruin Allison's lesson. A much kinder teacher response is to encourage Allison to think about how she might act differently in the future in order to be accepted on the playground.

RELATED CONSEQUENCES

Related consequences are useful when natural consequences won't work. Not only do school rules make natural consequences impossible at times, but also the natural consequences in many situations are unacceptable. Adults do have the responsibility of keeping children safe from harm. Obviously, no one allows a child to experience the natural consequences of playing in the street. Instead, adults watch carefully and plan related consequences to help youngsters learn to stay away from traffic.

Different teachers have varying views on the safety issue as it relates to consequences. Some let children use paring knives to prepare fruit salad, supervising the use but realizing that a small cut may be the occasional result. They feel that the minimally unpleasant experience is a natural consequence that will teach care with knives. Others might be willing to use that method with their own children but don't feel comfortable doing so with other people's children. It is a matter of personal comfort level, as are the varying amounts of risk that different parents allow their children. However, there is general agreement that children cannot be allowed to take risks that could result in serious injury. Therefore, adult-imposed consequences are often the only learning experiences available. Following are examples of several different types of related consequences. Note that the purpose in each case is to help children relate their behavior to its results.

Reciprocity

At home, Mrs. Jensen is likely to use a reciprocity consequence by not driving Betsy to her friend's house because Betsy didn't finish helping with household chores. This differs from punishment due to the connection between Betsy not helping her mom and her mom not helping Betsy. At school, it is more often the children who impose consequences of reciprocity. For instance, Nicole may not help Karina with her project because Karina got mad and messed up Nicole's project last time they worked together. Mrs. Jensen helps Karina to learn from this experience and doesn't insist on her inclusion. What if Sam hits Zach? Do you allow the consequence of reciprocity, in which Zach hits him back? Occasionally, Dennis decides that this response is the learning experience one of his preschoolers needs. Perhaps the child hasn't had enough social interaction to realize that hitting gets a negative response from peers. In that case, Dennis pretends not to notice what is happening; of course he cannot appear to condone hitting. In the rare times he might allow it, Dennis definitely keeps an eye out to be sure no one really gets hurt.

Exclusion

Usually, however, Dennis doesn't allow hitting and uses related consequences, as in the following example using the consequence Piaget (1965/1932) called exclusion:

> Sam wanted to play with Zach after nap time. Unfortunately, Zach was waking up slowly and just wanted to be left alone. Frustrated, Sam got increasingly aggressive and eventually resorted to physical contact to get Zach's attention. Action escalated from nudges to pushing, and then to hitting. Zach wailed and Dennis intervened. Sensing that Zach was in no condition to verbalize his need for privacy at the moment, Dennis chose to impose the consequence of removing Sam, explaining that he could not let him hit Zach. "Hitting hurts," Dennis

said as he calmly took Sam to the next room. He told the child, "You may go back to the sun room when you are ready to use your words instead of hitting. Zach is hurt and he needs to feel safe."

Notice that Dennis did not tell Sam how long he had to stay away from Zach. Instead of using his adult power to make all the decisions here, Dennis allowed the child to be in charge of how much time he needed. He allowed Sam to reflect on his own actions and to decide when his feelings were under control. This approach helped Sam learn to take responsibility for himself and become more autonomous.

There is a fine line between time-out and a related consequence of exclusion. Therefore, this type of consequence needs to be used cautiously and carefully. Time-out damages community by banishing a child from the group (Howes & Ritchie, 2002); related consequences seek to keep the child as part of the group while providing time space for reflection. Ideally, a teacher or aide can stay with the child to support the thinking process and encourage rejoining the activity as soon as possible. If there is only one adult with the group, then it is best to keep the child nearby, possibly participating from a different spot.

Deprivation

Chapter 1 mentioned the problem of Kenji knocking over other children's block constructions. In addition to helping Kenji learn a better way of showing that he wants to play, the teacher might also explain to Kenji that he cannot play with the blocks until he is ready to play without damaging anyone else's constructions. This is an example of the consequence involving deprivation: not being allowed to use materials that were misused. Dreikurs (1964) introduced the idea that children must be allowed to determine when they are ready to try again to get along with their friends. Telling Kenji he may not play in the block area until he decides he can play without knocking over other children's work is very different from simply removing him. Asking him to decide when he is ready to return gives him the message that you have faith in his ability to make the necessary adjustments in his behavior.

Restitution

The example from Chapter 1 in which Aaron wipes up the water he spilled is also a related consequence. Cleaning up the mess you make is a way of making restitution, a method that Piaget (1965/1932) recommends. Restitution is our favorite type of related consequence, one that isn't likely to get mixed up with punishment. An example of making restitution that we particularly like involves children who hurt each other through carelessness. If Dylan is throwing rocks and one accidentally hits Jessie, Dylan learns much more about the dangers of rock throwing by holding a cold cloth to Jessie's head than by being banished to the principal's office. Kenji and the block destruction could also be handled with restitution. If it seemed appropriate to the circumstances, the teacher might ask him to help rebuild what he knocked down. Making restitution helps youngsters see themselves as helpful people rather than bad ones. All of these examples describe ways of motivating children to build rules of conduct for themselves from within.

Consequences are not the same thing as punishment. Consequences teach understanding; they do not hurt or humiliate.

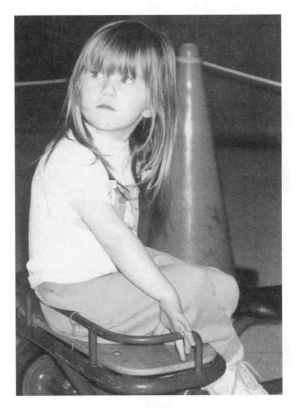

Combining with Other Teaching

In a situation like the one with Sam hitting Zach, be sure you don't ignore the child's feelings that lead up to an incident, although this doesn't mean you should interrogate the children to determine who started it. An interrogation would put the adult back in charge of the kids' behavior. Instead, think about how you can help the children deal with their feelings or learn needed skills.

Imposing consequences to stop the hitting doesn't preclude the use of other guidance techniques. For instance, after Sam and Zach have calmed down from the incident, you could work with them on the communications skills discussed in Chapter 7. Each boy could be helped to tune in to his feelings and put them into words. Hitting is often a primitive form of communication; learning higher-level communication skills can help a child give up hitting.

CONSEQUENCES OR PUNISHMENT?

Many people use the term "consequence" when they really mean "punishment." "He has to face the consequences," often means a spanking or loss of privilege. In this book we are trying to make a distinction between punishment and consequences. Consequences respond to a behavior problem in a way designed to solve the problem rather than to punish the child. As they were originally described (Dreikurs, 1964), consequences were not intended to be punitive. Yet many people began using that "nicer" term when they really meant punishment, and as a result the terms became confused. Alfie Kohn's (1996) position against consequences appears to be based on such misuse of the term.

Use Consequences with Caution

Nevertheless, related consequences can easily turn into punishment if the adult is not careful (Charney, 2002). Because the adult administers them, they demonstrate adult power over children. For this reason, other less-intrusive methods of discipline should be tried first. Prevention of problems is the least intrusive approach to discipline. Teaching by example, coaching, "I messages," and conflict negotiation all teach discipline without the use of adult power.

However, if none of those approaches works on the cause of the misbehavior, then another approach is needed. If a lack of understanding is the behavior cause, then consequences can be used to help the child understand. Also, there are times when judicious, respectful, and limited use of adult power is required in order to keep children safe. If safety guidelines are being tested, it may be time to plan a related consequence. These are the two reasons to rely on consequences as discipline: (1) to teach understanding or (2) to enforce necessary limits while you work on the cause of a behavior problem.

The big difference between punishment and consequences is in how they make children feel about themselves. Punishment convinces a child that he or she is "bad" and damages self-esteem. Consequences aim to empower children in their efforts at self-control and to help them see themselves as good people (Brady et al., 2003). An example of consequences empowering children is the emphasis on giving them the power to decide when they are "ready" to return to a situation from which they were removed. Restitution consequences are an example of consequences helping children see themselves as good people as well as people who can remedy their mistakes.

Plan Ahead

Sometimes it's hard to remember the judicious and respectful aspects of related consequences. Imposed consequences can quickly lead to a power struggle for the unwary adult. Remember Dennis's problem with the "no lunch until you clean up your mess" ultimatum in Chapter 4? Dennis had a practical rationale for that ruling: He wanted to clear the room for lunch. However, it was really Dennis, and not the situation, that was depriving Amy of her lunch. Amy's dress-up clothes weren't on the lunch table, and she couldn't see any reason why they had to be put away before she could eat. Dennis had only his power as an adult to enforce his hasty ultimatum, and that power led to the confrontation. Effective consequences strive for adult withdrawal from power rather than an application of power. Fortunately, Dennis's ego allowed him to back down, listen reflectively, and negotiate a solution with the child.

Related consequences take planning and forethought. The connection between the child's behavior and the results must be clear to the child. Dreikurs

(1964/1991) reminds parents that there is no relationship between not taking out the garbage and not getting to watch television. He suggests that there may be a relationship between a parent's refusal to fix dinner and a kitchen with smelly garbage. Therefore, being deprived of television is a form of punishment, while not fixing dinner is a consequence reasonably related to the situation.

Notice, too, that the adult must assert power over the child to enforce the no-television ruling, but refusing to fix dinner affects only the adults's own behavior. A bonus of this approach: You are much less likely to get into a power struggle if your consequence affects your own behavior instead of someone else's.

Watch Your Attitude

Even an excellent related consequence can be turned into punishment however. For instance, if the adult expresses anger about the garbage, then not fixing dinner will come through as a retaliation rather than a consequence. Instead, the parent might use an "I message" and say, "I don't want to fix dinner until the garbage is out. The garbage makes the kitchen smell too bad for me to be in there cooking." It is important to be calm and matter-of-fact about imposing consequences. In fact, it is important not to be angry, or your anger will be all that is heard. Effective consequences involve adult intervention without anger or recrimination (Brady et al., 2002).

If you use the impending consequences as a threat, that treatment also turns them into punishment (Dreikurs, Greenwald, & Pepper, 1998). "Take that garbage out before I come home from work, or no dinner tonight" is not in the spirit of related consequences. There are times when you want to inform children in advance of consequences, but it needs to be done in a nonthreatening and calm manner.

Variations of the "I told you so" theme are another way to ruin the educational value of related consequences (Dreikurs, 1964/1991). Perhaps, in addition to not fixing dinner, the parent might be tempted to say, "Maybe that will teach you a lesson." These words take the focus away from the actual problem and invite an angry power struggle. Often it is better to say nothing. Let the consequences speak for themselves.

The bottom line is respecting children. If you take away a child's dignity as you deal with his or her behavior, you damage that child. Sarcasm and humiliation have no role in teaching better behavior. Instead of trying to avenge a wrong, the helpful approach is to work on a solution to the problem. A constructive guidance approach using consequences looks for ways to make things right again. Helping a child make restitution to someone he or she has harmed is probably the most useful consequence of all.

SELECTING REASONABLE CONSEQUENCES

As a result of trying to think up reasonable consequences, Mrs. Jensen sometimes finds that there really is no good reason why some actions aren't acceptable. What was the reason for the rule against water in the sand table? She knows that children will more easily accept limits when they can see their value. She believes children deserve an explanation of reasons why certain behaviors are unacceptable. If she can't think of such an explanation, she is inclined to allow the behavior. Sometimes her decision means not conforming to school traditions, such as walking in lines.

> Walking through school hallways in regimented lines under the stern gaze of the teacher is a time-honored tradition. Yet Mrs. Jensen can't convince herself that lines are necessary or helpful.
>
> Why shouldn't youngsters be allowed to walk in quiet groups like adults? Won't they learn more about respecting others if they are in charge of their own behavior than if the teacher is standing guard? Won't many behavior problems be solved if kids aren't walking so close together and don't all have to go at the same time? Mrs. Jensen sees many children poking the child in front of them just from the sheer frustration of waiting until everyone is ready.
>
> She has been working to teach her students about walking through the halls without disturbing other classes or blocking the hallway for people coming in the opposite direction. She finds this approach a much more productive use of her energy than enforcing the lines.
>
> It is much easier for Mrs. Jensen to explain to her students the importance of not bothering others than to explain why they have to stay in a line. She feels good about the time spent helping children learn to be independent in the halls. She leads class discussions about what hall behaviors would bother other classrooms. During these discussions, Mrs. Jensen sees careful thinking; the children are definitely making progress in understanding the views of others. She sees children feeling important and proud as they practice being responsible for their own behavior in the hallway. Children who continually forget about thoughtful behavior can be helped to remember by experiencing a consequence. Mrs. Jensen simply asks forgetful children to walk with her until they think they can manage on their own.

You probably have seen a child being punished for hallway misbehavior by having to walk with the teacher and you may be wondering why we are calling this a consequence and not a punishment. Notice that the child only walks with the teacher until the child decides he or she can manage alone. Giving the child this power is important. Also remember that the adult attitude toward the child is a key factor in the difference between punishment and consequences. A helpful attitude is much different from an angry one and makes a child feel much differently about walking with the teacher. Of course, the way the child feels about the teacher in general also plays a part. Your relationship with each child is the foundation for any guidance or discipline approach.

Clear Teaching Goals

Living and working harmoniously in a group requires great mutual consideration and cooperation (DeVries & Zan, 1994). Related consequences can be very useful in helping children develop and remember these attitudes. Mrs. Jensen plans this part of her curriculum as carefully as the academic aspects. As she plans, she keeps in mind her goal of assisting the children's growth toward autonomy. She

Teaching social responsibility through related consequences requires as much careful planning as teaching academics.

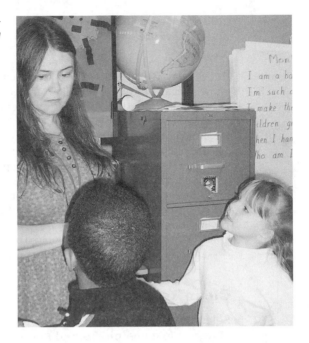

wants to give them freedom while helping them understand that freedom implies responsibility.

This responsibility includes not impinging on the freedom of others, such as the rights of other classrooms not to be disturbed. Mrs. Jensen's plans are also built around the principle of respect for each child, which she demonstrates through her belief in the child's ability and desire to behave responsibly. She firmly believes that all people, including children, have an equal claim to dignity and respect. She likes the way Dr. Seuss puts it in *Horton Hears a Who* (Geisel, 1954): "A person's a person, no matter how small."

Mrs. Jensen employs a variety of strategies to help her students determine the value of mutual consideration and cooperation. In addition to imposing related consequences, she also demonstrates desirable attitudes and behaviors through personal example. She makes sure that the class environment encourages harmonious social interaction, too. The best approach to guidance and discipline is usually a combination of approaches.

Careful Thought

Related consequences are supposed to help children judge the pros and cons of a certain behavior as they experience the ramifications. Therefore, consequences must be selected carefully. Besides picking something related to the behavior, you need to think of a consequence that matters to kids. Telling them they have to hurry up or they'll be late may carry no clout if being late isn't important to the child. The consequence also needs to be something that you can live with and are actually willing to follow through with, unlike Joanne's threat:

> The children kept running across the plot that had been rototilled for a garden at Midway Children's Center. They delighted in how the fluffy soil felt! The parent who had promised to build a fence to protect it kept putting off the job. Joanne tried steering the children away, telling them that the ground would get packed down too hard to plant in, but they had no concept of the problem. As yet another group raced through the garden area, she gave up. Crossly, she told them, "That does it! We just won't have a garden if you step in there again!" Intimidated by her anger, the children avoided the tempting dirt for most of the afternoon.
>
> Then Kenji blew it. Right before pickup time, he got carried away with a game of tag and tromped through the forbidden zone. A few minutes later, the parent volunteer arrived with an armful of tools to work on the fence. Olivia piped up, "We don't need a fence anymore. We can't have a garden 'cause Kenji stepped in it!" Embarrassed, Joanne looked at the confused parent. She wondered how she could get out of this one. She really wanted to have a school garden.

Clear Relationships

Selecting a consequence related to the action takes thought and understanding. Many people misunderstand and misuse the term *consequence.* They impose totally unrelated outcomes on children's behavior and call them consequences. They don't realize that without the relationship between the action and the result, there is no learning involved; the result is merely punishment (Curwin & Mendler, 1999; DeVries & Zan, 1994).

Public school discipline guides often list a variety of punishments they call consequences: losing a recess for chewing gum, staying after school for talking back to a teacher, or doing push-ups for hitting someone. Totally unrelated to children's behavior, these punishments teach resentment, calculation of the risk of getting caught, and consideration of whether the benefits are worth the costs (Kamii, 1984). Gum chewing might have a reasonable consequence if there is a need to scrape gum off floors and desks. Discipline for talking back to a teacher or hitting someone should depend on the causes for those behaviors. No pat solution could address all the various sources of those behaviors. Discipline solutions are of questionable value if they are not based on the cause of the behavior as determined by information about the nature of the individual child, the particular situation, and the relationship between those involved.

USING CONSEQUENCES

Because of the thought and planning required, you usually will not implement consequences the first time a certain behavior occurs. Typically, a teacher analyzes an on-going problem, trying out various hypotheses about the cause. When it becomes clear that the cause is not unrealistic adult expectations, missing skills, or unmet needs, the adult may decide that the cause is the child's lack of

COMPARING APPROACHES

You may find it helpful to compare punishment, natural consequences, and related consequences as they might be applied to a single behavior problem. Kids seem to love throwing sand, and teachers always get upset about it. They lecture endlessly about the dangers of sand in playmates' eyes. Here is how the different discipline approaches would look if Jimmie threw sand at Joshua.

Punishment

No doubt you have observed or experienced the punishment response to this behavior. There are many variations of punishment, ranging from sending Jimmie to the principal's office to having him miss recess for a week.

Natural Consequences

You probably would not see any adult deliberately use natural consequences for sand throwing, though such consequences certainly do occur accidentally. In this case, natural consequences might happen because you were unaware of Jimmie's behavior until Joshua or Jimmie got sand in his eyes. Then you could discuss what happened with them and help them relate the unpleasantness to the sand throwing.

Related Consequences

Related consequences involve adult intervention without anger or recrimination.

One type of related consequence, deprivation, is to remind Jimmie about the dangers of throwing sand and remove him from the sandbox until he thinks he can play without throwing sand. If he immediately goes back and starts throwing sand again, you need to impose a longer period away—such as the rest of the play period. Although it is preferable to encourage Jimmie to decide for himself when he is able to behave acceptably, some youngsters need guidance for such reflection.

Another type of consequence would also be appropriate if sand actually got into Joshua's eyes. Jimmie would be put in charge of helping Joshua go to the nurse's office, and then he would stay with Joshua while he got his eyes washed out. This would be a consequence of restitution. This experience should help Jimmie learn why throwing sand is dangerous.

understanding. At that point, the teacher must first decide whether natural consequences will suffice or whether related consequences are required. If related consequences are needed, the adult's challenge is to figure out something that will demonstrate the link between the behavior and the outcome. All this thought and effort would be reserved for a recurrent disruptive problem.

Family Situations as a Model

Mrs. Jensen frequently uses her experiences with her own children to guide her with her students. When she needs inspiration about how to apply related consequences at school, she reflects on the following successful use of them at home:

> Getting ready for school in the mornings had become an unpleasant ordeal. Mrs. Jensen not only had to get herself ready and out the door early, but she had four children who also had to get to school on time. If they missed the bus and she had to drive them, then she was late for work. It had happened once, and there were several other narrow escapes. The pressure of this situation was making her cross with the children as she hurried everyone along. It seemed that the more she tried to hurry them, the slower they moved. Her frustration was building, and her days were getting off to a bad start. Her children were leaving for school upset, too. She had to find a way out of this problem.
>
> How could she change the situation so that the children's behavior did not affect her personally? The part that was upsetting to her was the prospect of being late for work because of driving the children to their school. If only they lived close enough to walk when they missed the bus. The walk and their tardiness would be good learning experiences. But this natural consequence wasn't available because their school was 10 miles away.
>
> However, the city bus route was within walking distance. Her children were experienced bus riders. Sure, it was a long, slow trip, probably involving a wait for the bus and assuring tardiness, but those were learning experiences, too. Mrs. Jensen thought the idea might work. She bought a roll of bus tokens and showed her children where they were. Then she explained that she simply couldn't be late for work and that they could take the city bus to school if they ever missed the school bus.
>
> What a relief! Mrs. Jensen could relax and be cheerful with her children in the mornings. She could make sure she left the house on time, but it was up to the youngsters to make certain they did. Sure enough, before long it happened. The four children dragged sadly back to the house after seeing the bus pull away. Their mother calmly reminded them where the bus tokens were as she left for work.
>
> The problem was now the children's, not hers. She was not at all upset because she knew they would be fine. She was careful not to say, "I told you so." She merely waved as she drove off to work. That evening she could be truly sympathetic about how awful the long bus ride had been and how they felt about being tardy. However, she also sent the clear message that getting to the bus on time was their responsibility, not hers.

Allowing Consequences to Happen

This learning experience worked so well at home that it has become a model for Mrs. Jensen at school. She uses the same principles and procedures when she applies reasonable consequences with her students. She withdraws from any power struggle and turns the responsibility over to the children. This plan helps her remain calm and pleasant. She knows that any anger on her part will ruin the consequences by turning them into punishment.

She used these guidelines to solve the problem of children not keeping track of their own crayons and scissors. She has classroom boxes for crayons, markers, and scissors. Any of these items found lying around after clean-up go into the boxes and become community property. Children are free to borrow them and use them, but they now belong to the class. The boxes solve several problems at once. They provide a place for the things that have been left out, a source of needed supplies, and an incentive for children to keep their own things put away. With this solution in place, Mrs. Jensen is able to turn the problem over to the children.

Because of her experience with her own children, Mrs. Jensen is better able to help the families of her students find similar solutions. For instance, she can talk to Travis' mom about not bringing his gym shoes when he forgets them. And she can help other families to use related consequences as part of fostering children's independence.

Helping Children Make Connections

Preschoolers may be somewhat less adept at linking cause and effect, but they are able to learn from related consequences. Dennis and Maureen know that they can use related consequences to help their students learn. Adults can assist children in thinking about cause and effect as well as about how their actions affect

Teachers using natural or related consequences must be careful not to ruin the learning experience by adding sermons or scolding.

others. Therefore, experiences with related consequences are a valuable part of their preschool curriculum. As the following example shows, the teacher is careful not to ruin the learning experiences with sermons or scoldings.

> Celest and Kyle were being too rough with Pinky the guinea pig. As the frightened creature squealed and tried to pull away, Celest grabbed its fur. Tufts of fur came out in her hand. Kyle thought the tufts were neat and tugged off another bunch of fur. The teacher heard Pinky's cries and came to his rescue. As she examined his patchy coat, she decided he deserved a respite to recover. She moved his cage up out of the children's reach, explaining as she did so, "Pinky's hair has been pulled out, and I want him to have a chance to grow it back. He needs to be in a safe place for a while. After he gets better, and when you feel you can play gently with him, he can come back down."

Depriving the children of Pinky's company matches one of Piaget's recommended responses. Dennis finds that his young students respond to the inherent justice of such as consequence. They do not usually resent or rebel against a truly related outcome. Noting this fact, Dennis is challenged to think of the best possible consequences. Still, he keeps in mind that the behavior may be a symptom of another problem that needs attention.

Combining Approaches

Dennis wants to do more than merely stop the behavior; he wants to get at the cause as well. If the cause is simply that the child does not understand why an action is inappropriate, then consequences alone are sufficient. If the behavior is signaling an unmet need, as it may have when Sam hit Zach, that need must also be considered.

> When Sam was harassing and eventually hurting his friend Zach, Dennis stopped the escalating behavior by removing Sam—an exclusion consequence. If he thought that Sam's behavior was a symptom of an unmet need for attention, Dennis could have helped Sam get that need met. If Sam had complained that Zach wasn't his friend anymore, Dennis could have listened reflectively to find out more. Maybe Sam just wanted a playmate, so Dennis could have coached him in ways to play cooperatively.

CONCLUSION

Natural and related consequences are ways of helping children construct moral rules and values by reflecting on their experience. Like teaching through example, teaching through experience is an extremely effective method. Of course, just the experiences themselves are not sufficient for learning. The child must reflect on the experiences and try to make sense out of them. It is this process of thinking about the experiences that results in learning. Children construct their own sense of right and wrong in this way. Moral rules that children construct from within are compelling to them, unlike rules that have been imposed by others. Children are best guided by their own understanding. Similarly, the values they construct for themselves are more likely to guide their actions.

Thus, consequences teach self-discipline. They not only help children take responsibility for their behavior at the time, but they also assist with the development of lifelong autonomous behavior. When you help children move toward autonomy, you work toward the ideals of a democratic society. Instead of being imposed by authority, order is maintained by each person for the benefit of all. When schools employ democratic principles and treat students according to those principles, students will rebel less and learn more.

∽ FOR FURTHER THOUGHT

1. Observe an early childhood education program, watching for how often children experience the results of their actions and how often an adult protects them from those results. Are adults getting in the way of children learning, or are they merely protecting them as necessary?

2. Watch for situations in which making restitution would be the most educational consequence for inappropriate behavior. Are you quick to discover these situations, or is your thinking still locked in to more punitive approaches?

3. Practice planning and implementing related consequences. Do you have trouble thinking of actual relationships to the behavior? Is it hard not to use consequences as threats? Do you find times when there may be no real reason not to allow the behavior?

4. A problem to solve (use this chapter and the previous ones to help you): Chelsea knocked over Katie's block construction. Katie is yelling at Chelsea and threatening to knock down what Chelsea has built.

   a. Describe an appropriate related consequence.
   b. Describe other guidance approaches that might also be useful.
   c. Describe how this problem might have been prevented.

∽ RECOMMENDED READINGS

Butchart, R. E., & McEwan, B. (1998). *Classroom discipline in American schools: Problems and possibilities for democratic education.* Albany, NY: State University of New York Press.

Dreikurs, R. (1964). *Children: The challenge.* New York: Hawthorne Books.

Kamii, C. (1982). Autonomy as the aim of education: Implications of Piaget's theory. In C. Kamii (Ed.), *Number in preschool and kindergarten,* (pp. 73–87). Washington, DC: National Association for the Education of Young Children.

Piaget, J. (1965). *The moral judgment of the child.* New York: Free Press. (Originally published in 1932.)

9 Controlling Behavior Externally

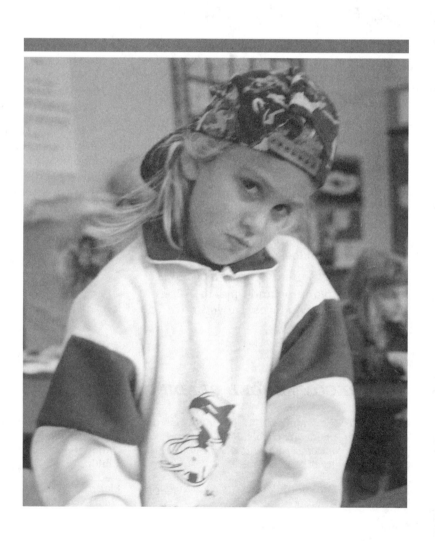

I n this chapter we will discuss the uses and abuses of Behaviorist theory for discipline. As explained in Chapter 1, our approach to guidance and discipline is based on Constructivist theory, a very different view. However, we recognize the validity of the basic premises of Behaviorism: Behavior that gets pleasant results is likely to be repeated. Behavior that gets unpleasant results probably won't be repeated. That is the natural response of both people and animals. This principle is used in training circus animals to perform, housebreaking a puppy, or getting laboratory rats to run a maze. Unfortunately, it is also widely used to control children's behavior. The method is called *behavior modification:* It sets up artificial reward systems designed to get children to behave in certain ways.

BEHAVIOR MODIFICATION

Behavior modification is based primarily on the research of Skinner (1965, 1971), who conducted experiments with laboratory animals, testing theories about using reinforcement to get rats and pigeons to perform, discontinue, or persist with specific actions. In looking for a "quick fix" to managing groups of children, schools have widely adopted and misapplied behavior modification to classrooms.

The authors of this book are opposed to behavior modification as a discipline approach. We are convinced that praise, stars, stickers, tokens, and other behavior modification reinforcement systems are counterproductive to the development of self-discipline and autonomy. (Yes, we said *praise* too.)

Behavior modification does not teach children why certain behaviors are more desirable than others; instead, it uses rewards in attempts to coerce better behavior (e.g., Kohn, 2001). Coercion then replaces teaching as a means of changing children's behavior. Performance based on rewards requires the presence of an authority figure who dispenses or withholds rewards; therefore, it is not consistent with the goal of autonomy. In addition, there is compelling evidence that rewards aren't really effective in changing behavior; they may actually be counterproductive (Kohn, 1999; Landy, 2002).

Don't Let It Backfire

We do not recommend this method to elicit desired behavior and we will further discuss our reasons later in the chapter. However, we think you need to understand how behavior modification works—because it does work. Even if you don't deliberately use the technique, it is an inevitable side effect of your interactions with others. It can work for you or against you. Your reactions are constantly affecting the behavior of others, just as their reactions are affecting your behavior. If the reactions are pleasant or meet a need, chances are the person will repeat the action.

In Behaviorist terminology, the behavior has been reinforced. When you smile at what someone says, your action is a pleasant response. When you pay attention to what someone is doing, your interest, too, can be a rewarding response. Chapter 2 explains that the need for attention is a basic human need. It is easy to reinforce undesirable behavior accidentally if you don't know about reinforcement theory.

Do the following examples seem familiar?

A. Have you seen an adult chasing after a runaway toddler? If so, you know the glee with which toddlers play this game. It is a lot of fun to have Dad or a teacher running after them and giving them so much attention. Of course, the attention encourages running away again.

B. What about adult laughter at a preschooler's rude or improper language? It may sound funny to hear such words come out of the mouth of an innocent child, but laughter as a response can unintentionally act as a reward and will ensure repetition of the inappropriate language.

C. Who tends to get the most attention from the teacher in a classroom? Is it the child who responsibly does what is asked or the one who never does? Is the teacher unconsciously rewarding the irresponsible behavior by paying attention to it?

You can more easily avoid these pitfalls if you understand how behavior modification works. It is essential to remember the link between the action and the reward. Rewards can take many different forms, depending on the person and the circumstance. Even a spanking may actually be a reward if it is the only way a child can get attention. Being aware of how this works can keep you from accidentally rewarding behaviors you want to stop.

Close observation of children will help you discover what reactions a child finds rewarding. In the following example, Sheri and Maureen make an important discovery through observation.

Max had been making life difficult at the children's center. He was throwing tantrums regularly and often chose the block area to do it. If there was a structure standing there, he knocked it over. If the blocks were on the shelves, he pulled them all off. If they were on the floor, he scattered them and threw them about. The staff had been trying hard to help him. They tried everything they could think of. Recently, they were implementing sanctions of reciprocity, but the method didn't seem to be working at all. Max helped to clean up the mess he had made, but then he went and did it all over again. Clearly, a different approach was needed.

Sheri was watching him as he went through his block-scattering routine; she was trying to figure out what the teachers could try next. As she watched, she caught Max glancing out of the corner of his eye to see if she was looking. Then Maureen came over and stopped the destructive behavior. While Maureen talked to Max about the problem, she held him on her lap and rubbed his back lightly with her hand. Max sat with a little smile on his face, not appearing to listen. Sheri thought the experience seemed to be a pleasant one for him. She began to think about the possibility that Max was getting what he wanted through his disruptive actions. Later, she suggested that perhaps the staff had been unintentionally reinforcing Max's tantrums.

The teachers made a new plan. The next time Max began his inappropriate behavior, they left the area. No one paid any attention to what he was doing. Pretty soon he stopped and went over to join a group listening to a story. He seemed quite content and under control. His teachers were amazed. Always before, his tantrums had gone on and on while adults worked to calm him down. This time he had calmed himself down. It appeared that Max got bored without an audience for his behavior. As the adults at the children's center continued to resist reinforcing his undesirable behavior, it disappeared.

This example demonstrates how mislearning occurs when an unproductive behavior is inadvertently reinforced. The child learns to use inappropriate behavior to get his needs met (Charles, 1996).

Reinforcement Theory

Understanding more about how behavior modification works will help you avoid having it backfire on you. Too many adults accidentally teach children to misbehave.

Rewards   The pleasant or rewarding responses that encourage behaviors are called *reinforcers* or *rewards*. Reinforcement is generally divided into two categories: social and tangible rewards. Smiles, laughter, and attention are social reinforcers, as are a hug, a touch, or even eye contact. Words of praise are commonly used social reinforcers as well. Food is often used as a tangible reinforcer. Raisins, Cheerios, or M&Ms are handed out to children to reinforce certain actions. Seals prefer fish, and puppies like dog biscuits. Common tangible rewards used in school include stars, stickers, and smiley faces. Because older children are better able to delay gratification, behavior modification systems for them often include points or tokens, which can be accumulated and redeemed for prizes.

Punishment   Remember, there are two sides to behavior modification: the pleasant rewards and the unpleasant punishments. Chapter 10 focuses on punishment and explains its dangerous side effects. Most proponents of behavior modification emphasize the positive aspects and usually deny that punishment is used. However, any time a hoped-for reward is denied, it can feel like punishment.

Miss Wheeler wanted to "motivate" Karin to finish her Excel Math worksheet on time. The girl always dawdled and just wouldn't stay focused. The teacher knew that Karin loved to use the math manipulative materials, so she said that if Karin got her sheet done by 10:30, she could join the advanced group working with the Unifix cubes. Enticed by the possibility, Karin worked diligently for 10 minutes. But the deadly worksheets soon took their toll, and she started daydreaming as usual. Her wandering gaze settled on the table with the Unifix cubes. She began wondering if she could make them into a horse. Then she remembered the time limit, glanced at the clock, and panicked: 10:27! She scrambled to finish the page, but it was hopeless. She'd blown it again! Discouraged, she thought, "I hate math!"

There are two sides to behavior modification: the unpleasant punishments as well as the pleasant rewards. Both are damaging.

Reinforcement Schedules   Behavior modification research provides guidelines for the most effective ways of using reward and punishment: responses must be immediate, specific, and consistent (Charles, 1996). These guidelines are designed to demonstrate the relationship between the action and the result. If you want to use behavior modification, this information is essential to its effective use. Those of you who have trained puppies have used these principles.

Although Behaviorist theory considers immediate and consistent reinforcement to be essential for initially getting the desired behaviors, it does not recommend it for long-term use (Wolfgang & Wolfgang, 1995). Not only is it exhausting to constantly have to watch for a desired behavior and then immediately reward it, but it also works better to gradually reduce the frequency of reinforcement. Behavior modification research indicates that, once a response is established, unpredictable intervals between rewards have a longer lasting effect (Charles, 1996; Miller, 2004). This is called an *intermittent, variable reinforcement schedule*: You keep the behavior going the longest with the least amount of effort in this way. Unfortunately, it also means you keep unwanted behavior going longer if you only give in to it occasionally.

Even though we don't recommend that you formally implement behavior modification, we think you should be warned that intermittent, variable reinforcement has the most lasting impact. This knowledge can save you from accidentally applying the principle to behavior you don't want. The parent who usually doesn't give in to her children's nagging or whining may, in fact, be teaching them to keep trying. If their behavior works sometimes, youngsters will be motivated to keep it up.

Similarly, the teacher who is trying hard not to reinforce attention-getting behavior may inadvertently be strongly encouraging it through intermittent, variable reinforcement. It takes practice and self-control to follow through with a strategy of "planned ignoring" (Grossman, 1990).

IS BEHAVIOR MODIFICATION THE APPROACH FOR YOU?

Behavior modification apparently gets results, so why do so many child guidance books advise against it (e.g., Charney, 2002; DeVries et al., 2000; Gartrell, 2004; Kohn, 1999)? And why do so many teachers and parents refuse to use it as their discipline approach? The answers can be found in careful analysis of the system. They include the effect on autonomy as well as self-discipline and intrinsic motivation. Adults who reject reward and punishment to control children's behavior do so primarily out of concern for the child's long-term welfare.

Many adults are also personally uncomfortable with using their power to coerce someone with less power. To do so violates their value system and models—a principle they reject (Greenberg, 1992a). The power involved may not be physical, but rather the power of access to resources that children desire. Because this use of power is effective, the system of reward and punishment is a method of forcing children into compliance.

However, schools often focus on compliance and ignore the price paid in damaged relationships and apathetic minds (McEwan, 1998). Rather than working on the unique causes of individual children's behavior problems, many educators want to believe there is one "magic trick" to solve them all. The promises of behavior modification feed this illusion.

Some teachers use behavior modification techniques without question simply because that is what their teachers did when they were in school. Even though they may have hurtful memories of their own school discipline, and even though they may acknowledge that it wasn't useful for them, they perpetuate the system in their own teaching. The common practice of teaching as you were taught—not in teacher education classes, but as a child in school—testifies to the powerful influence of role models.

Autonomy Destroyed

Moral autonomy means that a person will make decisions based on internally constructed convictions about right and wrong (DeVries, 1999). A morally autonomous person will be respectful of others whether or not someone in authority is watching. Both moral and intellectual autonomy require that a person be

 Moral qualities are not apt to be learned through techniques that are themselves of dubious moral value: manipulation, cajolery, punishment, bribery, and other "teacher tricks" (Butchart & McEwan, 1998).

skilled in thinking about issues and coming to personal conclusions (Kamii, 1982). These skills require practice. Behavior modification eliminates the opportunity for practice with decision making or self-evaluation of behavior options (Reynolds, 2000). The person with the rewards or punishments is in charge, not the child. With behavior modification, the child's thinking centers around how to get the reward or avoid the punishment, not about what is right under the circumstances (Kohn, 1999). Behavior modification creates moral heteronomy, which causes people to behave properly only when they think they will get caught if they don't.

By taking responsibility for the child's behavior, the adult denies the child the opportunity to learn by experience and by reflection on those experiences (Piaget, 1965/1932). When adults are constantly in charge of children's behavior, the message to the children is that they are not capable of making good decisions for themselves. Their confidence in themselves as thinkers and decision makers is damaged (DeVries, 1999). Therefore, behavior modification creates both a lack of experience with making decisions and a lack of confidence to do so.

It is ironic that schools advocate teaching critical thinking and problem-solving skills in academic subjects, but do just the opposite for social and emotional development (McEwan, 1998). This mix of incompatible approaches not only harms moral autonomy, it also counteracts the intellectual autonomy necessary for critical thinking. You cannot teach children to think for themselves about certain issues while simultaneously disempowering them in other areas (DeVries et al., 2000).

Self-Discipline Limited

With behavior modification, the teacher decides what the children should do and enforces that decision through reward or punishment. Many adults apparently think that children become self-disciplined by being bribed and coerced in this way. Actually, the opposite is true. When adults force children to behave appropriately, they deny children the opportunity to learn self-discipline. The hope of behavior modification is to make good behaviors a habit; however, the common result is to make reliance on external controls a habit (Kamii, 1982).

Making the decisions for youngsters takes away their chance to make the decisions for themselves. They have no opportunity to develop inner controls when adults are imposing external controls (Kohn, 1999). Young people who have been controlled by adults often have difficulty when they are old enough to be on their own. They don't know, or maybe don't care, what is right without the rewards. As soon as the rewards quit, the behavior quits.

Performance Decreased

It is a little-known fact that people who perform only for rewards perform at lower levels. This can explain much of the student apathy so observable in our schools: External controls cause students to become passive and to withdraw their interest and investment in learning. This is too often the price paid in the name of quiet, efficient, predictable classrooms (Beyer, 1998).

Many studies have compared groups of people doing the same task, rewarding one group and not the other. Results are clear that those who were rewarded for their performance did less well than those who were not (Kohn, 1999). Rewards backfire in many ways. For instance, a program to help people stop smoking found that those who were given rewards for quitting were most likely to be smoking again in 3 months (Curry, Wagner, & Grothaus, 1991). Trying to get people to buckle their seat belts by giving them rewards had a similar negative impact (Geller, Rudd, Kalsher, Streff, & Lehman, 1987). Surprised? You probably are, which goes to show how much society has unquestioningly bought into a false premise.

Ignores Cause of Problems

As long as the cause of a behavior problem continues, any efforts to change the behavior can only be superficial. Like the weed whose roots live underground, the problem will pop back up again soon. Long-lasting approaches to change have to search for the cause and work on that cause. Behaviorist approaches focus on the symptoms instead of the cause (Kohn, 1996).

If a teacher has to use rewards to keep kids on task with the learning activities provided, the obvious question is, "Why?" Why aren't students interested or involved? Perhaps it is because the school work is boring (Butchart, 1998). That means putting some teacher energy into a more meaningful curriculum. Some teachers put their energy into making learning interesting and relevant. Others put their energy into bribing or threatening children to keep them on task. Which teachers do you think have students who learn the most?

Think about behavior modification and causes of behavior problems. If Kayla behaves inappropriately because of missing social skills, does it help to put her name on the board? If unmet power needs cause Noah to act out, does it help to

Discipline using rewards and punishment gets in the way of self-discipline, hinders development of moral autonomy, damages relationships with adults, and ignores the cause of behavior.

send him to time-out? If a lack of understanding leads Tenzin astray, does it help to deprive the class of a popcorn party?

Relationships Damaged

As we have said before, caring, mutually respectful relationships are an essential component of teaching desirable behavior (DeVries et al., 2000; Kamii, 1982; Piaget, 1965/1932). Rewards and punishment both damage relationships (Brady, Forton, Porter, & Wood, 2003; Kohn, 1996; Reynolds, 2000). You probably already knew that punishment damages relationships; after all, who wants to be around someone who hurts you? But, isn't getting rewards just the opposite? The answer is no.

Getting rewards means you are dependent on someone else to judge you worthy of getting something you want. This causes you to try to impress or flatter the person who gives rewards; this is not an honest relationship. Such an unauthentic relationship cannot foster the trust and genuine caring that inspire students to do their best. In addition, the process of judging and rewarding is not respectful; it emphasizes the power and status differences between the person giving the reward and the person hoping to get one. Besides, if the authority figure withholds the reward, in essence the subordinates are punished by not getting it.

Relationships are damaged by the strict, rule-bound discipline typical of behaviorist theory. Behavior modification programs lay out the rules and also the punishment for breaking a rule (Canter & Canter, 1992). This focus on the rules does not take into consideration the reason a rule was broken; therefore, the relationships and contexts for the behavior are ignored (Noddings, 1992). This model does not teach children sensitivity to the needs and concerns of others, since their own needs and concerns are not considered.

Mutual trust is essential to caring relationships, but the impersonal nature of a reward and punishment system damages children's trust in adults. Rather than caring and compassionate protectors, adults become feared authority figures. The lack of trust goes both ways, as a teacher's use of such a management system implies adult mistrust of children as well. Teachers who believe that children want to be kind and cooperative will not feel the need for constantly monitoring and coercing children to do their bidding. Behavior modification is based on the belief that people will not do the right thing on their own (Beyer, 1998).

Intrinsic Motivation Destroyed

Intrinsic motivation means doing something for its own sake. The value lies in the behavior itself, and the reward is in how you feel about it: The reward is internal to you. Extrinsic motivation is the opposite; it means doing something for a reward. The value lies not in the behavior, but in what you get as a result of the behavior. The reward is external to you because it comes from someone else. Obviously, behavior modification relies on extrinsic motivation.

The relationship between self-discipline and intrinsic motivation is just part of the problem. Rewards can teach people to expect them and to perform only for them. Thus, the extrinsic motivation of rewards goes against the development of self-discipline and autonomy. Self-disciplined, autonomous people don't behave appropriately only when a reward is offered. They have come to appreciate the value of learning appropriate behavior as a reward in itself. They recognize the natural benefits of positive interactions and making good choices.

It is possible to destroy intrinsic motivation by rewarding behavior that a person was doing for personal satisfaction (Beyer, 1998; DeVries et al., 2000; Kohn, 2001; Watson, 1999). Such a counterproductive result is another aspect of the problem with extrinsic motivation.

> Mandy was in third grade but loved to go to her old first-grade classroom and help. She would frequently offer to stay after school and help clean chalkboards or tidy up the shelves. Helping made her feel good, and it also made her feel grown-up. Miss Wheeler decided she should reward Mandy's helpfulness and began giving the girl a prize each time she came in to help. Somehow helping wasn't as much fun anymore, and Mandy went to Miss Wheeler's room less and less often. Neither the teacher or the girl understood the relationship between the rewards and Mandy's lessened enthusiasm.

In this case, Mandy's reaction to rewards caused her to discontinue her volunteer work. Sometimes extrinsic rewards do more critical damage. It is possible to override a child's joy in learning and change the focus to getting rewards. As Kohn (1999) says, "The more you want what has been dangled in front of you, the more you may come to dislike whatever you have to do to get it" (p. 83).

NECESSARY MOTIVATION

Having emphasized the importance of intrinsic motivation, we need to examine sources of motivation. The previous discussion implies that the only choices are intrinsic or extrinsic motivation. Yet, there are many tasks and behaviors that are simply not intrinsically motivating. Does that mean we have to resort to extrinsic rewards?

Many people say, "What about the real world? Isn't it basically run by a system of rewards?" After all, who would go to work without getting paid? Isn't that extrinsic reward the reason you work? Maybe not. If you really like your job and are interested in what you do, the pay probably just makes it possible for you to follow your intrinsic motivation. It frees you from having to do something else to support yourself. If your work is boring or unpleasant, the reward of a paycheck is probably what Hymes (1990) called *necessary motivation*. You really do want and need food and shelter; therefore, you go to work. However, as stated earlier, people work less effectively if they work only for the payoff. Interestingly, paying according to the level of output ("merit pay") damages productivity the most (Jenkins, 1986).

Mrs. Jensen is aware that there are three kinds of motivation: intrinsic, extrinsic, and necessary. Many activities may not be pleasing in themselves, but they lead to goals that are. Therefore, they are done out of necessary motivation. Although teaching is intrinsically motivating to her, washing dishes falls into the "necessary" category for Mrs. Jensen. She doesn't like doing dishes, but she does appreciate a tidy kitchen. In this case, the clean kitchen provides necessary motivation. Mrs. Jensen tries to help students find such motivation for some dull tasks such as clean-up by focusing on a purpose for doing them. It is important to remember that the purpose needs to be the children's, not the teacher's.

COMMON FORMS OF BEHAVIOR MODIFICATION

Regardless of the criticism it receives, behavior modification is a tradition in the public schools. You have experienced it as a student, and you will see it as a teacher. We want you to recognize it when you see it so that you won't just go along with tradition, not realizing what you are actually doing.

Rewards and Punishment

You are probably most familiar with tangible rewards, such as stickers and stars. Your memories probably focus on how you felt about either getting or not getting the coveted rewards; you probably remember little about the actual purpose or content of the work. That fact is evidence of the damage done by rewards: they take attention away from what is truly valuable. Too often, schools take eager kindergartners who are excited about school and, by the fourth grade, transform them into bored students eager to escape school. This can partly be explained by the constant use of rewards in school: not only stickers and stars, but also popcorn parties, videos, awards, and (oh yes) grades (Kohn, 1996). Most children come to accept this system and believe that they need such help in order to do the right thing, as in the following example:

> Miss Wheeler's class coat area was a mess! The coats were all over the floor instead of on the hooks, and the boots and gym shoes were strewn everywhere. It took forever for children to find their own boots or gym shoes. Miss Wheeler decided to have a class meeting about the problem.
>
> She asked her students for ideas about what to do. The ideas ranged from punishment to reward: "Make us stay in from recess if our boots aren't where they belong," or "Give us candy if we clean it all up nice." These were the only options the children knew as their ideas were based on their experience. No one was able to think of problem-solving approaches or ways to help themselves be more responsible. Most already had experienced behavior modification discipline in kindergarten and preschool before getting to first grade.
>
> Given the choice between reward and punishment, the children naturally chose the reward. Miss Wheeler felt intuitively that something was wrong with giving children candy for organizing the coat area, but she didn't have a better idea, either. So, the children scurried around and tidied up, and Miss Wheeler got out her stash of reward candy. Of course, the boots, shoes, and coats were in the same mess the next day.

As we have said before, not getting a hoped-for reward is a form of punishment. Not getting candy when others do is sure to devastate a young child. It can also feel like punishment when the teacher says she likes how other kids are sitting, but she doesn't say your name when you are sitting nicely. Punishment may come in the form of not having your picture chosen for the display of good work, and it can come from being embarrassed by a public correction when you get confused about the rules. Many teachers who don't think they use punishment have students who feel punished. The nature of an authoritarian structure, with the powerful adult doling out approval or disapproval, sets up punishment situations.

Some teachers fool themselves into thinking they aren't punishing, but that children have made a choice. They say to a child who has not conformed to a rule, "I see you have chosen to give up your free time today." Or they will give a child a "choice" between two undesirable things, such as finishing the worksheet now or missing recess. These are not choices because they are not freely chosen; they are inherently dishonest way of trying to cover up the teacher's power to punish. Despite Behaviorist assertions to the contrary (Canter & Canter, 1992), such false choices do not teach responsibility, but rather breed all the negative outcomes associated with punishment described in Chapter 10.

Time-Out

Time-out is a pervasive school tradition. It is often used as a behavior modification technique and considered an improvement over the old stand-in-the-corner punishment. In actuality, there is often little difference between the two (Katz & McClellan, 1991). An analysis of the various ways in which time-out can be used may help you understand the differences between Behaviorist and other approaches to discipline.

> Joanne prides herself on her discipline during circle time at Midway Children's Center. When all the children are on their designated rug scraps in their circle spots, she begins singing, "I like the way that Christie sits; she's got her legs crossed, and her hands are in her lap. I like the way that Ling Ling sits; she's got her legs crossed, and her hands are in her lap. I like the way that Ashley sits; she's got . . . " until all the children are dutifully in position. Then she begins the "educational" presentation part of her circle program. If children get out of position, she says, "I need your whole body's attention, and you can't do it that way. Please sit up crisscross-applesauce style!" Some children continue to resist the rigid posture.
>
> Joanne's firm rule is that the second time they get out of position, youngsters are sent to a time-out chair for the remainder of circle time. Sheri, the aide, usually has her hands full supervising the time-out chairs by the end of Joanne's "well-behaved" circle time. She wonders if this approach is really working. The same kids are in those chairs almost every day, and the same few get the daily dose of praise. It sure doesn't seem to be teaching them anything.

Maureen uses a different approach to a similar problem, with more emphasis on self-regulation and less on external control.

> Maureen's story time before lunch has looser seating requirements. But even though children can sit where and how they please, there are still problems. Children get in each other's way or quarrel over who sits by whom. If their disagreements escalate into shoving and whining, Maureen tells them, "It's too hard for

me to read while you're not getting along (an " I message"). I can see you are up-set with each other (reflective listening). You need to go to the calming chairs in the other room until you can calm down enough to talk to each other about your problem. When you are ready to come back and listen to the story, you may."

Maureen views time-out as a related consequence of children's failure to be-have appropriately during an activity. Her term for the place, calming chairs, shows what she expects of their occupants. She leaves it up to the children to decide when they are capable of trying to be part of the group again—a critical feature separating consequences from punishment.

Dennis gives children a choice of not only when to return to the group, but when to leave, too. His approach gives youngsters the most control over their own behavior and helps them learn to self-monitor their feelings and needs.

Dennis knows the kids can be tired and irritable after a full morning of pre-school. If a child is having a particularly hard time getting along with his friends during story time, Dennis sometimes asks, "Might you feel better in a place by yourself for a while? Where could you go to get some alone time?" If the child does take him up on it, Dennis is sure to add, "Come on back whenever you feel like it!" Dennis recognizes when children are too upset or tired to be in a group. He helps them learn that time alone can help them get in touch with their feel-ings and gain control of themselves. He thinks that the most productive time-out is one you give yourself.

A cozy private space for cooling down emotions is very different from a time-out chair.

Mrs. Jensen uses yet another approach to help children get their cool-down and privacy needs met. She encourages her students to decorate a designated private space in the classroom, to make it a cozy and inviting place to go when anyone feels upset. Most years, children put cushions on the floor, take stuffed animals and books there, and put pretty posters or drawings on the wall. Mrs. Jensen helps children view this spot as a safe haven where they can choose to go when they need to be alone. She also makes sure that her students get help in dealing with their feelings.

Assertive Discipline

A program called *assertive discipline* (Canter, 1976) is one example of how behavior modification has been interpreted in classrooms. Although it is a misinterpretation that violates many basic behaviorist principles, it does come from that base. This program recommends a series of reward and punishment systems designed to gain student compliance.

> Miss Wheeler has just completed a summer training course in assertive discipline. She had watched the course videos and filled out the worksheets. Now she was excited to try it out. The authors, Lee and Marlene Canter, promised a well-behaved classroom if she followed the rules. She was all prepared to write names on the board and put marbles in a jar.
>
> On the first day of school, Miss Wheeler clearly told the children her list of firm rules. They were to sit in their seats until they had permission to get up. They were to follow directions the first time they were given. They were to raise their hands and wait to be called on before they spoke. The list went on.
>
> Next, she told them what would happen when anyone disregarded the rules. For a first infraction, the student's name would be put on the board. For a second failure, the name would get a checkmark by it, and the child would stay in for the first 5 minutes of recess. A second checkmark meant the student would lose the whole recess. Anyone who received more than two checkmarks would have his or her parents called. (She didn't tell the children that the course had recommended that she make a point of calling the parents at work to be sure to embarrass them.)
>
> On the bright side, Miss Wheeler said that whenever the whole class was following the rules nicely, she would drop a marble in a special marble jar. When the jar was full, they would have a popcorn party!
>
> Kayla was worried. She said, "But I'm allergic to popcorn." Miss Wheeler decided to use the girl as an example, saying, "You didn't raise your hand before you talked, Kayla. So I will put your name on the board to help you remember to do that." Pleased with herself for having used the opportunity to illustrate the system, Miss Wheeler went on with her classroom orientation. But Kayla wasn't listening to the detailed descriptions of how to use classroom centers properly: only one book from the shelves at a time, and so on. Kayla just kept staring at her name on the board, flushed with embarrassment.
>
> Delighted when her table was dismissed to the reading center, Kayla eagerly skipped over, taking three attractive books off the shelves and nestling into the beanbag chair to decide which one to read first. She had settled on *Frog and Toad Together*, one of her favorites from home, when she saw Miss Wheeler's feet next to where she had put down the other two books. Miss Wheeler looked

down at the girl and reprimanded her: "Kayla, because you didn't follow the instruction of one book at a time, you have chosen to have a checkmark by your name. You will lose part of recess now. You can use the time to think about the rules of our classroom."

Miss Wheeler caught the group's attention as she checked Kayla's name, saying, "I'm sorry, but we all need to work on remembering the rules. Maybe you can help Kayla learn so we can start getting marbles in the jar." Several children frowned at Kayla and she squirmed. She hated Miss Wheeler and her dumb rules. She hated school!

Like other forms of behavior modification, assertive discipline only deals with surface behaviors; it does not consider the child's feelings or the cause of behavior problems (Gartrell, 1987a; Hitz, 1988). Additionally, this approach doesn't consider maturation stages and the behaviors inherent in each. It uses power to gain compliance and ignores child development. Perhaps most damaging, it uses humiliation as a component of punishment, seriously damaging self-esteem. "The pain is forever!" wrote one college student, who became upset while reading about assertive discipline and remembering how it felt to have her name on the board as a child. Twenty years after experiencing it, she couldn't discuss the system without crying.

Group rewards, as in popcorn parties for marbles, also do serious damage to children. Kohn (1999) calls this "one of the most transparently manipulative strategies used by people in power." He also says it "calls forth a particularly noxious sort of peer pressure" (p. 56). It isn't too difficult for children to figure out that they are being deprived because of the behavior of another child. This system doesn't harm only the child who is always in trouble and who is therefore subjected to anger from classmates. The other youngsters are being used as the punishing force and therefore are embroiled in a negative classroom community. They are learning to be judgmental and punitive rather than caring and helpful to others.

Praise: A Verbal Reward

Praise is another form of behavior modification. Teachers and parents are often told to praise children for desirable behavior. It is common to hear teachers make these kinds of statements: "I like how Shelley is sitting so straight and quiet." They hope to make Shelley feel good and to make other children want to be like her. Often, it just makes the others resent Shelley as they hear the unspoken message, "Why aren't the rest of you as good as Shelley?" Even young children quickly learn to see through this type of insincere and manipulative comment. "I'm proud of you" is an even more dangerous type of praise because it is likely to make children dependent on you in order to feel okay (Kohn, 2001).

Praise is a type of reward. It has the same uses and the same side effects as other forms of behavior modification (Kohn, 1996). Certainly, it has the same effects on performance, self-esteem, moral autonomy, self-discipline, and intrinsic motivation as any other reward system. This is probably hard for you to believe, as most people have bought into the idea that we are supposed to praise children. However, there is compelling evidence that praise not only is counterproductive in increasing desired behaviors (Grusec, 1991), but actually has a negative influence even on self-esteem.

How can it make people feel less good about themselves to have someone tell them they are smart or pretty or capable? Think about the importance of unconditional love for self-esteem and then think about praise: Praise doesn't say "you are important and lovable because you are you." Instead it says, "I approve of you because you are smart or pretty or capable." Also think about the flip side of the praise coin: If a person judges you wonderful today, that same person can make a different judgment tomorrow. Instead of making kids feel confident, praise makes them insecure and fearful of rejection (Kohn, 2001).

Praise is often recommended as a tool for guidance and discipline, and most people consider it positive and helpful. Few seem to have considered that praise is an external judgment about another person (Katz & McClellan, 1997). When you praise someone, you are setting yourself up as an authority who knows what is best. This attitude implies that you are able to evaluate others' performance better than they are. These messages can make children dependent on others to tell them whether or not they are doing well. It keeps them from judging for themselves and developing autonomy. It is also condescending because it implies a power imbalance; rarely does a lower-status person praise a higher-status person (Brady et al., 2003). Would you tell your boss you are proud of her?

∞ PRAISE VERSUS ENCOURAGEMENT

Praise	*Encouragement Alternatives*
I'm proud of you.	I noticed that you helped Zeth with his coat.
	You got all the books back in their places.
	You did it!
	It looks like you're feeling good about that.
Good work!	How did you figure that out?
	What did you do to make it work?
	The end of your story made me laugh.
	I see you used a lot of purple paint.
	It looked like you enjoyed doing that.
I like how Emily is cleaning up.	Thank you for your help.

Giving Encouragement Instead

So, what *can* you say to kids? Should you never say another nice thing? You can learn to give positive verbal feedback that is not judgmental by substituting comments that help children learn to self-evaluate and self-congratulate. Instead of telling them what you think about their accomplishments, you can help children identify their own feelings of pride or success. We want to convey interest, appreciation, and respect but not impose our judgment on children.

Simply describing what the child did is one good alternative to praise (Kohn, 2001). For example, instead of giving your opinion by saying something like "You did a nice job" or "I'm proud of you," you could put more energy into the process and describe what it is you saw the child do. You could say, "I saw you share the doll buggy with Devon. That made her happy." You don't need to tell the child that she is generous or kind; it is better for her to draw that conclusion for herself (Faber & Mazlish, 1996). Describing instead of praising might involve such changes as saying, "You got all the blocks put away in their right place!" rather than "What a good worker you are." These examples take the focus away from praising the person and emphasize the behavior. In addition, they are specific about what the child did and therefore provide more useful information. Describing what a child did requires you to pay more attention to the child than is required for a judgment such as "Good job!" Children recognize and appreciate the difference.

Asking questions is another valuable alternative to praise. When a child shows you a drawing or other project, resist the temptation to judge. It is quick and easy to say something like "That's great." Or "How beautiful." But such responses actually *take away* children's confidence, interest, and pleasure in their work, causing them to do less well in the future (Kohn, 2001). Instead of judging the work, it is far more respectful and supportive to ask questions about their process.

> Luis has been at the paint easel for quite a while. Dennis stops by to see how he is doing and Luis asks, "Do you like my picture, teacher?" Dennis is working at using encouragement instead of praise and so he doesn't fall into the trap. Instead of a direct answer, he says, "Wow, look at all the colors in your painting! How did you decide which ones to use?" Luis responds that he used his favorite colors, so Dennis has a short discussion with Luis about why he likes those colors.
>
> Nearby, Dennis sees Nick and Tory, who have made an intricate block structure they want to show off. Dennis kneels down to examine it more carefully and asks, "What was the hardest part of building this?" When they mention the bridge, Dennis asks, "How did you figure out how to make this bridge stay up?" The boys explain their trial-and-error process in detail and Dennis listens attentively.

Responding to children by describing their actions and asking questions is often called *encouragement* rather than *praise* (Hitz & Driscoll, 1988). As shown in the examples, it doesn't require praise to show your enthusiasm for a child's efforts. Comments that focus children's attention on their own judgment of accomplishments and behavior helps them feel good about what they have done without damaging their autonomy.

Teachers who model honest communication are more likely to get it from their students. *Honesty* is the key word here. Honest expressions of appreciation or admiration are quite different from praise given to manipulate someone's behavior. As you work to reduce your use of praise, focus first on stopping manipulative praise, especially that which puts kids into competition with one another. A private statement to the child, rather than a public statement to the class about one child's performance, is less likely to be manipulative.

Encouragement as Effective Communication

It might be helpful to think about praise and encouragement in relationship to the communication skills described in Chapter 7. Praise is another of the "roadblocks to communication" described by Gordon (1970, 1989). In contrast, encouragement can be a form of reflective listening. This type of encouragement responds to the message sent by what a child says or does. If Blake calls you over to look at his block tower, you can tell by his expression that he is pleased with himself. Reflective listening and encouragement respond to that message about his own feelings. "It looks like you feel big for making such a big tower" tunes in to the child's feelings rather than judging what he has done.

Positive "I messages" are a form of encouragement also. For instance, when a child does something helpful for you, a sincere "thank you" gives a more respectful message than praise. If you decide you do want to give a value judgment, think about what you say to children in comparison to what you would say to an adult acquaintance. Then you might decide that "Congratulations," or "WOW!" is more respectful than "I'm proud of you."

Do you recognize the difference between praise and encouragement? Is it clear to you how examples of external adult judgment are different from helping children think about and evaluate their own behavior? Do you think the change is worth the effort? If not, read Kohn's article, *Five Reasons to Stop Saying "Good Job!"* listed in the Recommended Readings at the end of this chapter.

CONCLUSION

Behavior modification happens whether you plan it or not. Understanding how it works can help you keep it from working against you. Recognizing that many common discipline systems are forms of behavior modification can help you make more informed decisions about your own discipline plans. Thinking about the negative effects of behavior modification can help you decide whether to implement it purposefully or not.

This chapter has explained why behavior modification ultimately tends to be counterproductive. It has also discussed why rewards and praise are not compatible with a relationship of mutual respect. Such respect is crucial to the type of human relationships that nurture the development of caring, morally autonomous people. If autonomy and self-discipline are your long-term goals, you do not want to use behavior modification approaches to discipline.

∽ FOR FURTHER THOUGHT

1. Think about things you do just for the payoff or reward; think about those things you do purely for your own purposes. Which things do you put more effort into and get more pleasure from? What are the lessons for teachers?

2. Observe in a classroom, watching for the focus of the teacher's attention. Is inappropriate behavior or desirable behavior more apt to get attention? What are the consequences for child behavior?

3. Closely observe your own interactions with children. Do you accidentally reinforce undesirable behavior? What can you do to focus more on the desirable?

4. Talk to children about the stars and stickers they get for school performance. Do the children focus on the learning or on the prizes? How do you think getting rewards affects a child's education and attitude about learning?

5. A problem to solve: Courtney finally wrote something in her journal today instead of just drawing in it: a major breakthrough!
   a. If you were praising her, what might you say?
   b. If you were using encouragement, what might you say?
   c. How are the two approaches and their goals different?

6. Explain what's wrong with a teacher putting a marble into a jar when the class is especially cooperative, and then letting the class have a party when the jar is full.

7. How does the usual approach to time-out differ from a related consequence?

∽ RECOMMENDED READINGS

Canter, L. (1988). Assertive discipline and the search for the perfect classroom. *Young Children, 43*(2), 24.

Hitz, R. (1988). Assertive discipline: A response to Lee Canter. *Young Children, 43*(2), 25–26.

Hitz, R., & Driscoll, A. (1988). Praise or encouragement? New insights into praise: Implications for early childhood teachers. *Young Children, 43*(5), 6–13.

Kohn, A. (1996). *Beyond discipline: From compliance to community.* Reston, VA: Association for Supervision and Curriculum Development.

Kohn, A. (2001). Five reasons to stop saying "good job!" *Young Children, 56*(5), 24–28.

10 Punishment Versus Discipline

S ociety is gradually coming to recognize the negative effects of punishing children physically (Williams & Shaps, 1999). For example, spanking or slapping children is outlawed in most states. However, there are 13 states that still allow physical punishment in schools (CEASE, 2004). In addition, many other types of punishment are still commonly used to control and direct students. Although this chapter examines various forms of punishment and their negative effects on children, this book is primarily about alternatives to punishment. Chapters 4 through 8 explained how and why other approaches work far better. In those chapters, we explained which causes indicate the approaches described there. However, we do not accept punishment as an appropriate treatment for any cause of misbehavior.

Punishment is intended to hurt or humiliate a person in response to undesirable behavior; its goal is to make a person pay for misconduct (DeVries et al., 2000; Piaget, 1965/1932). Emotional pain is often more intense and lasting than bodily harm. You may have personal memories of intense embarrassment about being banished to the hallway for an offense. You might still be able to feel your childhood despair and frustration at being denied an eagerly awaited outing after an infraction of the rules. Or perhaps your worst memory of school is the shame and anger you felt from a teacher's sarcastic put-down. These are all punishments.

RESULTS OF PUNISHMENT

Most people who use punishment believe it will improve behavior. In fact, it can appear to stop the undesirable behavior because punishment may force negative behaviors "underground" (e.g., Butchart & McEwan, 1998; Straus, 1991). This quick result convinces many people that punishment is effective. However, extensive research proves that punishment is not an effective way of correcting behavior (e.g., Bredekamp & Copple, 1997; Dodge, Bates, & Pettit, 1990; Sabatino, 1991). It is clear that punishment does not improve behavior. Even if the action being punished does stop for the moment, worse behavior is almost sure to follow. Punishment creates seriously counterproductive feelings that are demonstrated in numerous ways.

Anger and Aggression

Anger is a common reaction to punishment. Children who are punished have a need to get even, to assert their own power after having been the victim of someone else's power. Because anger tends to be expressed as aggression, children often vent their anger by hitting and hurting others. The negative feelings inside these angry children inevitably surface. Having experienced punishment, they have learned from a powerful role model how to give punishment (Deater-Deckard, Dodge, Bates, & Pettit, 1996; Spieker, Larson, Lewis, Keller, & Gilchrist, 1999). Children who have been hit when they have displeased a big person are very likely to hit a smaller person who displeases them. This is very clear in the following example where Kyle seems to be echoing an adult as he tries to justify hitting Joshua:

Five-year-old Kyle and 3-year-old Joshua are working side-by-side with some magnets. Kyle decides he wants the magnet that Joshua has and tries to take it. Joshua resists by running away from the bigger boy, clutching the precious magnet. Kyle chases after Joshua, catches him, and hits him to get him to relinquish the magnet. As Sheri comforts the sobbing Joshua, Kyle keeps saying over and over, "He didn't pay attention. He didn't pay attention."

Children who experience other forms of punishment tend to be physically aggressive, too (Vissing, Straus, Gelles, & Harrop, 1991), and they will have also learned other methods of getting even. These kids might call other children names, ruin their work, or take their possessions. Such unacceptable behavior is then likely to be punished, creating further misbehavior. This negative cycle is behind the behavior of many "bad kids." Unfortunately, many parents use punishment as discipline at home (Springen, 2000). The teacher then has to deal with the results at school.

Mrs. Jensen chose her words carefully as she shared her concerns about Tony with his parents at their conference. "When Tony doesn't like what someone else is doing, he often hurts them." Looking concerned, his mother said, "Oh, dear. What does he do?" Referring to her observation notes, Mrs. Jensen described an incident. "When he didn't like a classmate's singing, he told her to quit it. She did for a while but started up again. Tony hit her and said, 'I told you not to do that!' He usually says that right after he hurts someone." A flash of recognition came across the mother's face. She knew where he got that line! And the hitting, too! She glanced accusingly at her husband. He retorted, "That sounds like a normal kid thing."

The father questioned Mrs. Jensen, "What do you do to him when he hits?" The teacher explained how she generally handled the situations, with attention to the hurt child and modeling alternative ways for Tony to get what he needs. Tony's dad leaned back in his chair and said knowingly, "Yeah, well, that soft-touch stuff just doesn't work with this kid. You have to tell him not to do something and then just don't let him do it! Giving him a quick wallop works at home." The mother stared intently at the pattern on the carpet, trying to avoid both the teacher's and her husband's eyes.

Mrs. Jensen could tell she had touched on a sensitive area with this couple. Still, she was glad she had brought it up. She promised to keep them updated on Tony's progress. In the meantime, she had some new insight about why Tony was exhibiting such physically aggressive responses; it seemed he was following his father's model.

∞ PUNISHMENT

Punishment does not appear to improve behavior. Even if the action being punished does stop for the moment, worse behavior is almost sure to follow. Punishment creates seriously counterproductive feelings that are demonstrated in numerous ways.

Damaged Relationships

Punishment also creates feelings of hostility and resentment toward the person administering it (e.g., Faber & Mazlish, 1996; Gordon, 1989; Thompson, 1998). This result is particularly serious when it damages relationships between children and their parents. Whether the negative feelings are aimed at parents, teachers, or other authority figures, those emotions get in the way of positive discipline teaching. People don't want to be around someone who hurts them or makes them feel bad. Certainly, no one is eager to listen to, or learn from, that person. Some children merely withdraw from contact, and others try to get even. Getting even takes many forms, depending on the experiences and the personality of the child. One child may be openly defiant and rude, and another may retaliate through helplessness and refusal to try anything. Still another may become a bully, using smaller children as substitute targets.

All of the above responses to punishment are self-defeating, and all are only made worse by further punishment. It isn't only relationships with punishers that are damaged; children who are punished tend to have trouble with peer relationships also (e.g., Hart, Olsen, Robinson, & Mandleco, 1997; Putallaz & Heflin, 1990). Because these youngsters use aggression to get their way, other children don't want to play with them. Being rejected for hitting or shoving truly confuses the child who has been punished; the experience of being punished teaches children that hurting others is an appropriate response when they don't get their way. They erroneously believe that their aggressive behaviors will have positive social outcomes. All too often these youngsters end up as social outcasts, exhibiting escalating antisocial behaviors in retaliation.

Damage to Self-Esteem

Punishment also damages self-esteem because children get their opinion of their worth from how others treat them (Miller, 2004). Being punished can convince youngsters that they are inferior (DeVries, 1999) and that they are bad (Vissing et al., 1991). Feeling like a worthless or bad person is likely to become a self-fulfilling prophecy, resulting in further undesirable behavior. Many children routinely experience verbal abuse at home, internalizing the labels such as "stupid" or "damn brat" and acting accordingly. A child who is verbally or physically punished does not feel respected or valued. Any kind of punishment attacks personal dignity by putting the child at the mercy of a more powerful person. Additionally, many punishments are humiliating, as shown in the following example:

> "Beep! Beep! Beep! Beep!" sounded the intercom, as the library light kept flashing. The secretary had two people on hold on the telephone and new parents at the counter needing forms. She switched on the speaker, "Yes, this is the office." The librarian sounded distraught. "Ian bit Serge and then ran out of the room. He's somewhere in the halls, and I can't leave the group to go find him." The secretary responded, "Sorry, but I'm the only person in the office, so I can't go look for him right now." Leaning by the message board, the custodian

Being punished can make children feel like "bad people" and damage their self-esteem.

overheard the exchange. He volunteered, "I'll go get him." Relieved, she called the library back and said, "George is going to go look for Ian. I'll let you know when we find him."

The custodian strode down the hall on his mission to bring in the wayward child. Not finding him on the first floor, he went upstairs. Still failing to see the boy, he checked the playground. Darn it, he needed to go set up the lunchroom soon. Where was that kid? Then he thought of the bathroom. Sure enough, there were two feet standing in the back corner of a stall. "Come on out!" ordered George. The boy froze, wondering if the custodian could see him. "Come out now!" he repeated. The other boys in the bathroom giggled as George crouched to look under the door and demanded, "Move it!" Ian slowly opened the stall door, his eyes darting around like those of a trapped animal. His mind raced as his playmates, Alex and Tory, teased him about being caught.

Once outside the bathroom, George scooped Ian up like a bag of potatoes. He hauled the boy past the library while the child flailed and demanded to be put down. His classmates crowded to the door to glimpse the spectacle. Humiliated, Ian's temper flared. He pounded on the back of George's leg, but the custodian just held him more tightly and headed for the office, proud to have successfully completed his mission. Dumping Ian in the detention room, George announced, "Here's your biter!" Ian felt about one foot tall as the custodian described the bathroom scene to the secretary. And Ian noted that the woman listening at the counter was his friend Kenji's mom. Ian wished he were invisible!

Unfortunately, this disrespectful treatment of children is not uncommon. The damage to a child's self-respect is immeasurable. The idea of mutual respect between adult and child is the absolute opposite of this scenario.

Fear

Punishment controls through fear (Brady, et al. 2003). This fear keeps some children from positive activities as well as negative ones. When they are punished without warning for something they didn't know was unacceptable, many children will tend to avoid any new activity. Their strategy is to use caution about anything that might possibly get them into trouble. Exploration and initiative are sacrificed to the need for safety and security. Therefore, fear of punishment can hamper academic learning. Remember Kayla in the assertive discipline example in Chapter 9? Scared of checkmarks on the board by her name and of classmates who blamed her for not getting marbles in the jar, Kayla rarely initiated conversation or joined activities. The following example of Beau and the broken bracelet shows the results of a different approach:

> Beau's face showed surprise as he held the two pieces of what had been Shayla's bracelet, and Mrs. Jensen could see that he had not purposely broken it. Mrs. Jensen acknowledged Shayla's concern and accepted Beau's protests of an "accident." She encouraged each child to hear the other's side of the story.
>
> That evening, Mrs. Jensen called Beau's parents and explained what had happened. She made it very clear that Beau had not been "naughty," just clumsy in examining the bracelet. She discussed the concept of making restitution and asked if they thought they could help Beau figure out a way to make it up to Shayla for her loss.
>
> A few weeks later, Beau arrived at school and handed a delighted Shayla a package with a small assortment of child-size bracelets. It had taken Beau those weeks to earn the money, buy the bracelets, and wrap them up to give to Shayla. Mrs. Jensen knew that Beau's heartfelt "You're welcome!" to Shayla's "Thank you!" could never have been the result of punishment. Beau understood the significance of his carelessness, but he felt good about himself for making things right. He saw himself as a good boy, not a bad one.

Sadly, many adults who were themselves punished, and suffered from the results, nevertheless use punishment to control children in their care. They may realize that it harmed them, but that model has been strongly imprinted on them (McEwan, 1998).

Missed Opportunity for Learning

Punishment actually undermines children's learning about appropriate and inappropriate behavior. Instead of youngsters thinking about the behavior that caused the problem, they end up thinking resentfully about the punishment. Punishment also focuses attention on what *not* to do rather than teaching what *to* do. Young children need information about acceptable ways of behaving, and they need help in understanding why certain actions are better than others (e.g., Hart et al., 1997). In other words, they need teaching instead of punishment.

> Caroline, the children's center director, was concerned about the row of sad faces in the back of the room during afternoon choice time. It was Joanne's policy to remove kids from play if they weren't able to get along with others. Caroline decided to discuss this policy with Joanne.
>
> Caroline met with Joanne and shared her concern that the children who most needed practice with social skills were not getting that practice. When they were removed from play, they were no longer in the learning situation. She asked Joanne to problem-solve with her about ways to help these youngsters learn to get along instead of just expelling them from play.
>
> As they discussed the kinds of learning experiences these problem children needed, Joanne began to think of ways to teach instead of punish. But she realized that the changes required more than one adult in the large playroom. "I'll have to ask Sheri or Maureen to work the blue room with me during choice time," she planned. That change, however, meant having fewer options available for children. The teachers would have to alternate between opening the woodworking center and the painting area. Joanne decided that the sacrifice was worth it. With two adults to intervene, teachers could help children individually resolve disputes.
>
> Caroline was pleased with the outcome of the discussion. She and Joanne reviewed the kinds of role modeling and problem-solving assistance that would be most helpful in teaching social skills. Joanne arranged a meeting with her assistants to go over this new plan.

Lack of Critical Thinking

Punishment doesn't just limit learning about acceptable behavior: it limits learning in general. Brain research shows that events that create fear, anxiety, or humiliation have negative effects on mental growth (Butchart, 1998). Even strict environments that require superficial, automatic responses can inhibit the growth of mental capacity. The gruff and threatening order to "Do as you're told!" and the expectation of instant obedience are examples of this type of environment. Children raised with this type of discipline usually have low motivation to think beyond parroting memorized answers. They tend to be submissive to the ideas of others and accept what others say uncritically instead of learning to think for themselves (DeVries, 1999). Such submissiveness may sound good to some parents, unless they realize that it will mean submitting to peer pressure when the child is a teenager.

In contrast, events that encourage reflection and other thinking promote mental growth and intellectual power. An example of an event that encourages thinking is Beau and the broken bracelet. Through his experience, he comes to realize the connection between his action and the broken bracelet, and then the connection between his work to earn money and making up for the damage. This type of discipline encourages children to think for themselves and strive to understand the world (DeVries, 1999). A brain that is exercised becomes stronger and more capable.

For some kids, fear of punishment becomes the only reason to behave in socially acceptable ways.

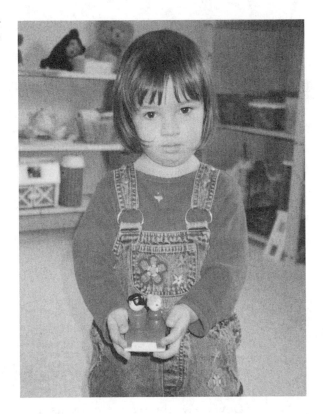

Lack of Inner Controls

For some kids, fear of punishment becomes the only reason to behave in socially acceptable ways. These youngsters are only likely to act appropriately when someone is there to catch them. Even then, the seriousness of the punishment is often weighed against the potential pleasure of the inappropriate action (Kamii, 1982). Often youngsters will choose to go ahead with the action and "face the music" later. Accepting the punishment can even become a sort of challenge to their courage. Not getting caught can become another type of challenge. Kohlberg's (1984) extensive studies of moral development concluded that punishment is ineffective in promoting moral development, whereas the opposite approach, a deemphasized use of adult power, assists the development of a child's internalized conscience (e.g., DeVries, 1999; Kochanska, 1991).

Deceitfulness

Many people whose only restraint comes from fear of punishment become incredibly sneaky (Kamii, 1982). They become skillful at lying and other forms of deceit. You have probably known people who have adopted this dishonest approach to life. They get what they want behind people's backs. Although they can act innocent, others soon catch on to them and learn to distrust them. Certainly, this behavior is not a desirable outcome of discipline.

Recent headlines tell us that juvenile crime is increasing alarmingly. The public response is to "get tough" and punish harder, while punishing the kids' parents, too. Suggestions such as publishing the names of juvenile offenders are evidence of how little most people understand about how to improve behavior. How can publicly labeling a young person as a criminal possibly help that child behave better? When suggestions focus on prevention of juvenile delinquency instead of punishment, the plans aim at older kids who are already in trouble. Kindergarten teachers can tell you which of their 5-year-old students are likely to end up in jail unless they get help; the problems begin early, and therefore need to be addressed early.

Those who would address the problems through punitive measures need to read the research showing that children who are punished are most likely to turn to crime (Straus, 1991). In 2001, nearly three of every hundred American adults had served time in prison, according to the U.S. Justice Department. Almost a third of those who had served time were still under correctional supervision, including parole, probation, and in local jails (U.S. Department of Justice, 2004). Punishment clearly isn't working, since building more and more prisons and incarcerating more and more people have not significantly reduced crime.

WHY PUNISHMENT IS USED

Obviously, the results of punishment are totally incompatible with the goals of self-discipline and autonomy. Punishment undermines the development of personal responsibility. Adults who rely on punishment are looking for the quick fix referred to in Chapter 1, but they may not get that result because some children are not submissive enough to give in.

Children's defiance leads to escalation of punishment and even greater defiance. When punishment clearly doesn't stop the behavior, many parents and teachers still persist in using it because they don't know any other methods. In the rest of this chapter we discuss this lack of skills and other reasons why some adults may use punishment.

ADULT STRESS

Even adults who really don't believe in punishment and know better than to use it sometimes resort to it (Sabatino, 1991). A survey of American parents found that 70 percent believed that yelling and swearing at children cause psychological problems (Daro, Abrahams, & Robson, 1988). Yet, that same study, as well as others, revealed that most parents had insulted or sworn at their children during the past year (Vissing et al., 1991). There are times when the stresses of life push people beyond their limits, when an adult's behavior doesn't live up to his or her personal expectations. If this is a frequent occurrence, counseling is needed. If it is a rare occurrence, it is best to forgive yourself and try to redeem the situation.

> Mrs. Jensen had such an experience several years ago when she was driving across the state on a very hot summer day with her four children in a van with no air-conditioning. The children were uncomfortable and fussy from the heat and from being confined in the van. Andrew was screaming that he wanted out of his car seat, and Joe was teasing John by snatching his hat. There was no place to pull over and deal with the problem sensibly, so Mrs. Jensen reached back and grabbed Joe's arm, yanking him into his place with a barking order: "Sit!" She just didn't know what else to do. Besides, it actually made her feel better at the time. But later she felt bad and apologized to Joe, explaining her frustration. When everyone was calm and cooled off, the family was able to problem-solve about the situation.

Such instances are less likely in the controlled environment of Mrs. Jensen's classroom. Sometimes, however, a child does push her beyond her limits. In her professional role, Mrs. Jensen maintains her professional ethics. She would never hit a child or even grab a youngster in anger. She knows the importance of being in control of herself to effectively deal with discipline problems.

> Robert began making screeching noises again during the Spanish lesson. Señora Lupita was trying to keep the group interested in the Spanish language songs and stories she was sharing with the class, but the group was clearly becoming distracted by Robert's antics. Mrs. Jensen tried to make eye contact with him to communicate with him, but he avoided looking at her. Finally, she went and sat beside him to calm him, but his disruptions only escalated.
>
> Out of respect for Señor a Lupita, Mrs. Jensen felt she had to remove Robert from the group. However, Robert was not receptive to the idea and was not co-operative when Mrs. Jensen tried to escort him away. He yelled louder and flailed around, kicking her in the process. It was an unpleasant scene, and Mrs. Jensen was very upset.
>
> She knew she shouldn't try to deal with Robert at that moment. Instead, she privately told him, "I'm feeling too angry to talk to you about this right now. When I'm feeling calmer, we'll talk about the problem."

Any time you feel angry, you run the risk of punishing behavior rather than teaching self-discipline (Curwin & Mendler, 1999). Chapter 8 described how anger can change related consequences into punishment, just by the inevitably negative tone of voice and body language. Similarly, anger destroys the technique of holding a child to calm him or her. Restraining a child when you are infuriated is different from the reassuring embrace needed by an out-of-control youngster. It is important to know when you are not emotionally able to provide helpful guidance to youngsters and to call in someone with a fresh perspective. This action also models for children an adult's personal time-out to calm down.

Misconceptions

Some adults say they don't believe in punishment and yet routinely rely on it. Apparently, they don't perceive their actions as punishment. Some teachers humiliate children in front of classmates and call it peer pressure. Others pride

ACHIEVING EFFECTIVE DISCIPLINE WITHOUT CORPORAL PUNISHMENT

The Association for Childhood Education International (Cryan, 1987) recommends the following measures to promote effective discipline in schools without resorting to corporal punishment:

- Improve school climate with support by all school personnel
- Provide in-service training to increase staff competence and help educators see the theory-practice link
- Improve teacher training by focusing it on techniques for student motivation and effective handling of discipline problems
- Identify children's potential problems early and follow up with counseling designed to prevent discipline problems

themselves on their "humor" when they cut down a child with a sarcastic response. Still others call it a "consequence" when they take away privileges totally unrelated to a behavior problem. All of these responses inflict hurt, create anger, and fail to teach. They are all punishment.

> Ahmed was notoriously slow at cleaning up before circle time. The truth was that he didn't like going to circle time, so he dragged his feet. It distracted Joanne to have a child otherwise occupied during her circle. One day she decided to break Ahmed of his habit. She announced in a voice that carried across the room, "We're waiting for Ahmed to join our group so that we can begin our circle."
>
> Embarrassed because all of the kids were staring at him, Ahmed hurried. Trying to carry both the basket of trucks and the box of animals at once, he dropped everything with a clatter. With his classmates laughing, he got even more flustered and put some trucks in the animal box. Joanne noted his error and asked, "Can anyone tell Ahmed which container the trucks go into?" "The orange basket!" taunted several children, enjoying what seemed to be the teacher's approval to pick on Ahmed. By now, Ahmed was nearly in tears, but Joanne couldn't see his face. She made another effort at using what she called peer pressure to bring his behavior into line. "Ahmed, we'll wait for 3 more minutes; then we'll have to start our circle. It's just not fair to keep your friends waiting." Throughly upset, he fumbled at putting away the rest of the toys. Finally, the teacher pronounced, "Time's up! Sorry, but you have used up too much of our time being a slowpoke." Steaming, Ahmed thought, "You're not sorry at all! I hate you!"

Lack of Discipline Skills

Many people fear that children will go wild without fear of punishment; it is the only discipline approach these adults understand (Gordon, 1989; Reynolds, 2000). They are not informed about how other approaches to discipline set limits and communicate expectations about desirable behavior. Not understanding these other approaches, they think their choice is either punishment or a total lack of discipline, as we discussed in Chapter 1. To many people, discipline means punishment. That was clearly the case with a father who told Mrs. Jensen, "I just don't know what to do with him anymore. Hitting him doesn't make any difference."

Any concern about a lack of guidance and discipline is justified. Overly permissive child rearing can be as damaging as a punitive approach. Freedom without limits or responsibility is chaotic and dangerous. There are times when adults must step in to keep youngsters safe as well as to help them learn. Children must be helped to learn socially acceptable behavior and respect for the rights of others. These understandings are good for the child who learns them, as well as for those around that child. Young people who don't learn socially acceptable behaviors are not pleasant to be around. They damage property and are rude and inconsiderate. Naturally, no one wants to spend time with them, which leads to feelings of rejections and damages their self-esteem. Understanding the rights and needs of others is also essential to the development of self-discipline. Self-discipline doesn't result from forced behavior, but neither does it occur by itself. It is a product of careful teaching through constructivist approaches to discipline.

Family and Societal Norms

Many truly loving and caring families are firmly convinced that punishment will have long-term, positive results (Springen, 2000). They mean well but are misinformed. Their beliefs are based on tradition rather than evidence. They are merely doing what their parents did with them, unaware of the negative effects punishment had on their own development. Education must be used as a tool to help these misinformed people learn the other, more useful approaches explained in this book. Most books on guidance and discipline are research-based and firmly reject punishment as an option. Unfortunately, a few are written by people without a background in child development or knowledge of relevant research; parents may not know the difference and can get led astray. Your suggestions of constructive discipline books or parenting classes may be a helpful way to introduce parents to effective discipline. In the Recommended Readings section at the end of this chapter and Chapter 7, we suggest some of our favorite parenting books.

Some people justify punishment for broken rules based on the model of our legal system. However, our legal system is merely designed to control behavior, not to teach acceptable behavior or to socialize citizens (Watson, 1999). In contrast to our legal system, parents and other educators could be the antidotes to punitive measures. "It does not make sense for educators to use the criminal-justice model as the first resort, before employing what they were professionally prepared to use—educational and mentoring approaches" (Gathercoal, 1998).

The violent traditions of society make it difficult for many people to give up punitive approaches to discipline. Movies and television promote violence as a legitimate way for the "good guys" to win. Many sporting events involve violence that is eagerly applauded, and world leaders still rely on force to settle differences. The use of force is continually glorified.

Yet, society also recognizes values that should counteract the use of force to discipline children. Respect for the rights of all people is increasingly evidenced in laws and attitudes. Minority groups are speaking up and insisting on respectful treatment. Perhaps the least represented group is the one with the smallest voice: the children. The U.S. Constitution guarantees equality, rights, and the protection of all. Perhaps children, too, will soon be included in this guarantee. Teachers can be effective advocates for the rights of young children. Professional organizations representing early childhood teachers, such as the National Association for the Education of Young Children (NAEYC) and the Association for Childhood Education International (ACEI), have been vocal about the subject of punishment (Greenberg, 1992a; Simmons, 1991).

CONCLUSION

We have hope that punishment will cease to be considered a reasonable means of discipline. We believe that when parents and teachers understand the dangers of punishment and learn more effective approaches to child guidance, the world will become a better place. There will be fewer angry people who need to get even with society through violence. There will be fewer people who have come to believe they are worthless. There will be less dishonesty and less energy spent to avoid getting caught. Personal inner controls and concern for others will become the norm among morally autonomous people.

∽ FOR FURTHER THOUGHT

1. Were you punished as a child? If so, what are your memories of the way you felt and what you thought about being punished? How do your memories of physical punishment differ from those of other types of punishment? How did each method affect your self-esteem?

2. Were you raised with no discipline? Did you wish for controls and guidance? How did this experience affect your attitudes about discipline? What was the impact on your self-esteem?

3. Were you given constructive discipline as a child? How has it affected your life, your attitudes, and your self-esteem?

4. Observe aggressive young children. Do they seem to be imitating a model of adult aggression?

5. Observe socially competent young children. Do they seem to have learned peaceful negotiation of conflict from adult models?

6. How would you explain to someone the fundamental differences between punishment and discipline? Can you relate those differences to the differences between moral autonomy and heteronomy?

∽ *RECOMMENDED READINGS*

Butchart, R. E., & McEwan, B. (1998). *Classroom discipline in American Schools: Problems and possibilities for democratic education.* Albany, NY: State University of New York Press.

Gordon, T. (1970). *Parent effectiveness training.* New York: Wyden.

Gottman, J. 1997. *Raising an emotionally intelligent child.* New York: Fireside.

Kamii, C. (1984). Obedience is not enough. *Young Children. 39*(4), 11–14.

Williams, M. M., & Schaps, E. (Eds). (1999). *Character education: The foundation for teacher education.* Washington, DC: The Character Education Partnership.

PART 3
Matching Discipline Causes to Discipline Approaches

Part Two explained the different approaches to discipline. Although this information is essential, its organization is not in the format most useful in real life. In the real world, we are first confronted with the behavior, not the discipline approach. Part Three looks at discipline from the real-world perspective: We start with the behavior and move backward to discover the cause, select the related approach, and then implement that approach.

Discipline is effective only if it addresses the cause of the problem. In Chapter 1 we explain this idea by comparing the guidance of children to gardening. Getting rid of unwanted behavior is like weeding the garden—the cause of the behavior is similar to the roots of the weeds. Because it is necessary to get at the roots of a problem, parents, caregivers, and teachers are constantly challenged to determine what is causing unwanted behavior.

In the following chapters we will look at some common behaviors that disrupt school and child-care settings. We hope the examples provide useful practice in matching behaviors to probable causes. We also hope that the process of matching discipline approaches to the cause of the problem becomes more clear as you read this section. Remember, we're matching discipline approaches to the causes, not to the behaviors.

11 *Immaturity*

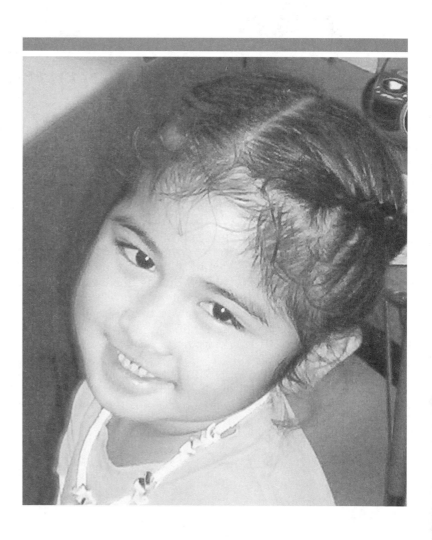

*I*t's playtime in preschool and the teachers are busy: Kyle just hit Sophie, El-lie has grabbed Olivia's toy, Meadow wet her pants, and Jack is sobbing hys-terically over something. This is a glimpse into a normal day with young children; these are examples of typical behaviors for little people with a lot to learn. Such immaturity is the cause of many behavior problems among children. This chapter examines the types of behaviors caused by immaturity. It also demonstrates some appropriate responses to the specific examples of immatu-rity. In doing so, we revisit the information presented in previous chapters about child development and appropriate child guidance.

The word *immature* means not fully grown; therefore, being young means be-ing immature. Although teenagers may use the term in a derogatory way to one another, even teenagers have a right to be immature. Just being young is often the cause of problems; the younger the child, the more this is so. Early childhood teachers face this issue daily as their students demonstrate a lack of skills needed for success in daily living. Experienced teachers of young children know that each day will bring spilling, falling, spitting, biting, hitting, crying, and screaming. These behavior problems can be directly traced to immature coordi-nation, undeveloped communication ability, childish social skills, and other per-fectly normal aspects of early childhood. Knowledgeable adults are able to distinguish between misbehavior and childlike behavior. This distinction is es-sential for helpful guidance.

Recognizing that immaturity naturally causes many problems gives you a more productive way to deal with those problems. Your challenge is to determine the exact cause of the problem so that you can provide the appropriate teaching for the child or make the needed change in the program. Because the exact same behavior can have different causes, you need to work at discovering the cause. This involves observing for patterns in individual children's behavior, listening and observing to determine a child's understanding of a situation, and commu-nicating with families so you have information about each child's experiences outside of school.

PHYSICAL IMMATURITY

Let's start by looking at problems typically related to physical immaturity. We will also examine emotional, social, and intellectual development as causes of unde-sirable behaviors.

Inability to Sit Still

Children often get into trouble for moving around when they aren't supposed to. The inability to sit still for very long is another example of the physical limitations of being young (Bredekamp, 1997). Forcing young children to sit still or control their bodies for long periods of time can cause problems. Unable to satisfy this unreasonable expectation, the young child will move around regardless of what the teacher wants. Chapter 2 described this aspect of early childhood development, and Chapter 4 explained the importance of allowing children to move around as a way to prevent discipline problems. Let's look more closely at ways to meet that need.

First the teacher must let go of plans that require children to sit still and be quiet for very long. The teacher's understanding and acceptance of young children's needs will go a long way toward solving some behavior problems. You certainly don't want to be the cause of the problem. However, if you find that you have been, changing yourself is much easier than changing someone else.

Then you need to analyze your classroom and your program for levels of physical activity. Boys, especially, tend to need a lot of large motor activity (King & Gartrell, 2003). Be sure to include activities that involve the arms, shoulders, and trunk muscles since these normally get used less than lower body muscles. A woodworking area is usually a big draw if it is well supplied with usable tools. Large, hollow blocks are also great for upper body development. If your program doesn't include them, large, hollow blocks would be an excellent investment. Then make sure there is plenty of time and space for using them. Varying the types of props to use with them will enhance children's interest. Pretend play can encourage physical activity too.

> Dennis set up a fitness center for children's play (King & Gartrell, 2003). Many of his students have parents who go to a gym to exercise before or after work, so the children are familiar with this type of activity and were excited about having their own workout area. Dennis included typical preschool materials such as the balance beam and climbing structure, and he created others.
>
> One of the parents volunteered to transform an old school tricycle into a stationary bike exercise center. Maureen and Sheri filled plastic bottles with sand to use as weights. Plastic floor mats were included for calisthenics and lively music for aerobics. Stable child step stools allowed for step aerobics.
>
> The teachers had fun playing with the children and demonstrating some of the less familiar activities. Both boys and girls were attracted to the area and it became a permanent part of the classroom throughout the winter when outdoor active play was less available.

Allowing children to move freely about the classroom and to find comfortable body positions lets children meet their need to move. Teachers who are aware of children's physical development provide meaningful reasons for them to move around. These teachers are also sensitive to the group's energy level. They recognize that squirming and children's frequent requests to move—to go get a drink, to go to the bathroom, to go!—as symptoms of their need for movement. These teachers know that sometimes the only reasonable thing to do is to have everyone push the tables back and play an energetic game or sing an action song!

Movement can be incorporated into many areas of the curriculum. Children can use large muscles when they do art projects that require large pieces of paper and large tools. For instance, children can be encouraged to paint with feather dusters on large cardboard boxes. Math activities can offer movement as children use large manipulatives or practice one-to-one correspondence by moving themselves around. The following example shows how even a normally sedentary activity like reading can accommodate the movement needs of young children.

Mrs. Jensen asked Andrea, her student teacher, to take a group to the library corner to read *The Three Little Pigs* together. Most of the children settled right in and found their place in their individual books. But Isabel, Jason, and Tomas couldn't get settled. They pushed and jostled for seats. They juggled their books into every conceivable position, flipping pages and occasionally dropping the books. Andrea was having a hard time keeping them still and focused on reading. How could she get them through the story with all of this activity and fighting? Deciding to ask for help, she excused herself from the group for a minute and described her difficulty to Mrs. Jensen.

Aware of the high energy level that morning, Mrs. Jensen suggested they try acting out the story. Andrea checked with the children to see if they'd like to do a play. Affirmative! She assigned the roles of three little pigs to—you guessed it—Isabel, Jason, and Tomas. They went to the adjacent block area to build their houses. She sent Brianna, a strong reader, along with them in the narrator/cueing role. Brianna brought the book to each construction site as the part came up in the story. Andrea read the part of the wolf to help pull the play together. The piglets frantically built while the narrator read. They read their pig parts with intensity. Then they squealed in delight and scrambled to the next house as Andrea huffed and puffed. There was no more pushing or dropping books; everyone was fully involved.

Andrea could have wasted a lot of energy trying to squelch the children's surface behaviors. Fortunately, Mrs. Jensen accurately recognized their off-task behaviors as symptoms of an undeniable need for movement. Her recommended discipline approach dealt directly with the cause of the problem.

Mrs. Jensen knows her students well and is in a position to know the cause of behaviors such as why Isabel, Jason, and Tomas had a problem sitting still. But the same behavior could have had a different cause. It is possible that the "troublemakers" might have been uncooperative due to their inability to read the material. Or the problem could have been just the opposite: The material may have lacked challenge for them. Similar disruption could have been caused by one child's attention-getting tactics. Often there are multiple causes, which create an even greater challenge for helpful adult intervention.

Without information about the children involved, it is not possible to diagnose the problem accurately. Without an accurate diagnosis, discipline approaches are likely to go astray. Knowing students well enough to guess fairly accurately about the cause of problems involves establishing authentic relationships with the child and the parents.

Immature Coordination

Spilled juice at snack time is an everyday occurrence in preschool. Usually it is a result of the immature coordination that is normal for young children. Providing child-sized pitchers and furniture increases children's successful independence, but it doesn't eliminate all spills. Adults with realistic expectations prepare for this inevitable outcome by having paper towels handy for clean-up. Piaget (1965/1932) calls it "making restitution" when children clean up their mistakes. We call it helping children take responsibility for themselves without making them feel bad. This approach to accidents is an example of using related consequences, as described

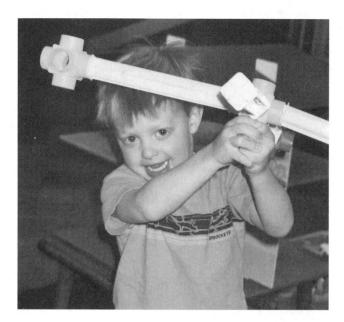

Without information about the children involved, it is not possible to diagnose a problem accurately. Without an accurate diagnosis, discipline approaches are likely to go astray.

in Chapter 8. Teachers also prevent spills from becoming a problem by locating snack tables on a washable floor surface. These preparations help teachers remain calm and allow for productive responses to mistakes. This attitude is a description of the approach to discipline we call *creating environments that prevent discipline problems* (see Chapter 4).

Unfortunately, not all adults realize that spilling is a natural part of learning to pour. Some act as if they think that yelling insults at a child will improve his or her pouring ability. Common adult responses to a spill are "Not again!" or "That's the third time today! Can't you be careful?" Other adults simply eliminate spills by denying children the chance to practice. Both responses are counterproductive to the child's skill development. Both approaches also damage the child's self-esteem and hinder the development of autonomy. Being yelled at makes youngsters feel ashamed and afraid to try, and having things done for them makes kids feel inept and unable to succeed. Both responses create helplessness. In contrast, related consequences help children feel capable and proud (Curwin & Mendler, 1999).

Young children frequently experience negative feedback for the clumsiness natural to their age. As a teacher, you may see a lack of sensitivity not only from other adults but also from the children's own peers. The following example demonstrates how an opportunity for making restitution can make everyone involved feel better about an accident. It is another example of a related consequence.

> Sophie and Anna were at the inventions table, busily cutting out pictures from catalogs and picking bits of ribbon, shells, and styrofoam to glue onto larger pieces of paper. Anna accidentally spilled some of the gooey white glue on Sophie's paper. Sophie started yelling in frustration and anger about her spoiled project. Anna kept saying over and over how sorry she was, but Sophie kept on screaming.

Maureen quickly came to the rescue. Anna looked frightened and fearful of punishment as the teacher came near. Maureen reassured her that accidents do happen and then turned her attention to the screaming Sophie. "I know you are angry about your paper, but such loud screaming hurts everyone's ears. Let's see what we can do to fix your paper. Anna feels bad about spilling on it, and I'm sure she will help you clean it up. What would be a good thing to wipe up glue with?"

Anna did indeed want to help. She suggested that Kleenex might work to wipe up the glue and ran to get some. Together, the girls carefully wiped away the excess glue, leaving Sophie's paper almost as good as new. Then they were able to continue working cooperatively together.

Such accidents don't stop when children reach grade school; they are still a normal part of the children's development.

Several second graders in Mr. Davis's class were busy painting for a class project. They were working on a countertop in the uncarpeted part of the room designated for messy projects. This was fortunate since it wasn't long before the blue paint had spilled on the countertop and was dripping down the lower cabinets onto the floor. The children happily and obliviously continued to paint, while making blue shoe tracks all over the tiled floor.

Mr. Davis saw the mess and said, "I see that paint drips a lot. It's going to be a lot of work cleaning it up when you're finished; what do think will be the best way to do it?" He also asked for their ideas about how they could keep from tracking the paint from their shoes onto the carpet. He helped them find the sponges and paper towels they decided they needed, but let them take charge. He was pleased to discover that his students figured out for themselves how to wipe their shoes off, as well as how to get all the paint cleaned up. In fact, the clean-up project turned out to be even more interesting than the painting, attracting help from many who hadn't even been painting. It didn't take long before there wasn't a trace of blue paint left.

Other Physical Limitations

"Someone wet on the floor!" Physical immaturity sometimes means a youngster doesn't make it to the toilet on time. The accident can be a serious blow to a child's pride and must be handled with care to preserve his or her self-esteem. Mrs. Jensen remembers how her kindergarten teacher publicly humiliated children who had accidents. They had to wash out their underpants, and then the teacher would hang them up to dry in the classroom for all to see. Mrs. Jensen is sure she can improve on that technique. She doesn't consider the incident to be a discipline issue; her only approach in the following example is to treat Meadow with compassionate respect. Mrs. Jensen knows this is not a discipline problem, but rather a maturation issue.

Meadow was working on a puzzle during choice time when she suddenly realized she had to go to the bathroom. She was very uncomfortable, but it wasn't time for the bathroom break yet. She knew she could ask permission to go any time she wanted, but it was just too embarrassing. Everyone would know

---

 SOME NORMAL BEHAVIORS OF YOUNG CHILDREN

Physical Immaturity Can Cause:

- spilling
- bumping
- wetting
- disrupting group time

Emotional Immaturity Can Cause:

- tantrums
- tears

Immature Language Ability Can Cause:

- misunderstanding
- hitting, kicking, biting
- tears and tantrums

Social Immaturity Can Cause:

- hitting
- kicking
- biting
- grabbing

Cognitive Immaturity Can Cause:

- being selfish
- telling "lies"
- taking things
- cheating

---

where she was going. She decided to wait until the scheduled time. Oh, oh! She couldn't hold it any longer. Meadow was mortified but hopeful that no one would notice the puddle on the floor around the chair. She quickly got up and moved away from the evidence. Her skirt didn't seem too wet and maybe no one would see that her underpants were soaked. Meadow just didn't think she could stand it if anyone knew what she had done.

"Mrs. Jensen! Someone wet on the floor!" shouted Jimmie indignantly. The teacher replied calmly, "I guess it will have to be wiped up. Just don't walk there for now." Mrs. Jensen noticed Meadow's damp skirt and furtive looks. She quickly put the pieces together and realized how distressed the shy girl must be. The teacher's challenge was to get the floor cleaned, help Meadow get dry, and still preserve the child's privacy and dignity. Mrs. Jensen noticed that recess was in 10 minutes, and decided to wait until then for the custodian to come and clean up. It would make much less fuss that way. Recess would also be a good time to get Meadow aside and quietly give her some dry undies as well as a plastic bag for her wet ones.

If wetting incidents became frequent, Mrs. Jensen would contact the child's parents and look further for a cause. However, this isolated incident appeared to be simply a case of waiting too long.

UNDEVELOPED COMMUNICATION ABILITY

Consider the activities of hitting, kicking, biting, and spitting. Although these behaviors are unacceptable, they generally only indicate a need to learn more productive approaches for expressing needs and feelings. One common cause of this type of behavior among preschoolers is their lack of communication ability. Young children are still beginners with language (Vygotsky, 1962/1934). They haven't yet had sufficient practice to find the exact words they need, and in times of stress what they do know may fall apart. A child who is angry, frustrated, or otherwise upset often has trouble expressing those feelings in words. Instead, the child hits, kicks, bites, or spits to communicate.

Productive discipline does more than simply stop the behavior; it doesn't just let kids know what not to do, it teaches them what to do. Therefore, when a lack of communication skills appears to be the cause of the behavior, adults need to help children express themselves with language. Teachers of young children can frequently be heard reminding them, "Please use your words," as in this situation with the rocking boat.

> Three children were in the rocking boat happily rocking and pretending to fish. Three-year-old Celeste went over to them and stood by the boat. The children kept on rocking. Celeste started whining and screaming at them, but used no words. The other children looked at her but did not stop what they were doing. Celeste kept on whining and screaming.
>
> Dennis came to the rescue. He bent down to Celeste and said, "You seem very upset." The child acknowledged her teacher's reflective listening with a nod and told him she wanted to play on the boat. Dennis asked her if she had used her words to tell the other children what she wanted. Celeste shook her head "No." So Dennis asked her to think of what words she could use. Celeste smiled at him and said to the children in the boat, "I want to ride."
>
> Thank heavens it worked! The children in the boat stopped and let her in, then the four of them proceeded to rock and fish. Dennis hoped that this successful experience would help Celeste remember to talk instead of scream in the future.

When a lack of language skills causes behavior problems, the proper discipline approach is to teach the missing skills. Possibly the most valuable communication skill is how to use an "I message," as described in Chapter 7. Notice how Mrs. Jensen helps Abby find a better way of expressing herself:

> Abby was reading by herself in a secluded spot in the room. She had had a hard day at school and needed to be alone. Suddenly Cole plopped down beside her and began reading his book aloud, laughing at how funny it was. Abby was in no mood for such nonsense, so she kicked him. Cole yelped and indignantly complained to the teacher. "I didn't do nothing to her!" As she comforted Cole, Mrs. Jensen thought about what might have brought this on.

She was aware of the conflicts Abby had experienced during the day and knew that Abby hadn't come out well in them. Mrs. Jensen had been pleased to see that Abby was making good use of the soft private area of the room to comfort herself. She hadn't noticed Cole go over there, however. Maybe she could use this situation as a teaching opportunity.

Mrs. Jensen went over with Cole to where Abby was pouting, her arms crossed and a big scowl on her face. Mrs. Jensen used some reflective listening to acknowledge what she thought Abby's feelings were. "It looks like you wanted to be alone over here," she said. Abby nodded, still scowling but perhaps more able to be reasonable.

So Mrs. Jensen decided to work on "I messages." She encouraged Cole to tell Abby how he felt about being kicked. "You hurt me and made me feel bad," Cole said. Then she tried to get Abby to use an "I message" to express her feelings: "Is there a better way for you to let Cole know what you wanted?" Abby was able to say, "I want to be by myself." And she spontaneously added, "I'm sorry I got mad and kicked you."

Another discipline approach might have been appropriate for this behavior if there had been a different cause. You may recall that we recommended in Chapter 8 that a child who hurts another child should help the injured youngster. Do you know why that wouldn't be the best learning experience in this case? Remember, you select your discipline approach based on what you believe the child needs to learn. Mrs. Jensen saw the need for communication skills here, apparently having reason to believe that Abby already knew that kicking hurts. Additionally, a child who desperately needs time alone is not in the best condition to offer nurturing help right then. The choice of discipline approaches was based on the teacher's perception of the child's current intellectual and emotional needs.

UNDEVELOPED EMOTION REGULATION

Hitting, kicking, biting, and spitting, as well as screaming, crying, and other out-of-control behaviors, can also be caused by an inability to regulate emotions. As explained in Chapters 2 and 6, learning to express emotions productively is not automatic, and some children require more assistance than others. Adults can support and coach children in the difficult process of learning to deal with emotions and express them productively.

Coaching Emotion Regulation

Being aware of a child's emotions and recognizing emotional moments as teachable moments are the critical first steps. Accepting children's feelings is also an essential part of helping them cope; you don't need to accept the screaming or hitting that may accompany them, but you do need to acknowledge the validity of the feeling. The reflective listening process described in Chapter 7 is an excellent way to show empathy and to validate a child's feelings. It also allows you to help the child verbally label emotions and provides an opportunity to support the

Inability to control emotions can lead to hitting, kicking, biting, and spitting, as well as screaming, crying, and other out-of-control behaviors. You can help children learn emotion regulation.

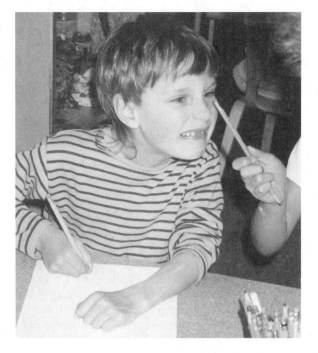

child in thinking about more useful ways of expressing feelings. Remember, we aren't trying to stop them from expressing how they feel, but rather to express their feelings in a reasonable way. Notice how Mrs. Jensen works on this process with Robert:

> Robert was involved in a math game when Mrs. Jensen gave the 5-minute warning for clean-up and lunch time. Robert immediately flung his cards and playing board into the air and wailed, "I didn't get to finish my game!" Then he got up and ran out of the classroom. Mrs. Jensen found him standing in the hall beside the door with his fists clenched, eyes shut, and face red. She could see that he was working on getting control of himself, but that trying to reason with him right then wouldn't work. She kept an eye on the students in the room, seeing that they were cleaning up. A couple of them were even cleaning up Robert's mess. Soon the others were on their way down the hall to lunch. "Have a good lunch," Mrs. Jensen said as they left.
>
> Then she had time to help Robert. He no longer had clenched fists, his eyes were open, and his face wasn't quite as red. He did have a few tears, though. "You really wanted to play that game, didn't you?" Mrs. Jensen said sympathetically. "Yeeeeeeeeeees, I never got to play that one afore. I want to play it!" replied Robert angrily.
>
> Mrs. Jensen asked Robert to come back to the room and look at the classroom calendar with her. She showed him that they would have math game time every day this week and the next and the next. Robert began to relax, and acknowledged that he could play the game tomorrow. "Can I go to lunch now?" he asked, obviously feeling much better.

As she walked down the hall with him, Mrs. Jensen asked Robert if throwing the game had made him feel better. "Yes, but I'm not supposed to do that, am I?" he answered. "What do you think?" smiled Mrs. Jensen. "No." Then Mrs. Jensen asked him why he thought he wasn't supposed to. "I don't want to hurt the game," he replied. It wasn't a perfect answer, she thought, but Robert had come a long way in these first 3 weeks of school. Last week he was spitting when he was upset.

Mrs. Jensen thought that in addition to needing help with emotion regulation, maybe he would benefit from more time to make transitions. Perhaps the pressure of a tight school schedule was making it harder for him to control his feelings. The next day Mrs. Jensen approached Robert a little before the 5-minute warning and asked him to be in charge of flicking the lights as the warning signal. This put Robert in charge and gave him a feeling of power over the situation that had been upsetting him.

Notice that Mrs. Jensen used a combination of guidance approaches, based on her assessment of the cause of Robert's outburst. She used reflective listening to acknowledge his feelings, she allowed him to express his feelings in words, and she helped him put the problem into perspective. All of these responses helped him with his emotion regulation. Notice, too, that she didn't try to do emotion regulation coaching until she had gotten the other children off to lunch. It is unwise to engage in such work when you are rushed or when you have an audience (Gottman, 1997).

In addition to working on emotion regulation with Robert, Mrs. Jensen used her observations of his behavior to determine that transitions were hard for him and that he might be helped by feeling more control over his day. So often there are interactive causes for a behavior problem; it is necessary to deal with all the causes.

Emotion Regulation Curriculum

Most children need help with emotion regulation; therefore, many teachers include that topic in their curriculum as a preventive measure (Hyson, 2004). Coaching and scaffolding children's emotion regulation during emotional moments is extremely useful, but some discussion during calmer moments can help too. Role play with puppets can be a fun way for children to practice better ways of expressing their feelings. Hyson (2004) suggests games to help children think about and talk about emotions.

Reading books about emotions with children can lead to important discussion of feelings and how to cope with them (Koc & Buzzelli, 2004). What children's books do you know that deal with the expression of feelings? Some children learn from the old favorite *Alexander and the Terrible, Horrible, No Good, Very Bad Day* (Viorst, 1972). Have you read *Spinky Sulks* (Steig, 1988) with children? Both provide examples of how not to express feelings, but offer children the opportunity to be wiser than the book character and offer suggestions for improvement. See the Recommended Readings list at the end of this chapter for some useful children's literature titles.

Class meetings often include discussions about feelings, offering the observant teacher valuable insights into individual children's thinking. Some teachers have pictures of faces showing various emotions and encourage children to pick the one that matches their feelings. Art projects offer a way to express feeling and journaling can be used by older children. Pretend play offers valuable outlets for children to express and explore emotions; observing children's pretend play can give adults valuable information about children's feelings.

It is valuable if children can plan ahead for ways to calm themselves when their feelings get too intense. Someplace they can retreat to while getting their feelings under control is essential. The soft and secluded classroom area we recommended in Chapter 4 provides for this need. Children can be encouraged to bring comfort items from home: for some children it is a special blanket, for others it might be a stuffed animal or doll. Taking a teddy bear and retreating to a beanbag chair away from other children can provide an age-appropriate, self-soothing process.

Helping children with emotion regulation requires a knowledgeable teacher; professional development specific to this topic is recommended for best results (Hyson & Molinaro, 2001).

UNDEVELOPED SOCIAL SKILLS

Learning the complexities of human interaction takes at least a lifetime. No wonder small humans with very little experience often have problems. To make matters worse, society groups these inexperienced beings into crowds where they have to compete for limited space and resources. Some children don't face this test until kindergarten, but many are in preschool or group care at much younger ages. They are expected to "get along" by "sharing" the attractive toys and being "nice" about letting others infringe on their play territory. When children are unable to rise to these challenges, adults generally consider it a discipline problem. Those who understand discipline as teaching respond in one way, but those who view discipline as controlling behavior respond in another way (DeVries & Kohlberg, 1987). You can observe this contrast in these next two examples.

> "Teacher! Kyle is messing up my cakes!" yelled Colette. Colette had been making cakes out of playdough and Kyle was making them into something else.
>
> Joanne immediately came to the rescue. "Kyle, you can't take the playdough Colette is using."
>
> "But I want to help her!" exclaimed Kyle. Joanne ignored his explanation; she gave Kyle another ball of playdough and set him up at another table. Kyle gave up on playing with Colette when teacher Joanne told him, "If you bother Colette again, you will go to time-out." Dejectedly, Kyle pounded on the playdough a bit and then wandered off.
>
> Sheri, the aide, watched this incident with interest. Because her hours at the center were from mid-morning to mid-afternoon, she noted the contrasting teaching styles of the morning and afternoon head teachers. Sheri had to admit that Joanne's style got the incident over with quickly, but children definitely got along better in the morning under Dennis' management system. The next morning, Sheri closely observed as Dennis handled a similar situation.
>
> Sarah was working with the large, interlocking tubes, trying to build a tower. Suddenly Dennis heard her crying and screaming at Jack, "No! No! Bad!"

Dennis saw that Jack was pulling apart the pieces that Sarah had been putting together, ignoring Sarah's cries.

"Whoa. Wait a minute here." Dennis said putting his arm around Jack and stopping the action. "What's going on?" He asked. Sarah was sobbing that Jack was wrecking her tower. Jack looked confused and said he wanted to help Sarah build.

"Does Sarah like what you are doing?" asked Dennis? Jack shrugged. "Look at her face," the teacher told Jack. "Listen to what she is saying."

Dennis got Sarah to stop screaming and crying and instead to use an "I message" to tell Jack how she felt. Then he got Jack to tell Sarah that he wanted to help her build. Things had calmed down enough now so that some negotiation could go on. Dennis scaffolded the process as Jack proposed how he could help and while Sarah made it clear that helping did not involve taking apart what she had put together. Before long, the two children were working happily together and Dennis was off helping other children.

Notice that Dennis not only scaffolded communication of feelings in this example, but also helped Sarah control her emotional outburst, and then assisted both children in interpreting one another's feelings. These are important social skills directly linked to peer acceptance (Landy, 2002).

Sheri could see that Jack was feeling more cooperative at the end of this exchange than Kyle had after his unsuccessful attempt to play with Colette and the playdough. Yet Dennis had to spend several minutes working with the youngsters on the problem. Sheri found a chance to ask Dennis, "Why didn't you just tell Jack to stop bothering Sarah instead of spending so much time with that problem?"

Dennis was glad to discuss his approach with Sheri; she seemed to have a good rapport with the children, and he hoped she would stay in this job for a while. He explained that children don't learn how to make friends if the teacher sends them away for mistaken approaches. He communicated his goals of teaching youngsters how to get along and helping them learn to consider the feelings of others. He told Sheri that he considered this knowledge one of the most essential outcomes of early childhood education; therefore, he was happy to spend his time working on it.

Dennis commented further on the time element, mentioning that he seemed to spend less and less time on arguments between youngsters as the school year progressed. Sheri was inclined to agree; Dennis spent more time on individual problems, but Joanne had many more continuing problems to deal with.

Sometimes a problem between children initially looks like it is about sharing toys or materials, but actually has another source. As shown in the previous examples, many young children don't know how to initiate play with another child (Ramsey, 1991). It is common for these youngsters to grab a possession away from someone they really want as a playmate. Sometimes they will punch or shove to get attention from someone they want as a friend. This behavior is a primitive way of saying, "I like you." Adults who don't understand young children's social development will simply try to stop the behavior. Adults who realize the cause of the problem will help children learn more productive ways of mak-

Children who don't know how to find playmates often hit, shove or grab things from the child they want to play with. These children need adult help to learn more effective approaches.

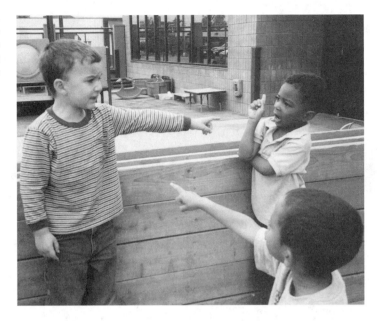

ing friends. It is difficult to stop unacceptable behavior unless you help children find another behavior to take its place. In the following example, Eric learns something about using one of the play entry approaches described in Chapter 3.

> Eric, a very quiet 4-year-old, was watching three girls who were engrossed in playing "puppy dog." One girl was the dog and the other two were leading her around, each one with a leash on the same puppy. Eric went up to them and tried to take hold of one of the leashes. "No, go away!" the girls told him.
>
> Dennis saw Eric's ineffective attempt at joining the puppy dog play and went to see if he could help. "You want to play with them, don't you?" he asked Eric. When Eric affirmed that he did, Dennis suggested a play entry strategy: "They have two leashes but only one dog; maybe they will let you be a dog too if you ask them."
>
> Eric went over to the girls but hesitated to speak to them, so Dennis supported the shy little boy by saying, "Eric wants to ask you if he can be a dog too, since you have two leashes." Then Eric was able to add, "I be dog?" The girls answered, "OK," and unhooked one leash from the girl being a puppy and hooked it into Eric's belt loop. Dennis was happy to see that the children played cooperatively until it was time for snack. This was a big breakthrough for Eric.

Children don't automatically figure out how to successfully enter play as they get older; many primary grade children still use inappropriate methods for gaining a playmate. It is not unusual for first graders to shove or grab something from a person they want to play with. These children still need lots of help figuring out how to accomplish their social goals. As they learn, there will continue to be conflicts. When you accurately diagnose the cause as missing play-entry skills, you can begin reducing conflict by teaching the missing skills.

EGOCENTRISM

Young children want their own way, and they want it now. Adults would actually like the same thing, but they have learned not to insist on it. Adults have learned that other people's wishes don't necessarily match their own. They have also learned that give-and-take is part of getting along with others. Young children need help in learning these things. In the meantime, their behavior often appears selfish and inconsiderate (DeVries & Zan, 1994) and is difficult to deal with. They wander off during group time and start a distracting activity, they take what they want regardless of who is using it, and they generally disregard others. That's because they are so concerned with their own wishes, they cannot think about anyone else's.

Many adults believe that such behavior should be punished, but those who understand child development know otherwise. Punishing selfish behavior doesn't make children more thoughtful; it only makes them more careful about being caught and resentful about sharing (Kamii, 1982). Youngsters will become more considerate and less selfish only when they are able to understand that other people have important needs and feelings, too. This understanding takes time to develop and requires experience in order to be learned. Constructive discipline gives children both time and experience.

> Luis was thrilled to see the new toy car that he could really ride in; he could hardly wait to get in it. As he drove around and around in it, he wore a huge grin on his face. But after about 15 minutes, other children began asking when they could have a turn. Zach finally decided to take things into his own hands; he climbed onto the back of the car and tried to force his way in.
>
> Nancy, the assistant preschool teacher, saw serious trouble brewing and hurried to head off any injuries. "One at a time," she cautioned as she gently removed Zach from the car. She assured Zach and the others who wanted a turn that she understood their desire to drive the car. At the same time, she tried to defend Luis' feelings. "How would you feel if someone got on the car when you were driving it?" she asked. However, it is hard for young children to understand another person's feelings. All Zach knew was that he wanted a turn. All Luis knew was that he didn't want to stop.
>
> To assure others that they would get a turn, Nancy helped them make a sign-up sheet for showing whose turn was next. The preschoolers had used this system for other situations and understood the significance of writing their names on the chart. But Katya still complained, "Luis is taking too long a turn!" Nancy agreed that something needed to be done with so many children wanting to use the attractive new toy.
>
> She asked the youngsters what they thought would be the right amount of time. Should it be the length of a song on a CD, or should they use an egg timer, or did they have another idea? Nancy knew that clocks were meaningless to these children and she didn't want to be the time-keeper: the "ogre" who makes people give up their turns. With Nancy's help, the children began learning ways of resolving such conflicts. By the end of the school year, they independently made sign-up sheets and turned on the CD player as a timer.

What if Nancy had taken a different approach? What if she had just solved the immediate problem either by forcing Luis to give up the car to Zach or by removing Zach to time-out for his behavior? Or what if she had just tried to distract Zach with another activity instead? Many people would consider those to be good solutions, yet they would not help the children learn anything useful. Notice the errors made by the adult in this next situation.

> Several preschoolers were lined up waiting to foot paint. Tory finally just couldn't wait any longer. He plunged past the others waiting in line and started shoving his way into the paint pan. The other children hollered at him indignantly. Teacher Joanne reacted quickly and firmly. She pulled Tory away and told him that he would have to go to the back of the line. Tory began wailing loudly. Needing to get back to supervising the messy activity, Joanne asked her assistant, Maureen, to quiet Tory. While Maureen was desperately trying to think of what to do, her eye fell on the gerbil cage next to Tory. "I think you are scaring Pinky," Maureen told the crying boy. Tory's attention was successfully diverted to the gerbil, and the problem was over for the moment.

Is this what we want to teach children about dealing with their own feelings? What about the feelings of the other children when Tory crowded them? Neither teacher tried to help him understand the viewpoint of those who were waiting in line. Tory needs help learning to deal with his own feelings and those of others. They are important realities that prepare a child to function effectively in society, whereas feigned concern about the gerbil's feelings is only a manipulative tactic.

A more productive approach to handling Tory's problem involves only a subtle shift in the teacher's response. The teacher could have used the guidelines (provided in Chapter 8) for implementing a related consequence. Instead of just pulling Tory away, Joanne could have told him to leave until he decided to get back into line and wait his turn. This method gives him some power over his own situation and focuses his attention more clearly on the problem. Instead of just thinking about how mean the teacher is, he is free to think about how he can change his behavior to get a turn (Curwin & Mendler, 1999). A related consequence addresses the immediate problem but needs to be supplemented with other approaches. Tory also obviously needs help with perspective taking—understanding the feelings of other children.

Therefore, it would be useful for him to listen to how they feel about his crowding. Tory also would benefit from the security of knowing that he would get a turn eventually. The sign-up sheet and the egg timer used with the trampoline line would address the children's needs in this situation. A combination of causes calls for a combination of approaches.

By the time they get into the primary grades, children usually have gained a little awareness of the needs of others. However, they still need help thinking about what others want when it conflicts with what they want. At this stage, they can make better progress with exchanging viewpoints through "I messages." Primary grade children can be helped to use "I messages" effectively as a starting place for negotiating resolution to conflicts, as these second-grade boys did.

> Henry, Anders, and Jeremy were playing a game they had made up that involved kicking a ball within the confines of a large box. Will was watching them kick the ball back and forth, asking if he could play but being refused. Will saw Mr. Davis on the playground and told him, "They won't let me play." The other

boys defended themselves by saying, "You play too rough and you always kick the ball out." Will retorted that he didn't kick the ball out any more than Henry did. Henry then replied, "You wouldn't let us play with you and your friends last recess so you can't play with us now." Jeremy and Anders nodded in agreement.

Mr. Davis asked will how he felt about not being allowed to play. Will said he felt bad. Then Mr. Davis asked the other boys how they felt when Will didn't let them play. They said they, too, felt bad; Henry especially seemed to feel that a payback was necessary. Mr. Davis acknowledged everyone's feelings, saying "It's not fun to feel bad." He could see by Will's face that he suddenly realized how his earlier rejection made his friends feel.

Mr. Davis decided to work on some problem solving by asking Jeremy, "Can you think of anything the four of you could do to solve this problem?" Mr. Davis addressed Jeremy because Jeremy's body language indicated he was less upset over the previous recess interaction and therefore could probably reason better. Jeremy stepped back, took a deep breath, and said, "Well, we could make a deal. If we let you play, you have to let us play." Will agreed to that, and Anders and Jeremy were willing to include Will. Henry was holding out, saying, "Not until next recess; this recess we want to play alone." But then Anders whispered to Henry, "This is the last recess of the day." "Oh yeah," acknowledged Henry.

Will saw his chance and piped up, "Come on, Henry. Two against two!" Anders said, "I'll be your partner, it will be us against them." Henry relented and all four boys went back into the box and played ball. At one point Jeremy fell

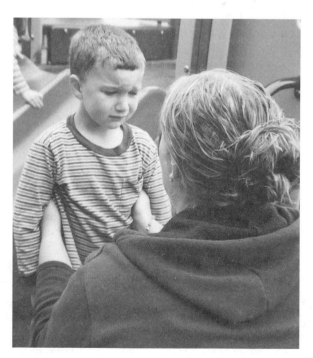

Emotion regulation helps children manage their own feelings; perspective taking helps children tune-in to other people's feelings. Both skills are essential to socially acceptable behavior.

down and Will ran over and pulled him up. He seemed to want to make up for hurting his friends' feelings earlier.

Class discussions, puppet re-enactments of class problems, and children's story books can be used to help children consider the viewpoints of others. The process is the same as using these techniques for emotional regulation, but the focus is different. Whereas emotion regulation helps children manage their own feelings, perspective taking helps children tune in to other people's feelings.

When you choose a book to stimulate discussion about feelings, be sure it is a book worth reading rather than just moralistic and simplistic. Look for lively, believable characters, a well-defined dilemma in a powerful plot, and a satisfying conclusion. The value of a story for emotion lessons lies in how well it promotes critical thinking and lends itself to follow-up activities such as role playing or art (Koc & Buzzelli, 2004).

OTHER IMMATURE PERCEPTIONS

Lying, stealing, and even cheating can be caused by children's lack of understanding. Before you decide you have a budding criminal on your hands, work on helping the child understand.

Lying

Young children often get fact and fantasy mixed up (Piaget, 1965/1932). Many adults get very angry when they believe a child is "lying." However, as explained in Chapter 3, the problem may be more a result of being young than one of immorality. Nevertheless, not telling the truth is unacceptable behavior in society. Children still need to learn how to sort out truth from untruth. They also need to learn why the truth is preferable. Effective communication strategies can help us teach both.

> Sam constantly bragged about his amazing exploits, patterned after those of cartoon superheroes. Dennis didn't want to call Sam a liar, but he did want the child to learn. Therefore, he responded with an active listening comment that read between the lines: "It sounds like you wish you were big and strong and could do all those things." This response got Sam onto a reality track for the rest of the conversation.
>
> When Sam told these stories to his preschool friends, they weren't so kind. They argued, "You did not!" Sam's reaction was to argue back and defend his incredible statements. Dennis decided Sam needed more specific feedback. He took the child aside and kindly but frankly told him, "Your friends can't believe you when you tell them things they know can't be true." Dennis continued with more information. "If you tell people things that aren't true, they might not believe you when you tell them the truth." Sam needed time to digest this idea, but Dennis was there to assist his growth over time. Dennis's goal was to help Sam sort out the difference between real and pretend without losing his joy in pretending.

Stealing

Almost everyone has an experience with "stealing" as they grow up. Taking what doesn't belong to you is a serious crime in society. Many adults believe they must harshly punish children for stealing to save them from a life of crime. Parents and teachers with more knowledge of young children realize the need for helping them learn about ownership (Curwin & Mendler, 1990). Punishment may stop kids from taking something if they think they may get caught, but it won't help them understand why it is unacceptable to take what isn't theirs. Related consequences will help children learn this concept and also increase the likelihood that they will respect others' ownership, even when no one is around to enforce it. A consequence for stealing involves making restitution by replacing what was taken. In the following example, Tory is helped to understand why taking the scissors is a problem, but he is allowed to return them without confrontation.

> Naomi complained that there weren't any of the new scissors left. Dennis was surprised. Only two people were cutting, and there should have been three pairs of new scissors. He checked the cubbies and noticed a bunch of cut-paper creations in Tory's. Thinking Tory might have inadvertently scooped up the scissors with his work and stuffed them into his cubby, Dennis picked through the pile. As he moved Tory's backpack aside, Dennis felt a scissors shape pressed against the cloth. A pair of scissors had been stuffed deep into the pack. There was a chance the pair was Tory's own from home, but it wasn't likely. Perhaps he just wanted a good pair of scissors at home.
>
> Rather than putting the boy on the defensive or making him feel guilty by accusing him of stealing, Dennis called a brief class meeting. He announced that one pair of scissors couldn't be found; now there weren't enough for the school. Dennis expressed confidence that they might show up. He concluded, "If anyone finds them, please put them in the lost-and-found basket in the back hallway." Tory looked self-conscious and trapped when Dennis began the meeting. But the final comment brought some relief to his face. No one could see the lost-and-found basket from the classroom. It was back by the cubbies! He could sneak those scissors into it, and no one would see.
>
> An hour later, Dennis glanced in the lost-and-found basket. There were the scissors. He brought them back into the classroom and put them on their tray. Seeing Tory eye them, Dennis offered, "Would you like to use them?" As the child eagerly reached for them, Dennis inquired, "Do you have a good pair of scissors at home?" "Nope," Tory frowned. Dennis replied, "I'll tell your parents where you can buy this kind. Okay?"

Cheating

How often do you hear complaints from your students that another child is cheating? Sometimes the accused isn't following the rules, sometimes the complainer doesn't understand the rules, and sometimes both are confused.

> Three boys are playing the Transportation game. The procedure is to roll a die, move your game piece the appropriate number of spaces, land on a picture of

a vehicle, and draw a card from the pile. If you land on a vehicle that goes on land and also draw a card that reads "by land," you get to keep the card. Having the most cards means winning.

Suddenly Blake calls out, "Teacher, teacher, Jason's cheating!" Mrs. Jensen comes to see and notices that Jason has five "by water" cards. He earnestly defends himself saying, "I'm not cheating." Mrs. Jensen asks Jason what he thinks the game rules were. "I have the boat (game piece), so I get to keep all the 'By water' cards," he explains. Blake is outraged at that explanation and insists, "You don't get to keep the card unless it matches the place where you land." The other child in the game agrees with Blake.

Mrs. Jensen helps the three boys look at the written rules for the game, which confirm Blake's view. She asks the boys if they want to play by the written rules or make up different ones, like Jason's. Jason is outvoted and he also realizes that he had misinterpreted the game. He is disappointed but agrees to play by the written rules.

Mrs. Jensen focuses on clarifying children's perceptions, not on placing blame. She knows that blaming a child for not understanding does no good. Rules are hard for young children, especially if the rules aren't working in their favor. Egocentrism contributes to this problem and is definitely a maturational issue that requires time and adult support.

FAMILY INVOLVEMENT

This book frequently mentions the importance of getting information from children's families as you try to figure out the causes of behavior problems. Listening to those who know children best is essential to understanding them. The communication lines need to go both ways, however, teachers also have an obligation to make useful information available to families. Few adults have studied child development and therefore many have unrealistic expectations for their children. It can be very helpful if schools can help families have a better idea of normal child behaviors; this can put into better perspective some of the frustrations of child rearing. Young children need families that understand and accept them, as well as teachers who appreciate them as they are.

CONCLUSION

This chapter provides only a few examples of the problem situations children encounter simply because they are young. Sometimes the problem requires only your respectful acceptance of the nature of young children, such as when you are dealing with wet pants or spilled juice. If youngsters can be part of fixing the problem, it helps them feel good about themselves. Sometimes the problem requires you to change your expectations to match the abilities of young children, such as adjusting your plans when youngsters can't sit still any longer. At other times you can help children's growth by teaching them a strategy for making friends, or a skill, such as modeling self-expression through "I messages." Adults can significantly aid children's social maturation by helping them try to understand another child's viewpoint, which is part of learning to negotiate solutions for interpersonal conflicts. Effective guidance for young children also involves knowing when behavior that looks like lying or stealing is really only a reflection of a child's point of view.

When you are searching for the cause of a discipline problem, be sure to consider lack of maturity as a possibility. Remember, your role as the teacher is to allow youngsters the time they need to grow as well as to provide the experiences they need to learn. It may help you to cope with frustration if you can also remember that it isn't their fault when they are inept.

∞ *FOR FURTHER THOUGHT*

1. A problem to solve: Jason grabs the ball that Tanya and Eric are playing with and runs away laughing. The other two children are hurt and indignant.
   a. Describe the probable cause of the problem.
   b. Describe the guidance approach that addresses that cause.

2. A problem to solve: It is group time at preschool and several children have wandered away to play elsewhere. Most of the children are enjoying the songs and stories in the group, but tend to get distracted by some of the other activities.
   a. Describe the probable cause of the problem.
   b. Describe a guidance approach that helps with that cause.

3. Analyze actual behavior problems and guidance approaches in a setting where you know the children. Cases in which you are the adult providing the guidance will probably prove most instructive.
   a. Describe the situation.
   b. Based on your knowledge of the children involved, state the probable cause.
   c. Describe the adult intervention that addresses that cause.
   d. Describe the children's response to intervention.
   e. If the approach was not helpful, was it unsuccessful because it did not address the actual cause or because one intervention was not enough?
   f. If a different cause is suggested, plan a different strategy for next time.

∞ **RECOMMENDED READINGS**

Bronson, M. B. (2000). Research in review: Recognizing and supporting the development of self-regulation in young children. *Young Children, 55*(2),32–37.

Landy, S. (2002). *Pathways to competence: Encouraging healthy social and emotional development in young children.* Baltimore: Paul H. Brookes.

Sample children's literature linked to emotion regulation

Bang, M. (1999). *When Sophie gets angry, very very very angry.* New York: Scholastic.

Barrett, J. (1988). *Animals should definitely not act like people.* New York: Aladdin.

Henkes, K. (1996). *Lilly's purple plastic purse.* New York: Greenwillow.

Lobel, A. (1982). Tear-water tea. In *Owl at home.* New York: Harper (a division of HarperCollins) Trophy.

Miranda, A., & Emberley, E. (1997). *Glad monster, sad monster: A book about feelings.* New York: Little, Brown.

Parr, T. (2002). *The feel good book.* Boston: Little, Brown.

Viorst, J. (1972). *Alexander and the terrible horrible, no good, very bad day.* New York: Macmillan.

Wojtowycz, D. (2000). *A cuddle for Claude.* New York: Dutton Children's Books.

Sample children's literature linked to perspective taking

Henkes, K. (1988). *Chester's way.* New York: Greenwillow.

Hughes, S. (1988). *Dogger.* New York: Lothrop, Lee & Shepard.

Luttrell, I. (1990). *Three good blankets.* New York: Macmillan Child Group.

Pfister, J. (1992). *The rainbow fish.* Transl., J. Alison James. New York: North-South.

Rosen, M. (1996). *This is our house.* Cambridge, MA: Candlewick.

Zemach, M. (1983). *The little red hen: An old story.* New York: Farrar, Straus, & Giroux.

12 *Unmet Needs*

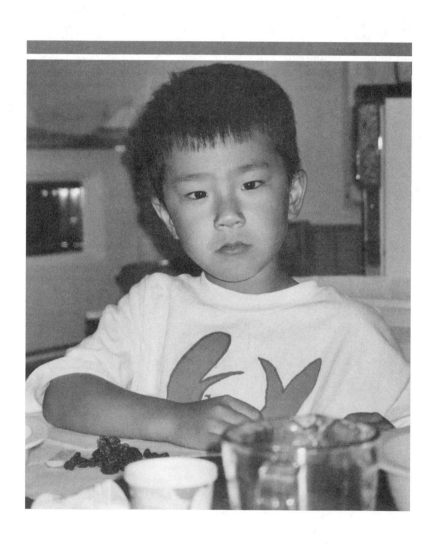

*L*ike a baby's cry, a young child's actions can signal a variety of unmet needs. Although they now have some words, young children may not be articulate enough to communicate their problems. Often they may not even be consciously aware of what they need. What's more, even if they do know what they need and can verbalize it, they may not have any idea of what to do about it. Thus, the adult's role is threefold: to help identify the need(s), to help the child learn to communicate them, and to facilitate problem solving so that the needs can be met. This chapter discusses some typical emotional and physical needs that cause problems if left unmet.

This book has used a gardening analogy to explain the importance of dealing with the cause of behavior problems: Discipline that does not focus on the cause of the problem is like weeding your garden without getting the roots of the weeds. The gardening analogy also seems to help explain the importance of meeting children's needs to improve their behavior. Consider the gardener's response to carefully planted seeds that are not growing as expected. Even a novice gardener knows the basic needs of plants—light and water. Checking these needs would be a first step: If the patio table umbrella is shading the plants, move the table. If the roof overhang is keeping rain off, bring the hose over. If you can't figure out the cause of the problem, then you get an expert opinion. But you never "punish" the plants for not growing: You continue to nurture them by meeting their needs to the best of your ability.

Sometimes plants grow, but not the way you wanted. What if you had a trellis for your sweet peas but they were growing along the ground instead? Would you be upset with the sweet peas or would you gently guide the tender shoots onto the trellis? Guiding the growth of children is a lot more complex and demanding than growing plants, but the attitude of the careful gardener can guide the teacher of young children.

DIFFERING NEEDS

Just as different kinds of plants require different treatment, the uniqueness of each child requires different treatment. Differences in gender, physical traits, chemical makeup, personality, and background combine to give each person a distinctive set of needs. If you try to treat each child exactly the same in an effort to be "fair," you are actually being very unfair. Fairness requires that each child has his or her unique needs met. That is why we warn against "one size fits all" discipline programs that tell you how to respond to different behaviors rather than to different children.

Each child has unique life experiences that contribute to different needs and different reactions to circumstances. Your classroom is likely to include a child whose parents are in the middle of a divorce, a child whose beloved grandparent has just died, a child who is having to move due to economic difficulties, and several children dealing with the birth of a new sibling. You may also encounter children dealing with abuse, parental alcoholism, incarcerated parents, and homelessness. Getting help for children coping with serious, long-term problems is discussed in Chapter 14. However, children facing the more common family occurrences usually can be helped through a partnership of supportive teachers and families.

Each child also has a unique temperament and personality: traits that seem to be part of the package at birth, as described in Chapter 2. Fewer behavior problems occur with children who adapt easily to new situations, who have a generally sunny outlook, and whose emotional reactions are fairly mild. However, we all know there are children who do not adapt easily, who expect the worse, and whose emotional reactions are intense (Landy, 2002). These children have greater needs and require more adult assistance in learning to meet them. With individual differences in mind, let's look at some types of behavior problems that are generally linked to unmet needs.

PRIVACY NEEDS

Adults, as well as children, often have difficulty properly identifying their own need for privacy. General grumpiness is frequently a sign of a need to be alone. In the following example, the cause of the child's antisocial behavior should have been recognized sooner. The youngster was finally helped to figure out how to get his need met, however. As we explained in Chapter 4, it is important that the school environment offers opportunities for privacy.

Cole yelled, "Don't talk! I'm trying to concentrate!" as he sat at a table with three other children who were sounding out words for their daily journal writing. The other children were carefully saying each word aloud in an effort to hear the individual sounds and figure out which letters were in the word. Cole was busy with an intricate drawing in his journal and appeared to be feeling very cross. He repeated his demands for quiet several times and finally crawled under the table to work.

Unfortunately, when Julie got up to show her work to the teacher, she bumped Cole's leg in the process, saying, "Sorry." The bump must have made his pencil move where he didn't want it to. Cole began sobbing and yelling, "She made me mess up! I hate girls! I hate that one girl!"

The tantrum was in full swing when Mrs. Jensen came over and told him, "You can lay under the table and cry for one more minute if you need to, Cole, but then you need to get up and figure out how to solve your problem. I'll help you as soon as you are ready." Then she quietly reassured the other children at the table that Cole was upset but he would get over it. She also acknowledged Julie's bumping Cole as an accident.

It was less than a minute before Cole stopped crying and came out from under the table. As Mrs. Jensen led him away for a private conversation, he again yelled, "I hate girls!" His teacher used reflective listening about his feelings, sympathetically saying such things as: "You were having a really hard time concentrating with other children around." And "You are very upset about making that scribble on your drawing." Mrs. Jensen put Cole in charge of solving his problems. She asked him what he could do if he needed to be alone to work and she asked him what he could do about the scribble.

Having his feelings accepted, Cole was able to think about solutions. He decided that he wanted to work alone at a desk, so Mrs. Jensen helped him find an acceptable one. He also admitted that he could erase the scribble since it was done in pencil. He calmed down and went back to work.

Mrs. Jensen recognized that Cole needed some time alone. He seemed more stressed than usual today, though he seemed generally high-strung. She berated herself for not intervening sooner and helping him find a spot alone before things escalated to the point they did. She also noted that Cole needed help with emotion regulation, since this wasn't the first time he had fallen apart over a fairly small problem. Cole's temperament made emotion regulation more difficult than normal, since his emotional responses are more intense than most children's. Of course, the unmet need for time alone made it harder for him to control his emotions. As is so often the case, there are interwoven causes for this behavior problem.

POWER NEEDS

Sometimes the more you try to get a child to do something, the more resistance you meet. She won't put her boots on, he won't eat, and nap time is a constant fight. Such behavior is often a symptom of a child's healthy desire to have some control over his or her own life. Arising conflicts can easily turn into fruitless power struggles. If the adult in charge insists, "You have to eat your lunch," the child insists, "I'm not hungry!" A limitation like "No, you can't go outside without your boots. There are puddles under the swings" evokes the response, "I hate those red boots!" To the statement, "Your mother still wants you to take a nap," the child replies, "I'm not tired!"

The problem may not be about hunger or boot color at all, and the child may actually be exhausted. These responses may be expressions of the need for personal power. Recognizing this need, the attending adult can, within reason, give the child as many opportunities for choice as possible (Katz & Chard, 2000). She must eat, but which food does she want to eat first, her apple or her sandwich? How does she want to eat her apple, like a worm nibbling through or around and around like a circling caterpillar? He must rest, but which nap story would he like: *Rumpelstiltskin* or *Strega Nona*? Does he want a back rub or to be rocked? She must wear her boots to play in the swings with the puddles under them, but if she wants to play in the fort or the playhouse, she can race out to them in her shiny shoes.

These are real choices, both desirable to the child and acceptable to the adult. They give children a chance to satisfy their need for control in a world governed by many rules they don't yet understand. And by allowing them some control at levels appropriate to their age, you will find that children are much more able to allow you to control decisions that must be made by adults. As they experience the desired power, they also develop valuable problem-solving skills. The following situation is an example of a child being allowed some power, choice, and opportunity for problem solving.

The youngsters at the children's center were going outside to play, and they were excited to get out after being cooped up indoors by bad weather. The joyful hustle and bustle of coats and boots was interrupted by Celeste's wail. She threw her boots across the floor and her coat on top of them. Then she sat crying and hitting her heels on the floor. Sheri, the aide in charge of helping everyone get ready, asked another staff person to help with the other youngsters and went over to Celeste to see what the problem was. It turned out that the little girl had new shoes, and she wanted to wear them instead of taking them off and putting on the boots kept at the children's center for muddy days.

Sheri explained carefully to Celeste that her new pink shoes would get ruined if she wore them out in the mud. Celeste continued to cry and say that she wanted to wear her new shoes outside. Sheri tried reasoning with the child while upholding the rule about not going outside without boots, but Celeste kept crying loudly. Suddenly Sheri remembered what she had learned from the head teacher, Dennis, about giving children choices. Sheri changed her tactics and asked Celeste what she thought she might do to protect her shoes if she kept them on.

Celeste's sobs ebbed as she began to talk about some ideas and possible solutions. Sheri stayed with her as the others trooped outdoors with another adult in charge. Finally Celeste decided to wear some big boots from the emergency supply box, which were large enough to fit over her beautiful new shoes. She was pleased with this solution and happily marched outdoors in the giant boots. Later, Celeste asked Sheri for help. She had decided to change into her own boots, explaining that it was hard to run in the other pair. Sheri noticed that Celeste's concern about wearing her new shoes seemed to evaporate once she had an opportunity to make a decision for herself.

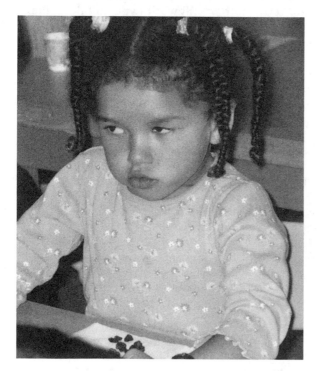

Power, privacy, and ownership are valid needs for children as well as for adults. Unmet needs can cause behavior problems.

Notice that the choices described for children were real ones. Sometimes people give children a "choice" between two undesirable things; that is not a real choice. Other times adults want to be nice, and so they ask children if they would like to do something when there is no other choice. If you say, "Would you like to go on a field trip to the zoo?" be prepared that some children may answer, "no." Similarly, many adults say things like: "Let's all get ready for lunch now, OK?" Unless you are able to accept "no" for an answer, the "OK?" question is not authentic communication.

OWNERSHIP NEEDS

"Naomi won't share!" This cry is familiar to all who spend their days with preschoolers. In Chapter 11, we explored both undeveloped social skills and egocentricity, both of which contribute to sharing problems. However, it is also important to consider whether or not it is necessary for a child to share at this time. Adults as well as children have a need for ownership of possessions and territory. Notice that office workers want their own designated spaces, and the contents of each person's desk are personal and private. Adults are not required to share the personal items they bring from home to make work more comfortable. Yet we routinely demand more generosity from young children. The need for ownership must be balanced with social expectations for sharing.

> Dennis addressed the problem of personal possessions at preschool by designating a large box as the "precious place." Youngsters who brought things from home that they didn't want others to touch could put their belongings there and be assured that they would be undisturbed. It was a child's decision when and if to bring something out for the group to enjoy.
>
> Mrs. Jensen found that putting a child's name on a personal possession helped children share. She figured out that having the item labeled as their own fulfilled the need for ownership and freed youngsters to be more generous. First graders enjoyed labeling, which became part of their emerging literacy activities. They began using the approach for staking temporary claim to class materials as well. Thus, when Eric was working on a jigsaw puzzle and had to leave it to go out for recess, he placed a sign on it that said, "Do not tuch. Eric." The children in the class respect such written notices, which solves many potential conflicts.

Both of these teachers defend children's temporary or permanent ownership rights. Rather than making children selfish, this defense of their rights actually helps them to be more generous. When children have their ownership rights respected, they learn how to respect those of others. When they are not busy defending their rights to an item, they are more likely to give it up voluntarily.

ATTENTION NEEDS

Often, behavior labeled as "disruptive" can actually be a plea for attention—a cry for help! It may take some reflection to realize that a child's irritating behavior is a cry for attention. You may know kids who get attention by showing off, and you have probably seen others who seem to deliberately seek a reprimand for misbehavior. Even negative attention, after all, is attention.

> Courtney's daily "owies" are almost microscopic in size, but she insists that they need a band-aid or a cold pack or a kiss. Mrs. Jensen wants to help her find better ways of feeling important and cared for. Courtney is a strong writer, so Mrs. Jensen helps her get attention and approval through sharing her writing with others. Gradually the "owies" diminish.
>
> Mrs. Jensen thinks Ashley's tattling probably comes from a need for attention, too. She knows that Ashley may not get a lot of attention at home in her large family. Mrs. Jensen makes a point of letting Ashley know that she is important: greeting her individually when she arrives, commenting about her activities, and noticing her accomplishments. Mrs. Jensen tries hard to give each child some undivided attention. It's so hard with a large class that she wishes she could clone herself.

The desire for attention is a legitimate need, yet it is often difficult to meet that need adequately in large group settings. Ratios of 10 or more students to one teacher can make it difficult for even the most conscientious childcare worker to give enough personal attention to each individual. Public school classes of 20 or 25 children create an impossible challenge. There is a limit to how many children you can fit into your lap at once! Levels of need vary among children, depending on their personality types and their stages of development. Levels also vary from day to day, and they are often related to the children's rest and stress levels. In addition, sometimes home life can fail to provide adequate attention.

A teacher's awareness of current home factors can provide valuable information, even about children from the best situations. A parent's absence or increased work hours, newborn siblings, or even visiting houseguests can create a need for extra attention. In the following case, teachers combine information from home with observations at school to solve the mystery of Alex's behavior.

> Alex was humming loudly and squirming around in his seat. Alicia, sitting next to him, complained that she couldn't hear the reading teacher. The teacher asked Alex if he heard Alicia. Alex was quiet for awhile, but soon began to hum loudly again and wriggle in his seat. The reading teacher became impatient and sent him back to his regular classroom with instructions to tell his teacher why he returned.
>
> After school, Mrs. Jensen talked to the reading teacher and asked about Alex. She said that as soon as she heard the door open, she knew it would be Alex walking through it. She had been having the same problem with him all day. Some checking revealed that Alex's mother was out of town for a meeting again. Mrs. Jensen remembered then that Alex always has this sort of problem when his mom is gone; she should have realized the cause sooner. It definitely would have been helpful to have been informed about the mother's travel.
>
> Mrs. Jensen made a special effort to give Alex individual attention when he came to school the next morning. She asked when his mother was coming home, and said, "I'll bet you really miss her when she's gone, don't you?" When

he went to his reading class, the reading teacher invited him to sit beside her and also talked with him about how long before his mom came home. With this support and extra attention from his teachers, Alex was able to cope with his unmet need for his mother's attention. The humming and squirming stopped.

In some cases, disruptive behavior for attention is not a temporary problem. Some youngsters have a well-learned pattern of trying to get attention and status by disrupting class. No doubt you remember these class clowns from your school days. Their behavior is a sad symptom of low self-esteem and a cry for help (Dreikurs, 1966). In addition to work on self-esteem, these children need to unlearn their counterproductive attention-getting strategies; however, as long as their disruptive behavior gets attention, they will continue it (Adams & Baronberg, 2005). We consider behavior modification acceptable when it means ignoring inappropriate behavior. This action helps correct mislearning by extinguishing previously reinforced unacceptable behavior. Chapter 9 describes behavior modification and explains that occasional reinforcement may actually entrench the behavior more firmly than consistent rewards do. But in the following example, a teacher manages to not reinforce negative behavior:

> A group of children was listening to a tape recording of a book about birds and following along in their own copies of the book. The children were enjoying the tape and the book; the vibrant and detailed illustrations helped hold their interest. Then Jeffrey quit listening and began to open and close his book loudly. The other children complained that he was making too much noise and they couldn't hear. Mrs. Jensen went over to Jeffrey and quietly asked him to please stop disturbing the other children. As soon as she walked away, he began the same behavior and got the same complaints from the other youngsters. Refusing to give attention to the behavior this time, Mrs. Jensen said nothing to Jeffrey but instead calmly walked over and turned up the volume on the tape recorder a little so that the others could still hear. Jeffrey's eyes showed his surprise. Because he was no longer getting any attention from his classmates or teacher, he began to follow the text again. Afterward, he had many comments about the birds in the book.

It takes time and patience, but eventually mistaken behavior learned through reinforcement will stop once the reward of attention stops. Mrs. Jensen was able to respond effectively to the cause of Jeffrey's behavior because she had made a special effort to understand him and his problems. She knew that Jeffrey not only needed to have his inappropriate behavior ignored, but also needed to have his desire for attention met in another way. Mrs. Jensen did want to give Jeffrey the attention he craved, but not in response to inappropriate behavior. She had been working with his parents on the problem and was making an effort to notice him when he was working well in school. Rather than make an issue over this minor incident, she appreciated that his inappropriate behavior was happening less and less frequently. They had already survived Jeffrey's initial surge of worse behavior, which Mrs. Jensen had known would be the first result of ignoring his inappropriate behavior. They were through the worst and on the road to recovery.

Although ignoring inappropriate bids for attention may be the best approach for some children's growth, there are many other children who may be inadvertently ignored. It is easy to overlook some very quiet children. The too-quiet ones should cause more serious concern than the too-loud ones because they may have given up. They may have quit trying to get their needs met. They often appear blank or unhappy, uninvolved in activities, and generally unsuccessful. Sometimes these children assume victim roles, but more often they seem to fade into the background. You may find yourself wishing that they would actively disagree with something, get upset, or show some strong emotion—even if it's disruptive! The source of this kind of problem generally lies outside the school and therefore is discussed in Chapter 14.

NEEDS FOR SUCCESS AND CHALLENGE

Youngsters who don't complete school assignments often get into trouble. Children who don't participate in planned activities in preschool worry both teachers and parents. There are reasons for their behaviors. Forcing a child to comply or punishing noncompliance does not address the reasons. The traditional loss of recess for not completing work is a classic example of counterproductive discipline. What should you do instead? The answer depends on the cause of the behavior.

You will get clues to the cause by observing the child's specific behaviors and by noting the circumstances surrounding the problem. Does the child look upset or anxious when confronted with the task? Or does the child appear distracted? Is the child interested in something else instead? If so, what is he or she interested in? What kinds of tasks go uncompleted? Does the child only avoid writing, for example, or does he or she avoid all work? Depending on the answers to these kinds of questions, you may decide that the child lacks the ability to succeed at the task, or you might decide that he or she is not sufficiently challenged by it. You may discover that the child does his or her math just fine but can't read the material to complete the science work. Each of these different findings suggests different responses. The goal is to address the problem in such a way that you help the child find success and satisfaction in his or her work. Treating each child as an individual is an important key in meeting this goal.

 OBSERVATION GUIDE FOR SCHOOLWORK PROBLEMS

- Does the child look upset or anxious when confronted with the task? Or does she merely appear distracted?
- Is she interested in something else instead? If so, what is she interested in?
- What kinds of tasks go uncompleted? Does she only avoid writing, for example, or does she avoid all work?

If Jacob won't read because the book is too hard, one useful response is to help him find a book at his level. Another response would be to help him improve his reading skill by inviting a volunteer to read to him daily. Perhaps reading in partnership with a friend who is a little more skillful would be more fun as well as more productive.

If Eli is acting up at math time because he is bored, find a more appropriate challenge for him. Help him find material at his level that is related to topics of personal interest. Yes, math can be relevant, too. Many teachers now help their students find math in the real world and use it to solve real problems.

If Madeline never uses the large-muscle equipment at preschool because she is afraid, help her find activities that will increase her confidence in her physical abilities. Perhaps helping her make friends with Kelsey, who is more physically active, would encourage her. Madeline spends a lot of time in the playhouse area; you could suggest large-muscle activities that fit in with her pretend play.

The need for success, coupled with the need for appropriate challenge, continues as the young child matures. Finding the right balance for each child is essential to avoiding the problem behaviors caused by either boredom or frustration. Protecting children from all failure and frustration is not the goal. A certain amount of frustration is often part of learning and can provide useful lessons in learning to cope with difficulty (Hyson, 2004).

NEED FOR SECURITY

Although adults generally focus on their obligation to keep children physically safe, children's behavior deteriorates if they lack emotional security (Koplow, 2002). Hyson summarizes the related research succinctly: "Feelings of security are the basic ingredient of a healthy personality" (Hyson, 2004, p. 37). Lack of security can be the cause of antisocial behavior and of nonparticipation in school activities.

Predictability

Children feel more safe when they know what to expect and what is expected of them. A predictable schedule for the day is part of this. A place for children to keep their belongings is also important, as is their knowing where to find school materials when needed.

When children arrive for preschool, Dennis is at the door to greet each one warmly. Each child has a cubby for his or her jacket and other personal belongings, so children can put away their things. Then they know that they can choose among a variety of activities and will have enough time to explore them. Many of the activities, such as blocks and the playhouse, are available every day; but something new and different is offered each day too. For instance, foot painting or snack preparation might be set up as a special event.

Lack of emotional security can cause anti-social behavior and non-participation in school activities.

Children know that group time comes after choice time and that they have snack after that. They know that outside play time follows snack and that they have story time when they come back inside. If there needs to be a deviation from the schedule, Dennis discusses it with the children and gives them advance notice about the change.

Starting School   This routine just described is well known and comfortable to the children after a month of school, but the the start of school was a different matter. A child's introduction to the school setting plays a crucial role in feelings of security.

Dennis tries to meet each child and his or her family on an individual basis before the child comes to school for the first time. Some families appreciate his offer of a home visit to get acquainted, while others wait to meet with him during the school visit prior to starting the program. During the initial meeting, Dennis works at making a connection with the child so he will be perceived as a friend when the child comes to school. Dennis also uses the meeting to get an idea of the child's prior experiences and parental expectations.

Family members are encouraged to stay with the child for awhile on the first day in the program. Dennis also suggests ideas to help children transition into the new setting. These include bringing pictures of family members and bringing a favorite blanket or toy. Dennis and his assistants offer nurturing support to young children as they adjust to the new setting.

Predictable Limits   Another type of predictability involves knowing class guidelines: what behavior is accepted and what is not. Just as they need safety limits set, children need to have clearly communicated and firmly held behavioral expectations. Although they naturally push against their limits, their tests help them find out where the boundaries are and if those boundaries are flexible.

Teachers who strive for mutual respect with children will involve youngsters in determining appropriate limits and help children understand the reasons for limits. It is wise to have much freedom for individual decisions and choice, but that freedom must have clearly defined limits that protect everyone. Mrs. Jensen, for example, is firm about kindness and safety for all people and animals in her classroom. She also insists on responsible treatment of equipment and materials. Her expectations can be condensed into three easy to remember guidelines: Be kind. Be safe. Be careful.

For children to feel secure in a group, they need to know that others will not be allowed to harass, humiliate, or threaten them (Howes & Ritchie, 2002). When adults observe such behavior, they need to interact to help the perpetrator recognize how the other child's feelings are being affected. It is time for the adult to accept an authority role and set limits.

A child having a tantrum may be a child who needs the security of limits. Children need the emotional security of knowing that someone will help them keep themselves under control. When they experience anger, they can actually terrify themselves with their rage and rapidly escalating emotions. Because they are still learning how to regulate their emotions, they can be overwhelmed by the strength of their feelings and be unable to escape them. Your intervention can actually be a relief, reassuring them not only that you won't let them hurt others, but you also won't let them hurt themselves. Calmly holding a child close and offering comfort will help some youngsters calm down. Others need to be left alone so as not to reinforce the tantrum through attention. However, children must be protected from doing damage to themselves, to others, or to their environment. As they fight to get control of their own actions, children are comforted by the reminder that there are limits outside of themselves.

Teacher Continuity What if a child gets to school and a stranger is there instead of the teacher? This can be very scary. Knowing that you can count on your teacher to be there is very important to children's sense of security. High staff turn-over in child-care programs is a serious threat to children's emotional security. Even having a substitute teacher can be a trauma. Being sensitive to the impact of such change on children, schools striving to provide emotional security help children cope. Instead of familiar caregivers disappearing and new ones appearing unexpectedly, proper good-byes are said and new staff are introduced gradually. If possible, teachers tell children in advance about substitutes and arrange to have someone known to the children be there with them.

Classroom Guidelines: Children need limits as well as freedom. These guidelines are easy for young children to learn: Be kind. Be safe. Be careful.

NEED FOR LOVE AND ACCEPTANCE

Feeling unloved and rejected can cause some dreadful behaviors. Wouldn't you think that someone wanting to be liked would try to behave in a likeable way? But no, that's not how it is (Landy, 2002).

Feeling loved and expecting others to like you is the result of successful attachment with parents and/or caregivers; attachment is necessary for the development of trust that you can count on other people. As explained in Chapter 2, attachment and trust are the earliest developmental tasks for an infant and they provide the foundation for future healthy emotional development.

When this foundation is not laid, people have difficulty with all other facets of life. In order to develop into fully functioning people, young children desperately need love and acceptance from the significant adults in their lives.

Family Histories

Some children have had experiences that spoil attachment and damage trust. Children's emotional development can be devastated by temporary or permanent loss of a family member due to divorce, military obligation, illness, death, incarceration, or other causes. A young child in child care who has known a caregiver for her entire one year of life can be similarly distressed if that person leaves the job. Some children's temperament is such that birth of a sibling can disrupt attachment and trust. You will be better able to diagnose behavior problems if you are able to get such information from families.

Good relationships between teachers and children will prevent many behavior problems and help resolve those that do occur.

Teacher Attachment

Children whose attachment and trust have been disrupted need a great deal of your assistance, but all children need to feel loved and accepted by their teachers (Howes & Ritchie, 2002). As explained in Chapter 4, good relationships between teachers and children will prevent many behavior problems and help resolve those that do occur. Time spent making connections with individual children is time well spent.

Dennis circulates among the children during choice time, frequently stopping to chat about a painting, a block construction, or some exciting event outside of school. He smiles acknowledgement to others and gives "high-fives" or a literal pat on the back as children go about their activities. Each child feels the teacher's recognition and affection.

When the children assemble for group time, Dennis often comments on what he observed during choice time, such as the theme of the pretend play or the creations made with playdough. He makes sure that all children know they have been noticed, especially those who need the most reassurance.

Group time often includes songs that help children feel valued and important (Gurian, 2001). One favorite is the familiar "name game" that plays with a child's name:

Tory, Tory bo bory.
Fe fi mo mory—Tory.

Another often requested is the "little box" song.

If I had a little red box
To put my Sarah in,
I'd take her out and (kiss, kiss, kiss)
And put her back in again.

Reasonable Expectations

Asking teachers to truly love all the children in their care may be unrealistic; however, it is reasonable to expect a teacher to have an enthusiastic approach toward children. This enthusiasm can be demonstrated by efforts to create an environment and a program that continually attempt to meet the needs of all the children enrolled. Your efforts are a way of giving love, whether you actually like a particular child or not. What is important is that you accept all children as they are, respecting each child's unique position and potential. The teacher's role is to care for, guide, and encourage all the children as they grow. Some children are just hard to like. Much as you try not to have favorites, you must admit that some kids (and adults, too) are just a lot more pleasant to be around than others.

Bailey was once again yelling at the other children, and Miss Wheeler again wished that Bailey hadn't been placed in her room. What a nuisance she was. She was always getting into fights with the others, and constantly talked out of turn but would never answer a question when called on. As if those difficulties weren't enough, Bailey lost everything. She never had a pencil, never knew where her reading book was, and always lost her lunch box.

Miss Wheeler had tried everything. It seemed that Bailey was constantly given time-out for interrupting or fighting. And Miss Wheeler had finally begun taking everything away from Bailey that she might lose. Bailey's only reaction was to pout and look like she was going to cry, but Miss Wheeler thought it was an act because there were never any tears. Now look at the child! She was crawling under the table instead of sitting on her chair. What next?

Miss Wheeler clearly doesn't like Bailey, and consequently neither do the child's classmates. Her behavior gets constant rejection from others. As a result of this rejection, Bailey has learned that she is a bad girl. The more she believes this lesson, the more she acts accordingly. As strange as it may sound, her reaction is normal and human. People who feel unlovable tend to act unlovable, which makes them feel worse and act worse (Rabiner & Cole, 1989). What a vicious cycle! The only hope for Bailey is to break the cycle by introducing experiences that teach her good things about herself. It won't be easy to change her self-image. At first, she will be so uncomfortable with positive feedback that she will act even worse. This behavior is the normal reaction of a person with low self-esteem: It is unsettling to be treated in any way incompatible with one's own self-image. Therefore, Bailey's first response to good feedback will be to act worse in order to show others who she really is. It takes dedication and perseverance to help a child unlearn a negative self-image. Planting a positive image in its place is essential to a child's success in life.

Changing Attitudes   The following example shows how adults can start the process by gaining a more positive perspective on a child.

At one staff meeting of Midway Children's Center, everyone was complaining about Leo, who was exhibiting particularly undesirable behavior. To relieve the negative focus, Caroline, the director, suggested an exercise. She asked everyone to think of just one thing they really liked about Leo. Some were embarrassed to find themselves struggling at first to come up with a positive point.

Gradually, though, they each brought to light one part of the child they could genuinely say they liked. Musical himself, Dennis said he liked Leo's singing. Even though Leo was usually disruptive during music time, at least he was on key! Nancy liked his eyes. Sure, they were constantly darting around, checking to see if anyone was observing his mischief, but Nancy had to admit they were bright, beautiful brown eyes, just like her mother's. Maureen respected his self-assurance. He may have been bossy, but at least he was capable, an attribute Maureen valued.

As the list grew, the teachers felt themselves coming to a new appreciation of the boy they had been complaining about earlier. It didn't erase their irritation with his behavior, but it did put that behavior into a little more positive perspective. They were then in a better frame of mind to brainstorm about ways to help him.

The children who are hardest to like are the ones that need your acceptance the most (Katz & McClellan, 1997). Their unmet needs for love may be acute, causing behavior that is extremely demanding. If you feel unable to meet their needs, they can become an irritation and a drain. Or they can become a challenge! It depends on your attitude.

It can be exciting to work with difficult children; although they may take the most out of you, they are also potentially the most rewarding. You will be delighted when a child who usually hits in anger progresses for the first time to venting that anger verbally. At that important moment, you can see the results of your coaching. A habitually disruptive child who makes it through a whole day, or even a whole hour, without having a negative effect on the group can give you hope for humanity! It also allows you to congratulate yourself on helping that child channel his or her energies more productively.

Peer Acceptance

In addition to needing a close relationship with adults, children need acceptance and friendship from other children. We have previously discussed peer relationships in terms of security and social development. This book has emphasized the importance of helping children understand that other people have feelings and thoughts different from theirs. But sometimes you encounter a child who doesn't seem to care how others feel and your best efforts at teaching perspective taking have no effect.

> By the end of the first week of school, Mrs. Jensen could see that Jason was going to be a challenge. He had been creating problems all week: grabbing things from classmates, pushing and shoving to get in front of others, and showing no remorse for hurting them. Mrs. Jensen had helped Isabel explain to Jason that it hurt when he shoved her, but Jason wasn't interested.
>
> Mrs. Jensen soon realized that Jason's problem wasn't that he didn't understand the impact of his action, but that he didn't care whether the other kids were upset. This was a bigger challenge than a child's lack of knowledge. Her job as a teacher was to figure out why Jason didn't care and then to work on that cause.

Mrs. Jensen found out that such children typically have a history of peer rejection (DeVries & Zan, 1994). They don't have friends and don't expect to have any. This puts them in a position of having nothing to lose by offending other children. As explained in Chapter 3, having a friend is critical to developing social skills. If Jason doesn't think Robert will play with him anyway, he naturally cares more about whether he gets the most clay than whether Robert is mad at him for grabbing it all. Therefore, the cause of disinterest in other children's viewpoints is an unmet need for acceptance from peers. Of course, this is a self-perpetuating problem: the less Jason considers other children's feelings, the less likely they are to accept him in their activities.

> Mrs. Jensen decides that what Jason needs most is a friend. She wonders if she can get Beau to take Jason under his wing. Beau is a popular boy with good social skills who would provide a useful role model for Jason. Mrs. Jensen privately asks Beau if he would be willing to play with Jason and teach him how. Beau lives up to her expectations of his compassionate nature and agrees.
>
> Being sought out as a reading buddy and a playground teammate by a highly desirable companion is a major change for Jason. Beau's sponsorship

gains Jason's temporary acceptance by others, but Beau reminds him that he has to share the ball if he wants to keep on playing. Now Jason does have something to lose by ignoring how others feel. As a result, Mrs. Jensen has a chance to help Jason learn perspective taking. Jason's whole life just took a turn for the better.

CONCLUSION

When children have behavior problems caused by unmet needs, effective teachers can help them get those needs met in acceptable and productive ways. Accurately determining when a child has an unmet emotional need and responding to that need can eliminate many unproductive discipline efforts. Additionally, you can make a difference in a child's whole future by intervening in the early years and not allowing the problem to escalate.

As you work at helping children get their needs met, you will come to appreciate the obvious "problem children." They are literally crying out for help; you can't ignore them. But they are also generally the survivors. The too-quiet child may have the serious problem. Consider this child as you read Chapter 14.

∽ FOR FURTHER THOUGHT

1. A problem to solve: Several children in your child-care center refuse to help at clean-up time before lunch.
   a. What is one possible cause? Describe the guidance approach that addresses it.
   b. What is another possible cause? Describe the guidance approach that addresses it.

2. A problem to solve: Jenny keeps forgetting to put her papers into her cubby. At the end of the day a mad scramble ensues, often accompanied by tears, while everyone searches for Jenny's papers.
   a. What is one possible cause? Describe the guidance approach that addresses it.
   b. What is another possible cause? Describe the guidance approach that addresses it.

3. Analyze actual behavior problems and guidance approaches in a setting where you know the children. Cases in which you are the adult providing the guidance will probably be the most instructive.
   a. Describe the situation.
   b. Based on your knowledge of the children involved, state the probable cause.
   c. Describe the adult intervention that addresses that cause.
   d. Describe the children's response to intervention.
   e. If the approach was not helpful, was it unsuccessful because it did not address the actual cause or because one intervention was not enough?
   f. If a different cause is suggested, plan a different strategy for next time.

∽ RECOMMENDED READINGS

Developmental Studies Center. (1998). *Ways we want our class to be: Class meetings that build commitment to kindness and learning.* Oakland, CA: Author.

Howes, C., & Ritchie, S. (2002). *A matter of trust: Connecting teachers and learners in the early childhood classroom.* New York: Teachers College Press.

Hyson, M. (2004). *The emotional development of young children: Building an emotion-centered curriculum.* New York: Teachers College Press.

Koplow, L. (2002). *Creating schools that heal.* New York: Teachers College Press.

13 Children Experiencing Disabilities

by Eileen Hughes

*T*eachers in child-care centers, preschools, and primary grades are now working with more diverse populations than they did in past years. Therefore, they need a broader and deeper understanding of teaching and learning principles. Educators in early childhood and early childhood special education are now working together to determine the most effective ways of teaching and learning for all children. The most current version of the NAEYC guidelines for developmentally appropriate practices (Bredekamp & Copple, 1997) includes recommendations for working with developmentally diverse children.

The following observation is an example of the "growing pains" the two fields experience as early childhood educators and special educators learn how to best provide a supportive environment that fosters meaningful relationships among all children. This observation took place in a community child-care center that has a history of including children with disabilities.

> Four-year-old Ben is swinging in the blue swing that was designed so he can sit independently. Ben has cerebral palsy, which affects his ability to speak and walk. Tonya, a girl with disabilities from another class is pushing Ben in the swing, and Joan, an instructional assistant, is standing next to him. Two other women surrounding Ben are professionals from the special education program who are visiting the center to gather information about Ben's development.
>
> Ms. Rucker is holding a clipboard and pencil, and is leaning in front of the swing as she talks to Ben. She says, "Isn't that nice she is pushing you?" Her tone reflects talk to a younger child. "Oh, Tonya gave you a big push" (she emphasizes the word *big*). And you like that." Ben smiles and laughs. She continues, playing what almost resembles a peek-a-boo game by moving her face away then moving back when the swing comes forward. Ben laughs hard as she continues.
>
> At one point Ms. Rucker asks Ben if she can swing, and he shakes his head, "No." A blonde girl sucking her thumb is standing back observing the playground. An adult asks her, "Can you use that swing?" The girl looks puzzled and says, "No, cause I am a big girl" (she emphasizes the word *big*). "Who is the swing for?" "Ben," the girl responds in a matter-of-fact tone.

Through their actions and words, the adults surrounding Ben send messages to the other children. The children on the playground may have perceived Ben as a younger child for several reasons. Ben was surrounded by several adults and was being talked to as though he was a much younger child.

The number of adults standing around Ben also sets him apart from the other children and is not common practice for the other children. Jerome Bruner (1987) discusses how the social context and language that children are exposed to contributes to the ways they will construct knowledge of their social world.

> It is by such subtle means, as well as by more direct linguistic forms such as metaphors and symbols, narratives and images, that the child picks up the vast array of messages about social categories, expectations of behavior, etc. that she needs to cope with the social and conceptual world. (Bruner, 1987, p. 24)

In the previous observation, Ben seemed to be included in his preschool setting; however, the teachers were not considering how their actions would influence other children's perceptions and their relationships with Ben. The goals of inclusionary practices go beyond merely placing children with their peers and teaching isolated "social skills." We must examine how approaches of teaching and learning reflect our image of children: all children and each child.

As young children with disabilities are being included in settings with their peers, we must create environments to support children's understandings about differences, commonalities, and abilities. At the same time we must create learning environments that support positive self-images where meaningful relationships and friendships are formed. All children need relationships as the basis for prosocial behavior.

PHILOSOPHY AND VALUES

Historically, different philosophical perspectives and practices have characterized the two fields of early childhood and early childhood special education. Early childhood special education has had a strong grounding in behavioral perspectives that, at times, promoted deficit-driven models, focusing primarily on what the child can't do. This focus resulted in teaching isolated skills instead of encouraging meaningful learning experiences in a relevant context. The field of early childhood special education has recognized the limits of a strict interpretation of applied behavioral analysis (Wolery & Wilbers, 1994).

Early childhood education has had strong roots in a more maturational, or developmental, view and continues to draw upon other disciplines and perspectives. Professionals in both fields are faced with the shifts in current research on teaching and learning. Thus, current practices are being influenced by a more comprehensive and deeper understanding of the ways in which young children learn.

In any field, theory gets translated to principles for teaching practices. In our daily lives as children, we make thousands of decisions as we work with students. Often we teach without the necessary time required for reflection or understanding of how our actions relate to theory, principles, or beliefs. Misunderstandings of theoretical perspectives can lead to the misuse of teaching practices. For example, one of the most misunderstood practices in the field of early childhood, or early childhood special education, is the use of "reinforcers." The use of reinforcers (verbal, activity/event, or tangible) can become a way of motivating children to do what we think is best. We see that children will "behave" if we give them a sticker or make recess contingent on finishing all their assignments. What is not so easy to see is that the desirable behavior is short-lived and the child is relying on an external motivator instead of learning to behave himself. Chapter 9 details the reasons why external motivation is counterproductive. Sometimes teachers in situations that demand immediate attention fall prey to the use of quick-fix thinking and strategies. At times, these strategies become applied to all children with little regard to what the individual child actually learns.

For example, a Head Start teacher explained how the staff she worked with was very discouraged with a child who had difficulty playing with other children. The child used language that was not appropriate for the classroom and had difficulty staying with most activities. The staff was quick to time-out the child and jump in to correct the child's actions. The Head Start teacher decided to videotape the child when he was engaged and interested to learn more about his interests. She found that on the playground he was very curious about the environment and took joy in explaining the bark on the tree or the ice that was forming on the ground. When the teacher shared her discoveries with the staff, they were surprised at the child's knowledge and the amount of time he was able to focus his attention. The Head Start teacher and her staff were learning to "reframe" the way they viewed the child's actions (Olson, Burgess, & Streissguth, 1992).

The use of praise is another strategy often overused with children with disabilities. Because the field of special education has promoted the use of reinforcers, teachers have become quick to comment on the actions of children. Sometimes, the teacher will say things such as "I like the way you _____" or "Good job." These comments tend to be frequent and are often almost automatic. Certainly, our intentions are to recognize the positive actions of the child; however, as discussed in Chapter 9, the teacher may be creating a dependency on teacher approval. Again, the children's actions are short-lived and probably for the wrong reasons.

Like our philosophical views, our personal values also influence the ways we interact with children. Self-examination of your own values and tolerance for resistent behavior is a critical starting place when considering positive guidance approaches. It is important to consider if the actions of a child are a problem to the child and to others, or merely irritating and inconvenient to you. The teacher must first ask if the behavior can be ignored. If the problem is inappropriate, then some intervention is definitely required.

As classrooms become more heterogeneous, teachers need effective classroom management systems for a wide array of disabilities. The authors recognize that there may be situations that require curricular modifications or individualized teaching strategies for some children. There are times when special educators

With more heterogeneous classes, teachers need effective classroom management systems for a wide variety of disabilities.

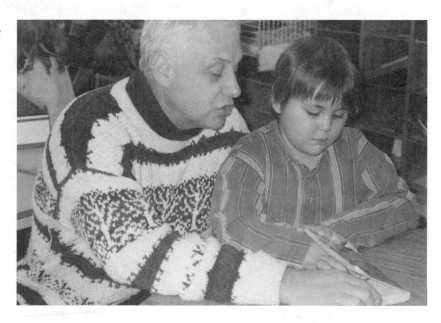

and early childhood educators must collaborate to determine ways to individualize or make curriculum modifications for a particular child. When educators work in teams, they can collaborate to make appropriate decisions related to objectives, teaching strategies, and curricular modifications. These decisions must be based in an environment and curriculum that support moral and intellectual autonomy, respect for others, positive self-concept, and problem-solving for all young children. The following sections discuss ways for thinking about a constructivist approach to guidance for children with disabilities.

THE SOCIAL ENVIRONMENT

Previous chapters explained why effective classroom management is dependent, in part, on the way children feel about themselves and each other. A classroom that supports the self-esteem of all its members will foster healthy relationships among children. When children observe you modeling respect and caring actions, they are more likely to have socially desirable behavior. Supporting children to become socially competent and to develop perspective taking is essential for effective classroom management. Social skills, including understanding the viewpoints of others, are necessary for children to resolve conflicts, understand the meaning of fairness, and build a community of learners.

Peer Interaction

As teachers, we must recognize the importance of the classroom as a place where young children learn about the roles, responsibilities, norms, expectations, and patterns of interacting. Corsaro (1985) suggests that young children come to understand themselves as members of a group through their peer culture. In the cultural context of their classrooms, young children acquire prosocial behaviors and come to understand the intricacies of relationships and ways of acting with others. Children co-construct their understanding about the values of the community and their classroom environment. Through interactions with each other, young children exchange their ideas and understandings to co-construct knowledge and assign meaning to experiences. In addition, adults in the environment provide ways of ascribing meaning to experiences or behaviors that give information about group norms. Thus, educational settings that support children of varying abilities must mirror the beliefs, perceptions, and "inclusive" values of its members.

Mallory and New (1994) suggest that the Social Constructivist theory offers a framework for understanding inclusionary education and that the Reggio Emilia approach from Italy exemplifies programs that demonstrate practices consistent with this theory. One of the many meaningful underlying principles of this approach is that all children are viewed as being capable, having "special rights," and making contributions to a community of learners (Edwards, Gandini, & Forman, 1998). Differences in children are recognized, valued, and used to develop knowledge about a child. When children with disabilities share the same educational setting with their nondisabled peers, there will be opportunities to create understanding related to "disability." We, as teachers, can construct with children the meaning of disability through our daily interactions that involve acceptance, understanding, and recognition of potential and capability.

Nondisabled children may be uncomfortable with unusual behaviors exhibited by children with disabilities. A child with a disability may not be able to communicate using speech and instead may use nonverbal actions. A child may have the power of speech, yet exhibit behaviors that are ambiguous and difficult to interpret. When a child's actions are misunderstood, or behaviors are disruptive to the classroom, a teacher must consider the actions she will take that will help the other children come to understand how to interact with the child with disabilities. Punitive actions or other actions that give negative messages about a child undermine the culture of the classroom. They are not consistent with a caring community that supports self-esteem; instead, they lead to an increase in conflict situations.

Helping nondisabled children to understand or assign meaning to atypical behavior teaches them perspective-taking and lessons about differences among people. Children in preschool settings often compare themselves to each other as it relates to their age or size. Using these dimensions to compare themselves to each other is what children at this developmental age know how to do. As young children step out of diapers and assert their independence with peers, they come to understand how they are alike and different. When children who have disabilities display behaviors that appear disruptive, children's usual ways of comparison must be extended. The way a teacher rejects or accepts differences, behaviors, or characteristics of children provides a model for the other children. At the same time that you are supporting understanding for nondisabled children, you can also build the self-esteem and self-image of the child with disabilities. Thus, the social context for young children should support (a) perspective-taking, (b) the strengths of each child, and (c) relationships among children.

Perspective-Taking

Perspective-taking helps children to (1) learn about multiple viewpoints and different ways of thinking, (2) problem-solve, and (3) accept other children who have different characteristics. Teaching children about "seeing" another view can help nondisabled children to understand children who exhibit unfamiliar or confusing behaviors. Children with disabilities may display behaviors that appear odd, confusing, or even frightening to other young children.

> Jaylyn, a 6-year-old child with significant disabilities, attends a community preschool and is the only child with a disability in her class. A 5-year-old boy in her class observes Jaylyn as she lays screaming on the floor. The boy comments to his friend, "She is a baby. She is 6 and I am 5. You know what? She wears diapers and she stinks." The boy's comments reflect a question about why Jaylyn, who is taller and older than himself, still wears diapers. Jaylyn's teacher responds to the young boy, "You wore diapers, I wore diapers, and Jaylyn needs diapers now."

Jaylyn's teacher views her role as being a guide for the children in understanding Jaylyn's behavior. She wants the children to accept Jaylyn, and she wants to support a positive image of Becky as a member of the group. Jaylyn's teacher knows preschool children compare themselves using physical characteristics to understand similarities and differences. She believes that Jaylyn's behaviors are confusing to the other children as they compare her to themselves. Further explanation in a private conversation between the teacher and the boy might alleviate the child's concern. By responding to the nondisabled children's concerns, teachers can help them to understand the behaviors of their peers with disabilities. This can lead to a supportive classroom environment and reduce conflict with children experiencing disabilities.

In another classroom, 3-year-old Cornado teaches us how to interpret the behaviors of a child with disabilities. His response reflects an acceptance of difference and shows perspective-taking.

Four-year-old Ben is in the same preschool class as Thomas. Ben has cerebral palsy, which influences his mobility and the ways he moves his arms. It is not uncommon that when Ben sits next to his peers he inadvertently moves his arm and hits them. Several of the boys in the class are bothered by his action and call for this teacher, Ms. Lowell. On one occasion, a boy next to Ben yelled out, "Hey, he's hitting me and I can't draw." Ben's intentions are sometimes unclear. His arm movement might have been involuntary, but over time it may have become intentional as he gained attention from others when he touched or "hit" them. Cornado, who often plays alongside Ben, is observed as he plays with a small, plastic playhouse. Ben is on the floor opposite the house and Cornado. Ben moves his arm and as he moves, he knocks the house over onto Thomas. Cornado looks surprised and replies, "Darn house." Cornado does not interpret Ben's actions as an intentional act to disrupt his play, nor does he call for the teacher.

A lesson to learn from Cornado is how nondisabled children can give meaning to behaviors in ways that build acceptance for the differences among children. Teachers can consider ways to extend Cornado's observations and use them to help other children who view situations less positively.

Perspective-taking is taught through the ways teachers invite ideas from individuals in a group. The goal is to help children realize there are other perspectives than their own—that other children also have things to say and want turns. In the following dialogue, Alex, who is diagnosed with ADHD, is trying to dominate the group discussion. Alex is still learning to take turns and sometimes has difficulty knowing how to express his ideas in a group setting. The teacher strives to include him in the group without removing or "punishing" him.

The following transcription is taken from a circle time activity with Jennifer, a preschool teacher. The children are in an ongoing discussion about dinosaurs. The dialogue reflects only a portion of the circle time discussion that started when Alex volunteered to share his "weekend." The children are encouraged during Monday's circle time to share stories about their weekend, and on this Monday Alex is telling about a dinosaur movie he watched at home.

Alex:	Quiet everybody! (yelling) It was my weekend!
Ms. Anna:	Let's listen to Scott for a minute.
Scott:	The dinosaurs umm, eat umm, dirt umm . . . they make it.
Alex:	No they don't eat dirt!
Ms. Anna:	Alex, Scott thinks that some dinosaurs might have eaten dirt.

Highlighting the abilities and strengths of all children helps them engage in healthy interactions with one another.

Alex:	They don't eat dirt!
Ms. Anna:	You might think that they don't.
Alex:	I know it's not dirt . . . I know it's not dirt.
Ms. Anna:	But this is what Scott thinks; you might think something different.
Scott:	They eat dirt and they eat whales except they're not s'posed to.
Ms. Anna:	And what do they eat that they're not supposed to?
Scott:	Whales that they're not s'posed to, the killer ones, killer whales.
Alex:	Scott did all my weekend, nobody gets a question.
Ms. Anna:	Geoffrey has something to say. Let's listen to Geoffrey.
Alex:	Nobody gets a question. (loudly over everyone) Nobody. Nobody gets a question! Mine.
Christopher:	I have my hand up.
Alex:	No you don't. I'm not gonna . . . put your hand down I'm not gonna let you have a question. . . . You can't have a question. (yelling) Nobody gets a question. Put your hand down!! Put your hand down!
Ms. Anna:	I'm sorry, Geoffrey. I couldn't hear.
Alex:	Put your hand down Christopher and do it now! (being forceful) Christopher if you s'pose to do that, I'm gonna tell.
Ms. Anna:	Alex, I'm having a hard time hearing Geoffrey.
Alex:	Nobody gets a question.
Ms. Anna:	I'm having a hard time hearing Geoffrey.

Alex:	Nobody does.
Ms. Anna:	We're having an open discussion.
Alex:	If you are gonna say that, I'm just gonna say the loudest words that I—.
Ms. Anna:	Will you listen to me for a minute? We started talking about dinosaurs. All of us are sharing our ideas. We're discussing about dinosaurs. Some people think differently and that's okay. So we're all discussing. Geoffrey is going to finish what he's saying and then we're going to let Austin and Christopher talk. If you would like another chance to talk just put your hand up and that will let me know.
Alex:	This is my weekend!
Ms. Anna:	I know, you told us about the movie that you watched. I was real excited to hear all of the fun stuff that you learned about dinosaurs. That was real interesting. I'm really glad that you shared.

Anna teaches the other children to express their ideas while at the same time teaching Alex rules and limits for remaining in circle with his classmates. First, Anna restates to the children their ideas, noting the children's different ideas about what dinosaurs eat. Second, Anna is patient with Alex, allowing him to express himself. Third, she helps Alex to remember the class rules by repeating that he must raise his hand and he must listen to the ideas of the other children. Anna is not used to working with children like Alex who have difficulty monitoring their own actions. However, Anna is working in collaboration with a special education support team to assist Alex in his community child-care settings. Anna and the special education team are learning new ways of supporting all children as they reflect on their observations.

Reviewing the transcript of the group discussion allows the classroom teacher and the special education teacher a way to revisit the experience, interpret the children's actions, and reflect on their own actions as a means for making decisions for classroom methods. Reviewing the situation with Alex, it might be that he needs more concrete ways to learn to limit his actions. For example, some classrooms use a card or object the child holds to indicate it is his turn in circle. Another idea might be to prepare Alex prior to the cirlce time and have him draw two ideas he wants to share. He can then use his drawing as a visual aide for limiting his ideas for discussion.

Thus, as you develop your approach to guiding young children in your classroom, you will need to consider ways to help all children learn about the differences among themselves.

Recognition and Strengths

We want to create an environment with capable children who view each other with respect and who value the attributes of each member. This means teachers must make visible the strengths and gifts of each child. In the following example in a kindergarten classroom, Miss Forrest prevents a potential classroom disruption. She observes Mark, a child with developmental delays, who squirms and bothers the other boys sitting next to him. Until this year, Mark has always had a teaching assistant assigned to his classroom. This year, in Miss Forrest's class, Mark is spending time away from the teaching assistant. Mark has difficulty in groups and seeks the attention of his peers by getting close in their face or hitting them. Children's reactions to this behavior often disrupt class activities. In the following example, note the way Miss Forrest anticipates Mark's actions and recognizes his interests; she also shifts her lesson in the midst of the classroom discussion in order to prevent the mounting conflict from the back of the room.

> The children in Miss Forrest's class are engaged in a group discussion about a wood carving experience from yesterday. A small group of boys in the back of the room begin to talk to each other and start to hit each other, causing others in the group to turn around. Miss Forrest is making a list of the children's ideas, writing down their comments on a poster board at the front of the room. She then observes Manuel getting restless and sees the other boys start to enter into interactions with Manuel. At this point, Miss Forrest calls Manuel up to the front of the class and asks him if he will draw something he remembers from yesterday. She rewords her direction to help him comprehend. She hands him the pen to draw on the paper and asks him to write some letters. Miss Forrest interprets Mark's actions to the class. She says that he is drawing an idea he remembers and that he is using his words to write about his idea. Manuel turns to his classmates, grinning as though pleased with himself, and gestures as he uses his limited speech.

In this example, Miss Forrest redirects Manuel's attention to avoid creating more problems for the group. She knows that Manuel has difficulty in large groups as he does not comprehend at the level of the other children; she also is aware that his way of seeking attention is to bother others. Further, Miss Forrest knows that Manuel takes an interest in drawing (making undistinguishable marks). She then interprets Manuel's "letters" for the children. Miss Forrest gives Manuel attention and prevents a further escalation of disruption. In addition, she makes Mark's abilities visible to the other children.

In the Reggio Emilia approach (Edwards, Gandini, & Forman, 1998), teachers acknowledge that a "handicap" is just one of many differences among people. In the previous instance, Miss Forrest was co-constructing with the children the ways that Mark was different. At the same time, she was building a sense of self for Mark that would support his relationships and positive associations with the other children. This guidance strategy is a very different approach than the common practice of giving "time-out."

By recognizing children's strengths and bringing them to the attention of the group, you create a climate for children to observe and interpret the variety of ways to understand "difference." When children learn that the differences among themselves are positive and can be strengths for the group, children will be better able to create healthy relationships with each other. Note the way the teacher in the following classroom observes ways to highlight the strengths of the children in her room.

Noah is diagnosed with ADHD and attends a local community child-care setting. Ms. Luman is aware that Noah has difficulty with other children. It is not an uncommon occurrence that children will move away from Noah when he tries to control a play situation. Ms. Luman is also aware of the different ways Noah sees an event, observation, or situation that the other children sometimes miss.

For example, at Christmas time four children are constructing a Santa Claus to hang in their playhouse. The children are on the floor, drawing the various parts of the Santa on butcher paper. One child decides to draw the head, another girl decides she will draw the body, and someone else decides to draw the legs. The children work next to each other on their separate parts. Noah, who is engaged in a playdough activity across the room, runs over to the children and says, "Hey you guys, that is never going to work." The children stop momentarily, then continue to work on their parts. Ms. Luman, overhearing Noah and observing the children, intervenes and comments, "Noah has an idea." One of the children looks up and says, "What, Noah?" Noah proceeds to explain that the parts won't go together. Ms. Luman asks Noah for his idea. Noah tells the children that some parts are too small for the head and it will look "funny." The children ask Noah what they should do. Noah says they should start over and make Santa bigger. The children exchange ideas with Noah and come up with the idea to trace Ms. Luman.

There are many ways the children could solve their problem. Ms. Luman, knowing that Noah has difficulty working with others, decides to use this opportunity for a learning situation. She focuses the group's attention to Noah's idea and supports Noah in his own way to gain entry into the group activity. Because the children have observed Noah to be someone who gets into trouble with the other children, the teacher facilitates an interaction with Noah. She also guides the other children to construct a more positive image of their peer who can offer creative and imaginative ideas.

In these examples, the teacher (a) recognized the child's action, (b) viewed the child's strengths, and (c) interpreted the action in a way to help the other children understand. When you highlight the strengths of children with disabilities you can also build their self-esteem. At the same time you can support opportunities for their further interactions with peers.

Friendship

As explained in previous chapters, friendship among young children is critical to their intellectual, emotional, and social development. Therefore, helping children make friends means less conflict in your class.

Young children with disabilities often have difficulties when socializing with their peers (Guralnick & Groom, 1988). Children with developmental delays can have difficulty initiating and maintaining interactions with other children. The attitudes and perceptions of nondisabled children can influence their relationships with children with disabilities. In Constructivist classrooms, teachers encourage children to work collaboratively to encourage the incidental, or spontaneous, op-

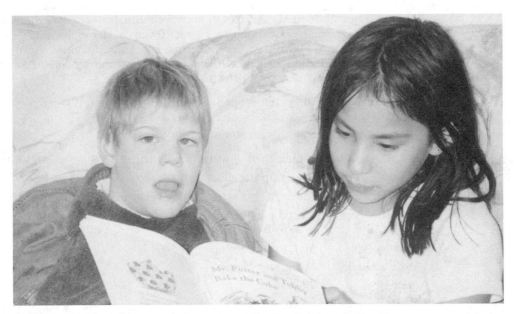

Children with disabilities need planned opportunities to interact with others; group work helps them find a place among peers.

portunities for social interaction. Children with disabilities will need even more opportunities to interact with others. At times you will need to modify your values, objectives, or activity routines to consider the social needs of the child with disabilities. In the following example, Miss Wheeler puts her own values first instead of the social needs of the children.

> Simon is painting alongside Martha and Vanessa. Martha blows paint from her paintbrush. Vanessa laughs and does the same with her paintbrush. The two girls continue giggling as they play a game. Simon watches the two girls and holds up his brush to his mouth to do the same. Because he has difficulty moving his arm, the brush hits his cheek and he ends up with paint on his face. Miss Wheeler sees the paint and, being very careful to keep Simon clean, wipes his face. The children watch as the teacher wipes Simon, then they return to their game. Simon tries again to enter into the game of the other children and again gets paint on his face. Miss Wheeler remarks to Simon, "I guess you are done." She wipes his face and hands and removes him from the table.

Miss Wheeler has good intentions. However, the way she interacts with Simon ends the potential for Simon's interactions with other children. Miss Wheeler did not recognize the potential for social interaction for Simon and the two girls at the time. If we value the importance of social and emotional development, we must create environments for all children that support interactions.

In the following observation, Ms. Kramer builds a classroom culture that fosters relationship building among children with disabilities who have difficulty with their communication skills.

Anne is a new child in Ms. Kramer's classroom. She is developmentally delayed and has an expressive vocabulary of about 10 words. Her classmates, Riley and Christopher, are playing with dinosaurs, blocks, and cars. Annie shoves Christopher and then she hits Riley. Both Riley and Christopher call Ms. Kramer to tell her that Annie is hitting them.

Ms. Hernandes:	Riley, tell Annie how you feel when you hit her.
Riley:	Stop.
Christopher:	Stop.
Ms. Hernandes:	Annie, Do you want to play with Christopher and Riley?
Annie:	[picks up the dinosaur]
Ms. Hernandes:	Annie, if you want to play you can say, "I want to play."
Annie:	[keeps playing with the dinosaur and grabs another dinosaur from Christopher]
Christopher:	My dinosaur, stop.
Ms. Hernandes:	Annie say, 'I play.'
Annie:	Play.
Ms. Hernandes:	[to Riley and Christopher] Can you think of a way that Annie can play too?
Christopher:	Annie, you play with this. [He gives her a dinosaur and a car.]

Ms. Kramer knows that Annie's language delays interfere with her ability to enter into play; the teacher interprets Annie's actions as a request to enter into play. Another factor to consider is that when two children at this age engage in play, it is typically difficult for a third child to enter into play. Thus, even without her communicative delays, Annie may have had difficulty given the social maturity of all the children.

Ms. Kramer tries to help Annie understand the consequence of her actions. It is difficult to know if Annie is able to do this; however, the teacher does model empathy for the other children. Ms. Kramer attempts to replace Annie's inappropriate actions with the use of words. In this interaction, the teacher also interprets Annie's actions for the boys. This helps the two boys understand that Annie has difficulty interacting and that her actions of hitting and taking toys may mean she is trying to say she wants to play. Finally, Ms. Kramer employs a strategy that invites the boys to problem-solve how to act with Annie.

In Miss Forrest's combined kindergarten/first-grade class, children work and play in very natural ways. In fact, the climate in the classroom strongly supports the five children with disabilities in their associations with the other children. From the first day of the school year, Miss Forrest has encouraged children to go to each other when they need help doing their school work. She identifies the strengths of each child to the group; the members in her class seek resources from each other as a natural part of their daily activity.

Children with disabilities, like all children, need to feel good about themselves. Sometimes teachers tend to focus too much on the child's "needs." Teachers may unintentionally give messages that work against building the self-esteem or enhancing the image of the child with the disability. In the example about paint brushes, Miss Wheeler could have allowed Simon to join in the play with Vanessa and Martha. Due to her misguided intervention, the girls saw Simon as messy and in need of being cleaned up instead of as someone to play with. Instead, teachers can help children to see different perspectives, to recognize strengths, and to support the children's need for interactions. It is in these ways that teachers can work toward effective classrooms that encourage healthy relationships and harmony among children.

Attention-Deficit Hyperactivity Disorder

Children act out due to many different causes—for example, environmental conditions, parenting styles, or any number of disorders that are associated with attention deficit problems. Currently, teachers report a high incidence of disruptive behaviors from children diagnosed with attention-deficit hyperactivity disorder (ADHD). Children with this disorder experience inability to pay attention and or distractabilty. Approximately 7.5 percent of students apparently have ADHD, which is more prevalent in males and tends to emerge in the preschool years. Approximately 85 percent of the children diagnosed in preschool continue to have problems in adolescence (Parker, 2002). See Appendix D for further information about diagnosing ADHD.

Students with ADHD may also have other conditions that contribute to learning and behavioral difficulties. Oppositional behaviors may be associated with an oppositional defiant disorder (ODD). These children may be defiant, stubborn, or become belligerent and will refuse to obey. Some children with ADHD may develop conduct disorder (CD) and exhibit a serious pattern of antisocial behavior. These children may be aggressive and lie, steal, or be inclined to get into fights with other children. A neurological disorder called *Tourette syndrome* can be associated with ADHD and causes children to yell out inappropriately.

The continuum of inattentive disorders is likely to have an impact on the child's school environments and academic performance as well as on the ability to form relationships with peers. Children may be unable to process and retain oral information. Their impulsivity and hyperacitivity may be frustrating to peers and teachers, leading to discipline problems. Other associated learning disabilities might include difficulty understanding sounds or words or difficulty with language; these difficulties cause problems with spelling, written communication, and math calculations. In addition, students may appear disorganized and unable to handle changes in routine or transitions; they may also be socially immature. We suggest that special educators be consulted for diagnosis and resources to develop intervention in the classroom.

Resistant Behaviors

Understanding the following four points about the nature of resistant behaviors can help you use more positive discipline. **First,** it is important to understand that the behaviors children exhibit signal some inner need or are a reaction to a past situation. Young children call for help or seek attention for many different reasons, and it's not always easy to know the cause for the disruptive behavior. **Second,** the behavior is usually controllable by the person who is acting out. **Third,** if you confront the child aggressively while he or she is acting out, you will "fuel" the conflict. **Fourth,** behavior can escalate from one level to the next and the higher the level of escalation, the harder the return to socially acceptable behavior. There are some days when a child starts the day calling for attention in a group and by the end of the day the child has hit, yelled, and created lots of discomfort in the classroom. Understanding the nature of the behavior, looking at your own values associated with resistant behavior, and examining the context are starting places for designing positive discipline approaches (Bailey, 2004).

When looking at the context it is important to consider the possible causes of the child's behavior. The behavior might serve to gain attention or express frustation, hurt, anxiety, independence, etc. The first step in understanding the cause of a behavior is analyzing the apparent purpose of the child's actions. Early childhood educators and special educators have been taught to use time and event sampling observation methods that can help with examining variables. It is important to note the context that might contribute to a given behavior. Does observation reveal patterns? Do problems occur at a certain time of day, during certain kinds of activities, or with certain children? After you examine your own values related to resitant behaviors and consider the nature of behaviors, then you are ready to analyze the context.

The Physical Setting

Previous chapters explained how the physical arrangement of the learning environment helps children understand the expected classroom behaviors and norms of the classroom community. When children with disabilities are included in environments that are developmentally appropriate, you may need to individualize aspects of the environment. If you pay attention to the social and physical dimensions of the environment, you can prevent the escalation of behaviors that might otherwise cause havoc to a class by the end of a school day. Some children with ADD, ADHD, FAS, or developmental delays have difficulty focusing their attention in the midst of noise and visual information typical to a classroom. Regardless of the type of disability, children who have difficulty focusing their attention may vary in their abilities to select or ignore information in the environment. For example, children may not be able to pay attention to verbal directions if they are attending to other noise in the classroom. Research suggests that reducing stimulation may help children focus their attention; however, a sterile environment void of materials may not be the answer (Jones, 1991). Children with ADHD may have difficulty inhibiting their own impulses also. Overall, children with attention problems will benefit from the same high-quality environments for all children that invite active participation and engage children in meaningful activities (Landau & McAninch, 1993).

In developmentally appropriate environments, as described in Chapter 4, the teacher will arrange the environment to allow children quiet time or privacy, mobility, and other comforts. However, a particular child may need you to tailor or adapt the physical structure of the environment to meet his or her individual needs. The following suggestions are guidelines to consider when you adapt the physical environment of a child who has difficulty with paying attention or who has another type of developmental delay.

Seating Arrangements

The arrangement of the classroom environment can influence the child's interactions with the environment and resulting behaviors (Landau & McAninch, 1993; Weaver, 1994). When a child has difficulty paying attention to the important information in the environment, you can seat the child in front of you or in the center of the group. When sitting in a visible location, the child can see you better in order to receive directions, both verbally and visually. Children with visuomotor integration problems may be distracted if they are seated too far from the teacher's presentations. It is also important to make sure distractible children are not seated close to environmental sound sources, such as fans, radiators, and so on. Children who are distractible may attend to these background noises and miss the verbal directions from the teacher.

In some instances, a child may need support to calm himself or herself in order to sit with the group. Sometimes teachers can plan relaxation exercises or warm-up exercises prior to "work." These exercises allow the child a chance to learn to focus by moving his or her body in space and to gain greater body control. There may be different types of strategies for calming or relaxing children depending on the individual child's characteristics. The following example is one way a preschool teacher helped relax a child with ADHD:

> Maureen found that when she holds 4-year-old Matthew on her lap for morning circle, he is able to listen to the other children for longer periods. Rather than punishing Matthew for his difficulties during circle time, Maureen finds that gentle touching and comforting on her lap provides a way to relax this child. Maureen helps Matthew to listen to the other children in this way. Over time, Maureen moves Matthew off her lap and places him next to her where she can put her arm around him when necessary.

Not all children will respond the same as Matthew. However, we can learn to observe when children need support. Sometimes a teacher might be quick to isolate or otherwise punish a child who cannot sit with others. In the previous example, Maureen is building a caring relationship with Matthew while providing the support and attention that allows him to remain a member of the group.

Asking the questions, "Why does the child want to leave his place in the group?" and "What types of support soothe or calm the child?" is the beginning for problem solving and identifying adaptations to the environment. Some teachers may question if Matthew is receiving preferential treatment by being allowed to sit on the teacher's lap. Teachers may believe that if Matthew is allowed to sit on their laps, then the other children will want the same treatment. Interestingly, Maureen is faced with the situation one morning when a new child to her class questions, "How come he always gets to sit there?" Maureen searches for a good response. However, before she can answer, a young girl in circle answers matter-of-factly, "Cause it helps him." Nothing more is said and the children continue with their circle time activity. The teacher concludes that the children are learning about caring, individual differences, and fairness through this situation.

In Miss Forrest's classroom, Manuel, who was introduced earlier in the chapter, will sometimes be seated in the front row for group discussions so that the teacher can move to be close to him if necessary. She makes sure not to always have Mark right next to her, but she knows that until he can remain with the other children without adult attention, she will need to observe his actions closely.

A child with ADHD may have difficulty returning to the same assigned place in the room for seating. In some instances, seating the child next to other children who can model accepted behaviors and provide reminders for expected classroom behaviors can be a support. Offering choices for seating that are acceptable can also be an alternative. For example, you might tell the child, "You may sit next to Joe or here next to Mary." You allow the child some choice, but provide appropriate options for his or her choice. For instance, in Ms. Forrest's classroom, Kelsey, who had a hard time focusing her attention, was seated next to Megan, who readily shared her journal writing with Kelsey. Over time Kelsey learned to look to Megan for ways to start her own journals to organize her work.

Sometimes thinking about the physical environment makes teachers forget about the social environment when they make decisions about classroom management. In the following classroom, the children are not socializing with Elena because of where she sits.

Physical isolation can become social isolation if the environment is not carefully planned to integrate all children.

Elena has difficulty sitting in the small chairs in her classroom. Because she falls out of the chairs, she is given a desk and a larger chair placed against the wall. Over time, the children in the class, as well as Elena, learn that the desk against the wall is "Elena's table." No other child or adult uses the chair, and this becomes a special place meant only for Elena. Because the table accommodates only Elena, the opportunities for social interactions are limited, and Elena's isolated physical place becomes her isolated social place in the classroom community. Another alternative is to consider adding more chairs with a wide base of support to prevent tipping. Elena would then have opportunities for interactions with the other children.

Organization, Activity Areas, and Material Selection

Early childhood classrooms generally offer an array of materials and activities to invite the participation of children with different interests and abilities, and of different ages. Some children with ADHD, and others who have a difficult time focusing their attention, may need more reminders, visual coding systems, or supports. For example, an environment that is carefully organized can reduce the risk of clutter and provide clear messages for the storage of materials. A child who is distractible needs to have a place that is clearly identifiable for organizing his or her personal belongings. Materials that are labeled and organized for easy classification help all children, especially those who have difficulty making associations. Visual cues, such as color coding, sometimes help children learn to organize and store their materials. All children may benefit when you have them clean out their book bags, cubbies, or desks regularly. A materials checklist can be used for children with organizational problems.

Some children may need support through the use of physical boundaries that designate their work area. Consider the following situation, which illustrates how teachers provide boundaries for Victor.

Victor has difficulty keeping his tools for drawing or painting on his own paper, and the other children are bothered by Victor's invasion of their space. The teacher defines Victor's work area by giving him a tray to work on at the table. Victor's teacher places carpet squares on the floor to define his area when he plays on the floor with materials that have many parts. Many teachers provide small decorative baskets or containers that help children to put materials away and keep a sense of order in the room. In addition to needing physical boundaries, some children may need to have a limited number of materials or types of choices available at one time. For example, when Victor has half a box of crayons to use instead of the entire box of crayons, he can organize his work place.

In early childhood classrooms, it is not uncommon that activity areas will change to reflect children's current interests. There may be some children, such as those with fetal alcohol syndrome (FAS), who will need more preparation or a longer period of time to adjust to changes in the environment. If the changes are unexpected, the children may have an even harder time adjusting. You can prepare the child for anticipated changes ahead of time or, better yet, the child could help to make the changes in the class. The child might be included by helping you to move or sort materials in preparation for making changes in the classroom.

There are times when you need to seek the support of other team members to identify alternative teaching strategies for a particular child. For example, some children are calmed or more attentive if they are in certain positions on the floor where they are given physical support and can move parts of their bodies. Some children can concentrate better with gentle rocking to soothe their bodies. Other children do not like to be touched and become bothered when sitting close to another child. Still others need physical boundaries to help them concentrate.

Special education staff can support teachers when making adaptations for children who have problems in the typical environment. In the following classroom example, the teacher and special education teacher work together to modify the environment for Elias.

> Elias has difficulty organizing himself and has a hard time putting on his clothes to go outside. In the process of trying, he often ends up in fights with the other boys. Ms. Ward collaborates with the special education staff in identifying that Elias has a hard time with the sequence of putting on his clothes. Understanding this helps the teacher to understand why he engages in fighting.
>
> Ms. Ward and special education staff figure out ways to use the environment to support Elias. The teacher finds that if she places his cubbie against the wall and provides a limited place for putting on his coat, Elias takes less time to put on his clothing. He can then be ready to go outside with the other children. The special educators provide a small bench for him to sit on to put on his boots. The additional boundaries allow Elias to remain in the area. The modifications in the environment provide boundaries that help Elias to focus on preparing to go outside.

An aspect of the Reggio Emilia approach that has meaning to the education of young children with disabilities is the belief that children have "100 languages" (Edwards et al., 1998). Italian educators have much to teach us about the different ways children have to express themselves. In the Reggio Emilia child-care system, you will find many different, wonderful raw materials for children to use to express their ideas, theories, and feelings. This concept, as applied to children with developmental delays, is meaningful especially for children who have limited use of verbal language for expression. If children can express themselves through the use of various media (sculpture, music, wire, paper, raw materials), they will have an outlet for feelings; this might reduce behaviors of frustration.

Identifying dimensions in the physical environment that influence the onset of a child's inappropriate behavior is extremely helpful. Such identification makes it more likely that teachers can understand the cause of the problem and the needs of the child in the environment. Special education staff can then provide meaningful support to the early childhood teacher and the child in the early childhood classroom environment.

ORGANIZATIONAL STRATEGIES

As noted in Chapter 5, a teacher can prevent problem situations by providing familiar routines and planning carefully for transitions, waiting periods, and group times. The same principles that you use to make decisions for typically developing children will especially help children with disabilities. However, as with other aspects of the curriculum, you may need to adapt or modify the principles when a child with disabilities has difficulty with the regular classroom routines or transitions. You will need to be sensitive to children who do not respond well to changes in the classroom routines or who cannot transition easily.

Routines

Several aspects of classroom routines can be individualized for the child who has difficulty with the usual approaches. First, a teacher can prepare children for the routines by having a visual calendar or a set of photographs for the routines posted. Children who have difficulty remembering the sequence of routines (for example, children with FAS) can be prepared at the beginning of the day and assisted during the day. Be sure that all parts of the daily routines are noted and not just topics or assignments. Having the schedule posted at the child's desk or table can also be a support.

Second, a child's individual routine can be altered, perhaps allowing an activity to continue longer. Third, you can help children who have difficulty making changes to prepare for any changes in the routine. Children are reassured if they can prepare in advance for the change of routines and be part of the planning for change. A designated place in the room can be used for notifying students of any changes to the weekly schedule or routines. You can also have a system for checking off the completed items or tasks of the schedule so the child has a visual tracking record. Fourth, having a daily routine for when homework assignments are collected and recorded can help students to organize their materials. Including these activities in the daily schedule will also help those students who have difficulty organizing themselves. For some students, having a partner to help them check their work or to check the schedule can prove effective and eliminate frustrations for everyone.

Transitions

It is not uncommon for children with ADHD or FAS to react negatively to the normal transitions that occur in an early childhood classroom. It is reported that children can spend up to 15 percent of the school day in some type of transition between activities or routines (Jones, 1991). Allowing plenty of time for transitions can help the child who has outbursts when he or she is asked to shift activities. The child may need individual directions, as well as the directions given to the group. In addition, the preparation for transition times can be introduced with visual drawings or photographs. The calendar of photographs of the day's activities previously suggested can also help a child prepare for transitions. You can also explain to the child in advance of the transition what will happen next and present positive aspects to the change of activity. It can also be helpful for you to explain the beginning and end of the activity in preparation for the change. Sometimes having rituals or established ways to transition are helpful. For young children, it may help to transition to different areas or tables so that the children have concrete indicators and receive a clear message about leaving one activity and starting another one.

RULES AND LIMITS

One of the goals of early childhood educators is to help young children learn to view themselves as capable and as competent decision makers. Guiding children to make decisions about their actions can support this goal. This is congruent with the research of Piaget and his colleagues related to the development of moral autonomy, which is the underlying principle of this book. Moral autonomy is a goal for children with disabilities as much as it is for other children. Therefore, the basic guidelines for effective guidance are the same for children with special needs as for others: Building mutually respectful relationships based on caring is essential to moral autonomy for all children. Planning that prevents behavior problems is probably even more important for children with disabilities than for others. Such planning helps keep problems from escalating and turning into power struggles.

It is important to understand that some children will need more support, guidance, or personal attention because of the nature of their individual learning patterns. Children with difficulty paying attention or following rules do not necessarily have "deviant" behavior. Teachers need to understand why children are making mistakes, ignoring rules, and calling for help or attention. When you know why children are acting out, you can make more appropriate decisions for when and how to individualize. We make informed decisions about why and when to bend the rules when we understand the characteristics of children who have disorders such as FAS or ADHD.

It is reported that teachers working with children who have ADHD tend to repeat directions over and over (Landau & McAninch, 1993). To avoid such repetition, teachers can anticipate these situations when they work with children who usually challenge the rules and limits. Some children with FAS will have difficulty expressing themselves and understanding language, or will have an inability to predict consequences for their behavior. Support from the special education staff or a school psychologist can assist the classroom teacher to determine when to modify teaching strategies. In some instances, it will be necessary to work with family members to seek resources that involve counseling or intervention beyond the classroom. Team members can exchange viewpoints and develop strategies for individual students.

Classroom Instructions

Children who are impulsive are likely to miss details while listening to group directions and will then make mistakes. There are several ways you can prevent or reduce this problem: preparing children to listen, focusing on important parts of class instructions and planning how to approach their work. The following suggestions might assist you when you work with children who have trouble listening and understanding directions.

Direct, brief, and concrete class directions will help. Combining auditory and visual information may also be helpful. For example, classroom schedules, rules, or instructions might be posted for visual reference, using pictures for younger children. Planning and offering time for children to ask questions will also help. We recommend providing children time to pause or longer times for processing during instructions for multi-task projects. Another strategy is to prepare students for an activity by helping them get organized. For example, you might ask children, "What do you need?" or "What do you do now?" These types of questions help children set up their workplace (Weaver, 1994). Some children might need more one-on-one contact.

Children who are impulsive may have frequent outbursts when asked to listen in a group or to remain at one activity. You can prevent outbursts by including the child in the class demonstration or giving the child a job. The teacher thereby engages the child and, at the same time, encourages self-esteem. Another suggestion is to allow these youngsters more breaks than the other children receive.

Even more than most of us, children with ADHD do not like to feel forced to comply. Power struggles and rebellious actions are not uncommon when teachers do not understand the characteristics of these children. Although these children need structure and predictable routines, they also need to feel as though they have choices. For example, the children may be allowed to choose when and where to take breaks outside or in the reading area.

Early childhood teachers and special education staff can work together to identify alternative teaching strategies for children with special needs.

It can be useful to help young children learn to monitor their actions when following directions. Concrete pictures of the appropriate responses can be used to ask the child if his action is okay. It may also be helpful for you to have someone record the ways you initiate and terminate a direction. Keeping the directions positive (do this) instead of negative (stop that) will create better compliance.

TEACHER COLLABORATION

As teachers in special education and early childhood special education come together to work with children in early childhood settings, they often need to study their actions and exchange points of view. In the following vignette, team members exchange viewpoints to decide how best to work with a child with developmental delays.

Malcom is playing at the table with the other children, who are given water, flour, and salt to mix and make goop. The children have this opportunity throughout the year and, over time, have become familiar with how much of the ingredients they need to make the consistency of goop that works best for them. Malcom sometimes has difficulty playing alongside other children, and sometimes tries to tell the other children what to do. He sometimes holds onto the cup so that the other children won't get a turn. On this day he is putting in more cups of water than the other children want. He is also splashing the water, and the other children are getting upset.

Ms. Luman and Ms. Dennis observe this situation. They use the observation for discussing their philosophies and to plan how best to work with Malcom in the early childhood classroom. Both the classroom teacher and the special education teacher feel they need to work with this situation, as it is becoming a problem for Malcom and the other children. Ms. Lumen listens to the special education teacher express her ideas about ways to deal with Malcom's behaviors. "I think Malcom needs to know his limits and that it is appropriate to take turns and to use only the amount of water necessary for the goop." Ms. Dennis suggests the following: "We should put up a sign on the wall that provides a clear visual cue that only one cup of water is needed for the goop. If he uses more than that, then he is put in time-out and he cannot play in the area any more."

After listening to Ms. Dennis, Ms. Luman responds, "I don't agree that Malcom should be timed-out. I don't believe in time-out for this class and that would be something different we do only for Malcom. Another thing is that I purposely don't put up a recipe at this time of the year because the children are learning how to transform the materials into the right consistency for goop. By putting up the recipe, I am giving them the answer instead of encouraging thought."

The two teachers are willing to listen to each other's point of view to decide how to best support Malcom. Each teacher explains her position while remaining open to the idea that her position might change after understanding the other teacher's viewpoint. In this case, Ms. Dennis listens to Ms. Luman's rationale and philosophy and poses the question, "How can we let Malcom know his behavior is not acceptable?" The early childhood teacher agrees that Malcom is being told too many times to cease his activity. At the same time, she does not want to punish him. She understands Malcom has more difficulty monitoring his actions than do the other children in the room.

The teachers then brainstorm a variety of ideas for helping Malcom realize he cannot continue to disrupt the play of others or control the play area. The teachers agree that a reasonable related consequence might be to exclude him from the activity, but that he needs to be part of the decision and needs to decide when he is ready to return. The teachers decide that Malcom also needs to be prepared for the related consequences on a daily basis or when there are activities such as these that are potentially "messy." The teachers explain to Malcom that he can choose to play where he wants but they clarify the expected behaviors. They then remind him, "If you have difficulty sharing the toys or if you splash water, you will need to make other play choices until you decide that you can share and not make a mess."

This example offers teachers ways to think about their work with special education staff when individualizing and adjusting the classroom rules to assist a child who has difficulty knowing his limits.

When the two teachers can work with all of the children, they all share a spirit of collaboration. For example, in Ms. Lewis's first-grade classroom, the children are busy working on a science project.

Alan is finishing his writing sample and wanders to another area before completion. This action is not uncommon for Alan, as he has trouble completing actitivites and tends to be implusive in his actions. Ms. Zina, the special educator in the room, is working with a child with vision impairments when Alan wanders over to the area. Ms. Lewis has just explained to a group of children that a "hypothesis is an idea they might have about how something works."

Ms. Zina, having heard Ms. Lewis' explanation, sees Alan wandering and says to a group of children, "Hey, did you hear Alan's idea?" The children are curious and begin to gather around Alan and his plant. Ms. Zina had focused Alan's attention to prevent him from bothering other children, gave him a role of leadership among his peers, and reinforced Ms. Lewis' lesson.

Thus, the ideal collaboration among special educators and classroom teachers is to co-teach and to work together in the instruction of young children with disabilities in ways that support the children and curriculum.

These examples illustrate the results of teachers who have established healthy professional relationships when dealing with resistant behaviors in the classroom. This type of relationship thrives on the problem-solving approach to classroom management. It is important that you approach your special education resource teacher with as much information as possible about a child; you and the family likely have more time with the child and know him or her better. You can offer time or event sampling records that identify elements of the behavior. When does it happen? What are the conditions that led to the behavior? Who is involved in the interactions with the child? How frequent is the behavior? When does it seem to escalate? In addition, you might be able to supply information about the child's apparent purpose for the behavior. The more accurate and clearly recorded your information is, the more prepared you are for a meaningful discussion with the appropriate resources.

Videotapes offer another valuable way for teachers to understand another point of view and to reflect on teaching practices. When teachers use videotapes for observation and documentation, they can review the tape several times. They can observe the actions of the children, the actions of the teacher, and the actions of the child with disabilities. Using the video as a means to revisit the teaching and learning experiences can be a tool for dialogue among the teachers. Videos also offer a way to really study children rather than merely observing them (Forman & Fyfe, 1998; Hughes, 1999).

RELATIONSHIPS WITH FAMILIES

The relationships that teachers develop with families are especially critical to establishing positive guidance for children with disabilities. The recognition of families as partners in the education of young children with disabilities is well documented (Turnbull, Turnbull & Rutherford, 2001) and is recommended practice for quality early childhood programs. In family-centered approaches, parents are regarded as knowing what is best for their child and are given partnership roles with the educational staff for planning ways to work with their children.

You can start off in a positive direction with families when you recognize that the child may act differently at home than at school. Acknowledging that families may experience different interactions will validate their knowledge of the child. Sometimes parents who have children with identified disabilities may not recognize behaviors as a symptom of disability. Or a family member may believe that you are not tolerant enough of the child's actions. It is advisable that you and the child's family reach agreement on the fact that all of you want what is best for the child. Parents need to know that the people and environments in their child's life are accepting and inviting.

There are some general considerations for working with families when developing intervention plans to guide children's behaviors. First, families should be asked, "What does your child offer to the classroom?" The question implies you are interested in knowing the strengths of the child. Families need to understand that the people working with their children are viewing the child's strengths and not just his or her limitations. Too often families are consulted only when there are problems with their child's behaviors. You provide families the opportunity to offer the knowledge of their children by asking them to help you understand the dispositions, abilities, and interests that characterize the child. When school staff invites families to share their knowledge of their child, then the relationships with families will likely start in positive directions. Because parents know their children in different environments, they can help us to understand the complex behaviors of some children with disabilities and can provide the information to help us interpret the children's actions. Parents inform you about their child's strengths, interests, and attributes will help you to create positive images of the child in your classroom.

Second, teachers might ask family members, "What do you want the child to learn?" All parents want their children to succeed in school and to perform well in academic subjects. Often, teachers hear parents also talk about wanting their child with a disability to have friends, to be accepted by others, and to be able to socialize with other children. Behaviors that impede interacting with others or that are confusing for other children will need intervention in ways that support the positive image of the child. Thus, the goal for intervention might be to help the child make friends, rather than to focus exclusively on eliminating a negative behavior.

Other considerations might include finding out about all the people who work with the child. Consistency in ways of guiding children is of particular importance to children with disabilities.

CONCLUSION

The principles related to guidance presented in other chapters also apply when children display inappropriate behaviors due to various disabilities. Understanding the nature and function of the behaviors and how they can be influenced by the curriculum and environment will help teachers to make decisions about ways to individualize. Viewing children with disabilities as contributing strengths to the classroom environment is central to the decisions about the modifications. Helping nondisabled children to recognize these strengths will support healthy environments and foster strong self-esteem in all children.

∞ FOR FURTHER THOUGHT

1. As a teacher in a child-care center or in a public school, you will have children with different types of disabilities in your class from year to year. Consider how you will prepare your class when you have a child with a disability who might scream or exhibit odd behaviors to communicate his or her frustration. How will you reduce the fear or confusion that the other children may feel? How will you model ways for the children to understand the confusing behaviors? How might you provide explanations that respect the child with a disability and consider the child's image with his or her peers?

2. A good practice in early childhood education is using the strengths of all children in your class. How will you design your curriculum and environment to support the strengths of all children? Consider how you will

recognize the strengths of children with disabilities. How can you observe for these strengths and bring them to the attention of the other children?

3. As an early childhood educator you may find yourself working with special education teachers. When you have a child in your class with resistant behaviors, how will you prepare to work with the special educator? What information will you collect? Why?

4. Videotaping our classrooms can offer a powerful tool for reflecting on our teaching practices and the learning environment. Consider how you might videotape experiences throughout the day to sample how your classroom supports the guidance approach discussed throughout this book. Look specifically at ways that your interactions with children, your

curriculum, and the design of your environment are positive for building self-esteem and work to help children make their own decisions. What supports are in place for the children with disabilities? Use the videotape as a means to have a dialogue among your team members. Focus on a particular question or issue.

5. Some children with disabilities will have difficulty following directions, classroom routines, or transitions. As an early childhood educator, you are interested in ways to prevent classroom problems. In what ways can you organize your classroom to individualize for a certain child and maintain the same rules for the other children? How will you prepare your classroom to prevent or reduce the disruption that might arise from an individual child?

∞ RECOMMENDED READINGS

Barkley, R. A. (2000). *Taking charge of ADHD.* New York: The Guilford Press.

Edwards, C., Gandini, L., & Forman, G. (1998). *The hundred languages of children: The Reggio Emilia approach—advanced reflections.* Greenwich, CT: Ablex Publishing Corporation.

Goldstein, H., Kaczmarek, L. A., & English, K. (2001). *Promoting social communication: Children with developmental disabilities from birth to adolescence.* Baltimore: Paul H. Brookes.

Mallory, B., & New. R. (1994). Social theory and principles of inclusion: Challenges for early childhood special education. *Journal of Special Education, 28*(3), 322–337.

Paasche, C. (2003). *Children with special needs in early childhood settings.* Florence, KY: Delmar-Thompson Learning.

Turnbull, A., Turnbull, H., & Rutherford, III. (2001). *Families, professionals, and exceptionality: Collaborating for empowerment* (4th ed.) Upper Saddle River, NJ: Prentice Hall.

Wender, P. H. (2002). *ADHD: Attention-deficit hyperactivity disorder in children and adults.* Bethesda, MD: Oxford University Press.

WEBSITES

http://www.surgeongeneral.gov/library/mentalhealth/chapter3

http://www.nimh.nih.gov./publicat/adhd.cfm

http://www.aota.org

http://www.schoolbehavior.com

14 Special Emotional Needs

by Lory Britain and Sierra Freeman

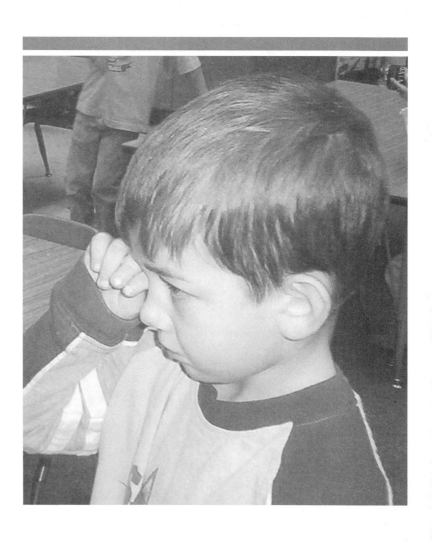

*M*ariah and Kwame have been working intently in the block corner for 20 minutes, carefully placing blocks in a trail around the edge of the rug in the block area. As they begin the next step of their plan to vertically place one pillar block on each rectangle block, Carlos enters the area. He selects a toy car and drives in along the block trail, knocking down some of the pillars. After Mariah and Kwame begin to protest, Carlos kicks the block trail, scattering blocks around the area and into other parts of the classroom. The teacher comes over to the area to facilitate the children's problem solving and to support Carlos in expressing his needs and emotions.

All teachers of young children have observed similar emotional outbursts and disruptions in children's play at one time or another. The task for a Constructivist teacher is to understand the meaning of the experience from the child's perspective and to find clues as to how to best respond.

Perhaps a child acting like Carlos simply didn't get enough sleep last night, or perhaps the teacher needs to look at how his or her classroom is arranged to encourage children to play cooperatively. Even a single event, such as the birth of a new child, could certainly provoke such emotional outbursts. However, for Carlos, the circumstances go much deeper.

Carlos's repeated exposure to family violence in his early years impacted several areas of his development. There are many ways children from stressful home environments might behave in the classroom. Carlos's difficulty entering into play and his low tolerance for frustration are just two examples. While one child with a similar history might frequently react by withdrawing from classroom participation, another child experiencing a short-term, disruptive home environment could behave similarly to Carlos.

This example highlights the challenges teachers face in supporting children with both chronic and temporary emotional and behavioral problems. These children come from many different environments. They may have had experiences that did not support their development in healthy ways and/or have traumatized or stressed them in significant ways. Helping all children to have successful classroom experiences requires us to consider how their experiences outside the classroom influence their behavior in the classroom. Understanding the relationship between children's life experiences and their development and emotional well-being is a first step.

This chapter provides background information on specific circumstances that put children at risk for emotional and behavioral problems. Strategies to provide constructive guidance for these children are presented with consideration to related issues in Chapter 12 (Unmet Needs) and Chapter 13 (Children Experiencing Disabilities). As an educator you will need to consider children's circumstances outside the classroom environment and their effects on classroom behavior, and to ask yourself the question, "What is my role here?" This chapter concludes with guidelines that help you answer this question.

RISK FACTORS

Even though the range of situations and environments that put young children at risk involve varied circumstances, there are commonalities when we view them from a child's perspective. Consider, for example, a home environment void of developmental stimulation where the television is blaring continuously. Children's books are absent and toys, if there are any, are broken and piled around the room with other objects and garbage. To this picture, add adults who are either physically or emotionally unavailable. They don't converse, offer verbal encouragement, or give affection to their children. Environments like this may be a result of parental drug abuse, adult mental health issues, or a traumatized parent coping with domestic violence. Regardless of the different causes of chaotic and neglectful home environments, children in homes like these often have a similar experience. It is difficult for these youngsters to view the world as a safe and predictable place that cherishes and encourages them.

In all children's lives, traumatic events or life-changing situations may occur. Events, such as the death of a significant family member, divorce, moving, or the birth of a sibling, disrupt children's views of the world. Some youngsters may not get the emotional support they need in difficult times like these. Special considerations in the classroom environment may be necessary for children in stressful family situations.

The Effect of Experience on the Developing Brain

We are discovering more and more about the influence of the environment on children's brain development, both before birth and during the beginning years of life. The Constructivist belief that children construct knowledge from their interactions with their physical and social world now takes on an even deeper meaning. Just as loving and nurturing environments help children develop empathy and trust, the opposite can also be true.

According to current brain research, abuse and neglect have far-reaching effects. "Prenatal development and the first two years are the time when the genetic, organic, and neurochemical foundations for impulse control are being created. It is also the time when the capacities for rational thinking and sensitivity to other people are being rooted—or not—in the child's personality" (Karr-Morse & Wiley, 1997, p. 45). Children's cognitive abilities can be profoundly affected, as can their capacity for the regulation of emotions and interpersonal responsiveness.

BEHAVIORS

A variety of risk factors and unmet needs can affect a child's development and behavior. Although the severity and kinds of situations that each child is faced with may vary greatly, they can provoke similar behaviors in different children. Some of the most common behaviors are tantrums, aggressiveness, distractibility, and inability to focus. Equally common are shutting down emotionally, acting clingy, crying, taking on an adult role, having unsafe boundaries, and poor academic performance. For example, a child who has not formed healthy adult attachments might seem emotionally distant, as might a child who is experiencing or witnessing abuse in the home. Likewise, children in similar circumstances or experiencing similar traumatic events may respond differently. For example, one child who has been exposed to domestic violence in the home might respond by withdrawing while another becomes unusually aggressive.

Some children who are experiencing short-term, abrupt disruptions, such as parental separation, might be extremely clingy and have separation anxiety, while others might react by showing signs of aggression and hostility.

As educators, you may not know enough about each child's developmental history or home life to confirm the source of a specific behavior. However, you can carefully observe the child's behavior and consider making changes in the classroom environment to support the child's learning and development. Sometimes teacher-child interactions, modifications to the physical environment, and individualized curriculum are not sufficient to meet the needs of a child; then it is time to consult with other professionals for support and services.

OBSERVATIONS

You can probably think of countless times when you have stopped to watch a child while he or she works at a given task, or when you have paused to observe a group of children during play. These observations provide useful information about what the child knows, feels, or can do. This information can serve as a guide for planning meaningful and relevant curriculum. Anecdotal notes give you an immediate picture of the children's activities and provide cumulative information over time (Chaille & Britain, 2003). Life in the classroom can be very busy, and stepping away from the children for even a few minutes can, at times, seem impossible. However, observations can be both formal and informal or scheduled and unscheduled.

One of the most valuable observation strategies to use when trying to figure out how to support children with behavioral difficulties is to look for patterns of behavior and events. How does the child begin the day? What precipitates the event or outburst? How does the child respond to the frustration? How do adults and other children respond to the child's behavior? And, finally, what is going on simultaneously in the room, such as loud noise or transitions?

There are many methods for observation that you can use in the classroom, and as a teacher you will need to develop the strategy that works best for your own classroom environment. Ideally, it is best to use a variety of strategies. Some educators find that having a time to sit back and observe without engaging the children is useful for gaining insight into the functioning of the class as a whole, as well as into individual children's needs and abilities. Taking time to do this can be difficult in a busy classroom environment and may take some planning and coordination with other teachers. Another useful method is to keep a note pad and pencil with you to jot down quick notes that you can use for reference later when

Observing to find patterns of behavior will help you figure out how to support children with behavioral difficulties.

you write more detailed observations or have a discussion with other professionals. Chaille and Britain (2003) recommend making an observation "necklace" by clipping a sticky note pad to a pencil and wearing it on a cord during class time. This allows teachers to have their hands free in the classroom but to still have their observation pad with them when they see a situation that they want to explore further. Videotaping classroom time can also provide a wealth of information about the classroom dynamics and about individual children's behaviors when reviewed at a later time.

Observations are essential for documentation if you decide to consult with a specialist or make a report or referral at a later date. Additionally, if a child has a Individualized Education Program (IEP) and is exhibiting behaviors that impede their learning or the learning of others, laws (Individuals with Disabilities Education Act Amendments of 1997 or IDEA, Public Law 105-17) require that the team examine the causes for the behavior and develop a plan for appropriate replacement behaviors. This process is called *Functional Behavior Assessment* (FBA) and the resulting plan is called a *Behavior Intervention Plan* (BIP).

In addition, objective written and verbal communication among teachers in different educational settings can help the child as well as provide teachers with better understanding and effectiveness. When challenging children move away suddenly, teachers can be left with an uncomfortable sense of unfinished business and of not knowing what will happen. On the other end, teachers who see a new student exhibit signs of emotional disturbances often don't have any background information to help them fully support the child.

THERAPEUTIC APPROACH: STRATEGIES AND TECHNIQUES

The Constructivist guidance and discipline approach presented in this book is useful for all children, especially those who present challenging behaviors. However, additional considerations, such as examining a child's needs both inside and outside of the classroom, are often needed for children with behavior problems stemming from emotional issues. Extra support and strategies for these children are sometimes called *therapeutic approaches*—strategies and techniques that provide healing, compensatory, and/or supplemental experiences for children under stress. These therapeutic approaches can strengthen the children's ability to cope with stress and to develop appropriately. To understand the concept of "therapeutic approach" as being healing and/or preventative, consider the following analogy: Hand lotion is often used therapeutically to heal our hands when they are chaffed from dry weather conditions or from the use of strong cleaning detergents. Lotion is also used preventatively so that the weather conditions do not dry out the skin. In the same way, the approaches presented in the following section help heal children whose environments have not promoted their well-being, and it helps prevent children from developing long-term emotional issues when their current circumstances are stressful.

Developmentally appropriate practices are central to a therapeutic approach, as well as to all quality early childhood and primary programs. In these programs, children's emotions, ideas, and explorations are honored. Occasionally, the nature of the issues that children bring into a classroom creates the need for particular attentiveness to their emotional development and their ability to develop trusting relationships.

Many researchers have looked at the characteristics and skills that help children face stressful situations. These skills and characteristics are generally accepted as indicating resiliency in children (Garbarino, Dubrow, Kostelny, & Pardo, 1998). These range from the ability to recognize and express emotions and being flexible, to having problem-solving skills and a strong sense of competence and self-esteem. Sociability, autonomy, the ability to comfort oneself by seeking comfort from others, adaptability, frustration tolerance, and competence are also part of this picture. As we describe these therapeutic strategies, you will begin to see the links among these strategies, meeting children's emotional needs, and supporting resiliency skills and characteristics. Equally important when selecting strategies to best support children with emotional and behavioral issues in the classroom is to reflect on "What is the meaning behind the behavior for the child?" and "How can I best support the child in getting his or her needs met in an appropriate way or healing way?" The following strategies will be useful for such times when a healing and/or preventative approach is called for.

CLASSROOM CULTURE

Each classroom has a culture of its own, similar in some ways to how we think of other countries and particular ethnic groups having a distinct culture. Classroom culture reflects the relationships among children, the issues and approaches each child brings to the classroom, and the routines that are established by the teacher in response to the needs of the children. Examples of the teacher's contribution include how the room is laid out, what activities are presented, the language the adults use in response to children, the daily schedule, conflict resolution approaches, and so on. You can see that this includes everything that has been presented in the book thus far. This classroom culture framework is based upon the belief that children construct meaning from interactions with their social and physical world. Consequently, it is important for a teacher to carefully observe and reflect on all of his or her classroom practices for consistency in values and goals.

Are all components of your classroom consistent with a therapeutic environment that supports respect, encourages problem solving, and also offers predictability and safety as well as flexibility and nurturing? Does your classroom encourage what was described earlier as "resiliency" characteristics? For example, creating an environment that encourages children to feel a sense of competence means more than words of encouragement. It also means that you will offer a range of easily accessible materials to facilitate children's exploration. This would include thinking about how many materials to have accessible or how to organize them in ways that are not too stimulating for sensitive children.

Another component of the classroom culture that is important to all programs, particularly programs including children with special needs, is the creation of a sense of classroom community. You can encourage and support collaboration and cooperation, rather than competition, by including several elements in the classroom. These elements include teaching and modeling empathy, valuing new ideas and variations, and focusing on problem-solving and child-centered decision making. Respect and encouragement for all children are basic to a classroom community (Britain, 1992).

Principle One: The physical environment should be arranged to be responsive to the issues and developmental levels of each child

Children with special emotional needs may require additional considerations in the physical environment. Consider the various home environments that can put children at risk and consider special circumstances that can be emotionally challenging to young children. As described in the beginning of this chapter, many home environments that do not support the child's developing sense of well-being may be unpredictable, traumatizing, void of stimulating materials, harsh, or unresponsive. In a different way, circumstances such as death, divorce, and moving might present the child with feelings of loss, fear, and insecurity. Thus, many different circumstances can contribute to children's needs not being met outside the classroom environment. Children's home environments, and subsequent behaviors as described earlier, can provide guidelines for thinking about the physical room arrangement.

Chapter 4 discusses the importance of considering traffic patterns, allowing for movement, and providing for privacy. Clear traffic patterns and visual cues can take on an even greater significance for children whose home environments are chaotic, cluttered, or constantly changing. Clear patterns not only can be re-

Children with special emotional needs may require special considerations in the school physical environment.

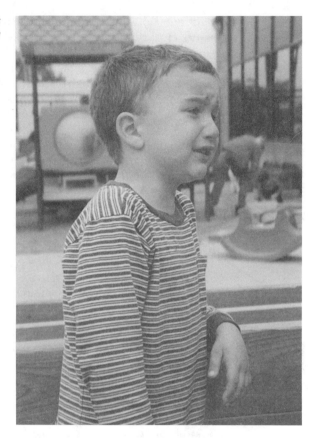

assuring to children, but can give them guidelines on how to move from area to area and make choices based on visual cues.

Mona's home has clothes, litter, and broken toys strewn all around. Naturally, she has little experience with looking around a room and seeing clear choices about what to do or how to play. When Mona first entered preschool, her teacher had the room arranged so that high shelves between learning areas blocked the view to all other areas of the room. Consequently, Mona remained all day in the first area that she saw. When the teacher analyzed the environment and realized the lack of clear traffic patterns, she rearranged the room so that each area was distinct and separate, but children could see the other areas and how to get to them. When the teacher made these changes, she also considered the importance of keeping each area free of distraction from the other areas, as discussed in Chapter 13. Gradually, Mona took her cues from the environment, began to make other choices and ventured into other learning areas. The teacher also made sure that materials were displayed within each area in a clear and organized way so that choices within the areas were apparent to Mona.

Similarly, children from unpredictable and/or chaotic home environments will probably have an unmet need for both privacy and calmness. Private corners in the classroom can meet that need and also provide a place for nurturing interactions between a child and teacher, something so critical for children in stressful circumstances. This arrangement can also give teachers the time for one-on-one reading to a child. Books that address emotionally relevant issues, such as divorce, family violence, and body issues, will be particularly helpful. Children who are aggressive toward others and who cannot be redirected with problem solving can retreat to the private space to cool down. This can be a place for children to learn to self-monitor their reactions to frustration. Teachers need visual access in these areas at all times to ensure child safety, especially for children with special social/emotional needs.

Creating a soothing environment for children can help meet their needs for relaxation and calmness. Children who have been traumatized by loss, abuse, or exposure to violence might react by being hyper-vigilant, clingy, and/or easily distracted and agitated. Subdued colors, soft lighting, and uncluttered walls with carefully selected pictures can be both child-centered and relaxing to these children. In these circumstances, more is definitely not better! Carefully consider the impact of visual and auditory stimulation on children's behaviors.

> In one toddler classroom, the teachers decided that playing classical music would be therapeutic and calming. Surprisingly, with the music, some of the children's activity levels escalated to the point that other children felt agitated. The teachers analyzed the situation and discovered that the music, as soothing as it seemed, caused the teachers to talk loudly to one another, and this contributed to a hectic-feeling environment. The music was subsequently turned off, and the children became calmer.

Sometimes, reducing noise levels requires more drastic solutions. When one therapeutic program moved into a new classroom with high ceilings, the staff discovered that voices echoed in the room, causing people to talk loudly, which in turn agitated children to the point that they would cover their ears. Eventually, sound-absorbing tiles were put in near the ceiling, the noise level of the room dropped, and the children and teachers became more relaxed.

In the same way that a soothing environment with allowance for quiet space can help children who are agitated or easily distracted, a quiet, protected space can help children who are withdrawn (an important behavior not to overlook). A critical strategy for developing a quiet space for withdrawn children is to have the space sheltered, yet allows children to view other activities and to eventually make choices to engage with others.

> The teachers suspected that Seth's life possibly included ongoing traffic of strangers in and out of his home throughout the evening. Seth was always reluctant to enter the classroom and would stand by the door looking vigilant. He was also startled easily. The teachers rearranged the room, allowing entry into the main part of the room from a private reading area, equipped with a rocking chair and books, that offered a clear view into the main part. Seth gradually developed the habit of entering the first area, reading a book while simultaneously looking around the room, and then transitioning into the main room and becoming involved with the other children and/or activities.

Similarly, a loft that overlooks the room and is cozy with soft surfaces and quiet materials and books, can provide a child with a simultaneous sense of security and a sense of power. Children need both security and power when those needs are not met at home.

Because children with emotional issues are often particularly challenged in their social interactions with other children, the teacher should analyze their physical environment to provide for social interaction with a variety of group sizes. For example, some areas might accommodate the larger groups of children working on a block structure or mural project, while other areas might be arranged to accommodate just two or three children. The size, shape, and positioning of tables, whether they are up against or perpendicular to a wall, all influence how children interact socially. Take the time to step back and observe what social interactions and groupings occur naturally in various areas of your room or around certain types of furniture arrangements. Consider the needs of individual children and how you might adjust the physical environment to help meet their needs.

Principle Two: The classroom routines should be predictable with an allowance for individual flexibility and responsiveness

In the same way that a carefully considered physical environment helps meet children's needs, classroom routines provide children with a sense of predictability, security, and safety. A challenge for teachers is to maintain predictability while still being flexible and responsive to children's individual needs. Sometimes these might seem like incompatible goals; however, several strategies can make this possible.

Establish your routine with consideration for the physical and emotional needs of the particular children in your classroom. Be sensitive to the individual pace of children. For example, are they arriving hungry? If so, can you have a meal available as soon as they arrive? Do the issues in their families' lives make their arrival time unpredictable? If so, establish a routine so that children can ease into the classroom activities without feeling like they are disrupting the established flow. Do some children need extra-long periods of self-directed activities either because they are slow to engage or because their lives at home are not relaxing? If so, consider how to accommodate the need. Do some children have unmet needs for physical activity? It is possible these children endure crowded living conditions at home with no outside play area and need large-motor activity during childcare or school time.

Discussions about the class schedule help children know what to expect. Such discussions also provide opportunities for children to make choices and, consequently, feel a sense of power. Empowering children and giving them choices has been a theme throughout this book. For children with emotional issues, who so often lack power over many aspects of their lives outside the classroom, it is critical to provide them with opportunities to make decisions in the classroom. Make sure that the choices you offer are realistic, especially for those children who require predictability. Offer clear options, such as extending choice time or returning to the same project after recess.

As described in Chapter 13, some children with developmental disabilities need supplemental cues for transition times. This is also true for children with social/emotional issues. This might include repeated verbal messages or visual cues, such as picture cards showing them what to expect next. This strategy can be an effective tool for children whose tolerance for frustration is low due to either environmental or developmental challenges.

Another way of honoring children's needs for both predictability and flexibility is to acknowledge that all the children do not always have to participate in the same routine. The following scenario describes how one teacher met a child's need for quiet and still helped her transition into circle time participation.

> Every time LaTanya came to circle time, she would become agitated and start to shove the children around her, eventually ending up rolling around and kicking in the center of the group. This extreme behavior not only perplexed and concerned the teacher, but was both upsetting and distracting to other children who eagerly came to participate in the circle time activities. The teacher decided to step back and observe LaTanya when she was relaxed and engaged in play activities in other times of the day. The teacher noticed that LaTanya was very focused on puzzles, working intently even with other children around her. The teacher's goal was to honor what seemed like LaTanya's need for individual time and to help her transition into group time. She set up a special tray for LaTanya with a puzzle on it and allowed her to sit just outside the circle if she could work quietly.
>
> Each day, the teacher would repeat the expectation of quiet during circle time and invite LaTanya to join the circle when she was ready to participate. Some days LaTanya would leave her puzzle work and participate in circle time for a short while and then, upon getting agitated, return to her individual work with gentle reminders. The teacher would remind LaTanya that it was her choice, but still made the expectations clear. After several months of this strategy, LaTanya eventually became more relaxed and fully participated in circle time activities with the other children.

Just as a well-thought-out physical environment and routine help children with special emotional needs to feel safe and secure, so does consistent teacher language and follow-through. Using the same repeated phrases such as "It is not a choice to hit" or "How can we solve this problem?" clarifies classroom expectations for children. When there is more than one teacher or adult in the room, it is important that they all use the same language for consistency.

Principle Three: Positive, nurturing relationships should be encouraged and supported with a focus on problem solving

Positive, nurturing relationships are essential for helping children face issues in their lives that challenge them emotionally. Thinking about children's unmet needs outside of the classroom environment can provide clues to what children's relationship and friendship needs are within the classroom. Although a relationship with a beloved teacher is not a substitute for a nurturing relationship with a parent or primary caregiver, it can be a positive force for emotionally challenged children and can provide a secure base for exploration of learning (Howes & Ritchie, 2002). Positive social interactions with other children are also essential; peer friendships promote development in all areas, including the cognitive domain. Helping children to develop good social problem-solving, conflict resolution, and play skills will benefit all children.

Each day, as children enter the classroom, teachers should ensure that all children feel beloved and cherished in that environment. This can be harder to accomplish with children whose behaviors sometimes create difficulties in the classroom. Teachers need to make sure they connect with these children in a positive and nurturing way on a daily basis. Several strategies are key to achieving this goal.

First, children need to feel unconditional acceptance for who they are and what they feel, as separate from the behaviors that they exhibit. For example, a teacher's remarks to a child who has just hit another child should focus on the hitting and the need to keep all children safe rather than that the child was "wrong" or "too wild." Validating and accepting all the children's feelings as neither right nor wrong is also part of this separation of behavior from who the child is. Often, children who are acting aggressively are the ones who need the most reassurance from you.

Second, special provisions will need to be made so that significant adults in the classroom have individual time with the children who need it. The staff-child ratio must be low enough to enable adults to respond to children's needs in a timely manner. In many classrooms, this is not an easy task! Student interns, community volunteers, and parent volunteers provide ways to enhance your ratio of adults to children. Analyze your classroom arrangement so that you have a private place for individual time and still have a clear view of the rest of the activities. Establish communication strategies with other adults in your room so that when you are spending individual time with a child, they can be extra vigilant of the other classroom dynamics.

And, finally, strive to respond to children's ideas and explorations in ways that show them unconditional acceptance. Thinking back on some of the home situations that put children at risk, it is easy to envision an environment where

Positive nurturing relationships are essential for helping children face emotionally challenging issues in their lives.

adults are not emotionally able to respond to children's ideas and suggestions, much less greet them with enthusiasm. Consider how important it is in the following example to greet a child's ideas with enthusiasm and openness, rather than negating feelings and ideas.

> One day a teacher turned around and saw Nathan standing barefoot in the sand table, saying, "Look, teacher, my toes can wiggle in the gushy sand!" Because the teacher realized that it was not safe for a child to stand in the sand table, she knew Nathan would need to get down. However, instead of telling him that it was not safe and to get down, the teacher said, "It must feel good to have your toes wiggle. I'm worried about you being so high on the table, though. What could we put the sand in on the floor so you could feel the gushy sand in a safe way?" Together they got a plastic tub, placed it on the floor, and filled it with sand. The teacher even took her shoes off to feel the sand, too. Instead of feeling shamed, Nathan felt that his idea was wonderful and felt safe with his special teacher time.

Most early childhood teachers are aware of the importance of children having positive interactions with their peers. The discussion and guidelines presented in Chapter 3 (Intellectual and Social Development Affect Discipline) are particularly meaningful for children who are experiencing special emotional needs. Sometimes, however, these children can challenge even the most experienced teacher's ability to facilitate positive social interactions.

Several factors might be relevant as you consider strategies beyond those usually used to assist successful social interactions. Are there unmet needs getting in the way of successful social interactions? Does the child have an unmet need due to an inadequate home environment or a disruptive event in his or her life? Can you meet that need in the classroom by such things as providing a nutritious meal for the child in the morning or creating special individual time for you and the child? Perhaps the child needs quiet, alone time because his or her environment outside the classroom does not provide for this, such as in the case of a child who lives in a homeless shelter. Do any developmental delays, coupled with emotional difficulties, create even more challenges for the child?

Sometimes children with emotional challenges are also delayed in areas such as their language development and symbolic play level. These children will need more sustained, attentive coaching for peer entry attempts and the development of play. Teachers sometimes need to remain in play time with the child longer than might otherwise be necessary as the child gradually gets involved in play. A perceptive teacher, in these cases, will stay involved in the play and gradually back off and observe as the child becomes engaged in a significant way with other children during classroom and recess time.

Consider the home environment of the child. What experiences might have provided inappropriate role models for social interaction, such as aggression; harsh, controlling words; and the use of physical force? It's important to be reflective and consider experiences from the child's perspective, but to still proceed with caution in your analysis. In these cases, you might need to make referrals and seek other professional support.

As with all strategies intended to provide therapeutic support for children who are experiencing difficulties, helping children achieve and maintain positive social interactions does not happen in isolation. Arranging your room, choosing curriculum materials, and making all children feel cherished—all contribute to social growth and success.

Principle Four: Support and validate children's feelings and help them identify and respond to the feelings of others in appropriate ways

At the core of a therapeutic approach is the support of children's emotional development. This concept is basic to most early childhood programs, and is especially important for some children (Hyson, 2004). A child's world outside the classroom can be frightening and seem out of control, leaving the child without a means to cope with his or her feelings. In many cases, you have little impact on the children's environment outside the classroom, but you can help them with their feelings and assist their development of important coping skills.

Supporting children emotionally can be broken down into more concrete components. The first step is helping children develop the ability to recognize and express their feelings. Planned curriculum such as literature, music, and circle time activities are all useful in this regard, but some of the most powerful supports involve in-the-moment responses by teachers.

> Tommy enters the classroom with an angry scowl on his face, shoving his way past the other children as he goes to hang up his coat. The teacher is aware that Tommy's parents are going through a divorce. She is also sensitive to the fact that anger is not the only feeling Tommy is experiencing right now. Sadness and fear have also come into play. The teacher knows that she must simultaneously keep the other children safe, set limits for Tommy, and support all of his feelings. What she decides to do first is support his feelings by saying, "I can see you're angry and I know you might be feeling sad and scared now about your Dad."
>
> Immediately, Tommy's face changes from an angry scowl to a sad look. Using eye contact to see if the other teacher can take over the classroom, the teacher asks Tommy if he would like to go in the library corner with her and read a special book about divorce she found for him. As they go off together, Tommy is able to learn more about his own feelings and feel validated and supported.

Recognizing feelings in others, and thereby developing perspective-taking and empathy, is the other side of emotional development. These are "abilities" that can be developed through activities such as group meetings, creating a story about a beloved pet who died, and reading carefully selected children's literature. However, "in-the-moment" opportunities may be the best way for children to learn how their actions affect others around them. For example, younger children sometimes need to look for visual cues, such as facial expressions, to identify how other children feel. Questions like the following can support this process: "Look at Melissa's face. Can you tell me how she might be feeling?"

Chapter 6 already explained the importance of accepting feelings and being a role model for children in learning to identify feelings in others. As discussed in other chapters, teachers can and should be role models for the self-expression of feelings. When children experience disruption in their lives or environments, they can be at risk for emotional difficulties and have confusing, conflicting feelings.

Children might experience an intense loss through death, moving, or even removal to foster care. Under these conditions, adults may not be sharing their feelings with them in an age-appropriate way. Children might be told too much or too little. Teachers who model an appropriate demonstration of adult feelings and help children identify their own feelings can contribute to children's sense of well-being and ability to cope.

Sometimes, a teacher might feel torn between supporting a child who is having difficulty and supporting other children who might be upset by the outburst.

> During snack time, Jenine was very agitated as she described a violent scene about hitting and people getting "bumped off." The teachers listened, thinking that she was describing something that happened at her house last night. Meanwhile, the other children were becoming quiet with frightened expressions on their faces. As it turned out, Jenine was describing a video game (still inappropriate for children to witness). In retrospect, the teachers wished they had said to Jenine in the beginning, "That sounds like it was scary and important to share. Let's go sit in the block area and we can talk."

When all teachers and adults in the classroom use consistent phrases, it helps to support children's feelings, gives clear messages about their acceptance, and provides a sense of safety.

Another important component of supporting emotional development is helping children develop the ability to comfort themselves, including seeking comfort from others. Children whose environments are chaotic or seem unpredictable and inconsistent might not view adults as sources of comfort. Similarly, they might not have many experiences identifying their needs and knowing when they need to retreat to a quiet corner of the room for relaxation. A perceptive teacher can help children learn when they need to quiet themselves and also what to do.

∞ **EXAMPLES OF PHRASES TO HELP SUPPORT CHILD'S FEELINGS**

Tell me how you feel.

Can you tell _____ how you felt when _____?

I can see by your face that you might be _____.

It seems to me that you are angry and I need to help keep you safe.

I feel _____.

Look at _____'s face. Can you guess how she might be feeling?

Let's look at this chart and see if you can pick a face that shows how you are feeling.

How did it make you feel when _____?

It's okay to feel _____, but I can't let you throw blocks at other children.

Use your words to tell _____ how you feel.

Ideas such as reading a book or holding a stuffed animal or other comfort object can help; strategies can also include asking an adult for comfort. Such strategies help children cope before they find themselves out of control or withdrawn in an unhealthy way.

Principle Five: Activities and materials appropriate to the needs and issues of the children can help provide healing and supportive experiences

As confirmed throughout this book and highlighted in Chapter 13, therapeutic goals and constructive guidance and discipline must be grounded in a developmentally appropriate curriculum; such curriculum is child-centered, flexible, emergent, and based on giving children choices and opportunities for problem solving. For a child with special emotional needs, the following curricular considerations are particularly important.

Chapter 13 discusses the importance of meaningful curriculum with topics driven by the children's interests and issues. For example, in a classroom with a child whose dog died, children might paint a mural of all the things the dog liked to do or how the children feel about it (Britain, 2003; Goldman, 2000). These sorts of activities can help children with emotional and behavioral needs to make sense of their environment and to develop appropriately.

Also, one classroom had several children whose families were either homeless or transient and had to use pay phones to make a call. The class designed and decorated a phone booth out of a cardboard box. The project involved a discussion of phone use and emergency calls. The class measured for the door, and problem solved about stability. The children were then encouraged to use the phone booth in symbolic play. This project also highlights the importance of selecting and/or creating relevant symbolic play materials. Look to the children's lives for inspiration about what might be appropriate. Family figures, cars, camping props, police stations, phone booths, babies, and baby items are but a few examples of props that might allow children to symbolically represent issues that are pertinent to their lives. Common traditional school curriculum at the beginning of the school year often involves activities that revolve around "self," "my body," and "my family." These concepts are meaningful throughout the entire year for children whose sense of self has been stifled by environmental conditions.

There is also the issue of children who do not seem to be able to participate in pretend play and other types of play (Koplow, 1996). For example, there are children who have taken on an adult role in their home environment, and there are children whose language and symbolic representational ability has been thwarted by relationship and attachment issues. Helping these children feel safe and secure in their environment, selecting relevant play props, and engaging in play with them can help them gradually participate fully.

In addition to play props that allow children to transform and represent their world symbolically, materials that can be physically transformed by children in shape, form, or substance (Chaille & Britain, 2003) provide a context for children to experiment and feel both powerful and soothed. Particularly empowering and

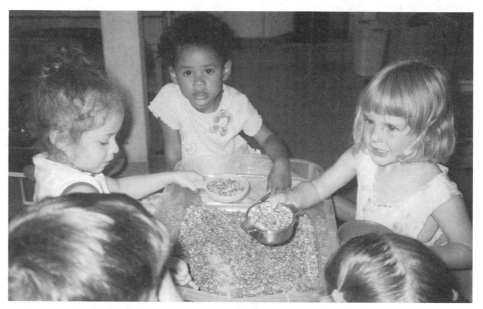

Transformational materials such as sand, water, playdough, cornmeal, mud, and dirt are empowering and soothing to children facing difficult emotional issues.

soothing to children are transformational materials—such as sand, water, playdough, cornmeal, mud, clay, and dirt—that change through mixing, combining, poking, and shaping. For many children with emotional issues, these tactile experiences are needed for their developmental progression and are often used in a therapeutic setting with children far beyond the preschool years. For children who need extra guidance with social interactions, these materials lend themselves easily to collaboration.

Painting, drawing, writing (including "pretend" writing), dancing, singing, and movement are all examples of ways children can express and represent their feelings and issues to themselves and others. This representational ability is related to children's ability to communicate with others. Unfortunately, some children's early experiences do not support the development of a positive, caring relationship with a trusted adult. These children might not learn appropriate communication and may need attentive support for representational experiences. Accessible materials, open-ended creative activities, and gentle encouragement with some adult participation are part of setting the stage to encourage children to express themselves through a variety of mediums.

Children's literature is a significant part of using representational materials therapeutically. The use of literature to support children's experiences and emotions is called *bibliotherapy*. Experienced teachers are well aware of both the magic and power of using a carefully selected book to help prepare children for an upcoming event or to validate and reflect the emotional impact of past or ongoing experiences. Books can suggest healthy strategies for children to use in challenging situations.

The power of books to help support children through troubled times lies in the teacher being familiar with existing books and having them readily available at the appropriate time. Children can't wait until library time to have their feelings validated or for solutions to troubling situations. For example, being able to pull just the right book about death off the shelf when a child comes in upset after attending his grandma's funeral can be a powerful and healing experience. The book *Unsmiling Faces: How Preschools Can Heal* (Koplow, 1996) has an excellent bibliography listing children's books on sensitive topics. Parenting Press, in Seattle, Washington, specializes in books that help children and parents through difficult times. Children's librarians in public libraries usually have lists on such topics as well.

There are key decisions you will need to make when you decide when or how to read books on difficult and/or emotional topics. One decision will be whether to read the book to the class or to an individual child; another is whether to have the book available on the children's bookshelf. A book about domestic violence, for example, might be too frightening and confusing to read to a group of children who have never been exposed to it; such a book might be best read to individual children or small groups of affected children so that you can monitor and support their responses. On the other hand, a book about personal touch, such as *It's My Body* (Freeman, 1983), would be valuable to read in a group with an interactive and supportive format. However, as with all sensitive issues, the teacher must be prepared to respond to a child who discloses sensitive information in a group context.

Using children's literature therapeutically involves the same principles as reading all books to children; these include creating an interactive format where children share their ideas and feelings, and accepting all ideas and feelings.

Another important consideration when planning a curriculum to support children is that many children who come from high-risk environments might not have had the opportunity to problem solve with materials and to explore cause-and-effect relationships. Constructivist activities involving physical knowledge, such as ramps, inclines, balls, pulleys, and pendulums, not only focus children on physical relationships, but also provide them a sense of power and choice over materials and their actions on the materials. Asking children to predict, "What would happen if?" when using these materials increases their awareness. These types of activities (Chaille & Britain, 2003) often will help children focus; children who otherwise act distracted and/or aggressive may focus on problem solving for sustained periods of time.

The storage and dispersal of materials in the classroom sometimes needs to be done in different ways for different children. For example, children whose needs for ownership and privacy may not be met in their home environment may benefit from having personally marked containers or backpacks with their school belongings in them. Homeless children who suddenly find themselves in unfamiliar places with little or no personal belongings or comfort objects will especially benefit from this strategy. Occasionally, particular habits related to hoarding food and/or materials indicate unfulfilled needs. Responding with a reassurance such as, "You may have more when you are done," and then providing the child with more food, can help the child feel satisfied and cared for.

Principle Six: Teachers need to be aware of issues particularly relevant to the lives of children with emotional needs

Part of your challenge in working with children with special emotional needs is to educate yourself about the multiple issues relevant to understanding the behaviors of these children. The following section about children's boundaries is an example of only one such issue and how it impacts teaching strategies.

Children who have been sexually abused, traumatized, and/or deprived of healthy relationships with trusted adults may nervously guard their personal boundaries. Sometimes this can be confusing for teachers whose natural instinct is to be physically affectionate and responsive with young children. These children might be too readily affectionate with adult strangers in the classroom or may not pick up on cues when other children do not want to be touched. On the other extreme, children may not want adults or other children near their bodies at all. In one therapeutic early childhood and family support program, the Relief Nursery, Inc. in Eugene, Oregon, a key goal is that children will maintain and develop a sense of self-protection of their bodies and personal space.

As a teacher, your role is to be educated about indicators of sexual abuse and other warning signs of serious emotional problems that warrant referral. Your role is also to support children in developing and recognizing appropriate boundaries. Modeling, helping children listen to each other's limit setting, reading books about appropriate and inappropriate touch, and role-playing are effective means to help children both recognize other children's boundaries and to be empowered to set clear limits for themselves. However, you must take care not to suggest that children are to blame if they cannot stand up to predatory adults.

As you educate yourself further about risk factors for young children and about children's special emotional needs, you will want to consider the implications for classroom practices and your role as a classroom teacher.

EXPANDING THE TEACHER ROLE

Bronfenbrenner (1979) discusses children's development with an ecological model. The ecological view points out how children's interactions and experiences in the family, neighborhood, and community all interconnect and play a role in child development and well-being. A teacher who understands children's development from an ecological model has new issues to consider, such as, "What is my role here and what part do I play outside of the immediate classroom environment?" Reflecting on these kinds of questions can help you respond appropriately to the needs of children while caring for your own emotional needs as a teacher.

Angelica, a child who is homeless, arrives at school during cold weather wearing only a thin sweater. From what you can gather from Angelica's comments at school, you have reason to believe that her mother has recently left a domestic violence situation and is considering returning to her partner. How do you support Angelica? What do you do, if anything, that might extend outside of the classroom? And, most importantly, how do you take care of yourself so that you do not continually wake up at night troubled by Angelica and her mother's situation?

Another type of situation that might challenge you to consider your role as a teacher is a child's father breaking down during a parent-teacher conference and confiding in you about the troubling details of his divorce situation. Again, what is your role here in supporting the child's development and how deep into this discussion with the father do you go? Sometimes these questions are referred to as "professional role" or "professional boundary" issues.

The NAEYC Ethical Code of Conduct (1998) provides useful guidelines to help early childhood teachers be clear about their role. For example, in the divorce case, it might be useful to remember that, "In cases where family members are in conflict, we shall work openly, sharing our observations of the child, to help all parties involved make informed decisions. We shall refrain from becoming an advocate for one party."

Referrals and Teaming with Specialists

As a teacher, you will no doubt encounter children whose emotional and behavioral issues require the support and expertise of specialists outside of the classroom. It will be important to understand when to seek support and to make referrals, as well as to know what resources are available in the school and community where you are teaching. It is vital to understand your school or agency's policies and procedures about making referrals.

Some emotional and behavioral problems are more than the classroom teacher can be expected to manage. They require the support and expertise of specialists.

Teaming with specialists can be a means of providing both direct support for a child and consultation services for you, as a teacher. Appropriate referrals for a child with special behavioral needs for example, might be for a special education evaluation or for mental health services. Your written or taped observations of a child in the classroom environment are especially useful when making a referral or sharing concerns with other professionals.

Your awareness of community social service, health, and basic needs resources will not only aid you in making the appropriate referrals, but can also greatly enhance your relationship with the parents of children in your class if you are in a role to share your knowledge with them. Because parents in stress often have difficulty taking the first step to locate resources to help themselves, a handout with community resources, phone numbers, and the name of a contact person can be more effective than just mentioning the names of agencies. Whether making a professional referral or helping parents or guardians find resources, remember that parents and guardians are your partners in supporting their children's development and well-being.

Reporting

The NAEYC Ethical Code of Conduct (1988) states that when we "Have reasonable cause to suspect child abuse or neglect we shall report it to the appropriate community agency and follow up to ensure that appropriate action has been taken." As an educator it is your legal responsibility to do so. This role is often called being a "mandatory reporter" and it is vital that you understand the reporting procedures of your state and your community. It is also important that you understand the reporting procedures for your own school or agency. It is necessary to have a clear grasp of these procedures before a situation arises that requires a report. Making reports can be both stressful and uncomfortable. It is valuable and often essential to debrief the situation with another professional for support and guidance.

Supervision, Professional Support and Development, and Self-Care

One of the most important steps in answering questions, such as ones presented in this chapter, is discussing troubling situations with a supervisor, principal, co-worker, or a team of other professionals. Seeking further professional development is another valuable approach. All of these approaches will help you maintain a clear professional role in troubling circumstances. Just as a Constructivist teacher provides support for children to problem solve, professional support can provide a safe environment for teachers to problem solve the best solutions for children with emotional challenges. Regular, reflective supervision not only helps you analyze and debrief about relevant child issues, but also provides guidance in maintaining clear professional boundaries.

Garbarino et al. (1998) talk about the importance of providing support for teachers to help them cope with the emotional intensity of dealing with traumatized children and children experiencing emotional difficulties. In recent years, more has been learned about the potential for "burnout" among professional caregivers, such as teachers, therapists, social workers, and health care providers who are helping others deal with troubling situations. Debriefing with supervisors and co-workers, paying attention to your stress levels and your own mental and physical health, and developing good self-care habits around relaxation and recreation are essential.

CONCLUSION

Sometimes, after learning about all the various conditions and events that can make children vulnerable, it is easy to feel overwhelmed and wonder how a teacher can possibly help children in these situations. While there are clear limits to the role of the classroom teacher, you should remember that a child's relationship with a beloved teacher can do much to ameliorate or "soften" some of the disturbing events or environments outside of the classroom. An early childhood teacher who carefully observes and maximizes the strategies to support the child in the classroom can exert a positive influence on the child's overall development and sense of well-being.

∞ FOR FURTHER THOUGHT

1. When families are in short-term or chronic states of crisis, they often have difficulty taking the first step toward accessing resources. Investigate what kinds of resources are available in your community to help families meet basic needs, such as food, shelter, and clothing, as well as medical attention and counseling. What other needs might families have? Collect brochures and/or phone numbers and contacts from the agencies to be able to help parents take that first step in meeting family needs.

2. This chapter provided resources for children's books that can be used to help children deal with difficult and challenging issues. Explore those resources and others to compile your own list of children's books. Organize the list by age group (i.e., preschool and elementary school age) and by topics that you feel are meaningful.

3. When children come to the classroom with special emotional needs resulting from issues in their lives outside of the classroom, teachers can be pulled in directions beyond their typical daily classroom role. What are some situations that would be especially challenging for you? How might you proceed? What would you need to take into consideration when establishing clear boundaries about your role as a teacher?

4. This chapter covered many different issues and discussed overlapping

emotional and behavioral responses to various stressful situations. How might the issue of family culture influence children's responses to stress? What would you need to take into consideration as you respond to children's needs? What other culturally sensitive situations would be challenging for you in your classroom as you support children emotionally?

∞ RECOMMENDED READINGS

Chaille, C., & Britain, L. (2003). *The young child as scientist: A Constructivist approach to early childhood science education.* New York: Longman Press.

Garbarino, J., Dubrow, N., Kostelny, K., & Pardo, C. (1998). *Children in danger: Coping with the consequences of community violence.* San Francisco: Jossey-Bass Publishers.

Howes, C., & Ritchie, S. (2002). *A matter of trust: Connecting learners in the early childhood classroom.* New York: Teachers College Press.

Hyson, M. (2004). *The emotional development of young children: Building an emotion-centered curriculum.* New York: Teachers College Press.

Karr-Morse, R., & Wiley, M. (1999). *Ghosts from the nursery: Tracing the roots of violence.* New York: The Atlantic Monthly Press.

Koplow, L. (Ed.) (1996). *Unsmiling faces: How preschools can heal.* New York: Teachers College Press.

Koplow, L. (2002). *Creating schools that heal: Real life solutions.* New York: Teachers College Press.

Slaby, R., Roedell, W., Arezzo, D., & Hendrix, K. (1995). *Early violence prevention: Tools for teachers of young children.* Washington DC: NAEYC.

15

Analyzing Discipline Problems

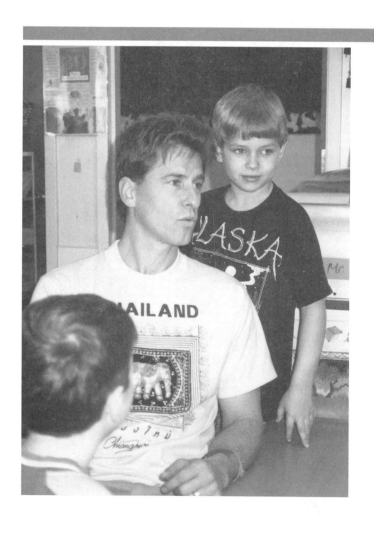

You have read about many approaches to discipline and many causes of discipline problems in this book. In case the information is whirling around in your head and you're not sure what to do with it, this final chapter presents guidelines for how to put it all together in a usable fashion. However, it is not a recipe for no-fail discipline, but rather assistance in the difficult task of analyzing discipline problems and matching them with appropriate discipline approaches. Each child and each situation is unique, requiring your professional judgment about discipline.

KEEPING GOALS IN MIND

The first step in exercising your judgment is to examine your goals for discipline. Chapter 1 discusses the importance of keeping long-term goals firmly in mind as you plan discipline strategies. This book has emphasized the long-term goals of enhancing self-esteem, self-discipline, and moral autonomy. It is crucial that no discipline approach damage a child's growth in these areas. We attempt to explain how inappropriate forms of discipline counteract progress toward these long-term goals. Rewards, punishment, and other coercive approaches to discipline have become mainstream practices; teachers must understand that these practices work against their long-term goals.

Short-term goals are also important, although meeting them must not conflict with long-term goals. There are certain behaviors that are so disruptive or dangerous that they must be stopped immediately, leaving the teaching aspect of discipline for the next step. If children's actions put them into danger, it is essential to act quickly and decisively. Talking directly to the children involved is much more productive than yelling directions across a room. An emergency situation may require a warning shout, which will be useful if the teacher's voice is usually calm and controlled. However, teachers who routinely raise their voices in an effort to control a group will find that a raised voice quickly loses effectiveness.

FINDING THE CAUSE OF THE PROBLEM

If the situation is not an emergency, or after an emergency situation is over, you are free to think about the most appropriate discipline approach for long-term goals. This step requires a search for the cause or causes of the discipline problem. Many times you will find several interactive causes of a problem. This means you need to address several causes in order to provide effective help. Discipline that deals only with the symptoms rather than the causes of behavior problems is doomed to failure; the problem behavior will continue to surface until the reason for that behavior is addressed. Too often teachers respond to the behavior instead of the causes (Flicker & Hoffman, 2002). This problem is well demonstrated in schools with posted sets of rules and the pre-planned punishments for breaking each rule.

The causes of a problem are not always obvious, and it may take serious study and even some trial and error to get at the root of the matter. The chart in

Matching Problem Causes to Solutions

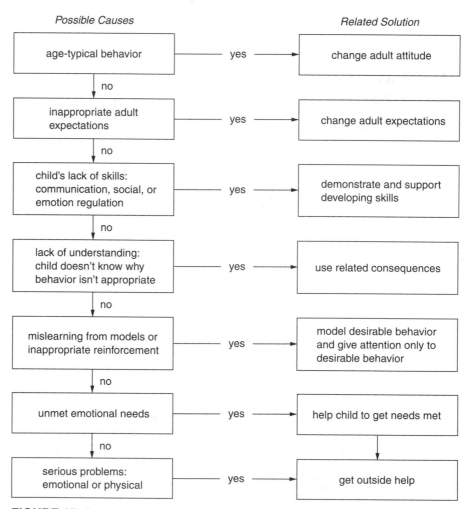

FIGURE 15–1   Matching problem causes to solutions.

Figure 15-1 may help you in the process of analyzing a discipline problem pattern for an individual child. The organization of this chart follows the organization of the book in moving from the least intrusive to the more intrusive approaches to solving behavior problems. First we consider the possibility that the adult needs to change and then gradually consider more and more serious needs of the child.

Age-Typical Behavior

As you start to search for the cause of a child's behavior problem, first ask yourself whether the offending behavior may simply be typical of that child's stage of maturation. Some adults don't realize, for instance, that a 2-year-old is not being naughty when she wets her pants. These adults might punish the child or try bribing her in efforts to change this behavior, unaware that a 2-year-old who isn't potty-trained is exhibiting maturationally normal behavior. The child can't change the behavior until she is older. Chapters 2 and 3, as well as Chapter 11, offer other reminders of age-appropriate child behaviors that may frustrate adults. Your soul-searching may reveal that the "problem" is actually adult intolerance or a misunderstanding of childlike behavior (Landy, 2002). In that case, the cause of the problem is the adult's attitude, therefore, that attitude, not the child's behavior, needs to be changed.

Inappropriate Adult Expectations

The next step in finding the cause of a behavior problem involves examining whether or not inappropriate adult expectations may have created the problem. Inappropriate adult expectations may include those that are incompatible with an individual child's temperament, those that conflict with a family's culture, those that do not reflect gender differences, and those that are a poor match for children's maturational levels.

Chapter 2 summarizes relevant information about child temperament. When we reflect on the unique personalities of children in our care, it is clear that we cannot have the same expectations of all. Chapter 3 examines behavior-related issues of diversity based on culture, class, and gender. As we become more aware of diverse ways of viewing and responding to experiences, we can better match interactions and expectations to those differences.

Chapters 4 and 5 describe many common ways in which well-meaning teachers and caregivers accidentally cause discipline problems. Adults create problems when they require young children to sit still and be quiet for more than a few minutes, to wait with nothing to do, or to engage in learning activities designed for older youngsters. The National Association for the Education of Young Children offers guidelines for appropriate programs (Bredekamp, 1997) and curriculum (Bredekamp & Rosegrant, 1995) that teachers can consult to make sure discipline problems are not being caused by an inappropriate environment.

If you suspect that the environment is causing children to react negatively, the solution is to change the situation rather than try to change the children. This preventive discipline approach saves both teachers and children a lot of trouble. The adult response in the following example demonstrates the value of planning to better meet a child's needs.

> After eating lunch each day, the children in the child-care program are expected to clear off their table setting and sit back down to wait for a teacher to call them to brush their teeth. Sometimes there is no wait time, but sometimes it can be a couple of minutes, depending on how many children have finished eating. Sheri knows this is not an ideal situation, but it seems to be the only way to handle the tooth brushing with 20 children and only two sinks.

The children don't seem to have a problem with this, with the exception of Sam. Sam sits down for about 10 seconds and then has to get up and move around the room, usually causing a disturbance in the process, or he wanders into the unsupervised kitchen.

Sheri has repeatedly reminded Sam about sitting and waiting his turn. He seems to know what is expected of him but doesn't seem to be able to do it. Sheri decides that this situation just isn't appropriate for Sam and makes a plan to accommodate his needs. The chairs need to be stacked to sweep the floor after lunch. This has usually been done by the staff after the kids leave school, but Sheri asks Sam if he would like to help out and be the chair stacker after lunch. Sam jumps at the chance to do this real and important work—and to get to move around and use his muscles instead of trying to sit still. Now Sam is the proud official chair stacker instead of the kid in trouble every day. What a difference this makes to his self-esteem!

The good news is that most solutions to undersirable behaviors can be found by rethinking adult expectations and overall classroom practices (Fox et al., 2003).

Missing Skills

Once you have satisfied yourself that you are accepting children at their maturational level and providing an individually appropriate environment and curriculum, you can go on to look for other causes of discipline problems. Young children have a lot to learn about how to get along, how to deal with their emotions, and how to communicate effectively. If you suspect that lack of skill in any of these areas is causing the problem, a discipline approach that works on needed skills is the solution. Most of us work at developing these skills throughout our lives, so it is to be expected that young children will need help with them.

Chapters 3, 6, 7, and 11 present ways of helping children learn social skills and effective communication techniques. Adults can demonstrate and assist in desirable modes of self-expression and interacting with others (DeVries, Hildebrandt, & Zan, 2000). Probably the most important and difficult lesson has to do with perspective-taking—understanding other people's viewpoints. This requires a combination of communication and social skills because people need to be able to express their feelings clearly in order to facilitate an exchange of viewpoints. Teachers can help children find words so that they can share their views and feelings with their peers, thus decreasing egocentricity. Helping children learn how to play with others and make friends goes along with teaching them perspective-taking. Other useful approaches include the use of "I messages" and problem-solving techniques to teach children effective conflict resolution (Gordon, 1989).

Emotion regulation, discussed in Chapters 2 and 6, is related to enhanced communication and perspective-taking skills. When children are able to find the words to express their sorrows and frustrations, they have a way of getting support and an acceptable way of letting off steam. When they begin to understand that there may be another side to a situation, they are often comforted. For instance, if children are able to understand that the child who wronged them did so by accident, it often has a calming effect. Similarly, beginning to learn that things don't always go their way because others also want their own way can help children cope with a disappointment. In addition, most children need specific assistance with learning how to comfort themselves and how to delay gratification. Teaching children social skills, perspective-taking, effective communication, and emotion regulation are important discipline strategies that promote lifelong, harmonious social interaction.

Lack of Understanding

Perhaps the child has the needed skills but has chosen not to use them. Sometimes children behave in unacceptable ways because they don't understand why they shouldn't. Perhaps the cause of the problem is a lack of knowledge about how to behave or about the results of certain actions. Young children need assistance in learning about cause-and-effect relationships. They need to learn that their behaviors have certain results or consequences (Brady et al., 2003).

Chapter 8 explains how natural and related consequences help youngsters to understand why certain behaviors are undesirable or desirable. Adults often have trouble allowing children to learn from experience because of the desire to protect them. Although you do need to keep children away from harm, you don't want to protect them so much that they lose the opportunity to learn. Finding out that you get cold if you don't dress for the weather or that you get hungry if you don't eat are valuable educational lessons. They are examples of natural consequences (Dreikurs, 1964). Related consequences are adult-imposed, but they link the behavior to a result that demonstrates why the behavior needs to be changed. Too often, adults expect children to learn from lectures and forget that experience is the best teacher. Natural and related consequences are effective forms of guidance that help children gain knowledge, which in turn guides youngsters in self-regulating their behavior.

Mislearning

Sometimes children have learned the wrong things. Chapters 9 and 12 describe how youngsters often get attention for undesirable behavior and how this attention encourages the behavior to continue. These children have learned to get their emotional needs met in counterproductive ways. In this case, the needed discipline approach involves reteaching. Children need to unlearn old ways of getting attention and learn new ones (Curwin & Mendler, 1999). Judicious use of behavior modification techniques guides teachers in ignoring undesirable behaviors and encouraging desirable ones.

Another type of mislearning is a result of undesirable role models. Chapter 6 discusses the problems of media violence and how it impacts the behavior of children and youth. The need to counteract this influence cannot be overstated (Levin, 2003). Sometimes the undesirable role models are older children, family members, or sports heroes. Additionally, educators frequently model power tactics that model a "might makes right" approach (Butchart, 1998).

Whatever the source, positive role models who build trusting relationships with children are desperately needed as the antidote. Teachers must be moral, caring, and socially skilled so they can demonstrate important skills and understandings

Mislearning causes much undesirable behavior. Sometimes mislearning is caused by accidental reinforcement of inappropriate behavior and sometimes mislearning is due to inappropriate role models

in word and deed (Watson, 1999). The most effective models "transparently" model desirable behavior by talking to themselves out loud, demonstrating the thought processes behind their actions (Dill, 1998).

Unmet Emotional Needs

If you are sure that a child knows better and is capable of behaving better, but is still acting out, you need to look deeper for the cause. Sometimes undesirable behavior is motivated by children striving to feel okay in spite of experiences that have left them with emotional deficits (Landy, 2002). Strong survival instincts motivate these youngsters to try to get their needs met, and they frequently act out in extremely disruptive ways that show misguided efforts toward "wholeness." Other youngsters with emotional deficits give up and retreat into their shells. The latter may be easier to deal with but are ultimately an even greater cause for your concern and attention.

Chapter 12 discusses how unmet needs in such areas as trust, pride, love, and power can contribute to discipline problems. If unmet needs are the cause of the problem, a truly effective discipline approach must involve attempts to help children get those needs met. These attempts might be made in conjunction with other approaches that will make the symptoms more manageable, such as related consequences. It is important to keep the cause of the problem in mind, however, and continue to work on helping the child get his or her needs met.

Serious Problems

Teachers frequently find that a child in their care has unmet needs or other problems that they cannot adequately address by themselves. Chapters 13 and 14 discuss ways to work with children with behavior problems stemming from causes outside the school setting. These problems, although manifested in undesirable behaviors, may not actually be guidance or discipline issues. Rather than being addressed through teaching, they may need to be dealt with by medical practitioners or social workers. In some cases, the child's entire family must be helped in order to benefit the child. There is a limit to what can be expected of teachers and caregivers, and they must insist on outside expertise to help children with severe behavior problems. Therefore, Chapters 13 and 14 discuss sources of help for children with serious problems.

Sometimes teachers find themselves at odds with parental preferences and are torn between what they believe is right for the child and their commitment to honoring families. These are times for consulting the NAEYC Code of Ethics included in Appendix C (Feeney & Kipnis, 1999).

Family Communication and Complexity of Causes

This list of possible causes for undesirable behavior (Figure 15-1) may make it appear that there is only one cause for each behavior problem. But, in reality, human beings just aren't that simple, are they? Typically several different causes are interacting with one another when a child is acting out. Teachers often need information from the child's home in order to get a clear picture of the possible causes. The following example shows how a teacher and a mother worked together, sharing information about the child to figure out why she had a hard day at school.

> Corrie had a terrible, awful, no-good day at preschool. She screamed and cried and clung to her mom at school. Her mother explained that she couldn't stay with her because she had to take Corrie's baby sister home for her nap, but Corrie continued to cry and insisted that her mother stay with her. After mother finally did leave, Corrie followed the teacher around and wouldn't engage in play with the other children.
>
> Dennis talked to Corrie's mother on the phone that evening in an effort to figure out the cause of her daughter's problem and keep her from having more such bad days. They took into consideration maturational factors: that Corrie was too young to understand other people's needs, so she naturally didn't respond to the explanation of what her mother needed to do. They also acknowledged that preschool-age children still have a long way to go in learning to control their emotions and express them appropriately. Young children can't distinguish between a momentary frustration and a true tragedy; therefore, they tend to respond in the extreme to all upsetting events.

Corrie's teacher and parents had previously discussed her innate tempera- ment: emotionally sensitive and also slow to adapt to change. Because she is more than typically emotionally sensitive, Corrie experiences her feelings deeply, making emotion regulation even more difficult for her. When she gets upset, she has great difficulty getting over it. Corrie's other identified temperament chal- lenge, difficulty in adapting to change, means that disruptions in her schedule upset her. Therefore, it is very significant that this was Corrie's first day back at school after a 2-week family vacation.

As Dennis and Corrie's mother talk, the mother acknowledges that Corrie was pretty tired after their trip and notes that she had been sick most of the time they were gone. In fact, given the day's problems, Corrie's mother now worries that Corrie may still not be feeling well.

Whereas she had previously been frustrated with Corrie, the mother now realizes that Corrie's distressing behavior was probably inevitable, given the combination of factors. The horrible, no-good day was a result of normal mat- uration limitations interacting with Corrie's individual temperament and com- pounded by unmet physical needs.

Rather than a list, a set of concentric circles might be a better way of analyz- ing some behavior problems (Figure 15-2). We could start with the behavior itself shown as a tiny circle in the center, and then make surrounding circles that show the context in which the behavior occurred. This way of analyzing a behavior problem may be helpful in connecting multiple, interwoven causes.

The next larger circle can be used to show any unmet physical or emotional needs involved. For instance, is the child tired, hungry, or ill? Could the child be worried, sad, or fearful?

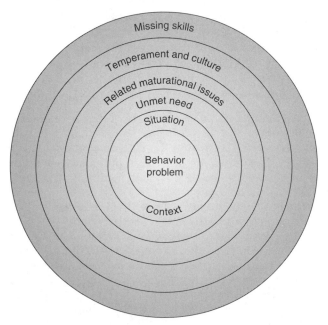

FIGURE 15–2   Complexity of causes analysis model.

Another larger circle around that one could show the related maturational limitations. Typically, you would expect that young children would not be good at perspective-taking, emotion regulation, or any type of logical thinking.

The next circle could be used to show the child's unique characteristics such as temperament and cultural influences. A final, outside circle might look at related learning: What missing skills might be involved? Does the child need help understanding why the behavior is inappropriate? Has the child learned inappropriate behavior due to poor role models and/or reinforcement of misbehavior?

This is just another way of looking at the causes of behavior shown in Figure 15-1. The concentric circle model might help you more easily discover how causes interact with one another.

MATCHING DISCIPLINE APPROACHES TO THE CAUSE

As you try to use the various guidance and discipline approaches described in this book, remember that each is useful only to the extent that it deals with the cause of the problem. Each discipline approach is aimed at a different type of cause. Using all available evidence to discover the cause is the first and most difficult step. The solution is usually fairly evident from there—if you keep in mind that the solution needs to aim at the cause. Too often, people forget that the solution is to treat the cause; they slip back into the old ways of responding to the behavior instead of the cause.

An Example

Perhaps it would be helpful to analyze an actual problem behavior using the chart in Figure 15-1. See how Mrs. Jensen worked as a "detective" to discover the cause of Shayla's problem:

> Shayla arrived late this morning and is very quiet during morning circle. When the class begins to work together on writing, Shayla sits alone. Since Shayla usually participates in writing groups, Mrs. Jensen is confused by the girl's behavior.

Given this evidence, do you think that Shayla's behavior is age-typical, or are the expectations inappropriate? Since the others are participating and Shayla usually does, neither of those possibilities seems to be the cause of the problem.

> Mrs. Jensen encourages Shayla to find someone to work with, but Shayla insists that the other children don't like her. The teacher decides to let her alone for the time being. A little bit later, she notices Shayla sitting under the table looking sad.

Mrs. Jensen thinks hard, trying to figure out what is going on. Shayla usually enjoys working with her friends and seems to be well accepted by the other children. Therefore, the teacher doesn't think that missing communication or social skills are the cause of the problem. Mrs. Jensen continues to explore other possibilities. She wonders if Shayla is testing the limits to see if there is any good reason to work on her writing.

Mrs. Jensen reminds Shayla that the class is working on play scripts for Friday Fun Day, when they will act out their plays for one another. Mrs. Jensen expresses concern that Shayla won't get to be in a play. Shayla makes no response.

The teacher decides she is giving Shayla far too much attention for her negative behavior. Mrs. Jensen wonders whether her urging and attention has actually been encouraging Shayla's pouting. She decides to shift her attention to the children who are writing.

After a little while, Shayla brings Mrs. Jensen a picture of a broken heart with a girl crying on it. Next to this picture, she has written her name. She looks so sad that Mrs. Jensen is concerned. She thinks this is starting to look like unmet emotional needs. She decides she must find out what is happening in Shayla's life. She gives Shayla a hug and asks her about her picture. Shayla only says, "That's me feeling sad."

At lunch time, Mrs. Jensen makes some phone calls and discovers that there had been some domestic violence at Shayla's house the night before. The police had been there and Shayla was aware of the trouble.

Mrs. Jensen revises her theory about the cause of the problem from unmet emotional needs to serious emotional needs. She knows that it will be especially important for her to provide a sense of love and security for Shayla at school.

This example explores all the possibilities on the chart, but you will find that most problem analysis stops far short of serious problems. Yes, it may seem like most of your discipline problems have a serious cause because a child with serious problems can take up so much of your time. But in actuality, you have dozens of minor incidents daily that are caused by lack of perspective-taking skills, lack of ability to enter play, or lack of communication skills. We hope you do not have many problems caused by inappropriate expectations. However, if you do, you know what to do about it (Landy, 2002).

Safety First

Discipline approaches aimed at teaching missing skills and understandings are different from your job of keeping children safe.

In an emergency you must first stop unsafe behaviors or assist an injured child. It is not a "teachable moment" when children are in danger, injured, or upset. However, this does not mean that you should ignore the needed teaching. After the crisis has passed and the children involved are comforted and calmed, you can work on the skills or understandings that can keep the problem from happening again.

EVALUATING GUIDANCE PROGRAMS

Many packaged guidance programs offer a set of discipline approaches. We hope you will use what you have learned from this book to evaluate those approaches. We hope you will not accept ideas that ignore the cause of behavior, use rewards, or that otherwise are not respectful of children.

Discipline problems with serious causes are troubling, but most discipline problems are among the dozens of minor daily incidents caused by lack of perspective-taking, social skills, or communication skills.

Much of the current curriculum material for guidance and discipline is in relation to violence-prevention, due to the recent tragic rate of school violence. Many violence-prevention guides focus on "managing behavior," which tends to be a focus on symptoms rather than on the causes of inappropriate behavior. The most consistent rule enforcement will not help the child who mistreats others due to unmet attention needs. The most detailed lessons in social skills will not help the child who lashes out due to low self-esteem. Genuine change will come only when the child's needs are met and self-esteem is secure. Superficial change due to a focus on symptoms may submerge the actual problems and allow them to grow more serious over time. These problems will eventually emerge again and be manifested through more serious negative behavior.

Teachers and caregivers working with young children have a unique window of opportunity to make a difference. Children's attitudes about themselves and their world are still malleable during the early childhood years (through age 8). By the time students are adolescents, it is often too late for them to change their views and their behavior.

WHOSE PROBLEM IS IT?

Another way to analyze a discipline problem is to ask yourself, "Whose problem is it?" Gordon (1989) suggests the usefulness of separating those problems that belong to the child from those that belong to you, the adult. You might be amazed at how often you are trying to get a child to solve a problem that is really yours; and how often you are trying to solve a problem that is the child's to solve. When you

ADULT'S PROBLEM	CHILD'S PROBLEM
DISCIPLINE APPROACHES	DISCIPLINE APPROACHES
Express "I message" Change expectations Change environment Change curriculum Remove yourself	Reflective listening Related consequences Coaching in skills Help with unmet needs

SHARED PROBLEM

Problem-solving negotiations
Conflict resolution steps

FIGURE 15–3   Whose problem is it?

know whose problem it is, you have a start on how to solve it (see Figure 15-3). To find out who owns a problem, look at who is bothered by the behavior.

Your Problem

If the child is perfectly content with the situation and you are the unhappy one, the odds are that you own the problem. If you are bothered by children's messiness, exuberance, or lack of logic, you definitely own the problem. These characteristics are part of being young and aren't likely to change until children get a little older. This type of problem leaves you with only one reasonable solution: Change yourself. Perhaps you can increase your understanding of youngsters to the point of increasing your acceptance of them. For some teachers, the solution is to find work with older children.

Other common examples of discipline problems that belong to the teacher include children taking blocks out of the block area, leaving the group at circle time, or talking out of turn. The children exhibiting these behaviors certainly are not bothered by it, and rarely are other children offended by these situations. If the problem is the teacher's, then the teacher is the only one motivated to find a solution.

Solutions to Your Problem

When you own the problem, you have several options. One is to change your expectations so that you no longer perceive the behavior as unacceptable. For example, you may decide to allow blocks to be used in other centers as long as they are eventually returned to the block storage area. You may also decide to allow children a choice about attending circle time, as long as they don't disturb those who are participating. You might even decide to allow more informal talking and not require raised hands.

Your options also include changing the situation to prevent the problem from recurring. You may decide to locate the block center next to the pretend-play area because the blocks so frequently get taken for use in playhouse scenarios. You may decide to shorten circle time and make it more lively so that the children's attention won't wander. You might decide to encourage more small-group rather than large-group activities, thereby reducing the need for formal turns in discussion. All of these solutions involve creating a more developmentally appropriate learning environment for young children, as discussed in Chapters 4 and 5.

If you cannot overlook the behavior or change it by modifying the situation, you still have other options. If the child is capable of changing the behavior, you might find an "I message" effective (Gordon, 1989). Matter-of-factly telling a youngster, "I can't read this book when you climb on my back," provides information about the situation and your wishes. It does not suggest that the child is being "bad," nor does it reinforce the behavior with undue attention. If you have established caring relationships with the children around you and have respected their feelings, they are likely to respect your feelings expressed as "I messages." Saying "I don't like to be hit" may be the way for you to deal with another problem. This approach also demonstrates to children how they can deal with some of their own interpersonal problems.

If that method doesn't work, you still have options. If you have tried the other approaches without success, you may decide that the behavior has a cause that needs attention. As Lillian Katz suggests, if you have tried the same discipline approach more than two or three times with the same child and it hasn't worked, you can assume it isn't going to be effective for that child (Katz & McClellan, 1997). Perhaps you need to investigate the possibility that the cause of the problem includes mislearned approaches for getting attention, as described in Chapters 9 and 12. In that case, the option of walking away from the offending child can not only meet your needs, but also can address the cause. When you withhold attention from inappropriate bids for it, you help the child unlearn the misguided behavior.

There are some behaviors, however, that are too disruptive or dangerous to ignore. When they occur, these instances may be good times for related consequences that teach why certain actions cause problems. These strategies try to make the problem also belong to the child by getting the child involved in a solution. However, remember the cautions in Chapter 8 about imposing consequences; they are dangerously close to punishment.

The Child's Problem

Many times the problem does belong to the child in the first place, but the adult takes it on. We described this situation in Chapter 8 when we introduce the mother who repeatedly brings the child's forgotten library book to school. Remember, children won't see a need to change behavior that is not causing a problem for them. Therefore, it is crucial that we acknowledge when the problem belongs to the child. Natural and related consequences can get the adults out of the way and let the child experience the problem. These approaches quickly teach youngsters what behavior needs changing. Through natural and related consequences, children experience the problem, understand its cause, and are motivated to solve it.

When a child's problem is of a social/emotional nature, reflective listening (described in Chapter 7) is useful. When you listen carefully and reflect back a child's words, you are not taking over the problem and offering solutions (Gordon, 1989). Rather, you are being a supportive sounding board to help the child arrive at his or her solution. This approach helps children learn to own their problems and demonstrates an effective communication technique for them. Reflective listening respects children's ability to solve their problems, which not only enhances their self-esteem but also provides practice in autonomous decision making.

Mutual Problems

Sometimes a situation arises that makes lots of people unhappy. But even if it only makes two people unhappy, the problem is a shared one. Perhaps a group of youngsters can't start their math game because they can't agree about who should have the first turn. Now mutual problem-solving skills are required: It is important to find a solution that is acceptable to everyone involved. Chapter 7 describes how to brainstorm solutions and look for one that pleases all participants. This process may be a formal and time-consuming operation with a large group, or it may be a quick negotiation between two youngsters or between an adult and a child. Using this process solves many discipline problems, and teaching it to children provides them with a lifetime tool (Levin, 2003).

TAKING TIME FOR DISCIPLINE

Some teachers and parents want solutions too fast. They don't want to take the time to work through problem solving. They provide their adult solutions instead of listening reflectively, and they even force desirable behavior through fear or coerce it through rewards. These adults are short-circuiting the learning process that defines constructive discipline (Watson, 1999). Instead of helping children become autonomous and self-disciplined, this quick-fix attitude makes them dependent, rebellious, and sneaky (Kamii, 1984).

Time for Children to Learn

Teaching desirable behavior is a process of helping children learn a complex set of concepts and skills. Adults need to understand that children's exploration of behavior and social interaction is as natural for them as their exploration and manipulation of a new toy or another interesting object. Children need to try out certain behaviors to see how they work in relation to themselves and others. Given a predictable environment, along with sufficient practice, guidance, and time, youngsters will discover through their explorations that there is a logical pattern or consequence of actions. Children need to experience repeated connections between their behaviors and the results of them. As they reflect on these ex-

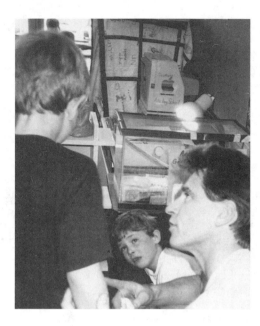

Effective discipline takes time: time to plan for it, time to teach children necessary skills, and time to cool down for clear thinking.

periences, they construct their knowledge of productive behaviors, which eventually allows them to self-direct their actions as morally autonomous people. Such an important process does not happen quickly. Understanding gradually evolves as the child internalizes experiences and information over time. But the results are important enough to be worth waiting for.

Time for Cool-Downs

It is hard to quit rushing. Sometimes teachers hurry to implement effective teaching techniques in a discipline situation. Perhaps two children are fighting. You know that they need to use their words to express their feelings and then negotiate a solution through problem solving. It is tempting to immediately start in on this important teaching as you separate the antagonists, but they are red-faced, short-breathed, and still swinging. Will they hear your voice of reason right now? A wise teacher allows a cool-down time before trying to teach more acceptable social skills. Of course, teachers sometimes need to cool down before they can offer the best guidance.

Time for Adults to Plan

Adults usually don't give themselves time to reflect on behavioral problems or to plan effective discipline. Behavior modification, with its emphasis on immediate feedback, has contributed to the common view that discipline must be instantaneous. Therefore, adults see a child doing something unacceptable and they feel pressured to respond immediately. However, thoughtful, reasoned responses on any subject take time. None of us does our best thinking without reflection time. Many teachers and parents confess to using discipline approaches they don't like simply because they couldn't come up with a better one at the time. It rarely occurs to them to allow sufficient time for effective planning in the area of discipline.

If you discovered a child had a language development problem, you would study the situation and consult others as you carefully planned proper intervention strategies. However, when the subject to be learned has to do with proper behavior, adults tend to act without thinking. Next time you are confronted with a discipline problem that you don't have an immediate answer for, try telling the child or children involved that you need time to think about it. Such a response demonstrates the seriousness of the situation and also models the use of thoughtful reflection in problem solving.

For ongoing and predictable discipline problems, it's possible to plan ahead and have a guidance plan ready to implement. The guides to discovering problem causes that are presented in this chapter will provide useful reflection content. Reflecting on the context of the problem and evaluating your previous responses will help you improve your next response (Flicker & Hoffman, 2002).

Most of us have learned some highly inappropriate discipline methods from our own childhood role models. When we react quickly instead of thoughtfully, our actions are often influenced by old models. The automatic response generally corresponds with the one our own teachers used. If we want to implement better ideas about effective discipline, then we must make a constant effort to override our automatic responses with rational ones. Be careful and take your time.

FAMILIES AND RESPECT FOR CHILDREN

Few of us experienced discipline with respect in our childhoods and therefore may not know what it means to show respect to children. American mainstream society says it values children but demonstrates little respect for them. Many of us experienced punishment and behavior modification—coercive tactics that damage both character development and intellectual development (DeVries, 1999). Adults in our lives may have also criticized us when they wanted to improve our behavior. Many parents believe that criticism helps people to improve. Yet, in fact, criticism discourages us and it does not improve behavior. When children's efforts result in feedback about their shortcomings, they are discouraged. Discouragement leads to quitting, not to trying harder. Alternatively, encouragement (described as an alternative to praise in Chapter 9) leads to trying harder. Families need to know these things and teachers may be able to communicate them.

Some families may need help realizing that respect accepts the child as a child, not as an imperfect adult. Respecting children means that we provide situations in which they can thrive while still acting their age. It also means that we give them as much choice as possible. When we respect youngsters, we don't force or manipulate them to bend to our will. However, that attitude doesn't mean they are allowed to run wild and be undisciplined. Respect for children guides us in helping them learn effective behaviors and understand the reasons for them. When we respect children, we help them to respect themselves. The resultant self-esteem combines with self-discipline skills to create morally autonomous people—something desperately needed in our society.

CONCLUSION

The teacher with the knowledge and the caring to implement this sophisticated approach to discipline deserves society's highest respect. Few observers realize how much effort and thought goes into a smoothly functioning program for young children. Teachers make hundreds of important initial decisions about the environment and the program, and they must make hundreds more each day as they implement their plans and keep youngsters constructively involved. We hope that this book is helpful to your own professional growth toward implementing the best possible approaches to discipline for young children. We hope that it helps you to envision and create educational relationships in keeping with democracy and human dignity.

∞ *FOR FURTHER THOUGHT*

1. Think about your goals for guidance and discipline. Do you feel clear about what you hope to accomplish?

2. Analyze an actual, ongoing discipline challenge using the chart in Figure 15-1 and the accompanying explanation as a guide. Does this analysis help you to consider your own possible role as a cause of discipline problems? Have you discovered a cause you had not previously considered? Have you discovered a need for outside help? Does this analysis approach help you to match guidance approaches to the causes of discipline problems?

3. Analyze another discipline situation using the chart in Figure 15-2. Have you been unsuccessfully trying to get children to take responsibility for your problem? Have you been inadvertently taking responsibility for theirs? Does this analysis help you to match your responses to the situation more effectively?

4. Practice taking your time with responses to undersirable behavior. Give yourself cool-down time and planning time. What are the children's reactions? Do they seem to learn from your example? Are your interventions more effective?

∞ *RECOMMENDED READINGS*

Butchart, R. E., & McEwan, B. (1998). *Classroom discipline in American schools: Problems and possibilities for democratic education.* Albany, NY: State University of New York Press.

Dill, V. S. (1998). *A peaceable school: Cultivating a culture of nonviolence.* Bloomington, IN: Phi Delta Kappa.

Williams, M. M., & Shaps, E. (Eds). (1999). *Character education: The foundation for teacher education.* Washington, DC: The Character Education Partnership.

Appendix A

Action Guide for Media Violence and Children

This appendix contains pages 1, 2, 3, and 5 of the *Action Guide for Media Violence and Children*, prepared by Teachers Resisting Unhealthy Children's Entertainment (TRUCE). The complete guide is available on-line at www.truceteachers.org.

TRUCE
Media Violence and Children
Action Guide   *2004-2005*

Media is a powerful force in children's lives. It influences most aspects of children's development and learning. Many children spend more time in front of a screen — with TV, movies, videos, computers and video games — than in school. Shows, advertisements and the toys and other products related to them control children's play and learning.

Too much of what children see on the screen is *violence as entertainment.* It undermines lessons we teach at home and school about how people treat each other, and encourages the use of violence to solve problems and to have fun. We have seen the effects of this glamorized violence in such events as school shootings.

Media violence is a public health issue that affects all our children.

Teachers and parents, please join the TRUCE Campaign Against Media Violence

Our Action Guide will help you to:

- Promote children's informed and responsible use of media.
- Counteract the negative effects of media violence on children.
- Take action to reduce media violence in children's lives and in society.

Facts About Children, Media, and Violence

What do we know?

- Children average 35 hours per week of screen time—including TV, video games and videos.
- Heavy TV viewers are less imaginative, more aggressive, and are more likely to have attention problems have lower academic performance, and be aggressive later in life.
- The average child sees 8,000 murders and 100,000 other violent acts by the end of elementary school.
- In July of 2000, a Joint Statement from the American Medical Association, American Academy of Pediatrics, and the American Medical Association concluded that viewing media violence can make children more aggressive, fearful, disrespectful and insensitive to the effects of violence.
- Playing violent video games has been directly linked to increased aggressive behavior.
- Violent movies and TV shows, like Star Wars, Spider Man, and wrestling, are used to sell violent toys and products to children even when these shows aren't rated as appropriate for their age.
- Toys linked to violent media encourage more violent play, which takes the place of imaginative and creative play.
- Young children are most at risk for the harmful effects of media violence.

For more information: TRUCE PO Box 441261, West Somerville, MA 02144
truceteachers@aol.com   **www.truceteachers.org**
PLEASE COPY AND DISTRIBUTE

*T*eachers *R*esisting *U*nhealthy *C*hildren's *E*ntertainment

What You Can Do

Parents and Children

◆ Protect children from exposure to media violence as much as possible.

◆ Get TV sets, video game systems, and computers out of children's bedrooms.

◆ Talk with children about your concerns about media violence. To help you begin, here's a letter from teachers that you can read and talk about together [See the letter below].

Dear Kids,

A lot of kids really love to watch TV and videos. Many of the shows they watch have lots of fighting. The fighting often seems fun and exciting and a great way to solve problems.

Many teachers are worried about the violence children see on TV. They say a lot of kids act out the fighting they see when they play. Teachers also say they think TV fighting is making more kids use fighting in school to solve their conflicts with each other.

Kids often answer, "But we're only pretending. It isn't real. We're just playing." They say their pretend violence is different from real fighting.

But teachers say that when kids pretend to fight like TV characters, other kids often really get hurt. And sometimes kids seem surprised when this happens.

Some kids agree they're surprised when someone gets hurt. They say they're the good guys & good guys have to fight bad guys, that's why they fight.

Teachers see that a lot of little kids look up to good guy TV characters and want to do what they do. So the teachers think violent TV shows can teach kids that it's okay to fight and hurt people.

Because teachers are worried about TV violence and kids are getting hurt, teachers want to help grown-ups and children talk together about it and decide what to do so everyone stays safe.

• WHAT DO YOU THINK ABOUT WHAT TEACHERS ARE SAYING?
• WHAT DO YOU THINK GROWN-UPS SHOULD DO ABOUT VIOLENCE ON TV & VIDEOS?
• WHAT CAN GROWN-UPS DO TO HELP CHILDREN BE SAFE & LEARN NOT TO FIGHT?
• WHAT CAN YOU AND OTHER CHILDREN DO?

Thanks a lot for listening to and talking about our letter,
From Many Teachers All Over the Country

For more information: TRUCE PO Box 441261, West Somerville, MA 02144
truceteachers@aol.com   www.truceteachers.org
PLEASE COPY AND DISTRIBUTE

*T*eachers *R*esisting *U*nhealthy *C*hildren's *E*ntertainment

◆ Talk to children about what they see on the screen, including media violence. Aim for a give-and-take discussion rather than a lecture where you give the answers. Listen carefully, find out their ideas and fears, clear up misconceptions, and share your ideas and concerns about media violence.

Parents and Children Can Talk Together about TV and Other Media *

- **Discuss** each others reactions (both positive and negative) to what you saw.
  - *What did you think about that show/game?*
  - *Did you like it when _____ happened? Why do you think it happened?*
  - *I didn't like it when _____. I wish they didn't have to hurt each other. What do you think?*

- **Help** them sort out fantasy from reality.
  - *What was pretend and what was real? How could you tell?*
  - *Help clarify confusion by saying things such as, "In real life things don't work that way. I wonder how they made _____ happen on that show."*

- **Help** them develop an understanding of advertisements and advertising.
  - *How can we tell the difference between these ads and the show?*
  - *I wonder why they made the ad like that?*

- **Compare** what they saw to children's own experience.
  - *Could anything like _____ happen to you? When? How could it be the same/different?*
  - *What would you do if you were in that situation?*

- **Talk** about the violence and other mean-spirited behavior that children see on the screen.
  - *What do you think about how _____ solved their problem?*
  - *If you had a problem like that what could you do / say?*
  - *Can you think of a way to solve that problem where no one gets hurt?*

- **Ask** questions that focus on stereotyped images and behaviors.
  - *I wonder why it's always men with big muscles that go to fight? Did you notice that?*
  - *The women always seem to need to get rescued by men. Have you noticed that? I wonder why?*
  - *I wonder why the "bad guys" have foreign accents? Wear dark colors? Have darker skin?*

* Adapted from *Remote-Control Childhood* by Diane Levin

For more information: TRUCE PO Box 441261, West Somerville, MA 02144
truceteachers@aol.com   www.truceteachers.org
PLEASE COPY AND DISTRIBUTE

Teachers Resisting Unhealthy Children's Entertainment

◆ Help children develop thoughtful and responsible media viewing habits.
  - Decide together how much "screen time" is okay each day or week. (With young children, we recommend starting with the least amount that can work with your schedule and your child's.)
  - Discuss and work out which shows and video games are okay and which are not.
  - Make a chart (with simple picture illustrations for non-readers) of shows which your children want to watch and which you can agree are good choices. Check the chart regularly to help you discuss how things are going.
◆ Encourage your child's play as a way to help them work out their own ideas and develop a sense of mastery. [Use the TRUCE Toy Action Guide available at www.truceteachers.org]

- Promote creative and imaginative play which children control, instead of play that looks like they are imitating what they see on the screen.

- Choose toys carefully.
  • *Provide play materials that can be used in many ways over a long period of time, such as blocks, play dough, dress-ups, and props for dramatic play.*
  • *Limit the number of highly realistic toys and other products (such as lunch boxes, tee shirts and breakfast cereals) that are linked to TV programs.*
  • *Avoid toys that are linked to movies, TV programs, and video games that are rated for older children or adults.*

Parents and Other Parents

◆ Talk about your concerns and approaches to media violence and media-linked toys.

- Help each other find solutions to problems media violence creates for you and your children (how to make good choices about what to watch and buy; how to turn off the TV while you're making dinner).

- Agree on how you'll deal with TV and other media when your children are at each other's houses.

- Support each others' choices to resist media's negative influence.

Parents and Teachers

◆ Ask your child's school to develop policies and educate parents about the problems created by media violence and how to deal with them.

◆ Work with schools to develop curriculum that incorporates healthy play, media literacy, and conflict resolution and violence prevention programs.

◆ **Promote school-wide activities which help create a community of aware parents and teachers**
  - *Sponsor school events such as a TV Turn-Off Week or a violent toy trade-in [see Organization Resources: TV-Free America and Lion and Lamb Project].*
  - *Create media resource library to help parents use media wisely.*
  - *Have the PTA organize workshops and guest speaker events for parents on this topic.*
  - *Sponsor school-wide activities to involve children in alternative activities such as after school clubs.*

For more information: TRUCE PO Box 441261, West Somerville, MA 02144
truceteachers@aol.com   www.truceteachers.org
PLEASE COPY AND DISTRIBUTE

Appendix B

Curriculum Guidelines from the National Association for the Education of Young Children

1. **The curriculum has an articulated description of its theoretical base that is consistent with prevailing professional opinion and research on how children learn.**

    Curriculum should be grounded in the most current knowledge of child development and learning. The prevailing world view reflects a developmental, interactive, Constructivist approach to learning that is not limited to the almost exclusively Behaviorist approach that has permeated curriculum and assessment in this country for the past several decades.

2. **Curriculum content is designed to achieve long-range goals for children in all domains—social, emotional, cognitive, and physical—and to prepare children to function as fully contributing members of a democratic society.**

    Curriculum should address the development and learning of the whole child. This means that curriculum in primary grade schools must attend to social, emotional, and physical goals as well as cognitive goals. Likewise, programs for 3- and 4-year-olds need to address cognition as well as social, emotional, and physical development. In addition, curriculum content and processes should reflect democratic ideals of community involvement, liberty, freedom of choice, equality, fairness, and justice.

3. **Curriculum addresses the development of knowledge and understanding, processes and skills, dispositions and attitudes.**

    The acquisition of knowledge and the mastery of skills is accomplished so as to ensure that children will be disposed to apply the knowledge or skill and so that children associate positive feelings with the learning (Katz & Chard, 1989). For example, if reading instruction is limited to a drill and practice on phonics and word-attack skills, children may choose not to read because they find no pleasure or satisfaction in reading or do not understand what they decode. On the other hand, if children are motivated to get meaning from reading, they are more likely to respond to instruction in the use of phonetic cues.

4. **Curriculum addresses a broad range of content that is relevant, engaging, and meaningful to children.**

    The human mind is a pattern detector; the child naturally attempts to make meaning out of every experience. As a result, what is meaningful is always more easily

From *Guidelines for Appropriate Curriculum Content and Assessment in Programs Serving Children Ages 3 Through 8.* A Joint Position Statement of NAEYC and NAECS/SDE (National Association of Early Childhood Specialists in State Departments of Education). Reprinted with permission from NAEYC.

learned, understood, and remembered. Effective curriculum develops knowledge and skills in a meaningful context, not in isolation. For example, children learn numerals and number concepts by counting real objects, not by filling in workbook pages. Children learn letters and their sounds from using them in their name, signs, or stories that are meaningful to them rather than by tracing them on a page or reciting the alphabet repeatedly. The younger the child, the more important it is to provide curriculum content that is close to the child's experience and therefore more likely to be meaningful.

5. **Curriculum goals are realistic and attainable for most children in the designated age range for which they were designed.**

Curriculum planning should adjust for normative differences in children's development and learning. Children should not be expected to comprehend abstract/symbolic concepts or master skills or content that can be acquired much more easily later on. To some extent, this guideline addresses the issue of efficiency in teaching and learning. For instance, first-, second-, and third-grade teachers all report that children cannot comprehend place value; teachers spend hours trying to teach this abstract concept, and children either become frustrated or resort to memorizing meaningless tricks. This is an example of an unrealistic objective that could be attained much more easily later on.

Curriculum decisions about when children are expected to acquire knowledge and skills are based on age-group, individual, and cultural expectations. Curriculum expectations of young children are flexible and dynamic rather than deterministic and lock-step since there is no universal sequence of skills development. The curriculum allows for children to work at different levels on different activities and does not require all of the children to do the same thing at the same time. Decisions about when knowledge and skills are introduced and/or expected to be accomplished are based on knowledge of the prior experiences of individual children in a group, knowledge of prerequisite intellectual structures, and knowledge about typical patterns of development and learning.

6. **Curriculum content reflects and is generated by the needs and interests of individual children within the group. Curriculum incorporates a wide variety of learning experiences, materials and equipment, and instructional strategies to accommodate a broad range of children's individual differences in prior experience, maturation rates, styles of learning, needs, and interests.**

Curriculum planning should anticipate the interests that are typical of children of different ages and should also emerge from the interests that children demonstrate. Interest can also be generated by exposing children to events, materials, and people that children would not experience otherwise. Educators must choose which of the children's interests to support and which to ignore. In addition, educators have a responsibility to nurture certain interests, particularly those that are tied to cultural values, such as the value of children's autonomy and creative experience.

7. **Curriculum respects and supports individual, cultural, and linguistic diversity. Curriculum supports and encourages positive relationships with children's families.**

The curriculum embraces the reality of multiculturalism in American society by providing a balance between learning the common core of dominant cultural knowledge (for example, the English language, democratic values) and knowledge of minority cultures. Curriculum accommodates children who have limited English proficiency. All of the cultures and primary languages of the children are respectfully reflected in the curriculum.

8. **Curriculum builds upon what children already know and are able to do (activating prior knowledge) to consolidate their learning and to foster their acquisition of new concepts and skills.**

    For example, there is no body of knowledge possessed by all children of the same age, just as there is no universal sequence of learning. Because children bring meaning to learning experiences based on their past experiences and individual development, different children acquire different learnings from the same experience. As a result, curriculum for young children should not be based on a rigid scope and sequence but should help children connect new learning to what they already know and are able to do.

9. **Curriculum provides conceptual frameworks for children so that their mental constructions based on prior knowledge and experience become more complex over time.**

    Conceptual organizers such as themes, units, or projects give children something meaningful and substantive to engage their minds. It is difficult for children to make sense of abstract concepts such as colors, mathematical symbols, or letter sounds when they are presented at random or devoid of any meaningful context.

10. **Curriculum allows for focus on a particular topic or content while allowing for integration across traditional subject-matter divisions by planning around themes and/or learning experiences that provide opportunities for rich conceptual development.**

    Children's learning is not compartmentalized or divided into artificial subject-matter distinctions. The purpose of integrating curriculum is to reflect the natural way children learn and also to help children make connections between what they learn at home and in the program, between what they learn in school and in the real world, and between different disciplines or subject-matter areas (British Columbia Ministry of Education, 1990). The curriculum provides for long blocks of time to bring naturally related subjects together and does not require minimal time allotments for instruction in discrete subject matter. For example, children read and write about a science experiment they have done, or measure and estimate the number of blocks they will need to build a store.

11. **Curriculum content has intellectual integrity; content meets the recognized standards of the relevant subject-matter disciplines.**

    Regardless of the age of the child, educators have a responsibility to respect the knowledge base of the appropriate disciplines when formulating curriculum. In an attempt to simplify content, curriculum developers sometimes present inaccurate, misleading, or potentially confusing information. If the specific content is related to a particular discipline, then it should be as accurate as possible (although children's constructions of knowledge will not mirror adult conceptions). For example, science curriculum should be factual and not promote magical thinking in children; likewise, children should be exposed to literature, poetry, and the works of art and music of recognized quality.

12. **Curriculum content is worth knowing; curriculum respects children's intelligence and does not waste their time.**

    Content should be included in curriculum for specific age groups because it is important for children to learn to function capably in their world. Content goals should include what children can learn efficiently and effectively at this time. Children and teachers should not have to waste time trying to address content that is meaningless or could be learned much more easily when the child is older.

13. **Curriculum engages children actively, not passively, in the learning process. Children have opportunities to make meaningful choices.**

    The curriculum provides for children's direct experience before moving to more abstract levels of understanding. The curriculum or learning experience builds on children's prior learning and previous knowledge; thus, sensory experience is not prerequisite in every situation but is vital when introducing new concepts or information. Encouraging and permitting children to make real choices fosters interest and engagement. For instance, children should have opportunities to express their own ideas in writing and to read books of their choosing as well as those that the entire group will address.

14. **Curriculum values children's constructive errors and does not prematurely limit exploration and experimentation for the sake of ensuring "right" answers.**

    Overemphasis on standardized test scores and the acquisition of basic skills has made teachers and parents uncomfortable with the natural process of the child's construction of knowledge. The fact is that teachers can learn a great deal about children's thinking and reasoning and level of cognitive development by attending to their "wrong" answers.

15. **Curriculum emphasizes the development of children's thinking, reasoning, decision making, and problem-solving abilities.**

    Curriculum emphasizes both content and process, what children need to know and be able to do. Curriculum content gives meaning to process, rather than focusing on isolated facts. Skills are taught in the context of activities that are meaningful to the child, rather than teaching skills in isolation (Lloyd-Jones & Lunsford, 1988).

16. **Curriculum emphasizes the value of social interaction to learning in all domains and provides opportunities to learn from peers.**

    Social interaction with peers and adults is essential for children to develop real understanding. Social interaction also provides opportunities for children to learn cooperation and other kinds of positive social behavior. Multiage grouping is one strategy to promote social interaction among individual children and their more capable peers, an effective way of enhancing language competence, and generally assisting children's progress to the next level of development and understanding.

17. **Curriculum is supportive of children's physiological needs for activity, sensory stimulation, fresh air, rest, hygiene, and nourishment/elimination.**

    Curriculum should respect and meet children's physical needs while also promoting children's independent functioning and ability to meet their own needs. Children should not be required to sit still for long periods without a break. Under no circumstances should children who need regular opportunities to move their bodies be kept indoors to complete tasks or be deprived of food as punishment.

18. **Curriculum protects children's psychological safety; that is, children feel happy, relaxed, and comfortable rather than disengaged, frightened, worried, or stressed.**

    Decisions about curriculum should respect children's psychological safety. For instance, the content itself should not generate fear or confusion, nor should the premature expectation of mastery of skills generate stress.

19. **Curriculum strengthens children's sense of competence and enjoyment of learning by providing experiences for children to succeed from their point of view.**

    Sometimes teachers seem to use the following as their primary criterion for selecting curriculum: "But the children just love it!" Enjoying the curriculum is an important but insufficient criterion for curriculum selection. Worthwhile curriculum does not have to entertain children; instead, children's enjoyment can derive from positive feelings about self and meaningful learning as they realize their own progress and growing competence.

20. Curriculum is flexible so that teachers can adapt to individual children or groups.
The curriculum suggests alternatives as well as assumes that teachers will use their own professional judgment.

Appendix C

Code of Ethical Conduct and Statement of Commitment

GUIDELINES FOR RESPONSIBLE BEHAVIOR IN EARLY CHILDHOOD EDUCATION

NAEYC recognizes that many daily decisions required of those who work with young children are of a moral and ethical nature. The NAEYC Code of Ethical Conduct offers guidelines for responsible behavior and sets forth a common basis for resolving the principal ethical dilemmas encountered in early childhood care and education. The primary focus is on daily practice with children and their families in programs for children from birth through 8 years of age, such as infant/toddler programs, preschools, child-care centers, family child-care homes, kindergartens, and primary classrooms. Many of the provisions also apply to specialists who do not work directly with children, including program administrators, parent and vocational educators, college professors, and child care licensing specialists.

Core Values

Standards of ethical behvior in early childhood care and education are based on commitment to core values that are deeply rooted in the history of our field. We have committed ourselves to:

- appreciating childhood as a unique and valuable stage of the human life cycle
- basing our work with children on knowledge of child development
- appreciating and supporting the close ties between the child and family
- recognizing that children are best understood and supported in the context of family, culture, community, and society
- respecting the dignity, worth, and uniqueness of each individual (child, family member, and colleague)
- helping children and adults achieve their full potential in the context of relationships that are based on trust, respect, and positive regard

Excerpted from NAEYC's brochure *Code of Ethical Conduct and Statement of Commitment* (Washington, DC: National Association for the Education of Young Children, 1998). Reprinted by permission of NAEYC.

Conceptual Framework

The Code sets forth a conception of our professional responsibilities in four sections, each addressing an arena of professional relationships: (1) children, (2) families, (3) colleagues, and (4) community and society. Each section includes an introduction to the primary responsibilities of the early childhood practitioner in that arena, a set of ideals pointing in the direction of exemplary professional practice, and a set of principles defining practices that are required, prohibited, and permitted.

The ideals reflect the aspirations of practitioners. The principles are intended to guide, conduct, and assist practitioners in resolving ethical dilemmas encountered in the field. There is not necessarily a corresponding principle for each ideal. Both ideals and principles are intended to direct practitioners to those questions which, when responsibly answered, will provide the basis for conscientious decisionmaking. While the Code provides specific direction and suggestions for addressing some ethical dilemmas, many others will require the practitioner to combine the guidance of the Code with sound professional judgment.

The ideals and principles in this Code present a shared conception of professional responsibility that affirms our commitment to the core values of our field. The Code publicly acknowledges the responsibilities that we in the field have assumed and in so doing supports ethical behavior in our work. Practitioners who face ethical dilemmas are urged to seek guidance in the applicable parts of this Code and in the spirit that informs the whole.

Ethical Dilemmas Always Exist

Often, "the right answer"—the best ethical course of action to take—is not obvious. There may be no readily apparent, positive way to handle a situation. One important value may contradict another. When we are caught "on the horns of a dilemma," it is our professional responsibility to consult with all relevant parties in seeking the most ethical course of action to take.

Section I: Ethical Responsibilities to Children

Childhood is a unique and valuable stage in the life cycle. Our paramount responsibility is to provide safe, healthy, nurturing, and responsive settings for children. We are committed to supporting children's development, respecting individual differences, helping children learn to live and work cooperatively, and promoting health, self-awareness, competence, self-worth, and resiliency.

Ideals

I-1.1— To be familiar with the knowledge base of early childhood care and education and to keep current through continuing education and in-service training.

I-1.2— To base program practices upon current knowledge in the field of child development and related disciplines and upon particular knowledge of each child.

I-1.3— To recognize and respect the uniqueness and the potential of each child.

I-1.4— To appreciate the special vulnerability of children.

I-1.5— To create and maintain safe and healthy settings that foster children's social, emotional, intellectual, and physical development and that respect their dignity and their contributions.

I-1.6— To support the right of each child to play and learn in inclusive early childhood programs to the fullest extent consistent with the best interests of all involved. As with adults who are disabled in the larger community, children with disabilities are ideally served in the same settings in which they would participate if they did not have a disability.

I-1.7— To ensure that children with disabilities have access to appropriate and convenient support services and to advocate for the resources necessary to provide the most appropriate settings for all children.

Principles

P-1.1— Above all, we shall not harm children. We shall not participate in practices that are disrespectful, degrading, dangerous, exploitative, intimidating, emotionally damaging, or physically harmful to children. This principle has precedence over all others in this Code.

P-1.2— We shall not participate in practices that discriminate against children by denying benefits, giving special advantages, or excluding them from programs or activities on the basis of their race, ethnicity, religion, sex, national origin, language, ability, or the status, behavior, or beliefs of their parents. (This principle does not apply to programs that have a lawful mandate to provide services to a particular population of children.)

P-1.3— We shall involve all of the those with relevant knowledge (including staff and parents) in decisions concerning a child.

P-1.4— For every child we shall implement adaptations in teaching strategies, learning environment, and curricula, consult with the family, and seek recommendations from appropriate specialists to maximize the potential of the child to benefit from the program. If, after these efforts have been made to work with a child and family, the child does not appear to be benefiting from a program, or the child is seriously jeopardizing the ability of other children to benefit from the program, we shall communicate with the family and appropriate specialists to determine the child's current needs, identify the setting and services most suited to meeting these needs, and assist the family in placing the child in an appropriate setting.

P-1.5— We shall be familiar with the symptoms of child abuse, including physical, sexual, verbal, and emotional abuse, and neglect. We shall know and follow state laws and community procedures that protect children against abuse and neglect.

P-1.6— When we have reasonable cause to suspect child abuse or neglect, we shall report it to the appropriate community agency and follow-up to ensure that appropriate action has been taken. When appropriate, parents or guardians will be informed that the referral has been made.

P-1.7— When another person tells us of a suspicion that a child is being abused or neglected, we shall assist that person in taking appropriate action to protect the child.

P-1.8— When a child-protective agency fails to provide adequate protection for abused or neglected children, we acknowledge a collective ethical responsibility to work toward improvement of these services.

P-1.9— When we become aware of a practice or situation that endangers the health or safety of children, but has not been previously known to do so, we have an ethical responsibility to inform those who can remedy the situation and who can protect children from similar danger.

Section II: Ethical Responsibilities to Families

Families are of primary importance in children's development. (The term *family* may include others, besides parents, who are responsibly involved with the child.) Because the family and the early childhood practitioner have a common interest in the child's welfare, we acknowledge a primary responsibility to bring about collaboration between the home and school in ways that enhance the child's development.

Ideals

I-2.1— To develop relationships of mutual trust with families we serve.

I-2.2— To acknowledge and build upon strengths and competencies as we support families in their task of nurturing children.

I-2.3— To respect the dignity of each family and its culture, language, customs, and beliefs.

I-2.4— To respect families' childrearing values and their right to make decisions for their children.

I-2.5— To interpret each child's progress to parents within the framework of a developmental perspective and to help families understand and appreciate the value of developmentally appropriate early childhood practices.

I-2.6— To help family members improve their understanding of their children and to enhance their skills as parents.

I-2.7— To participate in building support networks for families by providing them with opportunities to interact with program staff, other families, community resources, and professional services.

Principles

P-2.1— We shall not deny family members access to their child's classroom or program setting.

P-2.2— We shall inform families of program philosophy, policies, and personnel qualifications, and explain why we teach as we do—which should be in accordance with our ethical responsibilities to children (see Section I).

P-2.3— We shall inform families of, and when appropriate, involve them in, policy decisions.

P-2.4— We shall involve families in significant decisions affecting their child.

P-2.5— We shall inform the family of accidents involving their child, of risks such as exposures to contagious disease that may result in infection, and of occurrences that might result in emotional stress.

P-2.6— To improve the quality of early childhood care and education, we shall cooperate with qualified child development researchers. Families shall be fully informed of any proposed research projects involving their children and shall have the opportunity to give or withhold consent without penalty. We shall not permit or participate in research that could in any way hinder the education, development, or well-being of children.

P-2.7— We shall not engage in or support exploitation of families. We shall not use our relationship with a family for private advantage or personal gain, or enter into relationships with family members that might impair our effectiveness in working with children.

P-2.8— We shall develop written policies for the protection of confidentiality and the disclosure of children's records. These policy documents shall be made available to all program personnel and families. Disclosure of children's records beyond family members, program personnel, and consultants having an obligation of confidentiality shall require familial consent (except in cases of abuse or neglect).

P-2.9— We shall maintain confidentiality and shall respect the family's right to privacy, refraining from disclosure of confidential information and intrusion into family life. However, when we have reason to believe that a child's welfare is at risk, it is permissible to share confidential information with agencies and individuals who may be able to intervene in the child's interest.

P-2.10— In cases where family members are in conflict, we shall work openly, sharing our observations of the child, to help all parties involved make informed decisions. We shall refrain from becoming an advocate for one party.

P-2.11— We shall be familiar with and appropriately use community resources and professional services that support families. After a referral has been made, we shall follow-up to ensure that services have been appropriately provided.

Statement of Commitment

As an individual who works with young children, I commit myself to furthering the values of early childhood education as they are reflected in the NAEYC Code of Ethical Conduct.
   To the best of my ability I will

- Ensure that programs for young children are based on current knowledge of child development and early childhood education.
- Respect and support families in their task of nurturing children.
- Respect colleagues in early childhood education and support them in maintaining the NAEYC Code of Ethical Conduct.
- Serve as an advocate for children, their families, and their teachers in community and society.
- Maintain high standards of professional conduct.
- Recognize how personal values, opinions, and biases can affect professional judgment.
- Be open to new ideas and be willing to learn from the suggestions of others.
- Continue to learn, grow, and contribute as a professional.
- Honor the ideals and principles of the NAEYC Code of Ethical Conduct.

Appendix D
Three Subtypes of ADHD

There are three subtypes of Attention-Deficit/Hyperactive Disorder: (a) children who are primarily inattentive, (b) children whose main problem is impulsivity-hyperactivity, and (c) children who have all three problems to a significant degree: inattention and impulsivity-hyperactivity. This is called the "combined subtype" and is the most common.

According to the DSM-IV-TR (APA, 2000, p. 92), criteria for ADHD are as follows:

Either (1) or (2):

(1) Six (or more) of the following symptoms of inattention have persisted for at least 6 months to a degree that is maladaptive and inconsistent with developmental level:

Inattention
- Often fails to give close attention to details or makes careless mistakes in schoolwork, work, or other activities
- Often has difficulty sustaining attention in tasks or play activities
- Often does not seem to listen when spoken to directly
- Often does not follow through on instuctions and fails to finish schoolwork, chores, or duties in the workplace (not due to oppositional behavior or failure to understand instructions)
- Often has difficulty organizing tasks and activities
- Often avoids, dislikes, or is reluctant to engage in tasks that require sustained mental effort (such as schoolwork or homework)
- Often loses things necessary for tasks or activities (e.g., toys, school assignments, pencils, books, or tools)
- Is often easily distracted by extraneous stimuli
- Is often forgetful in daily activities

(2) Six (or more) of the following symptoms of hyperactivity-implusivity have persisted for at least 6 months to a degree that is maladaptive and inconsistent with developmental level:

Hyperactivity
- Often fidgets with hands or feet or squirms in seat
- Often leaves seat in classroom or in other situation in which remaining seated is expected

- Often runs about or climbs excessively in situations in which it is inappropriate (in adolescents or adults, may be limited to subjective feelings of restlessness)
- Often has difficulty playing or engaging in leisure activities quietly
- Often is "on the go" or often acts as if "driven by a motor"
- Often talks excessively

Impulsivity

- Often blurts out answers before questions have been completed
- Often has difficulty waiting for a turn
- Often interrupts or intrudes on others (e.g., butts into conversations or games)

References

Adams, S. K., & Baronberg, J. (2005). *Promoting positive behavior.* Columbus, OH: Merrill/Prentice Hall.

Adams, S. K., & Wittmer, D. S. (2001). I had it first: Teaching young children to solve problems peacefully. *Childhood Education, 78*(1), 10–17.

Adler, A. (1917). *Study of organ inferiority and its psychological compensation.* New York: Nervous Disease Publications.

Adler, A. (1927). *The practice and theory of individual psychology.* New York: Harcourt Brace Jovanovich.

Ainsworth, M. D. S., Blehar, M. C., Waters, E., & Wall, S. (1978). *Patterns of attachment.* Hillsdale, NJ: Erlbaum.

American Psychiatric Association. (2000). *Diagnostic and statistical manual of mental disorders* (4th ed., text revision). Washington, DC: Author.

Bailey, B. (2002). *Easy to love, difficult to discipline: The 7 basic skills for turning conflict into cooperation.* New York: HarperCollins.

Banks, R. (April 1997). Bullying in schools. *ERIC Digest,* EDO-PS-97-17.

Barrera. I., & Corso R. M., with D. Macpherson. (2003). *Skilled dialogue: Strategies for responding to cultural diversity in early childhood.* Baltimore, MD: Paul H. Brookes.

Baumeister, R. (2001). Violent pride: Do people turn violent because of self-hate or self-love? *Scientific American, 284,* 96–101.

Baumerind, D. (1967). Child care practices anteceding three patterns of preschool behavior. *Genetic Psychology Monographs, 75,* 43–88.

Bebeau, M. J., Rest, J. R., & Narvaez, D. (1999). Beyond the promise: A perspective on research in moral education. *Educational Researcher, 28*(4), 18–25.

Berger, K. S. (1998). *The developing person through the lifespan.* New York: Worth.

Berk, L. E. (1994). Vygotsky's theory: The importance of make-believe play. *Young Children, 50*(1), 30–39.

Berk, L. E. (2002). *Infants, children, and Adolescents.* Boston: Allyn & Bacon.

Beyer, L. E. (1998). Uncontrolled students eventually become unmanageable. In R. E. Butchart & B. McEwan, *Classroom discipline in American schools: Problems and possibilities for democratic education* (pp. 51–84). Albany, NY: State University of New York Press.

Bhattacharya, J., & Currie, J. (2001). Youths and nutrition risk: Malnourished of misnourished? In J. Gruber (Ed.), *Risky behavior among youths: An economic analysis* (pp. 438–521). Chicago: National Bureau of Economic Research, University of Chicago Press.

Bhavnagri, N. P., & Samuels, B. G. (1996). Making and keeping friends: A thematic unit to promote understanding of peer relationships in young children. *Childhood Education, 72*(4), 219–223.

Billman, J. (1992). The Native American curriculum: Attempting alternatives to teepees and headbands. *Young Children, 47*(6), 22–25.

Bloch, M. N., Tabachnick, B. R., & Espinosa-Dulanto, M. (1994). Teacher perspectives on the strengths and achievements of young children: Relationships to ethnicity, language, gender and class. In B. L. Mallory & R. S. New (Eds.), *Diversity and developmentally appropriate practices: Challenges for early childhood education.* New York: Teachers College Press.

Blount, J. (1998). The visceral pleasures of a well-worn rut. In R. E. Butchart & B. McEwan,

Classroom discipline in American schools: Problems and possibilities for democratic education (pp. 85–108). Albany, NY: State University of New York Press.

Bodrova, E., & Leong, D. J. (1998). Development of dramatic play in young children and its effects on self-regulation: the Vygotskian approach. *Journal of Early Childhood Teacher Education, 19*(2), 115–124.

Brady, K., Forton, M. B., Porter, D., & Wood, C. (2003). *Rules in school.* Greenfield, MA: Northeast Foundation for Children.

Brazelton, T. B., & Greenspan, S. I. (2000). *The irreducible needs of children: What every child must have to grow, learn, and flourish.* Cambridge, MA: Perseus Books.

Bredekamp, S. (Ed.). (1997). *Developmentally appropriate practice in early childhood programs serving children from birth through age 8* (expanded ed.). Washington, DC: National Association for the Education of Young Children.

Bredekamp, S., & Copple, C. (Eds.). (1997). *Developmentally appropriate practice in early childhood programs.* Washington, DC: National Association for the Education of Young Children.

Bredekamp, S., & Rosegrant, T. (Eds.). (1992). *Reaching potentials: Appropriate curriculum and assessment for young children.* Washington, DC: National Association for the Education of Young Children.

Bredekamp, S., & Rosegrant, T. (Eds.). (1995). *Transforming early childhood curriculum and assessment* (Vol. 2). Washington, DC: National Association for the Education of Young Children.

Britain, L. (1992). *Having wonderful ideas together: Children's spontaneous collaboration in a self-directed play context.* Unpublished doctoral dissertation, University of Oregon, Eugene.

Britain, L. (2002). *My grandma died: A child's story about death and loss.* Seattle: Parenting Press.

British Columbia Ministry of Education. (1990). *Primary program resource document.* Victoria, British Columbia: Author.

Brofenbrenner, U. (1979). *The ecology of human development.* Cambridge: Harvard University Press.

Bronson, M. B. (2000). Recognizing and supporting the development of self-regulation in young children. *Young Children, 55*(2), 32–37.

Brophy, J. E. (1981). Teacher praise: A functional analysis. *Review of Educational Research, 51*(1), 5–32.

Bruner, J. (1987). The transactional self. In J. Bruner & H. Haste (Eds.), *Making sense: The child's construction of the world.* New York: Methuen.

Butchart, R. E. (1998). Introduction. In R. E. Butchart, & B. McEwan (Eds.), *Classroom discipline in American schools: Problems and possibilities for democratic education* (pp. 1–16). Albany, NY: State University of New York Press.

Butchart, R. E., & McEwan, B. (1998). *Classroom discipline in American schools: Problems and possibilities for democratic education.* Albany, NY: State University of New York Press.

Canter, L. (1976). *Assertive discipline: A take charge approach for today's educators.* Los Angeles: Lee Canter and Associates.

Canter, L., & Canter, M. (1992). *Assertive discipline. Positive behavior management for today's classroom.* Santa Monica, CA: Lee Canter & Associates.

Chaille, C., & Britain, L. (2003). *The young child as scientist: A Constructivist approach to early childhood science education.* New York: Longman Press.

Chaille, C., & Silvern, S. B. (1996). Understanding through play. *Childhood Education, 72*(5), 274–277.

Charles, C. M. (1996). *Building classroom discipline.* White Plains, NY: Longman.

Clayton, M. K. (Spring 1997). Teacher tips: Helpful ideas for the responsive classroom teacher. *The Responsive Classroom,* 4–5.

Coie, J. D., & Dodge, K. A. (1998). Aggression and antisocial behavior. In Damon and Eisenberg (Eds.), *Handbook of child psychology* (pp. 779–862). New York: John Wiley & Sons, Inc.

Coloroso, B. (1994). *Giving your child the gift of inner discipline.* New York: William Morrow.

Concerned Educators Allied for a Safe Environment (CEASE). (Spring, 2004).

Corporal Punishment in America—2004. 25(1), 6. Cambridge, MA: Author.

Charney, R. S. (2002). *Teaching children to care: Classroom management for ethical and academic growth K–8*. Greenfield, MA: Northeast Foundation for Children.

Chess, S., & Thomas, A. (1996). *Temperament: Theory and practice*. New York: Brunner/Mazel.

Committee for Children. (2003). *Second step: A - violence-prevention curriculum*. Seattle, WA: Committee for Children.

Copple, C. (Ed.). (2003). *A world of difference: Readings on teaching young children in a diverse society*. Washington, DC: NAEYC.

Corsaro, W. (1985). *Friendship and peer culture in the early years*. New York: Ablex.

Corso, M. (1993). Is developmentally appropriate physical education the answer to children's school readiness? *Colorado Journal of Health, Physical Education, Recreation and Dance, 19*(2), 6–7.

Corso, W. A. (2003). *We're friends, right? Inside kids' culture*. Washington, DC: Joseph Henry Press.

Cryan, J. R. (1987). *The banning of corporal punishment: In child care, school and other educative settings in the United States*. A position paper of the Association for Childhood Education International. Wheaton, MD: Association for Childhood Education International.

Cunningham, P., Hall, D., & Defee, M. (1998). Nonability-grouped, multilevel instruction: Eight years later. *The Reading Teacher, 51*(8), 652–664.

Curran, J. M. (1999). Constraints of pretend play: Explicit and Implicit Rules. *Journal of Research in Childhood Education, 14*(1), 47–55.

Curry, N. E., & Johnson, C. N. (1990). *Beyond self-esteem: Developing a genuine sense of human value*. Washington, DC: National Association for the Education of Young Children.

Curry, S. J., Wagner, E. H., & Grothaus, L. C. (1991). Evaluation of intrinsic and extrinsic motivation interventions with a self-help smoking cessation program. *Journal of Consulting and Clinical Psychology, 59*, 318–324.

Curtis, D., & Carter, M. (2000). *The art of awareness: How observation can transform your teaching*. St. Paul, MN: Redleaf Press.

Curtis, D., & Carter, M. (2003). *Designs for living and learning: Transforming early childhood environments*. St. Paul, MN: Redleaf Press.

Curwin, R. L., & Mendler, A. N. (1990). *Am I in trouble? Using discipline to teach young children responsibility*. Santa Cruz, CA: Network Publications.

Curwin, R. L., & Mendler, A. N. (1999). *Discipline with dignity*. Alexandria, VA: Association for Supervision and Curriculum Development.

Daro, D., Abrahams, N., & Robson, K. (May, 1988). *Reducing child abuse 20% by 1990: 1983–86 baseline data*. Chicago: National Center on Child Abuse Prevention Research.

Davidson, J. (1980), Wasted time: The ignored dilemma. *Young Children, 35*(1), 13–21.

Deater-Deckard, K., Dodge, K. A, Bates, J. E., & Pettit, G. S. (1996). Physical discipline among African American and European American mothers: Links to children's externalizing behaviors. *Developmental Psychology, 32*, 1065–1072.

Denham, S., Mason, T., Caverly, S., Schmidt, M., Hackney, R., Cameron, C., & DeMulder, E. (2001). Preschoolers at play: Co-socialisers of emotional and social competence. *International Journal of Behavioral Development, 25*(4), 290–301.

Derman-Sparks, L. (1999). Markers of multicultural/_antibias education. *Young Children, 54*(5), 43.

Developmental Studies Center. (1998). *Ways we want our class to be: Class meetings that build commitment to kindness and learning*. Oakland, CA: Author.

DeVries, R. (1999). Implications of Piaget's Constructivist theory for character education. In M. M. Williams & E. Shaps (Eds.), *Character education: The foundation for teacher education* (pp. 33–39). Washington, DC: The Character Education Partnership.

DeVries, R. (2001). Constructivist education in preschool and elementary school: The sociomoral atmosphere as the first educational goal. In S. L. Golbeck (Ed.), *Psychological perspectives on early childhood education: Reframing dilemmas in research and practice* (pp. 153–180). Mahwah, NJ: Erlbaum.

DeVries, R., Zan, B., & Hildebrandt. (2002) Issues in Constructivist Moral Education. *Early Education & Development.*13(3)

DeVries, R., Hildebrandt, C., & Zan, B. (2000). Constructivist early education for moral development. *Early Education & Development, 11*(1), 10–35.

DeVries, R., & Kohlberg, L. (1987). *Constructivist early education: Overview and comparison with other programs.* Washington, DC: National Association for the Education of Young Children.

DeVries, R., & Zan, B. (1994). *Moral classrooms, moral children.* New York: Teachers College Press.

DeVries, R., & Zan, B. (1995). Creating a Constructivist classroom atmosphere. *Young Children, 50*(6), 4–13.

DeVries, R., & Zan, B. (1996). Assessing interpersonal understanding in the classroom context. *Childhood Education, 72*(5), 265–268.

Dill, V. S. (1998). *A peaceable school: Cultivating a culture of nonviolence.* Bloomington, IN: Phi Delta Kappa.

Dixon-Krauss, L. (1996). *Vygotsky in the classroom: Mediated literacy instruction and assessment.* White Plains, NY: Longman.

Dobson, J. (1970). *Dare to discipline.* Wheaton, IL: Tyndale House.

Dodge, K. A., Bates J. E., & Pettit, G. S. (1990). Mechanisms in the cycle of violence. *Science, 250,* 1678–1683.

Dreikurs, R. (1964). *Children: The challenge.* New York: Hawthorne Books. (1991 edition published by Plume).

Dreikurs, R. (1966). *Psychology in the classroom.* New York: Harper and Row.

Dreikurs, R., Greenwald, B., & Pepper, F. (1998). *Maintaining sanity in the classroom: Classroom management techniques.* Accelerated Development.

Drug Strategies. (1998). *Safe schools, safe students: A guide to violence-prevention strategies.* Washington, DC: Drug Strategies.

Duckworth, E., and Cleary, J. (1990). A story for Larry. *New Directions for Child Development, 47,* 71–76.

Educational Productions, Inc. (2000). *Supporting transitions: Easing the troublespots.*

Preventing Discipline Problems (video series). Beaverton, OR: Author.

Edwards, C., Gandini, L., & Forman, G. (1998). *The hundred languages of children: The Reggio Emilia approach—advanced reflections.* Connecticut: Ablex Publishing Corporation.

Edwards, C. P. (1986). *Promoting social and moral development in young children: Creative approaches for the classroom.* New York: Teachers College Press.

Eisenberg, N. (1992). *The caring child.* Cambridge MA: Harvard University Press.

Eisenberg, N. (2002). Emotion-related regulation and its relation to quality of social functioning. In W. Hartup & R. A. Weinberg (Eds.), *Child psychology in retrospect and prospect: In celebration of the 75th anniversary of the Institute of Child Development* (Vol. 32, pp. 133–172). Mahwah, NJ: Erlbaum.

Eisenberg, N., & Fabes, R. A. (1998). Prosocial development. In Damon and Eisenberg (Eds.), *Handbook of child psychology* (pp. 701–778). New York: John Wiley & Sons, Inc.

Elswood, R. (1999). Really including diversity in early childhood classrooms. *Young Children, 54*(4), 62–66.

Erikson, E. (1963). *Childhood and society* (2nd ed.). New York: Norton.

Faber, A., & Mazlish, E. (1996). *How to talk so kids can learn at home and in school.* New York: Fireside/Simon & Schuster.

Feeney, S., Christensen, D., & Moravcik, E. (2006). *Who am I in the lives of children?* Upper Saddle River, NJ: Merrill/Prentice Hall.

Feeney, S., & Kipnis, K. (1999). *Ethics and the early childhood educator: Using the N.A.E.Y.C. code.* Washington, DC: NAEYC

Feiring, C., & Lewis, M. (1991). The development of social networks from early to middle childhood: Gender differences and the relation to school competence. *Sex Roles, 25,* 237–253.

Ferber, J. (1996). Therapeutic teacher, therapeutic classroom. In L. Koplow (Ed.), *Unsmiling faces: Preschools that heal.* New York: Teachers College Press.

Fields, M., Groth, L., & Spangler, K. (2004). *Let's begin reading right: A developmental approach to emergent literacy.* Columbus, OH: Merrill/Prentice Hall.

Flavell, J. H., & Hartman, B. M. (2004). Research in review: What children know about mental experiences. *Young Children, 59*(2).

Flicker, E. S., & Hoffman J. A. (2002). Developmental discipline in the early childhood classroom. *Young Children, 57*(5).

Forman, G., & Fyfe, B. (1998). Negotiated learning through design, documentation, and discourse. In C. Edwards, L. Gandini, & G. Forman (Eds.), *The hundred languages of children: The Reggio Emilia approach— advanced reflections* (2nd ed.). Greenwich, Conn: Ablex Publishing Corporation.

Fox, L., Dunlap, G., Hemmeter, M. L., Joseph, G. E., & Strain, P. S. (2003). The teaching pyramid: A model for supporting social competence and preventing challenging behavior in young children. *Young Children, 58*(4).

Freeman, L. (1983). *It's my body.* Seattle: Parenting Press.

Froschl, M., & Sprung, B. (1999). On purpose: Addressing teasing and bullying in early childhood. *Young Children, 54*(3), 70–72.

Garbarino, J., Dubrow, N., Kostelny, K., & Pardo, C. (1998). *Children in danger: Coping with the consequences of community violence.* San Francisco: Jossey-Bass Publishers.

Gartrell, D. (1987a). Assertive discipline: Unhealthy for children and other living things. *Young Children, 42*(2), 10–11.

Gartrell, D. (2004). *The power of guidance: Teaching social-emotional skills in early childhood classrooms.* Albany, NY: Delmar Learning.

Gathercoal, F. (1998). Judicious discipline. In R. E. Butchart, & B., McEwan, *Classroom discipline in American schools: Problems and possiblities for democratic education* (pp. 197–216). Albany, NY: State University of New York Press.

Geller, E. S., Rudd, J. R., Kalsher, M. J., Streff, F. M., & Lehman, G. R. (1987). Employer-based programs to motivate safety belt use: A review of short-term and long-term effects. *Journal of Safety Research, 18*, 1–17.

Gibbs, J. (2001). *Tribes: A new way of learning and being together.* Sausalito, CA: Centersource Systems, LLC.

Gilligan, C., & Wiggens, G. (1987). The origins of morality in early childhood relationships. In J. Kagan & S. Lamb (Eds.), *The emergence of morality in young children.* Chicago: University of Chicago Press.

Gimple, G. A., & Holland, M. L. (2003). *Emotional and behavioral problems of young children. Effective interventions in the preschool and kindergarten years.* New York: Guilford.

Ginott, H. (1965). *Between parent and child: New solutions to old problems.* New York: Macmillan.

Goldman, L. (2000). We can help children grieve: A child-oriented model for memorializing. *Young Children, 51*(6), 69–83.

Gonzalez-Mena, J. (1993). The child in the family and the community. USR, NJ: M/PH.

Gordon, A., & Browne, K. W. (1996). *Guiding young children in a diverse society.* Boston: Allyn & Bacon.

Gordon, T. (1970). *Parent effectiveness training.* New York: Wyden.

Gordon, T. (1989). *Teaching children self-discipline: At home and at school.* New York: Random House.

Gordon, T., & Sands, J. S. (1976). *P.E.T. in action.* New York: Bantam.

Gottman, J. (1997). *Raising an emotionally intelligent child.* New York: Fireside.

Greenberg, P. (1987). Ideas that work with young children: Child choice—another way to individualize—another form of preventive discipline. *Young Children, 43*(1), 48–54.

Greenberg, P. (1992a). Ideas that work with young children. How to institute some simple democratic practices pertaining to respect, rights, responsibilities, and roots in any classroom (without losing your leadership position). *Young Children, 47*(5), 10–17.

Greenberg, P. (1992b). Why not academic preschool? (Part 2). Autocracy or democracy in the classroom? *Young Children, 47*(3), 54–64.

Grossman, H. (1990). *Trouble-free teaching: Solutions to behavior problems in the classroom.* Mountain View, CA: Mayfield.

Gruber, H. E., & Voneche, J. J. (Eds.). (1977). *The essential Piaget: An interpretive reference guide.* New York: Basic Books.

Grusec, J. E. (1991). Socializing concern for others in the home. *Developmental Psychology, 27,* 338–342.

Gunnar, M. R., Mangelsdorf, S., Larson, M., & Hertsgaard, L. (1989). Attachment, temperament, and adrenocortical activity in infancy: A study of psychoendocrine regulation. *Developmental Psychology, 25,* 355–363.

Guralnick, M. J., & Groom, J. M. (1988). Peer interactions in mainstreamed and specialized classrooms: A comparative analysis. *Exceptional Children, 54,* 415–428.

Gurian, M. (2001). *Boys and girls learn differently.* San Francisco: Jossey-Bass.

Hall, N. S. (1999). *Creative resources for the anti-bias classroom.* Albany, NY: Delmar Publishers.

Hannaford, C. (1995). *Smart moves: Why learning is not all in your head.* Arlington, VA: Great Ocean Publishing.

Hart, C. H., Burts, D. C., Durland, M. A., Charlesworth, R., DeWolf, M., & Fleege, P. O. (spring/summer 1998). Stress behaviors and activity type participation of preschoolers in more and less developmentally appropriate classrooms: SES and sex differences. *Journal of Research in Childhood Education, 12*(2), pp. 176–196.

Hart, C. H., Olsen, S. F., Robinson, C. C., & Mandleco, B. L. (1997). The development of social and communicative competence in childhood: Review and a model of personal, familial, and extrafamilial processes. *Communication Yearbook, 20,* 305–373.

Harter, S. (1998). The development of self-representation. In Damon and Eisenberg (Eds.), *Handbook of child psychology* (pp. 553–618). New York: John Wiley & Sons, Inc.

Hartup, W. W., & Moore, S. G. (1990). Early peer relations: Developmental significance and prognostic implications. *Early Childhood Research Quarterly, 5*(1), 1–18.

Hesse, P., & Lane, F. (2003). Media literacy starts young: An integrated curriculum approach. *Young Children, 58*(6), 20–26.

Hitz, R. (1988). Assertive discipline: A response to Lee Canter. *Young Children, 43*(2), 25–26.

Hitz, R., & Driscoll, A. (1988). Praise or encouragement? New insights into praise: Implications for early childhood teachers. *Young Children, 43*(5), 6–13.

Holland, J. J. (July 26, 2000). Games, media linked to violence. (news article). Washington, DC: Associated Press.

Honig, A. S. (2004). How to create an environment that counteracts stereotyping. *Child Care Information Exchange.* March/April, #156.

Honig, A. S., & Wittmer, D. S. (1996). Helping children become more prosocial: Ideas for classrooms, families, schools, and communities. *Young Children, 51*(2), 62–70.

Howes, C. (1988). Same- and cross-sex friends: Implications for interaction and social skills. *Early Childhood Research Quarterly, 3,* 21–37.

Howes, D., & Ritchie, S. (2002). *A matter of trust: Connecting teachers and learners in the early childhood classroom.* New York: Teachers College Press.

Hughes, E. (1999). If you have sun and you have rain you get a rainbow: Creating meaningful curriculum. *Journal of Early Childhood Teacher Education, (20),* 2.

Hunt, R. (1999). Making positive multicultural early childhood education happen. *Young Children, 54*(5), 39–42.

Hyman, I. (1997). *The case against spanking.* San Francisco: Jossey-Bass.

Hymes, J. (1990). *Teaching the child under six* (3rd ed.). West Greenwich, RI: Consortium Publishing.

Hyson, M. C. (2004). *The emotional development of young children: Building an emotion-centered curriculum.* New York: Teachers College Press.

Hyson, M. C., & Molinaro, J. (2001). Learning through feeling: Children's development, teachers' beliefs and relationships, and classroom practices. In S. L. Golbeck (Ed.), *Psychological perspectives on early childhood education: Reframing dilemmas in research and practice* (pp. 107–130). Mahwah, NJ: Erlbaum.

Jalongo, M. R., & Isenberg, J. P. (2004). *Exploring your role: A practitioner's introduction to early childhood education.* Columbus, OH: Merrill/Prentice Hall.

Jambunathan, S., Burts, D. C., & Pierce, S. H. (1999). Developmentally appropriate practices as predictors of self-competence among preschoolers. *Journal of Research in Childhood Education, 13*(2), 167–174.

Jenkins, G. D., Jr. (1986). Financial incentives. In E. A. Locke (Ed.), *Generalizing from laboratory to field settings*. Lexington, MA: Lexington Books.

Johnson, C., Ironsmith, M., Snow, C. W., & Poteat, G. M. (2000). Peer acceptance and social adjustment in preschool and kindergarten. *Early Childhood Education Journal, 27*(4), 207–212.

Jones, B. (1991). *A sourcebook on attention deficit disorder: A management guide for early childhood professionals and parents*. San Antonio, TX: Psychological Corporation.

Jones, E., & Nimmo, J. (1994). *Emergent curriculum*. Washington, DC: National Association for the Education of Young Children.

Jones, I., & Gullo, D. F. (1999). Differential social and academic effects of developmentally appropriate practice and beliefs. *Journal of Research in Childhood Education, 14*(1), 26–35.

Kagan, J., Reznick, J. S., Clarke, C., Snidman, N., & Garcia-Coll, D. (1984). Behavioral inhibition to the unfamiliar. *Child Development, 55*, 2212–2225.

Kaiser, B., & Rasminsky, J. S. (1999). *Meeting the challenge: Effective strategies for challenging behaviors in early childhood environments*. Ottawa: Canadian Child Care Federation.

Kaiser, B., & Rasminsky, J. S. (2003). Opening the culture door. *Young Children, 58*(4), 53–56.

Kamii, C. (1982). Autonomy as the aim of education: Implications of Piaget's theory. In C. Kamii (Ed.), *Number in preschool and kindergarten* (pp. 73–87). Washington, DC: National Association for the Education of Young Children.

Kamii, C. (1984). Obedience is not enough. *Young Children, 39*(4), 11–14.

Kamii, C. (Ed.). (1990). *Achievement testing in the early years*. Washington, DC: National Association for the Education of Young Children.

Kamii, C. (2000). *Young children reinvent arithmetic: Implications of Piaget's theory*. New York: Teachers College Press.

Kamii, C., & Ewing, J. K. (1996). Basing teaching on Piaget's constructivism. *Childhood Education, 72*(5), 260–264.

Kamii, C., Manning, M., & Manning, G. (Eds.). (1991). *Early literacy: A Constructivist foundation for whole language*. Washington, DC: National Education Association of the United States.

Karr-Morse, R., & Wiley, M. (1997). *Ghosts from the nursery: Tracing the roots of violence*. New York: The Atlantic Monthly Press.

Katz, L. G., & Chard, S. C. (1989/2000). *Engaging children's minds: The project approach*. Norwood, NJ: Ablex.

Katz, L. G., & McClellan, D. E. (1991). *The teacher's role in the social development of young children*. Urbana, IL: ERIC Clearinghouse Document, ED313168.

Katz, L. G., & McClellan, D. E. (1997). *Fostering children's social competence: The teacher's role*. Washington, DC: National Association for the Education of Young Children.

Kemple, K. M., David, G. M., & Hysmith, C. (1997). Teachers' interventions in preschool and kindergarten children's peer interactions. *Journal of Research in Childhood Education, 12*(1), 34–47.

King, M., & Gartrell, D. (2003). Building an encouraging classroom with boys in mind. *Young Children, 58*(4), 33–36.

Klein, C. (1975). *The myth of the happy child*. New York: Harper & Row.

Koc, K., & Buzzelli, C. A. (2004). The moral of the story is . . . Using children's literature in moral education. *Young Children, 59*(1), 92–97.

Kochanska, G. (1991). Socialization and temperament in the development of guilt and conscience. *Child Development, 62*, 1379–1392.

Kohlberg, L. (1984). *Essays in moral development. Volume 2: The psychology of moral development*. New York: Harper & Row.

Kohn, A. (1996). *Beyond discipline: From compliance to community*. Reston, VA: Association for Supervision and Curriculum Development.

Kohn, A. (1999). *Punished by rewards*. New York: Houghton Mifflin.

Kohn, A. (1999). *Punished by rewards*. Houghton Mifflin: Mariner Books

Kohn, A. (2001). Five reasons to stop saying "Good job!" *Young Children, 56*(5), 24–28.

Koplow, L. (Ed.). (1996). *Unsmiling faces: How preschools can heal.* New York: Teachers College Press.

Koplow, L. (2002). *Creating schools that heal: Real-life solutions.* New York: Teachers College Press.

Kostelnik, M. J. (1992). Myths associated with developmentally appropriate programs. *Young Children, 47*(4), 17–23.

Kostelnik, M. J., Soderman, A. K., & Whiren, A. P. (2004). *Developmentally appropriate curriculum.* Upper Saddle River, NJ: Merrill/Prentice Hall.

Kriedler, W. J. (Spring, 1991). Dispute resolution in education: Creating "peaceable classrooms" in elementary schools. *Forum: National Institute for Dispute Resolution,* 5–8.

Kreidler, W. J. (1999). *Teaching conflict resolution through children's literature.* New York: Scholastic.

Kritchevsky, S., Prescott, E., & Walling, L. (1969). *Planning environments for young children: Physical space.* Washington, DC: National Association for the Education of Young Children.

Kuhn, J. (2001). *Quality child care and partnerships with parents.* Research Connections Canada 6. Ottawa, Ontario: Canadian Child Care Federation.

The Lancet. (2002, September 28). Selling to— and selling out—children. *The Lancet, 360*(9338), 959.

Landau, S., & McAninch, C. (1993). Young children with attention deficits. *Young Children, 48*(4), 49–58.

Landy, S. (2002). *Pathways to competence: Encouraging healthy social and emotional development in young children.* Baltimore: Paul H. Brookes.

Lantieri, L. (2003). Waging peace in our schools: The resolving conflict creatively program. In M. J. Elias, H. Arnold, & C. S. Hussey, (Eds.), *Best leadership practices for caring and successful schools* (pp. 76–88). Thousand Oaks, CA: Corwin Press.

Lantieri, L., & Patti, J. (1996). *Waging peace in our schools.* Boston: Beacon Press.

Leppo, M. L., Davis, D., & Crim, B. (Spring, 2000). The basics of exercising mind and body. *Childhood Education, 76*(3), 142–147.

Levin. D. E. (2003). *Teaching young children in violent times: Building a peaceable classroom* (2nd ed.). Washington, DC: National Association for the Education of Young Children.

Levin, D. E. (2004). Beyond banning war and superhero play: Meeting children's needs in violent times. In D. Koralek, (Ed.), *Spotlight on Young Children and Play.* Washington, DC: National Association for the Education of Young Children.

Lillard, A., & Curenton, S. (1999). Do young children understand what others feel, want, and know? *Young Children, 554*(5), 52–57.

Lloyd-Jones R., & Lunsford, A. A. (Eds.). (1998). The *English Coalition Conference: Democracy through language.* Urbana, IL: National Council of Teachers of English.

Lubeck, S. (1985). *Sandbox society: Early education in black and white America—A comparative ethnography.* Philadelphia: Falmer Press.

Lubeck, S. (1994). The politics of developmentally appropriate practice: Exploring issues of culture, class, and curriculum. In B. L. Mallory & R. S. New (Eds.), *Diversity and developmentally appropriate practices: Challenges for early childhood education.* New York: Teachers College Press.

Mallory, B., & New, R. (1994). Social constructivist theory and principles of inclusion: Challenges for early childhood special education. *Journal of Special Education, 28*(3), 322–337.

Mallory, B. L., & New. R. S. (Eds.). (1994). *Diversity and developmentally appropriate practices: Challenges for early childhood education.* New York: Teachers College Press.

McAfee, O., Leong, D. J., & Bodrova, E. (2004). *Basics of assessment: A primer for early childhood educators.* Washington, DC: NAEYC.

McCune, L., & Zanes, M. B. (2001). Learning, attention, and play. In S. L. Golbeck (Ed.), *Psychological perspectives on early childhood education: Reframing dilemmas in research and practice* (pp. 92–106). Mahwah, NJ: Erlbaum.

McEwan, B. (1998). Contradiction, paradox, and irony. In R. E. Butchart & B. McEwan, *Classroom discipline in American schools:*

Problems and possibilities for democratic education (pp. 135–156). Albany, NY: State University of New York Press.

McLellan, F. (2002, September 28). Marketing and advertising: Harmful to children's health. *The Lancet, 360*(9338), 1001.

McNeilly-Choque, M. K., Hart, C. H., Robinson, C. C., Nelson, L. J., & Olsen, S. F. (1996). Overt and relational aggression on the playground: Correspondence among different informants. *Journal of Research in Childhood Education, 11*(1), 47–67.

Miller, D. F. (2004). *Positive child guidance* (4th ed.). Albany, NY: Delmar.

Mize, J., & Pettit, G. S. (1997). Mothers' social coaching, mother-child relationship style and children's peer competence: Is the medium the message? *Child Development, 68,* 312–332.

National Association for the Education of Young Children (1998) Code of Ethical Conduct & Statement of Commitment. Washington DC: NAEYC.

National Council of Teachers of Mathematics. (1995). *Assessment standards for school mathematics.* Reston, VA: Author.

National Research Council. (1994). *National science education standards.* Washington, DC: National Academy Press.

Nelson, J., Lott, L., & Glenn, H. S. (2000). *Positive discipline in the classroom.* Roseville, CA: Prima Publishing.

Noddings, N. (1992). *The challenge to care in schools: An alternative approach to education.* New York: Teachers College Press.

Noddings, N. (1995, January). A morally defensible mission for schools in the 21st century. *Phi Delta Kappan,* 365–368.

Olson, H., Burgess, D., & Streissguth, A. (1992). Fetal alcohol syndrome (FAS) and fetal alcohol effects (FAE): A lifespan view with implications for early intervention. *Zero to Three, 13*(1), 24–29.

Osofsky, J. D. (1997). *Children in a violent society.* New York: Guildford Publishers.

Paley, V. G. (1999). *The kindness of children.* Cambridge, MA: Harvard University Press.

Parker, L. (April 5, 2002). *Conditions.* Available: http://www.schoolbehavior.com/conditions.

Pettit, R. W., & Sugawara, A. I. (2002). Age, gender, socioeconomic status, race/ethnicity, temperament, and actual social cognitive competence as factors contributing to preservice teachers' perceptions of preschool children's social and cognitive competence. *Journal of Early Childhood Teacher Education, 23*(2), 125–136.

Phillipsen, L. C., Bridges, S. K., McLemore, T. G., & Saponaro, L. A. (1999). Perceptions of social behavior and peer acceptance in kindergarten. *Journal of Research in Childhood Education, 14*(1), 68–77.

Piaget, J. (1960). *The child's conception of the world.* Totowa, NJ: Littlefield, Adams. (Original work published in 1929.)

Piaget, J. (1964). *Judgment and reasoning in the child.* Totowa, NJ: Littlefield, Adams. (Originally published in 1928.)

Piaget, J. (1965). *The moral judgment of the child.* New York: Free Press. (Originally published in 1932.)

Pica, R. (1997). Beyond physical development: Why young children need to move. *Young Children, 52*(6), 4–11.

Planinsec, J. (2002). Relations between the motor and cognitive dimensions of preschool girls and boys. *Perceptual and Motor Skills, 94,* 415–432.

Plattner, I. E. (2003). Granting children their emotions. *Child Care Information Exchange, 152,* 34–36.

Porter. L. (2000). Young children's behavior: Practical approaches for caregivers and teachers (2nd ed.). Baltimore, MD: Paul H. Brookes.

Powell, D. R. (1994). Parents, pluralism, and the NAEYC statement on developmentally appropriate practice. In B. L. Mallory & R. S. New (Eds.), *Diversity and developmentally appropriate practices: Challenges for early childhood education.* New York: Teachers College Press.

Powlishta, K. K. (1995). Gender segregation among children: Understanding the "Cootie phenomenon." *Young Children, 50*(4), 61–69.

Powlishta, K. K., & Maccoby, E. E. (1990). Resource utilization in mixed-sex dyads: The influence of adult presence and task type. *Sex Roles, 23,* 223–240.

Pritchard, M. S. (1996). *Reasonable children: Moral education and moral learning.* Lawrence, Kansas: University Press of Kansas.

Putallaz, M., & Heflin, A. H. (1990). Parent-child interaction. In S. R. Asher & J. D. Cole (Eds.), *Peer rejection in childhood* (pp. 189–216). New York: Cambridge University Press.

Rabiner, D., & Cole, J. (1989). Effect of expectancy inductions on rejected children's acceptance by unfamiliar peers. *Developmental Psychology, 25*(3), 450–457.

Ramsey, P. G. (1991). Making friends in school: *Promoting peer relationships in early childhood.* New York: Teachers College Press.

Reinsberg, J. (1999). Understanding young children's behavior. *Young Children, 545*(4), 54–56.

Reynolds, E. (2000). *Guiding young children: A problem-solving approach.* New York City: McGraw-Hill.

Rightmyer, E. C. (2003). Democratic discipline: Children creating solutions. *Young Children, 58*(4), 38–45.

Riley, S. R. (1984). *How to generate values in young children.* Washington, DC: National Association for the Education of Young Children.

Rizzo, T. A. (1989). *Friendship development among children in school.* Norwood, NJ: Ablex.

Rizzo, W., & Corsaro, W. A. (1991). *Social support processes in early childhood friendships.* Paper presented at the biennial meeting of the Society for Research in Child Development, Seattle.

Robinson, C. C., Mandleco, B., Olsen, S. F., & Hart, C. H. (1995). Authoritative, authoritarian, and permissive parenting practices: Development of a new measure. *Psychological Reports, 77,* 819–830.

Ruckman, A. Y., Burts, D. C., & Pierce, S. H. (1999). Observed stress behaviors of 1st grade children participating in more and less developmentally appropriate activities in a computer-based literacy laboratory. *Journal of Research in Childhood Education, 14*(1), 36–46.

Sabatino, D. (1991). *A fine line: When discipline becomes child abuse.* Summit, PA: TAB Books/McGraw-Hill.

Schmidt, F., & Friedman, A. (1992). *Peacemaking skills for little kids.* Fresno, CA: Peace Works, Inc.

Schorr, L. (1989). *Within our reach: Breaking the cycle of disadvantage.* New York: Anchor Books/Doubleday.

Selman, R. L. (1980). *The growth of interpersonal understanding.* New York: Academic Press.

Selman, R., & Schultz, L. (1990). *Making a friend in Youth: Developmental theory and pair therapy.* Chicago: University of Chicago Press.

Shonkoff, J. P., & Meisels, S. J. (Eds.). (2000). *Handbook of early childhood intervention* (2nd ed.). Cambridge, UK, Cambridge University Press.

Siccone, F., & Lopez, L. (2000). *Educating the heart: Lessons to build respect and responsibility.* Boston: Allyn & Bacon.

Simmons, B. J. (1991). Ban the hickory stick. *Childhood Education, 68*(2), 69.

Skinner, B. F. (1965). *Science and human behavior.* New York: Free Press.

Skinner, B. F. (1971). *Beyond freedom and dignity.* New York: Knopf.

Slaby, R. G., Roedell, W. C., Arezzo, D., & Hendrix, K. (1995). *Early violence prevention: Tools for teachers of young children.* Washington, DC: National Association for the Education of Young Children.

Slavin, R. E., & Madden, N. A. (2001). *One million children: Success for all.* Thousand Oaks, CA: Corwin Press.

Smith, C. (1998). Children with "special rights" in the preprimary schools and infant-toddler centers in Reggio Emilia. *The hundred languages of children: The Reggio Emilia approach—advanced reflections* (2nd ed.). Greenwich, Conn: Ablex Publishing Corporation.

Soukhanov, A. H. (Ed.). (1992). *The American heritage dictionary of the English language.* Boston: Houghton Mifflin.

Spieker, S. J., Larson, N. C., Lewis, S. M., Keller, T. E., & Gilchrist, L. (1999). Developmental trajectories of disruptive behavior problems in preschool children of adolescent mothers. *Child Development, 70,* 443–458.

Spinrad, T. L., Stifter, C. A. Donelan-McCall, N., & Turner, L. (2004). Mothers' regulation strategies in response to toddlers' affect:

Links to later emotion self-regulation. *Social Development, 13*(1), 40–55.

Springen, K. (October 16, 2000). Family: On spanking. *Newsweek, CXXXVI* (16), p. 64.

Staley, L., & Portman, P. (2000). Red rover, red rover, it's time to move over! *Young Children, 55*(1), 67–72.

Steinbeck, K. (2001). Obesity in children: The importance of physical activity. Proceedings of the Kellogg's Nutrition Symposium 2000, Sydney, Australia, 8 August 2000. *Australian Journal of Nutrition and Dietetics, 58*, 28–32.

Straus, M. A. (1991). Discipline and deviance: Physical punishment of children and violence and other crime in adulthood. *Social Problems, 38*(2), 133–154.

Styles, D. (2001). *Class meetings: Building leadership, problem-solving, and decision making in the respectful classroom.* Markam, Ontario: Pembroke. (Distributed in the U.S. by Stenhouse.)

Tabors, P. O. (1998). What early childhood educators need to know: Developing effective programs for linguistically and culturally diverse children and families. *Young Children, 53*(6), 20–26.

Teaching Tolerance. (1997). *Starting small: Teaching tolerance in preschool and the early grades.* Montgomery, AL: The Southern Poverty Law Center.

Teaching Tolerance. (1999). *Responding to hate at school: A guide for teachers, counselors and administrators.* Montgomery, AL: The Southern Poverty Law Center.

Thompson, R. A. (1998). Early sociopersonality development. In Damon and Eisenberg (Eds.), *Handbook of child psychology* (pp. 25–104). New York: John Wiley & Sons, Inc.

TRUCE. (2000). *Media violence and children: A call to action!* (brochure). Sommerville, MA: Teachers Resisting Unhealthy Children's Entertainment.

TRUCE. (2003–2004). *Media violence and children: Action guide* (brochure). Sommerville, MA: Teachers Resisting Unhealthy Children's Entertainment.

Turnbull, A., Turnbull, H., & Rutherford, III. (2001). *Families, professionals, and exceptionality: Collaboratiing for empowerment* (4th ed.). Upper Saddle River, NJ: Prentice Hall.

Vance, E., & Weaver, P. (2002). *Class meetings: Young children solving problems together.* Washington, DC: National Association for the Education of Young Children.

Vissing, V. M., Straus, M. A., Gelles, R. J., & Harrop, J. W. (1991). Verbal aggression by parents and psychosocial problems of children. *Child Abuse and Neglect, 15*, 223–238.

Vygotsky, L. S. (1962). *Thought and language* (E. Hanfmann & G. Vokar, trans.). Cambridge, MA: MIT Press. (Original work published in 1934.)

Vygotsky, L. S. (1978). *Mind and society: The development of higher mental processes.* Cambridge, MA: Harvard University Press. (Original work published in 1933.)

Watson, M. (1999). The child development project: Building character by building community. In M. M. Williams & E. Shaps (Eds.), *Character education: The foundation for teacher education* (pp. 24–32). Washington, DC: The Character Education Partnership.

Watson, M. (2003, July). Attachment theory and challenging behaviors: Reconstructing the nature of relationships. *Young Children*, 12–20.

Weaver, C. (1994). *Success at last! Helping students with attention deficit (hyperactivity) disorders achieve their potential.* Portsmouth, NH: Heinemann.

Wheeler, E. J. (2004). *Conflict resolution in early childhood: Helping children understand and resolve conflicts.* Columbus, OH: Merrill/Prentice Hall.

Williams, M. M., & Shaps, E. (Eds.). (1999). *Character education: The foundation for teacher education.* Washington, DC: The Character Education Partnership.

Wolery, M., & Wilbers, J. S. (Eds.). (1994). *Including children with special needs in early childhood programs.* Washington, DC: National Association for the Education of Young Children.

Wolfgang, C. H., & Wolfgang, M. E. (1995). *The faces of discipline for early childhood.* Boston: Allyn & Bacon.

Yanghee, A. K. (2003). Necessary social skills related to peer acceptance. *Childhood Education, 79*(4), 234–238.

Children's Literature and Videos

Bang, M. (1999). *When Sophie gets angry, very very very angry.* New York: Scholastic.

Barrett, J. (1988). *Animals should definitely not act like people.* New York: Aladdin.

Brown, M. T. (1999). *The bionic bunny show.* New York: Little Brown & Company.

Carle, E. (1977). *The grouchy ladybug.* New York: HarperCollins.

Carlson, N. (1990). *Arnie and the new kid.* New York: Viking.

Carson, J. (1992). *You hold me and I'll hold you.* New York: Orchard Books.

Cosby, B. (1997). *The meanest thing to say.* New York: Scholastic Inc.

Cutler, J. (1993). *Darcy and Gran don't like babies.* New York: Scholastic Inc.

dePaola, T. (1975). *Strega nona.* Upper Saddle River, NJ: Prentice Hall.

dePaola, T. (1979). *Oliver Button is a sissy.* San Diego: Voyager/Harcourt Brace Jovanovich.

Geisel, T. (Dr. Seuss). (1954). *Horton hears a who.* New York: Random House.

Grimm, Brothers. (1967). *Rumpelstiltskin.* New York: Brace and World.

Havill, J. (1995). *Jamaica's blue marker.* Boston: Houghton Mifflin.

Henkes, K. (1988). *Chester's way.* New York: Greenwillow.

Henkes, K. (1991). *Chrysanthemum.* New York: Greenwillow.

Henkes, K. (1996). *Lilly's purple plastic purse.* New York: Greenwillow.

Hess, D. (1994). *Wilson sat alone.* New York: Simon & Schuster.

Hoffman, M. (1991). *Amazing Grace.* New York: Dial Books for Young Readers.

Hughes, S. (1988). *Dogger.* New York: Lothrop, Lee & Shepard.

Lobel, A. (1972). *Frog and toad together.* New York: Harper & Row.

Lobel, A. (1982). Tear-water tea. In *Owl at home.* New York: HarperTrophy.

Luttrell, I. (1990). *Three good blankets.* New York: Macmillan Child Group.

Milne, A. A. (1957). *The world of Pooh.* New York: _E. P. Dutton.

Novak, M. (1994). *Mouse tv.* New York: Orchard Books.

Pfister, J. (1992). *The rainbow fish.* (J. Alison James, Trans.). New York: North-South.

Rosen, M. (1996). *This is our house.* Cambridge, MA: Candlewick.

Steig. W. (1988). *Spinky Sulks.* New York: Farrar, Straus and Giroux.

Steptoe, J. (1987). *Mufaro's beautiful daughter.* New York: Lathrop, Lee, & Shepard.

United States Department of Justice. (2004). *Prevalence of imprisonment in the United States.* Available: http://www.ojp.usdoj.gov/bjs/crimoff.htm

Viorst, J. (1972). *Alexander and the terrible, horrible, no good, very bad day.* New York: MacMillan.

Wade, B. (1990). *Little monster goes to school.* New York: Lothrop, Lee, & Shepard.

Williams, A. (1996). *Dragon soup.* Tiburon, CA: HJ Kramer Inc.

Winn, C. M., & Walsh, D. (1996). *Box-head boy.* National Book Network.

Wojtowycz, D. (2000). *A cuddle for Claude.* New York: Dutton Children's Books.

Wood, A. (1985). *King Bidgood's in the bathtub.* San Diego: Harcourt Brace Jovanovich.

Yashima, T. (1976). *Crow boy.* New York: Puffin/Penguin.

Zemach, M. (1983). *The little red hen: An old story.* New York: Farrar, Straus, & Girouz.

Curriculum for Peaceful Classrooms

Committee for Children. (1991). *Second step: A violence-prevention curriculum.* Seattle: Author.

Gibbs, J. (1995) *Sausalito, CA: Tribes: A new way of learning and being together.* CenterSource Systems, LLC.

Kriedler, W. J., (1994). *Teaching conflict resolution through children's literature.* New York: Scholastic.

Kreidler, W. J. & S. T. Whittall, (1999). *Early childhood adventures in peacemaking: A conflict resolution guide for early childhood educators.* 2d ed. Cambridge, MA: Educators for Social Responsibility, and Boston: Work/Family Directions.

Schmidt, F., & Friedman, A. (1992). *Peacemaking skills for little kids.* Fresno, CA: Peace Works Inc.

Siccone, F., & Lopez, L. (2000). *Educating the heart: Lessons to build respect and responsibility.* Needham Heights, MA: Allyn & Bacon.

Teaching Tolerance. (1997). *Starting small: Teaching tolerance in preschool and the early grades.* Montgomery, AL: The Southern Poverty Law Center.

Teaching Tolerance. (1999). *Responding to hate at school: A guide for teachers, counselors and administrators.* Montgomery, AL: The Southern Poverty Law Center.

Author Index

Subject Index